ADVANCE PRAISE FOR *MALCOLM BEFORE X*

"I have known Patrick Parr since 2019. The original research he shared with me was extremely helpful in writing one of my own books, *The Awakening of Malcolm X*. I believe Patrick's new book is an important addition to the story of my father's life."

—Ilyasah Shabazz, author of *Growing Up X: A Memoir by the Daughter of Malcolm X*

"Patrick Parr has managed an extraordinary feat. In telling the story of Malcolm Little the child, the student, the burglar, the prisoner, he has helped us to more fully understand Malcolm X the orator, the leader, the radical thinker. Parr has unearthed remarkable documentary sources to tell the gripping and important story of the shaping of a great mind."

—Jonathan Eig, Pulitzer Prize-winning author of *King: A Life*

"Six and a half years in three Massachusetts prisons turned an aimless, twenty-year-old petty thief named Malcolm Little into the spiritual and intellectual powerhouse we know as Malcolm X. Patrick Parr's meticulously researched book gives us the most detailed account yet of this historic transformation—and offers lessons for today about the life-changing potential of prison libraries and educational programs."

—Mark Whitaker, author of *Saying It Loud: 1966—The Year Black Power Challenged the Civil Rights Movement*

"More than any other previous biography of Malcolm X that I have read, in *Malcolm Before X*, Patrick Parr delivers an air-tight, well documented chronology of the well-known episodes in Malcolm's early life combined with a compelling, revelatory portrait of the six and a half transformative years he spent in prison."

—Abdur-Rahman Muhammad is a scholar, historian, journalist, writer, activist, and authority on the life and legacy of Malcolm X

"Parr offers an extraordinary portrait of Malcolm by relying on a cornucopia of significant primary sources that, in many instances, no one—literally no one—has ever tapped before. His rare and extremely commendable detective work shows on virtually every page."

—Keith Miller, author of *Voice of Deliverance: The Language of Martin Luther King, Jr., and Its Sources*

"*Malcolm Before X* is strikingly original. Parr's prodigious research gives us the most richly documented book about Malcolm's early life that we will ever have. His account of how a good prison library can spark a personal transformation should resonate widely. A superb achievement."

—David J. Garrow, Pulitzer Prize-winning author of *Bearing the Cross* and *Rising Star*

"Patrick Parr has produced an extraordinary act of historical research and recovery. By taking Malcolm X's prison years seriously, Parr helps to restore the human being behind the legend. This groundbreaking book, which should be read by every student, researcher, and scholar of Malcolm X and postwar American history, offers the most detailed examination to date of Malcolm X's prison years. In so doing, Parr provides the most brilliantly nuanced understanding and analysis of Malcolm Little's transformation into Malcolm X. Magnificent."

—Peniel E. Joseph, author of *The Third Reconstruction: America's Struggle for Racial Justice in the Twenty-First Century*

"Patrick Parr has managed an extraordinary feat. In telling the story of Malcolm Little the child, the student, the burglar, the prisoner, he has helped us to more fully understand Malcolm X the orator, the leader, the radical thinker. Parr has unearthed remarkable documentary sources to tell the gripping and important story of the shaping of a great mind."

—Jonathan Eig, Pulitzer Prize-winning author of *King: A Life*

MALCOLM BEFORE X

MALCOLM BEFORE X

PATRICK PARR

University of Massachusetts Press
Amherst and Boston

ISBN 978-1-62534-816-6 (paper); 817-3 (hardcover)

Designed by Scribe Inc.
Set in Adobe Garamond Pro
Printed and bound by Books International, Inc.

Cover design by adam b. bohannon
Cover photo: Detail from Malcolm X original mug shot,
Malcolm Little Mug Shot, February 27, 1946. Malcolm Little
Prison File, Massachusetts Department of Corrections.

Library of Congress Cataloging-in-Publication Data

Names: Parr, Patrick, author.
Title: Malcolm before X / Patrick Parr.
Description: Amherst : University of Massachusetts Press, [2024] | Series:
African American intellectual history | Includes bibliographical
references and index. | Identifiers: LCCN 2024033110
(print) | LCCN 2024033111 (ebook) | ISBN
9781625348166 (paperback) | ISBN 9781625348173 (hardcover) | ISBN
9781685750879 (ebook) | ISBN 9781685750886 (epub)
Subjects: LCSH: X, Malcolm, 1925-1965—Imprisonment. | African American
political activists—Biography. | State Prison Colony (Norfolk,
Mass.)—Biography. | African American prisoners—Rehabilitation. | Black
Muslims—Biography. | Prisoners—United States—Biography. | African
American criminals—Biography. | X, Malcolm, 1925-1965—Childhood and
youth. | Little family.
Classification: LCC E185.97.L5 P377 2024 (print) | LCC E185.97.L5 (ebook)
| DDC 320.54/6092 [B]—dc23/eng/20240824
LC record available at https://lccn.loc.gov/2024033110
LC ebook record available at https://lccn.loc.gov/2024033111

British Library Cataloguing-in-Publication Data
A catalog record for this book is available from the British Library.

For anyone who has felt forgotten . . .

CONTENTS

ILLUSTRATIONS

FIGURES

CHARTS

TABLES

NOTE TO THE READER

Twenty-seven years and two months . . .

That is how old Malcolm X was on the day of his release from prison: August 7, 1952. For the next 12 and a half years until his assassination, Malcolm spoke firmly to frustrated, downtrodden Black Americans, and as writer Julius Lester put it a year after Malcolm's death, "His clear, uncomplicated words cut through the chains on black minds like a giant blow-torch."[1]

Malcolm Before X stops just before Malcolm becomes a public figure. Many valuable books have covered this period in his life. But what I have found lacking in Malcolm's ever-evolving scholarship are details of his time in prison. In the 10 years I've worked on this book, I have attempted to find sources that have either been ignored, are unknown, or have been overlooked by past authors—such as prison files, prison newspapers, and archival correspondence—and used them in conjunction with more well-known sources, like the *Autobiography*. The result is a narrative filled with people who were important parts of Malcolm's life but have yet to be mentioned, such as prison debater Murdo Margeson, incarcerated men such as Godfrey Joiner and John Noxon Jr., educational director and librarian George F. Magraw, and Norfolk superintendent Maurice Winslow, as well as other, more well-known figures who until now have only had their stories partially or incorrectly revealed, like Beatrice Bazarian ("Sophia" in the *Autobiography*), John Elton Bembry ("Bimbi"), and Malcolm "Shorty" Jarvis.

Malcolm X's prison transformation is one of the most inspiring stories of the twentieth century, and yet we know very little about it. The general public might recall that Malcolm read a lot of books, debated, and converted to Islam while writing to Elijah Muhammad. But these surface recollections undercut what is, when fully revealed, a very different story.

With this book, I have sought to provide an in-depth look at Malcolm's day-to-day life in prison. Part 2, "Inside," takes place almost entirely in prison, covering the years 1946–52. Specific attention should be paid to Norfolk Prison Colony (chapters 7 and 8), where Malcolm was given access to a well-stocked library and learned how to hone his skills as a debater. Norfolk, first envisioned by progressive penologist Howard B. Gill, was *way* ahead of its time, and its intensive focus on education and rehabilitation is a trait sorely lacking in many American prisons today. I have included maps, photos, and Norfolk's general philosophy to show a prison that's devoted to helping its incarcerated individuals prepare for life on the outside.

But in order to appreciate Malcolm's prison awakening, we need to understand the social conditions that brought him to prison in the first place. Thus, in part 1, "Outside," we'll first explore Malcolm's eight home burglaries (chapter 1) using newly available prison files, only to then flash back to 1815 (chapter 2), when his maternal and paternal great-great-grandparents were taken from Africa. From there we'll travel across generations to Omaha, Nebraska, Malcolm's birthplace, and follow him through his tragic and turbulent youth.

Black thoughts '71

[malcolm]

today, minus six yrs, minus
the life of a
black prince, minus foolish
misconceptions of
taking the fangs out
of the wolf's mouth by
nonviolently attacking
him.
dig that, brothers,
we thought that we
could nonviolent him
to death and he
laughed while we
gave more blood to
quench his vampirical thirst.
it was five years ago today

that the black prince
taught us how to add & sub.
yes, he taught us math.
how to add positive black
images & deeds & sub negative
inferiority complexes,
& got me thinking that
if he wasn't the supreme being himself,
AllahGodMunguJehovahRama
(after someone pulled my coat &
told me that he was a man the same
as me, it messed me around but i
got it together).
& what he was I am
capable of being plus some.
so I passed on from my math
lessons to graduate to the
battlefields,
to destroy empires &
build nations/to destroy
empires & build nations.
build nations
Build Nations
BUILD NATIONS so
the next malcolm will not
be a victim of
FRATRICIDE or another
name on the list headed
MENTAL GENOCIDE. & I pray
lead us not into deification.

—Written by Insan while serving a life
sentence at Norfolk Prison Colony.

MALCOLM BEFORE X

PART I

OUTSIDE

FIGURE P.1. Malcolm Little. Mug shot. November 29, 1944.
Sketch restored by Wayne Watson. Information on the
card was found by Watson in Malcolm's FBI file.

1

B&E

December 1945 to January 1946

Looking back, I think I really was at least slightly out of my mind.

—Malcolm X[1]

Francis E. Brown needed money. At 23, the man some in Roxbury called "Sonny" had become so despondent financially that he'd abandoned his wife. In return, Mrs. Brown went to the police. A warrant of nonsupport was issued, leaving Brown surrounded locally by loan sharks, white police officers, and an angry spouse.[2]

In early December 1945, Brown ran into his old friend, Malcolm Little, in Roxbury. The two young men had first met back in 1942, when a then 17-year-old Malcolm worked at Townsend Drug Store. Malcolm was just beginning to embrace Roxbury's hustling underbelly, arriving there to live with his half-sister Ella in the middle of February 1941. Brown, meanwhile, had lived and breathed the neighborhood for years.[3]

Fast-forward three years, and Brown was now standing in front of a more streetwise friend. From late July to early October 1945, Malcolm had been living in New York City, performing as an emcee at the Caribbean Club on 7th Avenue between 139th and 140th Streets under the stage name "Rhythm Red." He'd gambled, hustled, been arrested at least twice, snorted more than a few lines of cocaine, smoked "a stick a day" of marijuana, and drank a fair share of whisky. Both men were cash-poor and wanted to do something about it. Let's "break into some house[s]," Sonny suggested to Malcolm.[4]

And so they did.

On December 5, after the sun went down, Malcolm and Sonny drove in Sonny's car to Milton, a well-to-do, predominantly white suburb outside Boston. They drove around until they spotted a house without any lights on. As Malcolm would later explain, if you don't want to be robbed, "one of the ideal things [to do] is to leave a bathroom light on all night. The bathroom is one place where somebody could be, for any length of time, at any time of the night, and he would be likely to hear the slightest strange sound. The burglar, knowing this, won't try to enter."[5]

Unfortunately for the owner of 116 Brush Hill Road, a two-story home built around 1920, the bathroom light wasn't on, so Sonny stopped the car.[6]

When it came to burglary, Sonny—two years older than Malcolm—had a bit more experience, but with mixed results. Around 1938, Sonny, then a teenager, had been charged with B&E (breaking and entering). He'd committed the crime with several other teenagers, Malcolm "Shorty" Jarvis being one of them. In fact, Jarvis, 14 at the time, signed a confession keeping himself out of jail but causing Sonny to serve time at the Massachusetts Reformatory in Concord. Later, in 1940, Sonny served time at Norfolk Prison Colony.[7]

In short, Sonny had done this before.

Malcolm was given doorbell duty, since they were dealing with white people, and Malcolm's lighter skin and smile would seem like less of a threat.[8]

Malcolm got out of the car and rang the doorbell. He waited a moment, but no lights came on. Seeing no trouble, he went back to the car and waited as Sonny took a screwdriver and jimmied open a storm window on the back side of the house. Sonny then opened the front door, and Malcolm went in.[9]

They didn't get much. According to Malcolm's prison file, the men came away with "jewelry, clothing, and household goods" valued at around $100—hardly worth a jail sentence.[10]

Still cash-poor after their first break-in, the duo discussed the idea of expanding their group. For Brown, he'd need bigger scores than this to climb out of his debts. Malcolm, meanwhile, harbored hopes of accruing enough assets to start a business somewhere. To do this, they needed to know the area better.

MAKING A TEAM

From December 6 to December 10, Sonny and Malcolm made plans. At the time, Malcolm lived between two residences: 72 Dale Street, where Ella lived, and 4 Hollander Street, where Jarvis had an apartment. It was Jarvis who'd helped Malcolm out of some trouble in New York City and offered him one of the bedrooms in his apartment.

Jarvis and Malcolm were solid, but during this time, Sonny needed a place to stay as well. Jarvis acquiesced to Sonny and gave him the other empty room in his apartment. Whether he knew of their plans to break into houses or not, Jarvis had unofficially become the third member of the group.

Still, three young Black men burglarizing houses in 1940s white suburbia wasn't exactly covert. The group needed trustworthy white-leaning people, and Malcolm knew who to ask—his on-and-off-again girlfriend, Beatrice Bazarian, or "Bea." Bea and her sister Joyce lived at 352 Harvard Street and had invited Kora Marderosian, 21, to live with them since she had been going through a hard time with her parents. In early December, Jarvis drove Malcolm (who didn't have a car) over to see Bea several times, as he'd done in years past.[11]

By December 11, Malcolm and Sonny had largely kept their burglary plans to themselves, but at around 7:00 p.m., all six of them (the two Malcolms, Sonny, Bea, Kora, and Joyce) sat in the living room of Jarvis's Hollander Street apartment. Beatrice brought up the fact that there was champagne at the home of Samuel Kletjian, Bea's mother's new boyfriend. Bea mentioned that Samuel and her mother were in New York City, so with the house now empty, the group could head over to Samuel's home in Arlington and grab some free alcohol, since Bea and Joyce had a key.

Malcolm asked Jarvis if they could use his 1938 Buick, which was big enough to hold six. Jarvis was reluctant at first, but he eventually changed his mind. As he'd later explain to a prison official, he had no idea that Sonny and Malcolm were already beginning a scheme.

It was about a 15-minute drive on a snowy night from Jarvis's Hollander apartment to 100 Gray Street in Arlington. When the group arrived at the five-bedroom brick home, they saw the lights on inside. Apparently, Mr. Kletjian and Bea's mother had returned from New York earlier than planned. Bea and Joyce didn't want to introduce their three new male friends to their mother, so the group drove away from the house, disappointed and without champagne.[12]

Still driving up Gray Street, Malcolm asked Bea if this was a rich neighborhood. Bea acknowledged it was, and soon after, Malcolm asked Jarvis to stop the car less than a half-mile away from Mr. Kletjian's home. They parked near 248 Gray Street, the four-bedroom home of Philip and Nora Eberhardt, but no one, except perhaps Bea and Joyce, knew them. Malcolm took a quick look and noticed no lights were on. "It looks like a good deal," he said. Now that he had Bea, Malcolm asked her to go ring the doorbell. Sure enough, Bea did. Later, she (and Kora) told the police that there was a "thrill and excitement" to it all after going through such a difficult year with the birth and death of her child and her parent's divorce.[13]

Bea came to Jarvis's car and said there was no answer. That was all Sonny and Malcolm needed to hear. Sonny got out of the car, and Malcolm was poised to join him as soon as Sonny opened the front door from the inside. Sonny was able to remove a storm window, then opened an "unlocked window" and climbed in. Sonny then moved to the front door and opened it. Malcolm, Bea, Kora, and a reluctant Jarvis, who admitted later that he "wanted no part of it," left the car and walked toward the home.

According to a police report, "all rooms were ransacked."

Items stolen—Nora D. Eberhardt's Home

$1,200 fur coat
$300 cloth coat
$175 bracelet
$75 moleskin fur jacket
$40 clock
$10 Kodak camera
n/a combination clock and barometer
n/a silk purse containing four to five dollars worth of dimes
n/a string of solid gold beads
n/a quilted green box containing costume jewelry
n/a gold locket
n/a leather-cased travel clock

They packed the stolen goods—Bea carrying the fur coat—into Jarvis's car and drove back down Gray Street, going past Mr. Kletjian's house again. After three blocks, they turned right and parked near the three-bedroom home of 58-year-old Rollin W. Hoyt, a business executive for the International Equipment Company of Boston, and his wife, Lillian. Once more, after seeing no lights on and a doorbell check by Bea, Brown moved through the snow with gloves on and a screwdriver in hand. Brown chose a window in the "reading room" and used the screwdriver to pull it open. Police later found Brown's "footprints in snow under [the] window," but no fingerprints. Brown unlocked the front door, and in came everyone except Joyce and Kora.[14]

As the four again "ransacked" every room, Malcolm grabbed a bottle of Haig and Haig whisky out of the closet and took a few swigs, as did Jarvis, before putting it back.

The group left the door unlocked.

Items stolen—Rollin W. Hoyt's Home

$40 string of yellow gold beads
$35 Amethyst pendant
$33 Hamilton wristwatch
$25 Onyx pendant and chain
$25 oval-shaped pin
$10 string of pearls
$5 broach
$2.10 six five-pound bags of sugar
$2 in cash from pocketbook in bedroom
n/a Old Spice perfume
n/a French perfume
n/a two three-cell flashlights
n/a scatter rug

Jarvis drove back to his apartment, his car now stuffed with over $2,000 of stolen goods. When they reached 4 Hollander Street, the group got out of the car and walked toward Jarvis's third-floor apartment. At this moment, Malcolm pulled Jarvis aside to see how he was feeling about what had just occurred. Nervous, Jarvis shared his fears with Malcolm and told him "he was not going to do it again." Malcolm, sensing a problem, said this to his friend: "If you don't, and I get caught I'll tell the police you were with me."[15]

BECOMING THE BOSS

Back in the apartment, there was an atmosphere of excitement and fear, with most of the loot now placed on a table. For Beatrice and Kora, yes, it had been a thrill, but reality had now settled in. They had just officially committed a crime, and even Joyce risked being charged if they were ever caught.[16]

Malcolm needed the group to see how seriously he took this situation. "In any organization," Malcolm mentioned in his *Autobiography*, "someone must be the boss. If it's even just one person, you've got to be the boss of yourself."

In the *Autobiography*, Malcolm, via Alex Haley, described what happened next this way:

> Talking to them, laying down the plans, I had deliberately sat on a bed away from them. All of a sudden, I pulled out my gun, shook out all five bullets, and then let them see me put back only one bullet. I twirled the cylinder and put the muzzle to my head. "Now, I'm going to see how much guts all of you have," I said.
>
> I grinned at them. All of their mouths had flapped open. I pulled the trigger—we all heard it click. "I'm going to do it again, now." They begged me to stop. I could see in Shorty's and Rudy's eyes some idea of rushing me.
>
> We all heard the hammer "click" on another empty cylinder. The women were in hysterics. Rudy and Shorty were begging, "Man . . . Red . . . cut it out, man! . . . Freeze!" I pulled the trigger once more.
>
> "I'm doing this, showing you I'm not afraid to die," I told them. "Never cross a man not afraid to die . . . now, let's get to work!"[17]

Surprisingly, this moment is described similarly in Beatrice's and Joyce's prison files. When giving her own version of the robberies, Beatrice mentioned the above incident as the main reason why she didn't tell the police about what they did. In Jarvis's apartment, Kora and Beatrice "were told that they were deeply as guilty as the men which included breaking, entering and larceny in the nighttime and that they would be given a severe court penalty with prison sentences if they ever squealed."

To emphasize his point, Malcolm then demanded their attention. According to Beatrice's prison file: "Little then took a revolver out of his pocket, put three bullets into the revolver [and] held the revolver to his temple and told the girls that he had no use for his own life, that he could easily pull the trigger and that he would do the same to the girls. He then spun the gun around and fired two bullets into the room, both of which were blank cartridges. The third bullet discharged into the floor."[18]

In the version that exists in Joyce's prison file, the suicide attempt by Malcolm is mentioned, but more generally. She also implicates Jarvis and Sonny as well. "They threatened the girls and brandished guns, reporting that they did not care for their own lives and would not have any consideration for the girls if they made any attempt to 'squeal' on them."[19]

Decades later, Jarvis told the *Boston Globe* that Malcolm "pointed the gun at him" and fired. "The thing clicked, and the blood shot to the top of my head." Jarvis then admitted that he "stuck my .38 right in [Malcolm's] face. I said, 'If you ever do that again, I'll blow your brains out.'"[20]

For Malcolm, the act was necessary to keep everyone together: "I never had one moment's trouble with any of them after that. Sophia [Beatrice] acted awed, her sister [Joyce] all but called me 'Mr. Red.' Shorty [Jarvis] and Rudy [Francis 'Sonny' Brown] were never again quite the same with me. Neither of them ever mentioned it. They thought I was crazy. They were afraid of me."[21]

Beatrice played up this fear when questioned in prison. After Malcolm's threat, she explained that she "lost all sense of reason and was unable to discuss the matter with any family member or to report to the police." She and Kora did, however, retain enough "sense of reason" to take several of Ms. Eberhardt's bracelets and other jewelry back to their 352 Harvard Square apartment.[22]

The burglaries continued. On December 14, after allowing some time to pass to make sure the police were not on to them, the group of six drove to 101 Oakley Road in Belmont, a four-bedroom, two-bath home built in 1938 and owned by William T. Kelley and his wife. At around 8:00 p.m., it was Brown who once again broke into the home, "jimmying a bath-room window in the rear of the house on the first floor." The house was a three-mile drive south of Beatrice's mother's house, but it's unknown if Beatrice or Kora knew Mr. Kelley. Following a similar pattern as the other houses, the group (with Kora and Joyce in the car) "ransacked" the first and second floors, taking $2,400 worth of "fur coats, jewelry and silverware."[23]

On December 15, Stanley R. Miller of Brookline came back to his Heath Street home around 8:30 p.m. only to see that the front door was open, the glass broken "beside an inner vestibule door"; all Brown or Malcolm had to do after breaking the glass was "reach in and open the front door." Miller had been gone since 2:30 p.m., and as he walked around his home, he noticed "silverware, rugs . . . linen, liquor and jewelry" had been stolen, and the group had pulled down shades on the second floor. All told, around $10,000 of household goods were taken, including, according to Beatrice's prison file, a $6,500 urn—one of only two in the world, the other being at Boston's Museum of Fine Arts.[24]

But the real jackpot came on the night of December 16 at Robert F. Estabrook's home at 79 Shornecliffe Road in Newton. Estabrook, once the vice president of the New England Telephone and Telegraph Company, retired in 1945 and moved with his wife into a seven-bedroom, four-bath home.[25] Blocked by bushes, Malcolm and Sonny were able to gain access to it "by forcing a front window" open "with a jimmy." When Malcolm, Beatrice, Sonny, and Jarvis entered the 4,000 square-foot home, they opened a side door "to give" themselves "a means of escape." On the second floor, they found a locked cedar closet and forced it open. After going through all the rooms, the crew eventually stole thousands of dollars of merchandise and stored it in Jarvis's car. Jarvis, meanwhile, pocketed one silver diamond ring with a green stone and was able to hold on to it for the rest of his life.[26]

Items stolen—Robert F. Estabrook's Home

Yellow-gold earrings with a turquoise stone in the center
Woman's yellow-gold ring with five turquoise stones
Gold rings, a gold pin
$3 in pennies
Costume jewelry
Elgin wristwatch
Two silver Bon-Bon dishes
An antique gold necklace with a coral cameo pendant
One gold necklace with eight baroque pearls
One Italian hand-carved silver ring with green stone
Cigarette case, letter "F" on it

Old-fashioned necklace
Pair of long pearl earrings
A gold pendant and chain
Leather handbag
Silver candlesticks
A Masonic watch charm
Five silver dollars
A silver dresser set
Eight silver spoons
Travel clock
A gold shoulder pin
A string of coral beads
Coral pin
Gold class ring
A portable ivory Fada radio receiving set
15 bedsheets
Turkish towels
Personal books and papers
A suitcase with the initials E.P.E. (Estabrook's wife's name was
    Ethel.)
A vacuum cleaner
A cabinet
A phonograph and record changer
A bedspread
A velvet evening cloak
A blue evening cloak
Two fur jackets
A bathrobe
A Persian Lamb muff
A fox muff
A black fox fur piece and a raccoon hat
Estimated total value in December 1945 . . . $6,275
Adjusted for inflation, around $108,000 in 2024

It had been quite a week for Malcolm and his team. From Tuesday, December 11 to Monday, December 16, they'd broken into five different homes and come away with nearly $20,000 of cash and merchandise. With such a heavy haul, the group decided to begin selling off what they'd taken. The same night they robbed the Estabrooks, they drove to New York City and then stayed at the Hotel Victoria for a week.

Before they left, however, Malcolm and Beatrice concocted a way to grab a bit of cash before their drive to the Big Apple. At this time, Bea's mother, Alice Aghajanian, and her soon-to-be husband, Samuel Kletjian, were largely unaware of what Beatrice and Joyce were up to. On December 16, Beatrice brought Malcolm inside Kletjian's 100 Gray Street home. She introduced him as a "chauffeur who had been willed the articles and wanted to dispose of them because he was unmarried and had no use for the household furnishings." Kletjian, then a 49-year-old widower with two grown children, was the owner of the Cozy Corner Café over on Porter Square in Cambridge. When Kletjian mentioned his interest in seeing a few of the articles, Malcolm brought in a silver set, a silver tray, an automatic recorder, and a Hamilton Beach mix master. Kletjian didn't ask for any more information and handed Malcolm $90 in cash.[27]

During this month, Malcolm put on the chauffeur act two more times in front of Mr. Kletjian, coaxing $50 out of him for a Philco radio and silver candlesticks and $20 the final time for an Oriental rug. Meanwhile, Beatrice went ahead and took two evening gowns, an evening wrap, a phonograph, and a record changer up to a bedroom closet. When asked, Beatrice said that the daughter of the lady Malcolm worked for gave the articles to her as a gift.[28]

GETTING CAUGHT

For at least five nights, the group of six stayed in New York's luxurious Hotel Victoria, Jarvis's car still filled with fur coats, jewelry, and other items. The expensive 26-floor hotel was located on the corner of 7th Avenue and 51st Street, near Radio City Music Hall. Around the time they were staying at the Victoria, the Adrian Rollini Trio was playing in the as-advertised Candlelight Room, while the Don Christy Trio performed for guests (six dollars per person) in the Rendezvous Room.[29]

Not much is known about what the group did, exactly, but Joyce later told a prison official that she "had gone to New York for the express purpose of trying to gain admission to a dancing school for further professional train-ing," staying close to her sister. Meanwhile, Jarvis, Malcolm, and Sonny went into Harlem to try to sell a few items.[30]

After the trip, the group decided to split up, perhaps to avoid suspicion; the police had, after all, gone over to the Estabrooks the morning after the robbery and were beginning to suspect that the thefts in the area were connected. So on December 23, Beatrice, Joyce, and Kora took a train back to the Boston area while Malcolm, Sonny, and Jarvis went back in Jarvis's 1938 Buick. As far as what was officially recorded by the police, the group of six did not rob another house as a team again.[31]

But on Christmas Eve, Jarvis and Malcolm decided to go ahead on their own. They weren't done yet. Well, Malcolm wasn't. He once again convinced Jarvis to join him by telling his friend "that he wanted just a little more cash and he was going to go to Ohio." Jarvis, on edge ever since these burglaries started, had hopes that "it would be the last that he would see of" Malcolm.[32]

In Dorchester, on the night before Christmas, Jarvis and Malcolm went ahead and stole from a six-bedroom home (likely Ethel F. Swan's, a Boston University graduate and a Belmont high school English teacher), taking a suitcase, a silverware set, a watch, and a cameo pin.[33]

It was a minor haul compared to their past jobs. Two weeks passed, and on January 8, 1946, they traveled to the four-bedroom home of Isabella O'Connor, on 122 Ward Street, in Newton. It was the burglary of the O'Connor home that eventually led to Malcolm's arrest.[34]

At around 9:15 p.m., Malcolm attempted to force open the kitchen door with a crowbar but couldn't do it. Jarvis came over to help, and in they went. In Jarvis's account, he could only remember taking a fireplace screen from the O'Connor home, but he did see that Malcolm had gone up the stairs to the second floor. Quickly and quietly, Malcolm took the following items:

$100 light tan topcoat
$25 silver dollars
$25 crystal beads
$50 Lord Elgin watch
$32 Rosary beads
n/a box of perfume

Malcolm tried on the tan topcoat, but it was too small for his 6'2", 172 lbs. frame. So instead Jarvis, 5 inches shorter and 10 pounds lighter, gave it a try. Perfect fit.

They were out of there in less than 15 minutes. When Mrs. O'Connor arrived back at the house, she immediately called the police.

The next day, January 9, Malcolm took several of the stolen items to the Hollis Loan Company, a pawn shop on 34 Warren Street, only six miles away from O'Connor's home. The owner there, Al Beeman, bought the Rosary beads for $1.25 and also agreed to fix the Lord Elgin watch. Since O'Connor's report of lost items had already been relayed to the police, officers had been on the lookout for Rosary beads as well as the Lord Elgin watch, worth around $700 in today's money. In fact, the police were already on alert and had given surrounding pawn shops and jewelry stores lists of stolen items they were looking for. One item had already been flagged: a watch that Malcolm had given to a relative for Christmas Eve. The relative had then sold it to a pawn shop clerk, who notified the police.[35]

On January 10, Malcolm and Jarvis burglarized one final home in Walpole, stealing "jewelry, household articles, and personal property valued at more than $100" from a man named Frederick Tetrault. In less than 48 hours, Malcolm would be arrested.

It's worth noting how potentially self-destructive Malcolm's actions were at this time. First, Malcolm sold stolen items that were still "hot" to a local pawn shop only a mile away from his half-sister Ella's home on 72 Dale Street and a mile and a half away from Jarvis's Hollander Street apartment. This move was careless enough that he could've been caught. Still, by selling Rosary beads—a very recognizable item, and one not expensive enough for even the greediest pawn shop store owner to keep it a secret—and an already broken watch that O'Connor described in detail (*it's missing a crystal . . .*), the evidence acted as an invitation for police to intercept him.

On Saturday, January 12, Malcolm returned to the Hollis Loan Company to pick up the now-repaired watch. On him was a loaded .32-caliber pistol, tucked into a jacket pocket. He entered the store carrying the Fada portable radio he'd stolen from the Estabrooks that he may have hoped to sell. On his clothes, Malcolm also sported a "diamond stickpin," according to a *Globe* newspaper account.[36]

Malcolm placed the radio on the counter and paid Beeman for the watch. Once he did, an officer stepped out from a backroom entrance—Detective Stanley Slack, a large and imposing detective who lived in West Roxbury and had many years of experience working as a patrolman in and around the Roxbury community. "Step into the back," Slack said to Malcolm. The

20-year-old complied. At this moment, according to Malcolm's memory, "an innocent Negro walked into the shop. I remember later hearing that he had just that day gotten out of the military. The detective, thinking he was with me, turned to him." It was during this pause, when Slack's eyes momentarily left Malcolm for a few seconds, that Malcolm considered taking out his revolver. If he shot Slack, perhaps he'd be able to run and pick up whatever items he'd stowed away from the robberies and leave Roxbury for good.[37]

But he didn't shoot. Seventeen years later, when describing the moment to Alex Haley, he said, "Allah was with me even then." Instead of firing, "I raised my arm, and motioned to him, 'Here, take my gun.'" By not shooting his .32, Malcolm saved his own life, since another armed officer, John Manning, was nearby, waiting to assist. "They'd had me covered," Malcolm remembered. "One false move, I'd have been dead."[38]

Malcolm was put in handcuffs and taken by Detective Slack to the Boston police headquarters. Since this was 1946, Slack did not need to give Malcolm his Miranda warning—*you have the right to remain silent*. The now-famous *Miranda v. Arizona* case wasn't ruled on by the Supreme Court until 1966. As Malcolm's vital information was taken, such as his date of birth and contact information, anything he said or did could be used against him in a court of law, whether he knew that or not.

The police had questions. As Malcolm waited in a nearby holding cell, the officers compiled information based on the stolen items they now had in possession. The radio linked him to the Estabrook home and the watch and Rosary beads to the O'Connors'. In addition, according to Milton detective Stephen Slack (a cousin of Stanley's), Malcolm had pawned a wedding band with the initials of the burglarized victim on the ring. By the time he was questioned that Saturday night, Detective Slack knew that Malcolm may very well be responsible for a series of burglaries.[39]

"The detectives grilled me," Malcolm later explained. "They didn't beat me. They didn't even put a finger on me. And I knew it was because I hadn't tried to kill [Slack]." By the end of their session that night, Malcolm had at least "acknowledged taking part in a series of breaks in Brookline, Newton, Milton, Walpole, Belmont and Arlington."[40]

The next day, at the bottom of page 10 of the Sunday edition of the *Boston Globe* was a headline: "Roxbury Man, 20, Arrested at Gunpoint for Series of Breaks." It's unknown if Beatrice, Kora, or Joyce picked up the newspaper that day and figured it was Malcolm. The three-paragraph report did not mention his name or his race.

The timing of this article, however, could have been beneficial to Malcolm Jarvis and Francis Brown if they had read it on the thirteenth. If either of the men had read it "hot off the press," they'd have used what ended up being a 36-hour window and left town.

In Jarvis's case, there was a strong chance he didn't see the article. After taking part in the final January 10 robbery, Jarvis decided to move out of his Hollander Street apartment and move back in with his parents, both of whom were helping to raise Jarvis's two young sons. Jarvis had also started a job as a porter on December 28, 1945, selling sandwiches for the Boston and Albany Railroad Station (similar to a job Malcolm had back in 1941). When the January 13 edition of the *Boston Globe* hit the streets, Jarvis was taking orders from passengers on a train moving toward Buffalo, New York.[41]

That leaves "Sonny" Brown.

In the group of six, Brown remains the most mysterious of them all. After the trip to New York City, Brown all but disappears from any available records. In his *Autobiography*, Malcolm was impressed at how Sonny escaped. "To this day," Malcolm said, "I have always marveled at how [Sonny] somehow, got the word, and I know he must have caught the first thing smoking out of Boston, and he got away." Brown probably "got the word" from the *Globe* and left the Boston area for good, leaving his wife and his mounting debt as well.[42]

Malcolm spent January 13 and 14 answering questions from Brookline, Arlington, and Roxbury detectives. On Malcolm were "papers" with names of friends and associates as well as their contact information; Jarvis later wrote that Malcolm usually carried "two address books" on him. This means there were a lot of potential suspects for police to go through.

At some point during their discussions, the police offered Malcolm an olive branch. Since Malcolm had a .32 revolver on him, the two Roxbury detectives "said that they would drop the gun charges if [the] subject would name his accomplices." Malcolm considered his position. If he went in alone on armed robbery for a series of homes, he'd most likely be going away for 16–20 years—a daunting amount of time for a young man who'd never been to prison. Being Black didn't help either.[43]

Malcolm had two close calls with prison before. The first was due to a larceny charge from November 30, 1944. Malcolm had stolen Ella's fur coat and sold it to a pawn shop for five dollars. Ella, furious, made sure to press charges and send a message to her wayward younger half-brother, but Malcolm's sentence was suspended. On March 18, 1945, Malcolm was living with his older brother Wilfred in Detroit when he broke into a friend's home with Kenneth Pointer and stole a radio, a clock, and clothing totaling over $200. Wilfred put up the $1,000 bail, and Malcolm eventually left the state while the trial was pending, his unalert probation officer dropping the ball.[44]

But this was far more serious. Malcolm didn't have much of a choice. Eventually, after investigating the names in his "papers" or address book, the police discovered the identities of the rest of the group. So Malcolm "told [them] about the girls," but "only when he had been assured by the police that they would not be brought into court, and that charges against them would be dropped."[45]

Slack was an experienced officer, and he'd have known how to dangle promises that sounded good to the accused at first but in reality meant very little to the case. A gun charge was a minor offense, and given the grandiose way Malcolm burglarized eight homes in one month, Slack was looking at a bigger picture—one that involved more than one burglar. But Slack did deliver on his promise.

On January 15, 1946, Malcolm stood before Roxbury district court judge Samuel Eisenstadt and was given a one-year suspended sentence for carrying a .32 revolver. Slack took Malcolm back to his holding cell at Boston police headquarters. As Slack told the judge before leaving, Malcolm "was wanted in a number [of crimes around] town."[46]

The hunt for the others was on. Around the same time Malcolm was in court for the gun charge, Beatrice received a call from the police. She and Joyce had been listed by Malcolm as codefendants, and it was in her best interest to comply with the police as they investigated her 352 Harvard Square apartment. Soon after, she called her husband, Martin, who was still in Miami, waiting tables. Beatrice told Martin that she was in deep trouble and needed him to come back immediately. She didn't give him the details. Martin took the next plane out of Miami and managed to reach Beatrice's late at night, "arriving at approximately one thirty A.M. on the morning of the arrest."[47]

The police found plenty at Beatrice's apartment, a "radio, clock and jewelry" being a few of the items. With the items matching what had been reported stolen, Beatrice and Joyce were handcuffed and taken to the Cambridge police department. The police dismissed Beatrice's explanation that the items were "gift[s]." On the same day, as Beatrice and Joyce were being held at Belmont police station, they were questioned by Arlington officers. There, they confessed to taking other stolen items that were still at 100 Gray Street, kept in an upstairs bedroom closet. Sure enough, the police found a white crepe evening gown with a gold neckband, a red evening gown, a wine-colored wrap, four sets of candlesticks, an evening bag, two more dresses, and a wrap with a fur collar. That's a lot of "gifts."

Around this time, Beatrice and Joyce also told the police of Kora's whereabouts. This is based on a letter written by Martin Bazarian to Beatrice while she was in prison. Angrily sarcastic, he wrote, "I can remember the brave, heroic detectives who crashed our apartment, got all the help they needed to make things easier for them. I can also remember who helped them catch the other party involved in the case." Kora was soon taken into custody in Arlington.[48]

As for Jarvis, he was on a B&A train now coming back from Buffalo, his wage $45 a week, including the tips he was getting as a basket waiter. Cambridge police officers searched his parents' house on Waumbeck and found very little—just "one bullet." Still, he'd most likely been implicated by Beatrice and Joyce, and his name was also in Malcolm's address book—which was enough alone to bring him in. Jarvis described how, at a routine stop in Newtonville, "the police boarded the train." Taking a break from his duties, Jarvis took "an empty seat to relax in [the nondining] car. Three men passed by me, heading to the dining car [where Jarvis was supposed to be]. Moments later, upon my return [to the dining car], two of them passed me again." Jarvis grabbed a seat and tried to lay low, but "the third one spied me lying down in the seat. Beckoning the other two, they surrounded my seat. The one nearest me gave me a poke asking, 'Are you M. Jarvis?'"

"Who wants to know?" Jarvis asked.

"Do you know a Malcolm Little?"

Jarvis "became quiet," and the police asked to see his ID. Jarvis moved his hand toward his pocket, startling the officers, but to "everyone's relief," Jarvis produced a wallet, not a firearm. They saw his ID. A match. "You are under arrest for breaking and entering in the nighttime."[49]

In Jarvis's pockets were pawn tickets for several of the items that were reported stolen, and as if the cake needed any more icing, he was wearing the tan topcoat from the Newton home he broke into.[50]

THE SENTENCE

On February 8, bail for Malcolm and Jarvis was set at $10,000 each ($140,000 in 2024). The girls, viewed as not much more than accomplices, had their bail set at $1,500 each. Joyce and Beatrice were able to avoid spending weeks in a holding cell thanks to funds from Samuel Kletjian, their mother's boyfriend. Kora's situation was different, however. Held as a material witness after being the first to plead guilty, Kora could have been released on bail, but her family did not have sufficient funds, nor did Samuel Kletjian decide to help.[51]

Kletjian did not escape his own punishment. The police refused to buy Kletjian's "I didn't know" angle; Kletjian was awfully close to Beatrice and Joyce. On March 21, Kletjian ended up paying a $200 fine and was given two months of probation for purchasing stolen items from Malcolm.

Malcolm and Jarvis's bail amount may have been astronomical for two reasons. First was the fact that Sonny was still on the run and might in some way help the two men escape their predicament. The second one is clear—they robbed *eight* homes, and both men had previous robbery charges on their records.

From Malcolm's perspective, the court set the bail high enough that "they knew we [would be] nowhere near able to raise" the funds in time. Jarvis's family couldn't afford it, but Ella could, *if* she put up "her property as collateral." But Ella had become disappointed with the choices Malcolm had made, and her half-brother's "flippant attitude" was not putting her in the mood to open her wallet. "He showed no remorse about what he had done to himself and his family," Ella said many years later. "I regarded his getting into trouble with those white women and hanging out with Jarvis, whom he knew we regarded as a bad influence on him, as a sign of disrespect that I just couldn't support. As much as I cared for my brother, I wasn't prepared to let him continue on a path to destruction."[52]

February 27, 1946, was the day of sentencing. Because they had not made bail, Malcolm and Jarvis were led into the courtroom in handcuffs and placed inside a cage with iron bars extending from the ceiling to the floor. As they sat in captive humiliation, Joyce, Beatrice, and Kora were seated near the front with their poised yet expensive lawyer, Walter McLaughlin.

Both Malcolms sitting in their no-bail cage could feel the strength of white society's "deck stacked against us." Jarvis recalled a man, possibly the district attorney, casually walking past the cage, saying, "If we had you Niggers down

South, we would hang you." As Jarvis's anger intensified, Malcolm took in the hostile glares coming from the lawyers and attendees, most of whom were white, except for his brother Reginald, Ella, and Jarvis's family. As Malcolm later recalled, "Before the judge entered, I said to one lawyer, 'We seem to be getting sentenced because of those girls.' [The lawyer] got red from the neck up and shuffled his papers: 'You had no business with white girls!'"[53]

In walked the stern, owl-eyed, bespectacled 69-year-old honorable judge Allan G. Buttrick, a four-decade veteran of the Massachusetts district and superior courts. Buttrick, a married thirty-second-degree freemason with a 27-year-old daughter, listened to McLaughlin's defense of the three women. They were victims, McLaughlin explained, who "lived in a constant state of fear."[54]

If Buttrick's sympathies lay anywhere, it was with Kora Marderosian. Kora, who'd spent over a month in the Middlesex County Jail and helped the case as a material witness after pleading guilty, influenced the perspective of the parole officer, Miss Bachelder, and told her that Beatrice had persuaded her to join in on the robberies.

In addition, Judge Buttrick had been briefed on the comments made by the landlord of the 352 Harvard apartment where Beatrice and Joyce had resided. The landlord spoke poorly of Beatrice, Joyce, and Martin Bazarian, saying they were a "tough . . . loud and profane" group who often "drink and gamble." Even Joyce, according to the landlord, "can make a nice appearance but when she is with the crowd is as tough as the rest of them."

This along with Kora's statement doomed the sisters' chances of escaping jail time.

It's worth noting that Kora was not exactly respected by Beatrice's family. Later on, Beatrice; her mother, Alice; and Martin would say that Kora had a "poor reputation" and was "put out of her own home." In a letter dated April 31, 1946, after the trial, Martin called Kora a "bum . . . even her own family had nothing to do with her." In the same letter, Martin all but confirmed the landlord's "profane" claim, calling the state government "stinking bitches."

In the end, Judge Buttrick delivered his verdict. Not all the burglaries were included—just those of the Arlington, Newton, and Belmont homes, since they were in Middlesex County. The rest of the charges, except one, were from Norfolk County, to be determined in early April; the other charge was to be taken care of in Suffolk County in November.

Kora Marderosian was given a suspended sentence. Later, she was given two years of probation under the supervision of the Framingham Reformatory for Women.[55]

Joyce Caragulian was found guilty on two counts of breaking and entering in the nighttime and was sentenced to five years and one day in the Framingham Reformatory for Women.[56]

Beatrice Bazarian was found guilty of three counts of breaking and entering in the nighttime and larceny. She was also sentenced to five years and one day, to be served at Framingham. Bea was given an extra "count" (larceny) due to confessing to going into the Estabrook home with Malcolm, Jarvis, and Brown.[57]

Malcolm Little and Malcolm Jarvis eventually pled guilty after Jarvis's lawyers, John Drew and M. Arthur Gordon, went over to the cage and told them they'd receive a less severe sentence if they did so.

For Jarvis, the entire trial was a surreal experience. "Looking around the courtroom," he'd later write, "I saw people, but I heard nothing. I felt like I was floating in space, like my mind had left me." Buttrick found Jarvis guilty of four counts of B&E in the nighttime and larceny—for the two homes in Newton, the one in Arlington, and the one in Belmont. Jarvis was sentenced to 8–10 years, to be served concurrently.[58]

Jarvis's aunt, Priscilla King, sat three rows back in the middle aisle with her sister. When she heard 8–10 years, tears came to her eyes. Then she saw Ella stand up and yell at Judge Buttrick: "Prejudice, prejudice! Nothing but prejudice!" Then, as King recalled, "the judge took the mallet and knocked on that thing. 'Get 'em out of here! I'll lock 'em all up!' And my sister and I cried like a baby."[59]

When Jarvis heard the judge read each count aloud and the words "eight to ten years," he "lost his mind" and shook the iron bars, screaming, "causing a scene in the court room."

Years later, Jarvis remembered the moment he was sentenced this way: "I was in mental shock. I felt like I had been hit in the head by a blunt instrument and knocked senseless." Eventually, he shouted at Judge Buttrick: "Why don't you find me guilty of murder and kill me? I'd rather be dead than to spend my life in prison."

Malcolm tried to calm his friend down. *Life?* Malcolm remembered that "the bailiffs had to catch and support [Jarvis]." Only later did Jarvis ask what "concurrently" meant. After hearing "eight to ten years" repeated for each crime,

Jarvis had believed that, yes, he'd spend life in prison, or 96–120 years. Soon enough, he was told that concurrently simply meant "at the same time"— prison time in layers.

As for Malcolm, Buttrick pinned the most on him. From the available evidence, Buttrick concluded that Malcolm was indeed the ringleader of the group. Thus, his prison record states he was charged with "conspiracy to break and enter with intent to commit larceny." Malcolm was found guilty of five counts, and his "conspiracy" charge was "filed."

Still, like Jarvis, he also heard the tormenting echo of "eight to ten years." The two young men were taken out of the courtroom and out of society. Soon, they would be forced to endure ancient six-by-eight jail cells inside the infamous Charlestown State Prison—one of the oldest and most dilapidated prisons in the country.[60]

In a way, Malcolm was ready. His entire life up to that point had been one long endurance test. In fact, Malcolm's bloodline had been enduring an oppressive American system ever since 1815.

2

ORIGINS

Africa to Omaha

1815 to 1925

The African slave trade was supposed to be finished.

On December 2, 1806, President Thomas Jefferson, owner of around "six hundred" slaves in his lifetime, spoke before Congress and demanded that the "importation of persons" end on January 1, 1808. He framed his decision as a moral call to the nation, but being a Virginian, the end of Africans being transported by ship across the Atlantic also meant a financial advantage for his own state. During this time, Virginia controlled the largest population of landed slaves in the still-forming country. Once the Atlantic slave trade ended, they'd have control of the market of slaves being sold to other states.[1]

Slave traders in one city in particular, Charleston, South Carolina, were not happy about this. For decades, Gadsden Wharf had been the arrival point for hundreds of slave ships coming from Africa. But when Jefferson made his announcement, those who made their living delivering slaves went into a panic. According to Emory University records, between 1805 and 1808, the number of "Trans-Atlantic Slave Voyages to the Carolinas" nearly tripled—merchants were attempting to maximize their profit before the January 1, 1808, deadline.[2]

As voyages declined, the resolution of the War of 1812 had brought the US and Britain into a truce, and a new period began, coined the "Era of Good Feelings." In February 1815, the official peace treaty from that war, titled the "Treaty of Peace and Amity," included 11 articles for both countries to adhere to. The tenth article read as follows: "Whereas the traffic in slaves is irreconcilable with the principles of humanity and justice, and where as both His Majesty and the United States desirous of continuing their efforts to promote its entire abolition, it is hereby agreed that both the contracting parties shall use their best endeavors to accomplish so desirable an object."[3]

Evidently, their "best endeavors" didn't include stopping Charleston from accepting illegal slave ships into their harbors . . .

AFRICA TO CHARLESTON, SOUTH CAROLINA

As family historian Oscar V. Little revealed at a reunion in 1985, Malcolm X's roots can be traced back to 1815, to the south of Mali in West Africa. It was in this region, among the Bambara people, that Hajja, Malcolm's paternal great-great-grandfather, lived. Details are scarce regarding Hajja, but by being a member of the Bambara, he was familiar with the root meaning of his people's name, *Banmana*, which, roughly translated, meant "the ones who refused their masters."[4]

For centuries, the Bambara were resistant to Islam, often rebelling against neighboring kingdoms as they kept a faith similar, in certain respects, to animism. Over time, they developed states of their own—Kaarta and Segou, the latter's major city being the secluded and powerful Timbuktu—but by 1815, they were under threat from several nearby African enemies, such as the predominantly Muslim Kong Empire to the south, but also from within their own empire.

The circumstances surrounding Hajja's capture and enslavement are, as one can imagine, largely unknown. Still, one can speculate . . .

It all starts with the illegal American slave ship. It's unknown whether West African merchants were attempting in any way to support the 1815 peace agreement made between the US and Britain, nor were they under any obligation to obey Thomas Jefferson's earlier 1808 decision to end the Atlantic slave trade. Most likely, the scenario was similar to hundreds before: sailors came off the boat and offered guns and ammunition in exchange for "human cargo."

As for Hajja, it's uncertain if he'd been a criminal, a prisoner of war, or simply taken by force. Regardless, the six-week, 5,000-mile journey on this slave ship was without question a daily hell, due mainly to the illegal nature of the ship, which meant that hiding the slaves in tight, closed spaces was the top priority.[5] It's unlikely that, as Hajja struggled mightily to survive, he could have known of the nearly two million African bodies—of men, women, and children—that had been consumed by the waters of the Atlantic Ocean.

Nor could Hajja have known of the lifelong hardships and subhuman treatment waiting for him in Charleston, slavery's "Ellis Island."

It's unknown how close Hajja lived to the center of Charleston, a city that, according to an 1820 census, had an astounding "57,221" Black residents (mainly slaves) and only "19,376" white residents.[6] With this gap, Charleston police set a zero-tolerance standard. For example, it was against the law for slaves within the city limits of Charleston "to appear in daylight . . . wearing fine clothes, smoking a cigar, playing a musical instrument, or carrying a walking stick." It's assumed that "fine clothes" was a vague enough term to allow police to search any Black man or woman walking around town when the sun was out.[7]

Slaves in Charleston were also not allowed out at night, and the police force created a system all could understand, no matter what language they spoke. As the sun set, one lone Black servant was forced outside the police station with a drum. Over and over, he'd play a familiar drum tattoo—*ratatat-tat*—loud enough for all nearby slaves to receive the message: stay inside until "sunrise the next day"; otherwise, you will be thrown in jail and whipped until your master arrives and pays a fine.[8]

This was the Charleston culture Hajja may have endured. It's important to note that during those initial years when he lived in South Carolina, a magnificent uprising was being plotted by 60-year-old freed Black carpenter and Charleston resident Denmark Vesey. Between the years 1817 and 1822, Vesey, who'd won his freedom in 1800 thanks in large part to winning $1,500 in a "pick-4" lottery, managed to galvanize around 9,000 members of the slave community and convince them to "fight for freedom." Vesey's rebellious example spread throughout Hajja's environment, especially since Vesey—who at any time could have left Charleston and lived a more comfortable life in the North—talked with Black slaves "as far as forty or sixty miles from the heart of the city."[9]

Vesey's planned rebellion failed after several within his inner circle betrayed him by telling white officials details of the attack, but his indomitable spirit and belief in his people remained in the hearts and minds of Black slaves for years to come. "We must not stand with hands in pockets," the trilingual Vesey expressed to Charleston slaves. And as one man recalled, Vesey believed "that if we did not put our hand to the work and deliver ourselves, that we would never come out of slavery."[10]

As for Hajja, it appears the white broomstick of history has swept away much of his life's record. According to *Seventh Child*, a family memoir cowritten by Malcolm's nephew, Rodnell P. Collins, Hajja was a skilled carpenter and became a father as well. Hajja's son, Tony, remembered him as "a rebellious African" and "one who was never anybody's nigger."[11]

But perhaps early in Tony's life, Hajja "mysteriously disappeared" from the plantation. It's unclear whether Hajja fled or was sold, but Tony never saw his father again.

Around 1840, Tony's owner sold him to a young settler named Allen Little. Perhaps with help from his white family, Little soon acquired at least 690 acres of land near Edgefield, South Carolina. More land meant more work, especially for Tony, who was "considered very valuable property" because of the carpentry skills he'd learned from Hajja.[12]

Near the beginning of his time with the Little family, Tony met Clarrie, who'd been acquired to work mainly as a cook. On the surface, Clarrie went about her duties, but within her was an anger toward "whites," who she thought of "as thieves." Her bloodline was a mix of African and Native American peoples, so she had to endure the double tragedy of witnessing the American government push her family off land that was rightfully theirs and be forced into bondage to serve their needs.[13]

In 1847, Allen Little saw an opportunity to accrue even more land in Georgia, where certain sections of the state were "wide open for exploitation." Bringing Tony and Clarrie with him, Little targeted Talbot County, and thanks almost entirely to the relentless work of several dozen slaves, Little eventually acquired and maintained 1,200 acres during the 1850s. His methods were encouraged by the state of Georgia, which, during the decades before the Civil War, passed a law requiring landowners to have at least one slave per "fifty acres of land purchased."[14]

As they hoped for systemic change, Tony and Clarrie stayed together, becoming parents to 22 children—4 girls and 18 boys, one being Malcolm X's grandfather, John. In 1865, the end of the Civil War brought emancipation—and with it, the end of Allen Little's financial authority. Still, there remained one decorative link to Allen Little that Tony and Clarrie could not shake as they moved toward purchasing their own land.[15]

Hajja may have had a last name from his birthplace in Mali, but since his whereabouts were unknown, Tony could not recover any semblance of his African identity. Even if Hajja had remained near Tony and uttered his family name, government officials (many of whom were defeated Southern soldiers) weren't interested in taking the time to process a new listing or making an exception. Instead, Tony and Clarrie, along with hundreds of thousands of emancipated slaves, were asked, in various ways, "Which plantation did you come from?" When Tony replied with "Master Little's," the documentation was complete. "Your owner was Little, so you are Tony and Clarrie Little." It was official—the African couple could finally become American landowners, but the cost was more than 2,000 years of African history.

When questioned about the name "Little" on a television show over a century later, Malcolm said this: "I never acknowledge it whatsoever."[16]

AFRICA TO GRENADA

As Tony and Clarrie labored under the Little family in the 1840s, an African named Jupiter was kidnapped off the coast of West Africa and forced onto an illegal slave ship. Jupiter, Malcolm's maternal great-great-grandfather, was originally from a region located within what is now Nigeria and was born around 1825,[17] according to scholar Erik McDuffie.[18]

Jupiter, however, was spared the same fate as Hajja, who'd been kidnapped before the British Royal Navy (BRN) had devoted ships to stopping the illegal trafficking of Africans across the Atlantic. By the 1840s, the BRN had more knowledge of the common routes being taken by ships potentially hiding away captive Africans and attempted to intercept as many ships as they could track down.[19]

The British should not be considered selfless heroes. To be given that distinction, they could have worked with the slaves and taken them back to a different region of Africa, where they could have been given a second chance. Instead, the British Royal Navy redirected Jupiter and the other "now-free" Africans to the island of Grenada, then a British colony. It was by far a better destination than, say, Charleston. Also, Grenada was a "former slave society," slavery there ending in 1834, which meant that the predominantly African population was at least making a conscientious effort to treat one another as fellow human beings.

Still, Jupiter wanted no part of Grenada's mainstream communities. Despite their recent emancipation, major cities in Grenada were still at least in some way controlled by the British and "deeply stratified by race, gender and class."[20]

Upon landing, Jupiter acquired a last name, "Langdon," and proceeded to start his life in La Digue, a small, quaint village on the east side of Grenada. La Digue's remote location was ideal for Jupiter to put his carpentry skills to use, as he grew "determined to be free and independent from whites." Malcolm's great-great-grandfather, as McDuffie writes, "built a home on the property in which several generations of the Langdon family lived, including Louise Little."

Malcolm's eventual belief in self-reliance can be traced back to his mother's side of the family, living on a small island in the Caribbean Sea. It was here where Jupiter purposely separated himself from the racial inequality he saw in the bigger Grenadian cities, such as St. George, and built a house next to his own vegetable garden. It all belonged to him and, eventually, to his children. In the late 1860s, Jupiter met a Black woman named Mary Jane, and they went on to have six children, one being Edith Langdon, Malcolm's grandmother, born in 1882.

Jupiter and Mary Jane were disciplinarians, often using straps to keep their children in line. This style of punishment lasted at least two more generations. Still, despite the severity, the family remained close. Then, in 1893, a white man invaded their family bubble.

He was a Scotsman named Edward Norton, and he met 11-year-old Edith in La Digue. Details are scarce, and Norton's age at the time is unknown. Was he a 16-year-old sailor looking for a good time, or was he, as McDuffie describes, a "loafer . . . who had a penchant for sexually assaulting African-descended women"?[21]

The relatives McDuffie interviewed believe it was rape, but another Grenadian scholar, John Angus Martin, interviewed relatives who believe it was consensual. Just how consensual a sexual encounter with an 11-year-old can be is strongly debatable, however. One possible scenario was that Norton was a teenager and met Edith while his ship was docked. Perhaps he promised many things and then left for good soon after, leaving Edith feeling abandoned and confused. Or, Norton was an adult predator and assaulted Edith. McDuffie cites an account by the great-grandnephew of Louise Little, Terance Wilson, writing that Norton "fled Grenada soon after his assault of [Edith] Langdon in order to escape the wrath of the Langdon family."[22]

Regardless of which story is correct, a young girl was impregnated and abandoned by an older white man. At the very least, a solid case for statutory rape could be made. As for Malcolm, his white grandfather's act lightened his own skin: "I learned to hate every drop of that white rapist's blood that is in me."[23]

On January 2, 1894, Malcolm's mother, Louise (Langdon Norton) Little, was born. Her mother passed away several years later after giving birth to two more children. When interviewed decades later, Louise was direct: "I never knew my mother and father." Thus it was up to her mother's sister, Gertrude, to raise her in the home of Louise's grandparents, both of whom were proud Africans, their hearts still connected to their motherland.[24]

They didn't hold her "sea-blue" eyes against her.[25]

EARL'S GEORGIA

Back in rural Georgia, Tony and Clarrie Little, along with their 22 children, had started to settle "in and around" Talbot and Taylor County, becoming landowners. For the rest of the nineteenth century, the next three generations of Hajja's descendants maintained their own land, free of white control. "By purchasing land," said Ella Collins, herself once a resident of this area, "the Littles were able to avoid the vicious trap of sharecropping," which, by its suffocating economic restraints, soon became the post–Civil War version of slavery. From Hajja to Tony to "Pa John" (1859–1940) and, finally, to Malcolm's father, Earl, a desire for self-reliance and free will remained.[26]

On July 29, 1890, J. Early Little was born in Reynolds, Georgia, the fourth of eight children born to John and Ella Little. Malcolm's father grew up learning how to farm from "Pa John," and the family remained in rural Taylor County for his entire childhood, relocating at least once from Reynolds to an even smaller town, Carsonville, 20 miles away. Relatives described Pa John as being "over six feet five inches, very dark skinned, lean, muscular, and strong, fearless, hardworking, commanding, and completely devoted to his family." He'd outlive his son Early by nine years, passing in 1940.[27]

Surrounding Early during his childhood were a host of racial issues, all revolving around what many white newspapers were calling "the negro problem." Two weeks before his birth, a prominent Georgia bishop of the African Methodist Episcopal (AME) Church, Henry McNeal Turner, stated in the *Atlanta Constitution* his full support for a "back to Africa" bill proposed by white South Carolina senator M. C. Butler. The "Butler Bill" asked that Congress appropriate five million dollars to help Black people leave the US if they so desired. "Yes, I do favor it with all my heart," Turner said, "provided the conditions remain the same as now—leaving it optional to go or remain, and provided, too, that any colored persons who may see fit to emigrate may have Africa for their destination. I am opposed to any measure of emigration that does not have Africa as a first consideration."[28]

The bill wasn't voted on, but it was not difficult to see the motivation for such an idea. As Early grew up, segregation and racial conflicts persisted across the South. Mob violence and lynchings (both Black and white) occurred on a weekly basis, some being carefully documented in local newspapers. As Malcolm recollected to Alex Haley, his father, while growing up in Georgia, "had seen four of his six brothers die by violence, three of them killed by white men, including one by lynching."[29]

Many newspapers published detailed accounts of lynchings. This first example shows a paper's use of vague language—"outraged"—to describe the crime and also the sheer communal force that went into a lynching:

Nashville, Tennessee, August 16, 1890.

Henderson Fox, the negro who outraged Miss Annie Dowling, was lynched at Trenton to-night by a mob of about two hundred men from the neighborhood where the crime was com[mitted]. The sheriff and the jailer did all in their power to prevent the mob getting at the prisoner and summoned a large guard, which surrounded the jail. The mob was determined, however, and ran over the guard and demanded the keys of the jailer. He was compelled to give them up. The prisoner was taken out and hanged to a tree.[30]

In particular, young Black men in the South had an incredibly narrow margin for error, and Early Little understood through family and friends how quickly a community can turn on someone. This second example occurred two weeks before Ella gave birth to Early and exemplifies how a young Black man in Georgia was expected to behave and how the white community believed they held a moral supremacy:

Elberton, Georgia, July 13, 1890.
160 Miles from Reynolds.

There came very near being a lynching about six miles south of
Elberton Thursday. A young lady had a school in the settlement
there, and sent one of her pupils—the daughter of a gentleman
living close by—to the spring for water as was customary in the
school. There was a negro boy plowing in a field near by the path
that led to the spring. The boy seeing the little girl, who was ten
or eleven years old, pass to the spring, left his plow and secreted
himself behind a stump on the path, and as the girl came on
back with the water, he jumped out in the path and seized her.

The little girl screamed at the top of her voice, which frightened the negro and he ran off. The father of the little girl soon
heard of the circumstances, and summoning his brother and
one or two neighbors, soon had the negro in their custody. After
mature deliberation they decided that whipping was the best
punishment for him, which they at once proceeded to inflict;
and while the negro is not seriously injured, he received such
a whipping that he is not likely to forget it soon. While some
citizens think the negro ought to have been lynched, the more
conservative element think the parties pursued the right course.[31]

There were many other public executions—Erastus Brown was hanged in
1897 in Statesboro (150 miles away) after killing another man, his death viewed
by hundreds; Henry Campbell was a Black man who in 1908 was hanged in
Lawrenceville, GA (120 miles away) in front of thousands despite stating his
innocence. One notion was clear to Early throughout his childhood: remain
on your segregated farm and try not to upset the white majority. After receiving around four years of formal schooling, Early dropped out and focused on
farming and carpentry—educating himself on how to live independently.[32]

Choosing to live a life based on hard, outdoor work, Early developed his
muscles. By adulthood, he'd grown, as his first son Wilfred recalled, to "six
foot four in height, no fat—muscle and bone . . . a very strong man, not only
physically, in other ways too."[33]

Having enough of a land-based education to live free of his parents,
around the age of 18, Earl attempted to put down roots of his own and in 1909

unofficially married a young Black Georgian woman named Daisy Mason. Three children soon followed, the oldest being Earl Jr. (1912), followed by Ella (1914) and Mary (1916).[34]

For the next seven years, Earl struggled with his new reality as a husband and father living on his own land and working as a carpenter in racially tense rural Georgia. During the 1890s and into the 1900s, the Populist Party's message of biracial unity—an idea spearheaded by Georgia politician Thomas E. Watson, who later reneged—helped bring the party the support of new Black voters, but it simultaneously enraged white segregationists. Year by year, Black politicians were elected to serve in counties with a Black majority, and mostly white labor industries such as carpentry experienced a healthy dose of competition from skilled Black workers such as Earl. As Georgia went through growing pains during a decade-long economic depression, so too did Earl, who most likely faced angry white competitors, all of whom were strapped for cash. Mob rule and lynchings continued—perhaps none more terrifying than the September 1906 Atlanta Race Massacre.[35]

Originally labeled by Northern newspapers as the Atlanta Pogrom—a Russian word meaning "to destroy without pity"—the devastation of the riot left over 20 African Americans dead and embarrassed the country enough that the *Brooklyn Times* wrote that "the crimes" committed by the racist white mob "have sunk the United States to the level of the darkest Russia," which had carried out its own anti-Jewish pogrom in July of the same year. The Atlanta riots lifted the personality of then Atlanta University professor and activist W. E. B Du Bois into the national conversation and dimmed the efforts of Booker T. Washington, whose vision of accepting segregation was displayed in his 1895 speech, which Du Bois later dubbed "the Atlanta Compromise."[36]

At the time, Earl's personal feelings about race most likely fell somewhere between Du Bois's and Washington's. As he continued to endure poverty and racism, he had reservations about simply "casting down his bucket" and accepting his circumstances as he incrementally moved toward self-improvement and eventual racial integration, goals similar to those of Washington's Tuskegee Institute. On the other hand, the intellectual highbrow fire of Du Bois's *Souls of Black Folk* (1903) might not have resonated with an expert carpenter who'd chosen to make his living outside of the classroom.[37]

On March 25, 1917, a Jamaican-born printer named the Honorable Marcus Garvey spoke at the Big Bethel AME Church in Atlanta, located on the corner of "Sweet" Auburn Avenue and Butler Street. It's unknown whether Earl attended the talk, but around this time, he'd done a bit of Baptist preaching, shaping his own message of hope and strength.[38]

Earl was in trouble. Besides enduring hardships—an alleged October 1915 conviction of larceny with his cousin Wright potentially standing as one example—Daisy's family had not exactly accepted his "brawling ways." Soon a confluence of stress—impoverishment, Southern racial tension, and a lack of family support—caused Earl Little to flee his wife and three children. He yearned for a fresh start and found it in Montreal.[39]

LOUISE'S GRENADA

The story of [my mother, Louise's,] life was an epic one. The epic began in Grenada, continued in [Montreal,] Canada, and ended here in the States. In all three countries there are parts of her life waiting to be resurrected.

—Wilfred Little, Malcolm's oldest brother[40]

For the first 23 years of her life, Louise Little absorbed Grenadian culture and its threefold identity. The French—ever since causing the last group of Carib Indians to plunge to their deaths off a cliff now called Leapers Hill—first put down their cultural roots in 1651. For 130 years, Africans were delivered to Grenada's shores along the Atlantic Ocean's North Equatorial Current, and soon the established French language collided with African dialects, the result being Grenadian French Creole, or Patois. By 1763, Britain had taken control of the island, and two decades later, the official lopsided population of Grenada was 996 white residents and 24,620 slaves—a ratio of 1:25.[41]

With numbers such as these and Grenada (unlike Charleston) being a somewhat isolated island, perhaps rebellion was inevitable. Late at night on March 2, 1795, Julien Fedon, a mixed-race planter angrily motivated by promises made by the French but reversed by the British, organized vicious attacks on two port towns.[42]

One year of fighting ensued, and an estimated 7,000 slaves were killed. The sting of Fedon's Rebellion endured, however, becoming a source of pride for many who remained on the island. A feeling lingered among many Grenadians that "agitating for inclusion produced results." Sure enough, Britain abolished slavery in 1834, and as the decades passed, Louise saw firsthand the interconnections of French, British, and African cultures.[43]

It was a unique combination, and for a time, Louise embraced it. She completed five years of education at a local Anglican school in La Digue, its curriculum inspired by the ideals of its ever-malleable Book of Common Prayer. Louise had at least completed introductory courses in English, French, Math, and Science. Louise's "Grenadian teachers taught her to recite poetry and helped her develop a love for words," a love she'd soon share with her own children.[44]

As she mastered the fundamentals in each subject, her teachers followed strict disciplinary procedures, striking students on the arms or legs if they fell out of line. Back then, corporal punishment in school was not generally considered cruel—in fact, to Louise, it enlivened her. "When the teacher lashed me," she said more than half a century later, with a bit of a smile, "he woke me up. He made me feel. When you feel the sting of the lash, it enables you to feel."[45]

As the years passed, Louise also helped in and around the Langdon home. Besides learning English and French, she picked up a third language, Patois, a local African-French Creole language spoken by longtime residents. As Aunt Gertrude continued to look after her, Louise gained a sense of self-reliance.

All was not idyllic, however.

By 1913, her uncle Edgerton had decided to leave Grenada behind and move to Montreal. Nineteen at the time and questioning her own future, Louise started to become a financial burden on the family. Her choices were limited: marry and remain on the island, work modestly on her own in a small economy that revolved around the 1,000-plus acres of sugar plantations, or leave the island.[46]

After enduring several years of "emptiness and loneliness" living apart from her family, Louise chose to leave La Digue and Grenada behind, never to return, but she continued to correspond.

After spending about one month on a boat moving north along the East Coast, Louise stepped foot on Canadian soil on June 26, 1917. From St. John's, New Brunswick, she traveled to Montreal, where her uncle waited, the powerful message of a 28-year-old Jamaican printer already on his mind.[47]

FIGURE 2.1. Louise Little. Passport photo. 1917.

TOGETHER IN MONTREAL

I remember seeing the big, shiny photographs of Marcus Garvey
that were passed from hand to hand. My father had a big envelope of them . . . the pictures showed what seemed to me millions of Negroes thronged in parade behind Garvey riding in a
fine car, a big black man dressed in a dazzling uniform with gold
braids on it, and he was wearing a thrilling hat with tall plumes.

—Malcolm X[48]

On May 9, 1916, Edgerton Langdon made his way from Montreal to Harlem's St. Mark's Hall. There he sat in a packed house to listen to a stocky, well-dressed man with a thick Jamaican accent. Marcus Garvey had a determined look in his eyes, as if trying to will into existence the reality he desired. "He had a tremendous voice," recalled activist A. Phillip Randolph, a fellow Harlem "soapboxer" who'd met Garvey shortly after the Jamaican's ship had brought him to America's shores on March 23, 1916.

Prior to arriving in New York, Garvey, along with his eventual first wife, Amy Ashwood, had established the foundations for the UNIA (Universal Negro Improvement Association) in Kingston, Jamaica, on August 1, 1914. His passion for helping Black people was sparked during a tour of Central America, where as an experienced journalist and newspaper printer, Garvey was devastated to see such labor-filled suffering in so many countries. To Garvey, Black people were enduring life-or-death struggles to complete the Panama Canal, all so that they could receive little-to-no pay and face complete disregard for their own needs and desires. The African race was still being exploited on a global scale.[49]

Near the end of his travels, Garvey read Booker T. Washington's 1901 memoir, *Up from Slavery*, and as a young journalist who'd learned to understand the power of the printed word, he couldn't help but be inspired by Washington's story of hardship. Visions soon appeared to him of a global alliance of Black people. "I read *Up from Slavery*, and then my doom—if I may so call it—of being a race leader dawned on me."[50]

Before his debut at St. Mark's Hall, Garvey had used his valuable newspaper skills to create buzz, printing attractive flyers, "handbills and . . . tickets." Louise's uncle had already heard of the man who hoped to unify the Black populations scattered across the world.

Still, Garvey was a rookie to the Harlem community, and his public speaking skills paled in comparison to others who'd stood on the same stage (two accounts report that Garvey was nervous and even fell off the podium). Poor performance aside, Garvey's galvanizing message was clear and direct enough to create a ripple through the Black community, and after learning a few tips from the Isaiah-possessed white preacher Billy Sunday, Garvey toured North America, visiting Montreal briefly in 1917.[51]

It was perhaps Garvey's passionate response to the bloody East St. Louis Race Riot that sparked newly arrived Montrealer Earl Little to become a Garveyite:

For three hundred years the Negroes of America have given their life blood to make the Republic the first among the nations of the world, and all along this time there has never been even one year of justice but on the contrary a continuous round of oppression. At one time it was slavery, at another time lynching and burning, and up to date it is [wholesale] butchering. This is a crime against the laws of humanity; it is a crime against the laws of the nation, it is a crime against Nature, and a crime against the God of all mankind.[52]

One of the few facts we have about Earl Little and Louise Langdon Norton is their shared passion for Marcus Garvey's beliefs. Less is known of Earl than of Louise, who lived with her uncle at 150 St. Martin Street, a 15-minute walk from what soon became the first UNIA branch in Montreal. Around 1918, during an association meeting, Louise met Earl.

They fell in love amid the tension of World War I. The white Montreal population was harshly divided over Prime Minister Robert Borden's decision to initiate the Military Service Act in 1917. While British Canadians believed it to be important to help serve their home country in what was turning out to be a long and bloody fight, the French Canadians, such as those surrounding Earl and Louise at the time, were furious over being pressured into risking their lives for a country they held no real allegiance to. In Montreal especially—after French-speaking antielitist mayor Mederic Martin overwhelmingly won his 1914 election, running on a take-sides platform of pro-working-class French Canadians against the snobby English bankers—protests and even minor riots often took control of the downtown area from 1917 to 1918.[53]

Earl and Louise had the fortune of watching the action from the sidelines. It was old news for Louise to witness France and England being hostile toward each other, since the two countries often collided over islands such as Grenada and also other regions in Africa. Still, as the conflict played out and she became more acquainted with Earl, Louise used her French language skills and fair skin to her advantage, finding work "as a shop assistant and a domestic."[54]

As for the way they appeared as a couple, their oldest child Wilfred remembered them next to each other: "She was a small-boned and slender woman, five-feet-eight inches tall, and she carried herself well. Because she always held herself erect, she looked taller, but beside my six-foot-four father, she looked short." On May 10, 1919, they took the plunge and married in Montreal. It can't be known for certain how much Louise knew of Earl's past family setup in Reynolds, Georgia, but according to Malcolm's prison file, Earl did go out of his way to secure a divorce from Daisy Mason after he traveled to Boston, Massachusetts, where Daisy and the children had relocated.[55]

NOMADIC GARVEYITES IN LOVE

The Littles attached photos to their UNIA applications and added 35 cents each—the membership fee—stating in writing their "pledged" support for Marcus Garvey's organization. At the top of the application was one line: "We believe in one God, One Aim and One Destiny, and Because of This Belief, We Associate Ourselves Together."[56]

They were officially Garveyites, and soon after their marriage was official, the couple relocated to Philadelphia. They had chosen to follow a man who many in the UNIA called "the Negro Moses." Garvey's status as a powerful and untouchable leader grew even after he was shot three times at his Harlem office by George W. Tyler, a frustrated Black businessman, on October 14, 1919. Tyler had been seeking to collect a debt of $25 from Garvey, and after making threats to secretary/soon-to-be-first wife Amy Ashwood, he shot Garvey near his right eye and twice in the right leg. Forty-eight hours later, Tyler fell from a third-story Harlem prison window, fracturing his skull and later dying, fueling conspiracy theories that Tyler was merely a plant by the FBI.

In what seemed at first to be a miraculous feat, Garvey left the hospital with a cane and spoke at Philadelphia's People's Church. In magnanimous fashion, Garvey declared to a near-worshipful crowd that "if the shots caused the organization to advance 2,000 per cent, then I am satisfied to die."[57]

Now living in America, Earl and Louise hoped to find specific roles in Garvey's organization. While they believed in the UNIA's potential for social change, Earl was looking for the movement to add a religious component. Garvey was a "nominal Catholic," and in the early stages of forming his organization, he was hesitant to give the UNIA a designated denomination. Still, he had among his followers many preachers eager to tie the movement to the church. Enter the Reverend James Walker Hood Eason, who in December 1917 founded the People's Metropolitan A.M.E. Zion Church in Philadelphia, on the corner of 15th and Christian Streets. Eason's church quickly became a fixture in the local Black community, offering members a "relief" wage of seven dollars a week if they became sick.[58]

The "silver-tongued" Eason was wildly popular in Philadelphia and Harlem. Just before accepting the unofficial title of American president for Black people, serving in the "Black House," Eason wanted to do anything in his power to help the American Black man, "from the blacking of boots to the purifying of souls."[59]

Around Eason's church in Philadelphia, Earl and Louise were surrounded by Garveyites. By 1920, membership in Philadelphia had reached nearly one million. On February 12, 1920, Louise gave birth to their first child, Wilfred. With a cause to fight for and a community to support them, the Littles spent their short time in Philadelphia soaking in the ideals of the UNIA and figuring out how best to make an impact.

For as supportive as Philadelphia was, the Littles were somewhat different than many of the other, more urban members. Earl had grown up on a farm in rural Georgia, and Louise's experiences in French-inflected, faraway La Digue were vastly different from her encounters in the loudness of a rapidly growing Philadelphia. "I always remember," Wilfred said later, "that [my mother] didn't like to live in the city, and my father didn't like it either."[60]

This desire—to take more control over their livelihood—meant looking west. The UNIA was always looking for members to help expand the organization outside the bounds of Philadelphia and New York. In the South and out west, there were horrific accounts of racial violence and lynchings. None, however, were as visually horrific as the killing of Omaha's William Brown in September 1919.[61]

After the end of World War I, America's cultural landscape quaked. There were fears, fanned in part by then-president Woodrow Wilson, that the ideals of Russian Bolshevism could infiltrate or undermine the minds of impoverished people tired of feeling like they were second-class.

While the "red" paranoia festered, many African Americans had started to carve out places in the country. The second great migration had taken tens of thousands of Black men and women out of the Jim Crow South and into Northern cities, such as Omaha. Jobs were abundant during the war, and white managers needed to fill positions to keep up productivity. In Omaha, the Black population doubled between 1910 and 1920, from around 5,000 to over 10,000; still a small number when compared with the white population of 191,000.[62]

Still, fortunes were changing. With national voices such as Garvey's UNIA along with W. E. B Du Bois and the NAACP, Black Americans had begun to feel a bit more self-confident about their future prospects. Black American soldiers who'd fought in Europe in segregated divisions had hoped serving their country would entitle them to more dignity.

It didn't work out that way.

During the 1919 "Red Summer," according to Omaha scholar Orville D. Menard, it was "sensation-seeking newspapers" that created "an atmosphere receptive to rabble rousing" and an acceptance of violent acts of mob justice, such as lynching. Over two dozen cities experienced racially motivated violence that summer, Omaha being one of them. But back then, the word *racism* was not often labeled as a cause of the underlying anger. More political terms, such as "anarchists," "sovietism," and "Bolsheviks" blanketed the fear and anxiety the white majority felt toward an increasingly confident and growing Black population.[63]

In Omaha on September 25, 1919, a young white couple, Milton Hoffman and Agnes Loeback, had just finished watching a silent movie and were making their way home. As they walked, a man who was allegedly Black (he could have been wearing blackface) pointed a gun at them. He took Hoffman's "watch, money and billfold, plus a ruby ring from" 19-year-old Agnes. This man then "ordered Hoffman to move several steps away then dragged [Agnes] by her hair into a nearby ravine and raped her." A local newspaper reported the next morning that the suspect was a "black beast" whose "ravishment" had been "consummated."[64]

A widespread search commenced. Besides police, a mob of around 400 Omaha residents joined. No clues or evidence was found, but one resident told the mob of a "suspicious negro" who lived with another Black man and a white woman. Apparently, that was enough. The mob surrounded the house and used shotgun fire to demand they come out. Eventually, they broke in and found a Black 40-year-old coal laborer with "chronic rheumatism . . . hiding under his bed." His name was William Brown, or Will for short.

Back at Agnes's home, the mob had brought Brown to her. Was this the guy? At first, Agnes said yes, but she later went on record saying she "can't say whether he is the man or not." Unfortunately for Brown, a still-enraged, looking-for-revenge Hoffman came in, stared at Brown, and stated with absolute certainty that he was the guy.[65]

Calls for a lynching ensued, and a rope was thrown around Brown's neck, only to be wrestled off him by police. After a mob frenzy, Brown was taken to the county jail. As word spread around Omaha, Brown pleaded to the police that he was innocent, but the spark had been lit. It mattered little that a lawyer and a local reporter strongly doubted Brown's ability to even complete such an assault, since his rheumatism had become so advanced.

Two days later, Hoffman was still furious. He rallied a few hundred young men and teenage students from a school. They reached the courthouse, and after three hours, the crowd became 5,000-strong. Breaking windows with rocks and bricks, they demanded the police hand over Brown; they demanded "justice" to show that white women deserved to be protected. A gun store was "broken into for revolvers and rifles." When the mayor of Omaha, Ed Smith, came out of the courthouse in the hopes of promoting a sense of calm, "he was hit with a baseball bat," among other objects. The mayor stood his ground, hoping to change the mind of the mob. "I will not give up this man. I'm going to enforce the law even with my own life." The mob seemed to mentally shrug and took the mayor's sacrificial comments literally, noosing his neck and stringing him up on a "traffic signal tower." He stayed up long enough to lose consciousness and was saved by sympathetic Omaha residents.[66]

When it came to Brown, however, there was no sympathy. Eventually, the mob's intensity grew so maniacal that the courthouse was set on fire.[67] When the firefighters came with water and ladders, the mob chopped up the hoses and used the ladders to get closer to Brown. Eventually, the prisoners, police officers, and administration trapped inside had no choice.

Menard describes the next hideous hour:

> Beaten and bloody, [Brown] was taken downstairs and handed over to the waiting horde, anxious to hang him from the traffic tower at Eighteenth and Harney. Several men pulled Brown's body into the air as the crowd cheered. The swaying body became a target for gunfire. Lowered after twenty minutes, Brown's remains were tied to the end of a police car that the mob had seized, and dragged to Seventeenth and Dodge streets. There he was burned on a pyre fueled with oil from the red signal lanterns used for street repair. Brown's charred remains were then dragged behind an automobile through downtown streets.[68]

The Omaha Race Riot became national news, and around 4,000 federal troops were called in to secure the city. In the next several days, nearly 2,000 Black residents left Omaha, most choosing to head south by train to Kansas City.

If Earl and Louise Little had not heard the details of this incident in Philadelphia, they may have eventually viewed what can only be described as the single most heinous picture this author has ever seen. As Brown's body "burned on a pyre," there happened to be an *Omaha World-Herald* photographer nearby. As part of the white mob crowded close together, proudly trying to make sure their faces were visible, the photo was snapped as Brown's body "sizzled" in front of them. The photo was reprinted by several newspapers across the country, though due to the sinister visual, the *New York Daily News* covered Brown's body by placing a block of text over it, deeming it too "revolting for publication." The photo even reached the desk of W. E. B. Du Bois, who eventually published it in the monthly NAACP magazine in 1920.[69]

Without question, Earl and Louise ultimately heard about the trouble in Omaha, and even though thousands of Black men and women had left the city, the violence did not scare them into remaining in Philadelphia. Instead, around a year and a half after William Brown's lynching (most likely in the middle of 1921), the young couple and baby Wilfred traveled 1,200 miles west and moved into a home at 3448 Pinkney Street in North Omaha. Their goal was to help establish a UNIA outpost.[70]

It may be tempting to imagine the Little family moving to an all-white city and alone defending the rights of Black people. While, yes, the Littles most likely chose Omaha because of its rural location and underrepresented Black population, the fact is that there were several organizations already established when they arrived in the middle of 1921. An NAACP chapter had been in Omaha since 1915, and there were at least three Black newspapers, the Omaha *Monitor*, founded by Rev. John A. Williams, being the most influential. If Earl and Louise wanted to carve out any kind of change in Omaha, communicating with Williams was a smart starting point.[71]

North Omaha was where the majority of the Black community lived, a red-lined, unofficially segregated district that had doubled its population due to the meat-packing industry actively recruiting Black Southerners because of labor shortages during World War I. At the beginning of the *Monitor*'s run, John Williams went a step further, offering to reimburse the travel expenses of any new Black resident willing to relocate and settle in Omaha. As new residents came, took up land, and accepted jobs at lower wages, racial tension began to grow.[72]

Earl and Louise started slowly in North Omaha, and on October 22, 1921, they added a daughter, Hilda, to their family. To put food on the table and keep their home, Earl worked as a freelance carpenter. It's unknown how Louise, in addition to raising two small children, contributed financially, but she later sewed clothes and sold copies of Garvey's the *Negro World*. In any case, their UNIA post remained small during those first two years.[73]

About three miles south of their home on Pinkney Street was the meeting location of the Omaha Ku Klux Klan (KKK). Much has been made of the Klan's threats against the Little family, none more famous than Malcolm's mention of them on the first page of his *Autobiography*. But especially after the 1919 race riots, Omaha officials had placed a zero-tolerance policy on public assembly. So when the Klan started a new Klavern in Omaha in 1921, they were only allowed to meet privately, at 41st and Farnam Streets. When one of the KKK leaders, Edward Young Clarke, came in hopes of organizing a large initiation ceremony in Omaha, James Dahlman, the new mayor (Ed Smith wasn't reelected), squashed the idea, banning any "public demonstration" in Omaha by the Klan.[74]

The Klan held a stronger influence in nearby cities such as Lincoln and other rural Nebraska towns, but in Omaha, they were publicly criticized, perhaps most relentlessly by the *Monitor*, which in print called the Klan "an association of cockroaches." Another short-lived Black newspaper, the *New Era*, had no fear in printing that "we . . . serve notice that we will not stand for any intimidation or imposition from the KKK or any of their sympathizers." Again, Earl and Louise were not alone. By the time Earl and Louise left Omaha, two of their fellow Black residents had won legislative seats.[75]

Most of Omaha's white community denounced the Klan as well, remembering far too well the national humiliation brought upon them by the mob-ruled 1919 riot. The University of Nebraska declared that "any student joining the Klan would be suspended." The predominantly white-subscribed *Omaha World-Herald* announced their disgust with the Klan in print as well.[76]

Earl and Louise also had to deal with a bit of UNIA damage control, courtesy of their fearless leader. On June 25, 1922, Marcus Garvey traveled to the KKK's headquarters in Atlanta and met with Edward Young Clarke for two hours. Garvey believed the two organizations had somewhat similar agendas, mainly the idea of keeping the races separated. Garvey's meeting was widely criticized, and it embarrassed many of his UNIA followers. The organization, already beginning to sputter because of financial mismanagement from Garvey's steamship corporation, known as Black Star Line, now had to face ridicule from not just the NAACP but its own leadership. James Eason, appalled at Garvey's attempt to find some sort of common ground with a fundamentally discriminative organization, made plans to begin his own organization. But in early January 1923, he was shot dead in New Orleans, most likely by Garvey loyalists.[77]

Earl and Louise were committed Garveyites, and these events did not dissuade them from participating in the UNIA. After all, it was Garvey's cause that bonded the couple and gave them their future vision. They carried on along Pinkney Street, Louise giving birth to Philbert, their third child, on May 4, 1923. On June 18, Garvey was convicted of mail fraud and sentenced to five years. He was taken to a prison in New York City called "The Tombs" but was released in September after $15,000 of bail money was collected by his wife, Amy Jacques Garvey. Legally required to remain in the country until he was sentenced, Garvey and his wife toured the United States, and it is during this stretch of a year and a half, most likely January of 1925, that Garvey visited Earl and Louise's UNIA-Omaha outpost.[78]

Their oldest child, Wilfred, remembered Garvey visiting their home. In describing the encounter more than a half century later to Grenadian author Jan Carew, Wilfred said he "can never forget that when Marcus Garvey was on the run from the FBI, my mother hid him in our house and wrote letters and dispatches for him." Garvey was never technically "on the run," but he was in a precarious state of freedom, awaiting his final sentencing while no doubt being tracked by unseen federal forces. Wilfred was almost five years old.[79]

To further the case that Garvey visited Omaha in January 1925, John A. Williams published an editorial of Garvey in his *Monitor* newspaper on January 23, 1925, disagreeing with Garvey's plan "to migrate to the land of its forefathers . . . by vast multitudes." The *Monitor* did remain respectful of Garvey, though. "When one views the growing prejudice against Negroes in America," the editorial explained, "it is easy to account for Garvey's contention and those who believe as he does. When, however, one notes other significant facts one cannot agree with him."[80]

In late January, Louise was close to five months pregnant with Malcolm, and it was at this time that the first paragraph of Malcolm's *Autobiography* begins:

> When my mother was pregnant with me, she told me later, a party of hooded Ku Klux Klan riders galloped up to our home in Omaha, Nebraska, one night. Surrounding the house, brandishing their shotguns and rifles, they shouted for my father to come out. My mother went to the front door and opened it. Standing where they could see her pregnant condition, she told them that she was alone with her three small children, and that my father was away, preaching, in Milwaukee.[81] The Klansmen shouted threats and warnings at her that we had better get out of town because "the good Christian white people" were not going to stand for my father's "spreading trouble" among the "good" Negroes of Omaha with the "back to Africa" preachings of Marcus Garvey.[82]

History's obsessive attention to the Klan has caused other related supremacist organizations to remain in the shadows. Take Omaha mayor James Dahlman, who at first glance appears to be a man bent on preventing the KKK from holding public rallies. A closer look at Dahlman, however, shows that on May 2, 1923, he was named the president of an organization called "Fascisti of America," an unauthorized branch of fascism used in Italy that brought Benito Mussolini to power. Dahlman's picture was published in many newspapers across the country, and the *Sacramento Bee* summarized the group's mission this way: "Purposes of the [Fascisti of America] include the upholding of the federal constitution, the engendering of 'pure Americanism,' prevention and elimination of causes of mob violence, protection of pure womanhood and 'upholding the rights of a free and enlightened people to choose their own religion.' Its symbol is a black shirt with an outstretched golden eagle over the heart."[83]

On May 19, 1925, Omaha was a mess. As pregnant Louise experienced contractions, the Little family found themselves deeply rooted within a city containing two fascist organizations—one with black shirts, and one with white hoods—and a financially frustrated white community. In the middle of prohibition, hundreds of Omaha bootleggers smuggled in whisky and gin mixed in unsanitized bathtubs. In North Omaha, their UNIA outpost battled for community respect against the more established NAACP as their leader, Marcus Garvey, sat in an Atlanta jail cell, the *Negro World* still circulating thanks to his loyal wife.[84]

Into this environment, Malcolm Little was born. He had a five-year-old brother named Wilfred, a three-year-old sister named Hilda, and a two-year-old brother named Philbert.

They would outlive him by decades.

3
THE MIDDLE CHILD

Omaha to Mason

1925 to 1940

All of our experiences fuse into our personality. Everything that
has ever happened to us is an ingredient.

—Alex Haley and Malcolm X, *The Autobiography
of Malcolm X: As Told to Alex Haley*

As Louise had done with Wilfred and Philbert, she gave her third son the
name of one of his Grenadian uncles. Malcolm Orgias had grown up near
Louise in La Digue and followed family members to Canada. It's unknown
to what extent Orgias had lived around the Montreal area, but Louise had
wanted to hold on to her island roots and pass on the memories of her relatives to her boys.[1]

Wilfred, five-and-a-half at the time Malcolm was born, could see immediately that his new brother was different from his other siblings. Sure, his
skin was light enough that their father sent a telegram to his parents in
Georgia, saying, "It's a boy, but he's white, just like mama!" But Wilfred
focused more deeply on the noise the newborn made in those first few
months. "Malcolm demanded attention from the day he was born," he told
a Grenadian author. "I remember that when my mother brought him home
from the hospital in Omaha, Nebraska, he used to bawl his head off, and
my mother would say, 'Wilfred, give this child a bottle, I don't have enough
milk to breastfeed him the way he wants me to'; and with Malcolm red in
the face and making himself heard, she'd say, 'This one is going to grow up
to talk to people.'"[2]

Louise, Wilfred recalled, had a mother's sense, a clairvoyance for knowing her children's future. In Wilfred's case, Louise believed he'd "always be helping those in need," as he had a gentle soul. Hilda, meanwhile, kept to herself and followed the rules, offering wry humor and contributing where and when she could. From an early age, Philbert was combative and confrontational—and now he had a bit of competition. "She had a way of forecasting what each of us would do from early on," said Wilfred, "and every one of her predictions came out just like she said."[3]

Both Earl—who'd begun to make a few business connections 500 miles away in the more economically dynamic city of Milwaukee—and Louise continued to manage their UNIA outpost with very little local support. If anything, they wondered why they remained in a city with very few opportunities for Black residents outside of North Omaha.

During the first week of October 1925, the American Legion held its national convention in downtown Omaha. On October 6, President Calvin Coolidge and his wife came to Omaha and gave their support to the organization, formed by war veterans in 1919, its motto being "For God and Country." Coolidge delivered a message of hope, emphasizing his desire for more peace and unity in the country: "Whether one traces his Americanism back three centuries to the Mayflower, or three years to the steerage, is not half so important as whether his Americanism of today is real and genuine. No matter by what various crafts we came here, we are all now in the same boat."[4]

If the Little family had decided to attend the event, perhaps to catch a glimpse of President Coolidge, they'd have seen a sea of white faces and a humongous 48-star American flag. Declared by one local paper as "the largest flag in the world," it weighed around 700 pounds and was 90 feet long and 165 feet wide. The flag had been hung across the entire north side of a Brandeis department store, located two blocks from where William Brown had been lynched six years prior. Perhaps Brandeis, who paid for the flag as the administration's gift to the American Legion, was hoping to recast the city's image as positively American.[5]

Due in large part to strict segregation measures and racial housing covenants, there was not much of a consistent Black presence in Omaha's white culture. African American representation in Omaha's white districts was led mainly by the Dan Desdunes jazz band, composed of 25 Black musicians who traveled to local fairs and parades across the state. In newspapers, white Omaha locals may have followed boxer Harry "the black panther" Wills, whose name in 1926 was most commonly linked to a potential bout across the "color line" against white heavyweight champion Jack Dempsey.[6]

The Little family remained in North Omaha until the end of 1926, and as Malcolm and his siblings grew, Earl and Louise held UNIA meetings once a month on Sunday afternoons at their own "Liberty Hall," located at 2528 Lake Street, about a mile away from their Pinkney Street home.[7]

Most of the meetings followed a particular format and were led by Earl, the president.

First, the group stood and sang "From Greenland's Icy Mountains," a hymn composed by an Anglican missionary in the early 1800s. One of several official songs of the UNIA, Garvey may have chosen it because of its nostalgic "back home" melody and its first verse:

> From Greenland's icy mountains
> From India's coral strand
> Where Afric's sunny fountains
> Roll down their golden sand
> From many an ancient river
> From many a palmy plain
> They call us to deliver
> Their land from error's chain

The white missionary who wrote the song couldn't have imagined it being used by an organization like the UNIA. Garvey may have interpreted "error's chain" to mean the long-lasting error of Africans all over the world being displaced from their home countries.[8]

After the three-minute hymn, the group sat, and Earl Little led them through a prayer and a preamble, the latter containing recent news and concerns, like Garvey still being in an Atlanta jail cell. Once Earl finished his remarks, there was a "musical selection." One song commonly used in many UNIA meetings was "Ethiopia, Thou Land of Our Fathers," written by A. Josiah Ford from Barbados:

> Advance, advance to victory,
> Let Africa be free;
> Advance to meet the foe
> With the might
> Of the Red, the Black and the Green.

Often, after the musical selection, a special guest spoke about the cause, sometimes a reverend or a professor, and directions were made to help boost membership.[9]

On May 22, 1926, a brief Omaha report was written, most likely by Louise, and published in the *Negro World*: "Omaha Division held its regular mass meeting on Sunday, May 9. Mr. E. Little delivered the principal address. This division is small but much alive to its part in carrying on the great work." To Garvey, it was important for solidarity's sake that as many outposts as possible publish their reports, no matter how small or uneventful. Along with Omaha, there were reports from 23 other cities, some as small as Massillon, Ohio; Gulfport, Mississippi; and Tampico Alto, California.[10]

FROM MILWAUKEE TO LANSING

By the end of the year, however, Earl and Louise had decided to uproot their four children and relocate to Milwaukee. In Malcolm's *Autobiography*, he mentioned the ever-growing threat of the Ku Klux Klan, but it was also a business decision made by Earl. The Klan were just as prevalent in Milwaukee as they were in Omaha, but Milwaukee's Black population in the late 1920s was on the rise.[11]

Malcolm was too young to recall much of Milwaukee, but Wilfred had a few memories: "I remember that when we lived in Milwaukee, we had a little store and a storefront, with an apartment next door." Wilfred also recalled his mother using her expert skills as a seamstress, often making the children's clothes herself. To make money, she "used the store to sell her merchandise," making "jackets and knickers" for boys and "dresses with bloomers" for girls. Also in Milwaukee, Louise was able to, in a roundabout way, reconnect with her Grenadian spiritual self by visiting a Native American reservation just outside Milwaukee. "The Indians treated her like one of their own," Wilfred said, "and she'd sit with them and join them in singing their chants." In her childhood, Louise had bonded with Grenadian Caribs, who'd first settled in Grenada back in the fourteenth century. "So this [in Wisconsin] was just connecting her to an experience from her past," Wilfred recalled.

Wilfred deeply respected his mother. "She was brave, and she was a fighter."[12]

In the middle of 1927, Louise was pregnant again, this time with Reginald. With the Little family about to grow again, Earl gave his time to Milwaukee's division of the UNIA. On Sunday, January 2, 1927, the "ex-president of the Omaha, Neb. division" was invited to speak at their 3:00 p.m. service.

Here is the program for that afternoon, in the order that it was printed in the *Negro World*:

Opening Ode: "From Greenland's Icy Mountains."
Meeting Called to Order: Mr. Odie Hall
Prayer: Mrs. J. E. Ferrell, Lady President of Milwaukee
    Division
Hymn: "God Bless Our President."
Opening Address: Robert Finney, ex-treasurer
Address: John Armond
Music Selection by the Band
Address: Mr. Odis Wedgeworth
Address: Mr. Washington, ex-president of Chattanooga, TN,
    division
Reading: "Aims and Objects," Mrs. J. E. Ferrell
Solo Performance: J. C. Scott
Reading: Front page of the *Negro World*, by UNIA-Milwaukee
    Secretary
Address: Earl Little
Closing Remarks: Perry Love, UNIA-Milwaukee President
Offering: Donations collected
Closing Hymn: National anthem[13]

On January 9, Earl Little had settled into his role as UNIA-Milwaukee's "spiritual adviser," a role that required him to lead a weekly religious service at 11:00 a.m. on Sunday mornings at their Liberty Hall location. Louise often brought the children with her—Wilfred (7), Hilda (5), Philbert (3.5), and baby Malcolm (1.5)—to listen to Earl preach. S. E. Rouguere, the UNIA member assigned to send in reports to the *Negro World*, mentioned that these religious services "were making wonderful progress under the leadership of Elder E. Little and . . . have put new life into the division."[14]

As for his business affairs, within six months of leaving Omaha, Earl had become the president of Milwaukee's International Industrial Club. On June 8,

1927, he used this title when writing a letter to President Coolidge. Cosigned by two fellow UNIA-Milwaukee members—his secretary, W. M Townsend, and his treasurer, Robert Finney—Little hoped to persuade the president to release Marcus Garvey from prison. Using loftily respectful language, Little made his case, starting this letter with "Honorable Sir:" "We now humbly petition your excellency in the Name of the God who created all men to dwell upon the face of the earth, to consider our request, that by the power vested in you, you release Marcus Garvey from the five-year sentence withou[t] deportation which shall be your priceless gift to the Negro people of the world thus causing your name to be honored with generations yet unborn. Your petitioners in duty ever pray."[15]

Earl wasn't the only one sending the president these kinds of letters regarding Marcus Garvey, and apparently, the amount eventually pushed Coolidge into action. Six months after the date on Earl's letter, Garvey was released from prison, but under one condition: he was to be immediately deported.

On December 3, 1927, a weary but still combative Marcus Garvey boarded a train traveling from Atlanta to New Orleans. Waiting for him was the SS *Saramacca* and thousands of supporters standing in the rain. As rain poured down, Garvey addressed the enormous crowd. He wanted them to understand that they had already come so far since he arrived 10 years ago. One of his last quoted sentences on US soil was this: "I sincerely believe that it is only by nationalizing the Negro and awakening him to the possibilities of himself that his universal problem can be solved." And with that, the *Saramacca* set a course for Kingston, Jamaica. He returned to his home country a hero, his work in the US only half finished.[16]

Early in 1928, Earl and Louise decided to give up their lifestyle in Milwaukee and uproot their family yet again. This time—their newborn son Reginald joining infant Malcolm and three other siblings—they settled in Albion, Michigan, only a couple hundred miles east of Milwaukee.

It's unclear why they decided to move, but there may have been an opportunity for the family via Earl's brother, Jim, who lived in Albion at the time. By August 6, 1928, the Littles were mentioned in the *Battle Creek Enquirer* as if they were already residents of Albion: "Reginald, one-year-old son of Mr. and Mrs. Earl Little, [717] Sheridan road, underwent an emergency operation at the Sheldon hospital Saturday afternoon [August 4]." Almost two weeks later, he was discharged.[17]

The family didn't stay there long. Albion was small and had few opportunities. By 1929 they had moved 40 miles north to Lansing, which was eight times the size of Albion and had a larger Black population.

It's in Lansing that young Malcolm's memory was given a jolt.

A NEAR-DEATH EXPERIENCE

On Thursday, November 8, 1929, around 2:30 a.m., the Little family slept soundly. Their six children had been in their beds since 7:00 p.m., newborn Yvonne in her crib. Suddenly, the sound of a strong "blow up" awakened Earl, and he "yelled for everybody to get up." At first, Malcolm remained asleep, but "I remember being suddenly snatched awake into a frightening confusion of pistol shots and smoke and flames." At four-and-a-half years old, Malcolm had not retained any impactful memories of Omaha and Milwaukee. Instead, his first "vivid memory" was of being in Lansing, surrounded by smoke and fire.[18]

Louise raced up and down the hallway and alerted the children. "She got us outta the house," recalled Philbert, "otherwise we would've all been cremated." Earl, meanwhile, grabbed his shotgun and ran out the front door. He could see, in his words, "the blaze whooping up on my house." In the distance, he saw someone suspicious leaving the area, so he shot at them once before running back into the house to help Louise and the children.[19]

What followed, according to Wilfred, was chaos. "Everybody was running into the walls and into each other, trying to get away." Eventually, Louise and Earl were able to rescue their six children and bring them out onto the front lawn. The fire roared and soon engulfed the house, leaving not much time to "bring anything else out."[20]

Still, Louise tried. The night air was chilly, even with the fire, and they were soon to be without a home, so Louise entered the burning house and took "whatever she could grab," such as blankets and quilts. In such a panicked state, Louise or someone else momentarily placed a few blankets over three-month-old Yvonne. As the fire consumed the house, Louise checked on her six children, but couldn't find Yvonne. A rush of terror came over Louise's mind. Hadn't she brought her out?

As Wilfred remembered, "My mother almost lost her mind. I mean [Dad and some of us] were hanging on to her to keep her from going back into the house. And then finally [Yvonne] cried [from under some blankets], and they knew where the baby was."[21]

Malcolm also recalled their desperation. "I remember we were outside in the night in our underwear, crying and yelling our heads off."[22]

According to a police report, the fire department "refused to come" and help stop the Little's home from burning down. By the time the police came, the Littles were homeless.[23]

The police felt compelled to start a case of suspected arson against Earl. Their reasoning was thin. Weeks before the fire, neighbors "resented the presence of the colored family" and used a racial covenant written into the deed for the house to start "proceedings for their removal."[24]

The covenant's language, written by the Capital View Land Company, which held ownership over the subdivision, read as follows: "Only persons of the Caucasian Race shall have the right of habitation or dwelling in any of said premises."[25]

The judge deemed the racial exclusion clause as fair enough grounds to rule against the Littles. They were soon to be evicted from their Westmont neighborhood home, and it was in this precarious state that the police began concocting the idea that Earl set fire to his home to collect a $2,500 insurance payout. There were several problems with this theory, however.

First, Earl, with backing from the local NAACP chapter and pastor George R. Collins of the AME Church, was in the process of appealing the judge's decision to uphold the racial exclusion clause. They had sold him the house anyway, so there was at least a chance they could keep the house or be in a position to negotiate. Second, Earl had actually failed to keep his insurance payments up-to-date, and only on November 9 did he go into his local insurance agency to make a payment. Last, and most important, why would Earl risk the lives of his entire family, his wife and six children, and his own, only to stage a home-destroying fire to collect $2,500?[26]

Twenty hours after the fire, the police took Earl to the city jail as they pursued leads, embarrassing Earl and the family. The Littles stayed with Herb Walker's family over at 732 Clark Street, in Lansing. Earl was released several days later, charged only with the possession of an "unregistered revolver."

Left with nothing, Louise must have felt devastated and unprotected. As Malcolm recalled, there was a "friction" between his mother and father: "They seemed to be nearly always at odds. Sometimes my father would beat her." In the *Autobiography*, Malcolm placed the blame on Louise for using her advanced education and superior linguistic skills to "correct an uneducated man." Louise was deeply concerned about the current state of her family, and it was natural for her to doubt Earl's priorities. Even though Earl certainly didn't start the fire, his fearless, never-back-down attitude toward neighbors may have provoked the attack on their home.[27]

Wilfred, since he was the oldest, saw his father's character clearly: "Knowing that my father didn't intend to stop what he was doing—he was always speaking in terms of Marcus Garvey's way of thinking and trying to get Black people to organize themselves to work in unity toward improving their conditions—in those days if you did that, you were still considered a troublemaker."[28]

Not only was Earl stigmatized as a "troublemaker," but he also went to extremes to keep his family away from being offered charity, handouts, or favors. "My father," Philbert recalled, "didn't want anybody to exercise authority over his children. He wanted to exercise the authority, and he did. And he didn't want anyone to sell him some house that was worn out. He wanted his own home, and he built it."[29]

After the fire, the Littles moved six miles away to East Lansing, at 401 Charles Street. It was temporary, since Earl still desired to build a home. By 1930, he'd completed enough of a four-bedroom home in South Lansing for the family to move in and get settled. Finally, the Littles had a property that was detached from the oppressive system surrounding them.[30]

The Littles had acquired enough land to grow vegetables in their backyard and kept a cow, chickens, and rabbits, but it took quite some time for Earl to complete the house's construction. As Wilfred recalled, "Every payday he'd buy whatever he needed and do some more to the house, and get it to where we could move into it." Earl went section-by-section, first building the frame, then he "had it covered, had the roof on, had the windows in, and had it partitioned off, so we moved in on the sub-floor . . . the wide boards [before the fine floor]." As the family sat on the subflooring, Earl eventually finished the house. Through this process, "he could [have a home] without getting in debt, and it would be his."[31]

Besides carpentry, Earl continued to work in some capacity as a spiritual advisor, buoyed by the philosophical outlooks of Garvey and the make-your-own-way discipline of Booker T. Washington. It was during these UNIA meetings that Malcolm would best remember Earl: "My father would drive in his old black touring car, sometimes taking me, to meeting places all around the Lansing area." At many of these events, Malcolm watched from his seat as Earl ended his speech "saying, several times, and the people chanting after him, 'Up, you mighty race, you can accomplish what you will!'"[32]

After the event, the Little sons felt empowered. "When you'd leave there," Wilfred recalled, "you'd feel proud of yourself . . . you'd be proud that you were Black. You know that you had been somebody and you're gon' be somebody now if you got the chance, and you looked for every opportunity to accomplish that."[33]

By the early fall of 1931, the Littles were a "structured family," independent from the community, yet together as a unit. "When we got out of school," said Philbert, "me and my brothers and sisters, we'd come right home and go to work in the garden, clean up the chicken shed, and get ready for the night. We'd pump the water and bring it in the house and all this. To not do this brought the consequence of a whipping. Everybody knew what they had to do and did it. We children were under check."[34]

A TRAGIC LOSS

On the night of September 28, 1931, however, their structure would come unhinged . . .

Wilfred, Hilda, Philbert, Malcolm, Reginald, Yvonne, and baby Wesley were home; the four oldest had been at school earlier in the day. "My mother and father were having one of their arguments," Malcolm said. It was about dinner. From what Malcolm saw, Earl went out into the backyard where the rabbits were kept (Malcolm: "We raised rabbits, but sold them to white people.") and pulled one out of the cage. With a quick "twist of his big black hands," Earl decapitated the rabbit "and threw the bleeding necked thing back at my mother's feet." With tears in her eyes, Louise reluctantly "started to skin the rabbit, preparatory to cooking it." In Malcolm's memory, this is when Earl, "so angry," left and headed toward town.[35]

Philbert remembers it differently. "We had supper together," he recalled, "and my mother was holding Wesley . . . she may have been nursing him, cause she was at the table and fell asleep, nursing, holding the baby. And my father had gotten up and went in the bedroom to clean up and to go to the north side of Lansing and collect chicken money."[36]

Where Malcolm and Philbert's stories begin to converge is how Louise reacted right after Earl decided to leave . . .

PHILBERT: She woke up and said, "Earl, Earl, don't go down-town. If you go, you won't come back." And so my father said, "Oh, Louise, get away." And she said, "Earl, please don't go." But he left.[37]

MALCOLM: After Earl "slammed" the door and left, "it was then that my mother had this vision. She had always been a strange woman in this sense and had always had a strong intuition of things about to happen. And most of her children are the same way, I think. When something is about to happen, I can feel something, sense something . . . my father was well up the road when my mother ran screaming out onto the porch. 'Early! Early!' She screamed his name. She clutched up her apron in one hand, and ran down the yard and into the road. My father turned around. He saw her. For some reason, considering how angry he had been when he left, he waved at her. But he kept on going."[38]

Although the details are different, what is shared is Louise's clairvoyance—an innate sense that she'd felt when she was a child with Carib Indians in Grenada, and again with the Native American tribes in Milwaukee and Lansing. "She told me later," Malcolm said, "that she had a vision of my father's end."[39]

Tragically, her sense was right. Around 9:30 p.m., near the unlighted intersection of East Michigan Avenue and Detroit Street, Earl Little was run over by the rear wheels of a streetcar. The coroner, W. Ray Gorsline, reported the death as an "accident" and said that the driver of the street-car, William Hart, hadn't seen Earl before the accident. Since streetcars often remained in motion as passengers hopped on, the coroner believed that Earl must have been running to catch the streetcar and as he tried to jump up to enter the rear door, he slipped and fell, his left arm and left leg nearly severing.[40]

Here is the summation provided by the *Lansing State Journal*:

Coroner Gorsline found that [Earl] Little had taken another car which passed about 12 minutes before the car operated by Hart. [Earl] reached for his pocket when he boarded [the first car], but told the motorman to let him off at the next corner. He did

not have an overcoat on at this time, it was said, but did have
an overcoat on when the accident occurred. It is believed that
he discovered that he had forgotten his coat when he reached
for his purse, and that he got off the car to go back for it. The
coroner was unable to discover where he left the coat. When he
was found his purse and a street car check were in the overcoat
pocket.[41]

To the demoralized Little family, it just didn't feel right. Doubts crept
in about whether someone had pushed him under the streetcar. In fact, on
Friday night, October 2, the KKK did hold a meeting of 250 local Klansmen
in Lansing, so there was a possibility that members of the group were around
the intersection where Earl was run over. Had Earl momentarily angered a
passenger, who then violently pushed him?[42]

If so, then Earl, who remained conscious on the street for nearly two hours,
decided not to tell police officer Laurence J. Baril, who arrived on the scene
at around 10:00 p.m. "It was dark, of course, and the streets weren't as well
lighted as they are now," Baril said several decades later. "We had him taken
to Sparrow Hospital." At the hospital, Baril recalled that Earl "told police that
he had missed his footing in attempting to hop aboard the rear of the trolley."
Baril, meanwhile, had the responsibility of driving over to Louise, who by
this point was deeply worried.[43]

"We all finally went to bed," Philbert remembered, "and late that night
somebody [Baril] banged on the door—and my mother screamed, she said,
'Earl!'; like that." When Louise answered the door, Baril or the other officer
with him said, "Louise Little, your husband has been injured. Would you
come with us please?"

Malcolm and the other children remained in their rooms. "I knew there
were children," Baril said, "but I never got to see them." Baril had been with
the state police for two months prior to September 28, making Earl the "first
fatality" of his career. Baril often in his mind returned to that dark and tragic
night, agreeing for the rest of his life with the coroner's jury report. "It was
an accident."[44]

By the time Louise reached the hospital, Earl had died from internal bleeding. "My mother," Wilfred said, "never really got a chance to talk to him and
find out what it is that he wanted to pass on to her before he died. This had
a devastating effect upon her."[45]

It also devastated Wilfred, who could see that he was now the father figure by default. Before Earl's funeral, Louise drew upon her spiritual strength and delivered a valuable lesson to Wilfred about death:

> She took me aside and told me, "Listen. When we get there, don't you get caught up in that." She says, "because you'll find yourself crying and carrying on and going on and grieving just like they're doing." She says, "So let me explain to you what death is." She says that when the physical body dies, the soul itself still lives, the soul never dies. So when that physical body dies, the soul has to get out of it, it can't stay in it. It has to get out of it and go on to what its next existence is. It can't take anything from this world with it. So that physical body has to be left there, and we have to dispose of that body for them. So she said, "When you get there and you look in that casket, realize that that's not your father in that casket. That's just the body that he had."[46]

It is difficult to pinpoint Malcolm's exact feelings about his father's death and whether he believed it was an accident. During his years as a public figure, Malcolm accused racist organizations such as the Black Legion of killing his father. But while incarcerated at Charlestown State Prison, Malcolm wrote a letter to a Muslim sister named Beatrice Clomax. Dated June 11, 1952, a little less than two months before his release, Malcolm explained it this way, the "devils" being white America and "colored masons" being Black Americans who didn't mind selling out their own race:

> When I was six (in 1931), my father was found all ground up beneath the wheels of a street car. He was a rabid Garveyite, and must have also heard the Teaching in Detroit [NOI] for he began to preach (already being a minister) something that had the whole town of Lansing Michigan in a stir . . . so one night he met his death: you can imagine what happened to him. The devil went to the "colored masons" and told him that my Father was giving out their secrets so they did the devils' dirty work . . . that left my Mother with Seven Hungry mouths to feed and we starved.[47]

• • • • • • • •

I think a lot of what made Malcolm the angry man he was
happened in our childhood. Malcolm didn't hate white people.
He hated the system.

—Yvonne Little, as quoted in William R. Macklin, "Spike Lee
Movie Prompts Sister of Malcolm X to Break Silence"

MAMA FINDS A WAY

Accident or not, Louise was now in deep trouble. Financially, a $1,000 insur-
ance policy was paid out to her, but after paying $99 to Dr. Ulysses S. Bagley
for helping to deliver Yvonne and Wesley and providing treatment for Philbert
when he had pneumonia, $762.76 in funeral expenses to Ingham County, $93.47
in land rent and property tax to John L. Leighton, *and* $113 to a dentist for giv-
ing Earl eight fillings and two gold bridges, Louise was left $68 in the red, with
nothing to call her own except the land, an old car, and the house, her seven
children still walking around on subflooring as a cold winter approached.[48]

Relief came in the form of weekly three-dollar checks (one per child) from
a Michigan pension law that sought to help "poor families with state-approved
guardians." The bottom line: the state government was providing Louise with
about $84 of welfare a month to support her entire family.[49]

"They weren't enough," said Malcolm.

Wilfred, about to turn 12, could see his mother's difficulties clearly: "Here
all of a sudden, here's a lady that's in her mid-thirties, with a house full o'
children, and her husband's gone. It's just like you have to start everything
from scratch." And as for the welfare checks, Wilfred knew how difficult it
was for her to "accept welfare," mainly because "this put [the government]
into her business, which she just didn't like."[50]

Still, Louise attempted to offset welfare's help. Her three acres of land
were valuable, so she went into sharecropping, providing "garden space" to
local farmers. "We had a [garbage] dump behind our house," recalled Yvonne.
"She rented that out." Louise also sewed and "crocheted gloves" for anyone
looking to buy, trying as much as she could to escape "a welfare mentality."[51]

As Louise attempted to create a new normal after Earl's death, Wilfred,
understanding that he was the man of the house now, went in and around
Lansing looking for odd jobs to help alleviate his mother's financial burden.

"Wilfred, I know," said Malcolm, "was particularly her angel." Even at a young age, Malcolm sensed the pressure his older brother was now under to provide. "I think he had the sense to see, when the rest of us didn't, what was in the wind for us. He . . . took any kind of job he could find and he would come home, dog-tired, in the evenings, and give whatever he had made to my mother."[52]

Hilda also felt her mother's plight. At 10, Hilda helped take care of Yvonne and baby Wesley. The quietest child in the family, Hilda still found moments to contribute to the family's running dialogue. "[Hilda] had a deadpan sense of humor," a longtime friend of the family wrote, "which was almost certainly lost on those who weren't quick enough to keep up with it." Hilda also "had a fantastic memory and . . . was very much her own person." When Louise, a "Grade-A sewer," worked on crocheting gloves, Hilda was not far behind, learning from her and sewing simpler garments to sell.[53]

With Wilfred and Hilda pushed into adult roles, and Yvonne and Wesley too young to pitch in, the three middle boys—Philbert, Malcolm, and Reginald—were left to explore the area without the threat of a disciplinary father figure at home. "We got looser and looser," admitted Philbert. "Young boys just coming along, just finding out how far we could spit, really."[54]

Malcolm was a bit blunter: "Philbert and I didn't contribute anything. We just fought all the time—each other at home, and then at school we would team up and fight white kids." As for Reginald, Malcolm knew his younger brother "looked up to me." Due to his herniated condition, such that he couldn't do any heavy lifting, Reginald couldn't help much around the house, so at times he stayed close to Malcolm, Philbert perhaps a bit too old and intimidating to ally with. Reginald and Malcolm eventually became "very close."[55]

In those first few years after Earl's death, Louise kept her seven children together by emphasizing education. Not the typical education Wilfred, Hilda, Philbert, and Malcolm were beginning to receive at all-white schools, but rather through her own international experience. "My mother . . . would teach us at home when we came home from school," remembered Wilfred. "We would give her what we had learned that day, and she would then re-teach it to us and give it to us in a way where it would do away with some of those negative things that they had incorporated in there. Because in those days, black children and white children could go to school, listen to the same teacher, read the same books, and when they would come out, that white child would have a superiority complex, and the black one would have an inferiority complex . . . she never allowed us to fall victim to that."[56]

One can safely say that Louise Little was Malcolm's first influential teacher. Newspapers such as Marcus Garvey's *Negro World* and Grenadian T. A. Marryshow's *West Indian* were often placed on the table. Louise used these newspapers to give her children more of a global outlook and helped them see past the rigid system around them. "A strong-minded mother," Malcolm wrote in prison, "has strong-minded children."[57]

Louise also didn't forget the fundamentals of education. "When we would come home from school," said Wilfred, "she had a dictionary on the dining room table, and she had picked out things in the newspaper for us to read. And we would have to stand there and read it to her. She'd be ironing, or cooking, or whatever, but she's hearing you. And whenever you made a mistake, she'd stop you and make you go to that dictionary, look it up, 'syllabize' it, get the meaning of it, and that way you began to improve your vocabulary. And we ended up, at that age, reading at a grade level beyond our age. . . ."[58]

During those difficult years, when money and food were scarce and their status as outsiders became grating, Louise used her own education and heritage to give her children an escape from their oppressive reality. "At night before we would go to bed," recalled Philbert, "we would all gather around the stove, and my mother would tell us stories. Or we would sing our alphabets, or we would sing our math, and then she taught us French—we could sing in French. And then, she would tell us stories about our ancestry."[59]

At their local school, Louise believed her children were being told a much smaller, marginalized story of their place in American society, and she tried to enlarge and empower her children to be more than what they saw around them. "She didn't tolerate us being treated as a negative or as subhuman," said Philbert. "She told us we came from great people that were onetime rulers."[60]

Years later, Malcolm wrote to Philbert about their mother, who taught Sunday school at a nearby Christian church in Lansing during the Depression.[61] He'd recently converted to the Nation of Islam and was reflecting on how he arrived at such a frame of mind. In an indirect manner, "we were taught Islam by Mom," he wrote while incarcerated at the Norfolk Prison Colony in August 1949. "Everything that happened to her happened because the devils knew she was not 'deadening' our minds." Malcolm went on, pouring his heart out to Philbert: "'Tis true, that my accomplishments are yours and yours are mine . . . because we are all brothers and sisters . . . but all of our achievements are Mom's . . . for she was a most Faithful Servant of Truth years ago. I praise 'Allah' for her."[62]

THE STARVING REBEL

In prison, Malcolm had time to reflect and learn to appreciate his mother. But during the years of the Great Depression, young Malcolm wasn't as grateful for Louise as Wilfred, Hilda, or even Philbert were. He didn't need to be. With his older siblings shouldering most of the responsibility, Malcolm was free to push boundaries. By around 1934, Malcolm, then nine years old, had started to see that the way he used words coaxed reactions out of his siblings. Verbally, he'd started to stand out partly due to being the literal middle child, walking the communicative divide between his three older and three younger siblings.

Yvonne once recalled a time when she, Malcolm, and Reginald were sent by Louise "out in the fields to work." As they pulled weeds, checked the chicken coop, pumped water, or tended the garden, "Malcolm would start talking, and we would start working." Yvonne then noticed that Malcolm was "laying under a tree with a straw in his mouth." She didn't mind. "Malcolm was telling these stories, but we were so happy to be around him that we worked—and Malcolm was using psychology, and we didn't realize it."[63]

At Pleasant Grove Elementary School, Malcolm had a new environment to master. The only African American in his class, Malcolm did attempt to fit in. In the third grade, he gave a Valentine's Day card to a girl named Phyllis, a photo of himself and the rest of the class inside. At that age, Phyllis was unaware of the struggles Malcolm was going through. "I was a shy girl," she recalled many decades later, "and I am sure some of the things that happened to him may have rolled right over my back."[64]

Over time, Malcolm struggled with elementary school. According to his prison file, he had a "poor scholastic rating" and a "poor attitude." Part of it came from his mother undermining the lessons he learned at school. Again, because Wilfred and Hilda were thrust into adult roles and pressured to provide and excel, Malcolm had enough idle time to question and absorb the predominantly white system surrounding his family.[65]

This desire to rebel or resist also came from seeing the way his mother interacted with the white community. "My mother was, above everything else, a proud woman," Malcolm explained, "and it took its toll on her that she was accepting charity. And her feelings were communicated to us." On weekly errands, Malcolm watched as his mother spoke "sharply to the man at the grocery store for padding the bill"—calculation was done by pen and paper back then—"telling him that she wasn't ignorant, and he didn't like that." But Louise saved her strongest anger for the state welfare workers who were obligated to routinely check in on how Louise was handling raising seven children without a main provider. "She would talk back sharply to the state Welfare people," Malcolm said, "telling them that she was a grown woman, able to raise her children, that it wasn't necessary for them to keep coming around so much, meddling in our lives." And just like the grocery store worker, "they didn't like that."[66]

Malcolm's mother also didn't like the way Malcolm and Philbert continuously tested each other. "I had my own garden [in the backyard] at home," Malcolm wrote while in prison in Charlestown. "[Philbert] used to swipe some of the crops and then he and I would fight all over the yard. Of course, I always lost, but it was lots of fun, now that I look back on it. . . . Once after he had given me a good beating, I took a pot shot at him with a 22 rifle. You should have seen the spanking mom laid on me . . . I couldn't move for a week. But as soon as I recovered from one spanking, I would earn another one (smile) until finally mom decided that she was wasting her time."[67]

Hunger was a constant problem for the family. As the children grew, dinners seemed smaller, and with only bits of income trickling in from government aid, sewing sales, and Wilfred's contributions, there didn't seem to be much hope in sight. Still, while the majority of the community around them predicted a breakup coming, they did have a few allies. "The Little family had a dignity," said Jenny Washington, who lived in Lansing and was a friend of the family. "When you think of how difficult it was for them, yet they didn't expect any sympathies, nor did they act like they should get it. They probably had had a rough time, but you'd never know it. I certainly was proud to call them my friends."[68]

Dignity alone didn't put food on the table, however, so the Littles had to devise ways of stretching their income. "We used to buy a hundred-pound of day-old bread for five cents at Old Castle's Bakery in Lansing," recalled Philbert. "But that day-old bread actually was about a month old. My mother knew how to fix it—she would take it and cut off the mold and put sugar on it and put it in the oven and soften it with water. We ate like it was the last supper."[69]

In these dire years, Reginald was often by Malcolm's side. In late 1937, Malcolm and Reginald started walking a couple of miles to the newly opened Peter Pan Bakery in Lansing. The store had its own plant and made its own bread. At the end of the day, the store needed to throw out any surplus or expired bread. There Malcolm and Reginald stood, buying at a steep discount ("a nickel") a "tall flour sack of day-old bread and cookies." Some months, when their social welfare check ran out, that haul of bread kept the large family's stomachs full. "Our mother knew . . . dozens of ways to cook things with bread and out of bread," Malcolm recalled.[70]

And she did. "Stewed tomatoes with bread, maybe that would be a meal. Something like French toast, if we had any eggs. Bread pudding, sometimes with raisins in it. If we got hold of some hamburger, it came to the table more bread than meat. The cookies that were always in the sack with the bread, we just gobbled down straight."[71]

Dinner for eight is a tall order for any cook, let alone a Black single mother on welfare living in rural white America during the Depression. "Relief food" provided by the government went out to low-income families, a message stamped onto the sack: "Not To Be Sold." For poor families like the Littles, it became a scarlet letter of poverty and broadcasted to other well-off families in the neighborhood that they were struggling. "It seemed that everything to eat in our house was stamped Not To Be Sold," said Malcolm. "It's a wonder we didn't come to think of Not To Be Sold as a brand name."[72]

But there were some days when there just wasn't enough food to go around, and Malcolm became "dizzy" with hunger. If he had been Wilfred, he could have gone and looked for work and felt the need to make his mother proud. If he'd been Philbert, he could have entered the boxing world and occupied his mind with training in the Golden Gloves league. Eventually, Malcolm did try to spar with Philbert, but as he continued to walk that narrow middle-child line between younger and older, his own flickering identity in need of direction, Malcolm succumbed to stealing. "Sometimes, instead of going home from school, I walked the two miles up the road into Lansing," Malcolm told Alex Haley, and "I began drifting from store to store, hanging around outside where things like apples were displayed in boxes and barrels and baskets, and I would watch my chance and steal me a treat. You know what a treat was to me? Anything!"[73]

As the oldest, Wilfred saw the perils Malcolm faced being the middle child in such a large family. "It brings a lot out of you because in order to survive you have to be able to cover your space. . . . He was always busy. He was always questioning everything, always challenging. . . . Just busy, busy, all the time."[74]

Eventually, Malcolm was caught stealing, and "state Welfare people began to focus on me when they came to our house." Louise "would whip me for stealing, and I would try to alarm the neighborhood with my yelling. One thing I have always been proud of is that I never raised my hand against my mother."[75]

Malcolm continued challenging and pushing boundaries at Pleasant Grove. With his best white friend, Ores Whitney, Malcolm sometimes threw messages across the classroom "via paper airplane." The teacher grew furious, but Malcolm and Ores didn't stop. After a failed attempt to crack a ruler over Ores's knuckles, the teacher "stood both boys in separate corners and proceeded to stack books on their outstretched arms." In the sixth grade, Malcolm continued to march to his own beat, and once, after not completing his homework yet again, a teacher "ordered him out of the classroom." But this time Malcolm "wouldn't budge." According to a biographer who interviewed many of Malcolm's teachers, Malcolm "clung to his desk." The teacher called in the custodian to carry him out, but the man was quite old. Still, he tried, but "Malcolm . . . grabbed a foot-long tin of water colors and declared, 'I'll club you with this if you lay a hand on me!'" Malcolm stayed, but he failed the class.[76]

After school, the nearby Lincoln Community Center (LCC) gave Malcolm a different way to learn and share with others. Opened in February 1937, the LCC had its own library and put on a wide range of activities—basketball, Ping-Pong, choir, board games, social dancing, group discussion—many being geared toward the impoverished community in West Lansing. Malcolm dabbled in several things, but most valuable were the chances he had to participate in open discussions with adults and same-aged kids.

All who participated had a chance to express their opinions, but young Malcolm didn't yet have his trademark verbal precision. He was frustrated, a teenager still searching for a way to be. At the LCC's group discussion events, Malcolm sometimes "spoke so fast that he forgot what he had intended to say." When it came to his opinions, Malcolm hadn't yet developed his own perspective and went back and forth between extremes. As one onlooker put it, "Either Malcolm wouldn't say anything or you couldn't shut him up."[77]

THE FALL OF LOUISE

In late 1937, hope arrived for Louise—a boyfriend. It had been borderline miraculous that Louise had kept such a large family together for six years, but if this Lansing man, described by Malcolm as "big and black . . . something like my father," decided to stay and provide, he could give Louise and the seven children the stability they needed. Yvonne liked him enough to call him "a very nice man." When this "nice man came on the scene," Yvonne saw that her mother, for the first time since Earl died, "was real happy, she glowed."[78]

But around the Christmas holiday season, Louise became pregnant with her eighth child. As the months passed, that nice man came over less and less.

Wilfred, now 17, didn't hold much animosity toward the man. "How is a woman that's got seven children gonna get married? Who's gon' marry a woman with seven children," Wilfred said. "They can fall in love with her, yeah, but who's gon' marry her?" With one more child coming, a boy, Yvonne could see that Louise had "lost her glow." A stark reality was beginning to set in, and each month, as her belly grew, social workers judged her ability to make sound decisions.[79]

If her Grenadian baptismal certificate is accurate, Louise was 44 years old on August 31, 1938, when she gave birth to her eighth child, Robert. Wilfred was nearing graduation from high school, as was Hilda. Philbert, Malcolm, and Reginald could have picked up work and pitched in a few dollars, and Wesley and Yvonne were both old enough that they were attending elementary school most of the day.[80]

But especially in 1938, as their pregnant mother faced a whole new set of financial issues, the social welfare workers began taking each child aside, planting "seeds of division" in their minds, as Malcolm called it. Their questions were calculated and probing: *Do you feel neglected? Don't you think you'd feel more supported within a smaller family environment? Wouldn't you like to live in a completed home with proper financial backing? Can't you see that your mother is under extreme psychological stress? Don't you think she needs professional care . . . someone who can help her?*[81]

"I was the first target," Malcolm recalled. "I stole; that implied that I wasn't being taken care of by my mother." The doubts that the social welfare workers planted in Malcolm's mind came to the surface in 1938. Twice in prison letters and again in his *Autobiography*, Malcolm recalled the day John Doane Sr. came over to their house offering two skinned pigs. The Doane family was

Black, and John, Charlice, and Watoga lived "in the next house down the street" from the Littles. Over the years, the two families had reached out to each other, and on this particular day in 1938, John Doane had an especially charitable gift to offer Louise and her hungry children: two whole hogs.[82]

Malcolm remembered the moment in a letter to Philbert in 1949, while at Norfolk Prison Colony: "When she refused those two pigs from Mr. Doane that time I thought she was crazy herself (as hungry as I was). And [the welfare workers] sowed their lying seeds in our heads . . . but she suffered the [most] abuse of all."[83]

In a letter to Sister Beatrice Clomax in 1952, Malcolm again remembered that day, but in a more reflective manner: "One day the man next door butchered his hogs and offered two of them to her free, and she refused them. Everyone had been saying that she was crazy, and when she refused all that meat, I began to believe what everyone was saying." Sitting in prison, just two months before his release, Malcolm felt guilty about how he had started to listen to the welfare workers: "So you can see how I feel today," Malcolm wrote, "having condemned my own Mother for nearly ten years just because the devil constantly whispered in my ear (as a child) that she was crazy."[84]

By the time his *Autobiography* was published, Malcolm, then a national figure with a professional writer interpreting his thoughts, had made peace with his mother and instead emphasized the role the welfare workers played. "But I can distinctly remember hearing 'crazy' applied to her by them when they learned that the Negro farmer [Mr. Doane] who was in the next house down the road from us had offered to give us some butchered pork—a whole pig, maybe even two of them—and she had refused. We all heard them call my mother 'crazy' to her face for refusing good meat. It meant nothing to them even when she explained that we had never eaten pork, that it was against her religion as a Seventh Day Adventist."[85]

At that time, Louise had indeed found some support at a church, but Wilfred knew that his mother didn't favor one faith. Instead, Louise used religion to enliven her own personal spirituality: "[She said], 'Stay away from religion, as far as joining, but I want you to study them all, because all of them have something, but you have to be able to sort it out for yourself.' And she said, 'Study them, whatever you see that you can use, accept that, and the rest of it, just put it on the shelf.'"[86]

The welfare workers refused to put anything "on the shelf." Louise's list of bad choices continued to pile up, and Malcolm, then an impressionable

13-year-old boy tired of being hungry, started to look at his mother as if she had lost her mind. In late December 1938, Louise went for a walk with four-month-old Robert. She was "barefoot," walking "along a snow-encrusted road," and Robert "was covered head to toe with sores." That day she was taken to the Kalamazoo Mental Hospital. On January 3, 1939, a man named Dr. E. F. Hoffman examined Louise and certified that she was "an insane person and her condition is such as to require care and treatment in an institution."[87]

Later that month, on a cold winter night, court-appointed officers came to take Louise away. Hilda and the others tried to object, but it was too late. "My mother had to go without even a coat," Hilda recalled many years later. "She was taken away in only her nightclothes and her slippers. There were two white men; one man had hold of either side of her as they took her out of the house to the car. She lost one of her slippers on the way out."[88]

DIVIDED

After losing their mother's presence and most of the financial support from welfare, Wilfred and Hilda were allowed to remain where they were. Philbert, meanwhile, was taken in by a local family with the surname Hackett. Reginald and Wesley went to the Williams family, and Yvonne and Robert headed over to the McGuires.[89]

As for Malcolm, one family, the Gohannas, had often welcomed Malcolm into their home during the Depression years, and in early 1939, they took him in full time. It was a day-to-day improvement over his family home, but Malcolm still had to share a room with another young boarder, Dave Roper, or "Big Boy." Even though it was nice having a bit of same-age company, Malcolm missed his "blood brothers," and the excruciating experience of having to watch his family splinter did not sit well in his memory. Rightful blame was placed on the failures of a flawed social welfare system, but that institution was, after all, simply a reflection of a biased culture. "I have no mercy or compassion in me," Malcolm later said, "for a society that will crush people, and then penalize them for not being able to stand up under the weight."[90]

Malcolm saw a different side to life under Mabel and Thornton Gohanna's roof. Besides receiving consistent meals, Malcolm and Dave also went fishing, but the long, slow hours tested his patience: "Neither [Dave] nor I," Malcolm wrote later, "liked the idea of just sitting and waiting for the fish to jerk the cork under the water—or make the tight line quiver. . . . I figured there should be some smarter way to get the fish—though we never discovered what it might be." Malcolm also hunted rabbits with his father's .22-caliber firearm. Mr. Gohanna, from his own tragic experience, may have cautioned Malcolm to take care of his gun. In September 1899, when Thornton was a teenager, he and three of his friends were out shooting a revolver when, suddenly, it jammed. One of the friends attempted to fix it, but as he tried, the revolver went off, and 18-year-old Fred Peterson was killed right in front of Thornton's eyes.[91]

As for Mabel, she was well known in the community for helping down-and-out residents, and she completed a "Red Cross home hygiene and care of the sick course" in May 1936. Malcolm had always carried a degree of respect for the couple, since they'd also supported his father's preaching before his death, and while sharing a room with Dave, Malcolm "began to sweep and mop and dust." A feeling of normalcy was beginning to settle in.[92]

The Gohannas were deeply religious, and they dragged Malcolm and Dave to their church each week. Malcolm had experienced a few Baptist services, but the Gohannas' church services seemed like they took place in another world. "The preachers and congregations jumped even higher and shouted even louder than the Baptists I had known. They sang at the top of their lungs, and swayed back and forth and cried and moaned and beat on tambourines and chanted. It was spooky." With so much of his own childhood already having been a grind, experiencing an "atmosphere" of "ghosts and spirituals and 'ha'nts,'" Malcolm was relieved to head back home from the "Holy Rollers" church.[93]

A bit of respite came in the form of employment. One longtime Mason resident, Dr. Gertrude O'Sullivan, gave Malcolm a job. In 1939, Dr. O'Sullivan was 73 and was deemed by a local paper to be "one of the nation's pioneer female physicians." By the time Malcolm started working for her, O'Sullivan was a widow with no immediate family and had faced a fair amount of gender discrimination since she opened her own practice 40 years ago. She needed a "house worker" and "chauffeur," and Malcolm did what he could to help her for an unknown wage.[94]

While Malcolm continued working for Dr. O'Sullivan, living with the Gohannas just wasn't working out. Whether it was due to the long bouts of monotonous fishing, the excessive religious fever, or simply the end of his school year, Malcolm left the Gohannas and headed back home to live with

Wilfred and Hilda. With the house emptier, Malcolm was primarily on his own, his siblings occupied and living within their own schedules.

This didn't sit well with Mr. Maynard Allyn, a social welfare official who'd kept his eye on the Little family. In what may have been a mutual decision, Malcolm became "a ward of the county court, placed on probation, and housed in a juvenile home."[95]

Malcolm was sent 10 miles south, to the Ingham County Juvenile Home on 304 East South Street in Mason, Michigan. His guardians were now James and Lois E. Swerlein, a white couple whose job it was to manage the children in the home. Thirty-eight-year-old Mrs. Swerlein was Malcolm's main supervisor, or matron, and she ran a tight ship. Children always needed to report their whereabouts. One 11-year-old, for example, left the house on a Thursday morning while playing in the front yard with other children. Swerlein immediately pushed the local paper to put out a notice the same day.[96]

Malcolm responded positively to "Ma" Swerlein's disciplined approach. As her bulky frame walked through the house, leaving behind the scent of "Gold Dust soap powder," Malcolm did his fair share of housework and even had his first-ever solo bedroom. He sat at "long tables" and ate full-course dinners with white children and adults. Malcolm remembered the well-liked Ma Swerlein several decades later as "a big, buxom, robust, laughing woman."[97]

But there was an undercurrent of falsity in his new home. "A hundred times a day," Malcolm recalled, "they used the word 'nigger.' I suppose that in their own minds, they meant no harm; in fact they probably meant well." At first, Malcolm suppressed this awkwardness—after all, he did have his own room, home-cooked meals, and adults who took care of him.[98]

MASON VERSUS WEST LANSING

At his new school, Mason High, Malcolm entered the eighth grade at 6'0" and a year older than most of his fellow students. He was also the only Black student in his class. His popularity soared, but Malcolm questioned why. Was it because he was merely "a novelty," or the token Black kid in class, thought of as some curious oddity? Or was the charisma he'd been cultivating for years around his siblings finally starting to show?

Malcolm managed to push through his first semester, but problems arose. One of them came early on, courtesy of 33-year-old Mr. Otto Grein, Malcolm's civics teacher. Grein was a local basketball legend who'd led Western Michigan University to their only undefeated season in 1930. At 6'0" and 170 pounds, Mr. Grein was one of the few teachers who could meet Malcolm eye-to-eye. During the "first week of school," Malcolm walked into the all-white classroom, and Grein, perhaps attempting to be some sort of playful provocateur, started singing "The Cornfield Medley," a song sung during the Reconstruction years: "Some folks say that a nigger won't steal / Way down yonder in the cornfield." Malcolm shook it off. Later in the semester, when the class reached the "Negro History" section of their textbook, Malcolm saw that "it was exactly one paragraph long." Mr. Grein let out a jocular laugh, then read the section out loud, adding a joke he'd learned years ago, that a Black man's feet were "so big that when they walk, they don't leave tracks, they leave a hole in the ground."[99]

Malcolm pushed through Grein's class and random sharp elbows in the hallway, excelling in school for the first time in his life. His grades were strong enough to be third in the class. He joined clubs and sports teams and earned the nickname "Harpy" for the way he'd *harp* or keep on about a topic. He showed this ability to express himself at length in English class, when the teacher at times called on him to expound upon a theme in the book they were reading. Malcolm, according to a student, stared at a hidden blank piece of paper and improvised, delivering thematic insight on the spot, or at the very least staying on the teacher's good side.[100]

At Mason, "Harpy" had decided to use his new nickname to run for class president. Signs could be seen taped to hallway walls: "Harpy for President." It worked. By the time the second semester started, Malcolm Little had received the most votes. He was Mason High School's eighth grade class president. "I was unique in my class," Malcolm said later, "like a pink poodle. And I was proud [of being elected]; I'm not going to say I wasn't."[101]

At school assemblies, his newfound position extended to crowd management. Assemblies occurred in the gym, and many students filed into the balcony. Usually, a somewhat annoyed teacher was assigned to stand and monitor the balcony crowd, but Malcolm convinced the school that he could manage his fellow students without teacher supervision. The school shruggingly complied, and the white students obeyed his commands.[102]

As Malcolm's confidence soared, he often traveled back to West Lansing and spent the weekend checking in on his siblings. His family noticed a new air about him. "When Malcolm went to Mason," his brother Wilfred recalled, "you could see a change in him. Some for the better, some for the worse. After a while he started feeling somewhat at home."[103]

This idea of feeling at home was complicated. Yes, he'd been accepted by his students at Mason, but the generic vibe of it all nagged at him. If he'd been white, would he have received the same adulation?

In West Lansing on the weekends, Malcolm attempted to reconnect with his roots. He'd visit Reginald, Wesley, Yvonne, and baby Robert and offer a bit of spending money he'd earned from Dr. O'Sullivan and also from washing dishes part-time at a downtown Mason eatery called Matthew's Restaurant, a job Mrs. Swerlein had secured for him. On Saturday nights, Malcolm was often seen "gawking around" certain West Lansing bars and restaurants. He'd hang around jukeboxes blaring big band trumpeter Erskine Hawkins's southern-dipped *Tuxedo Junction* and jazz duo Slim Gaillard and Slam Stewart's 1938 breakout hit "Flat Foot Floogie."

Also in West Lansing, Malcolm was able to hear the echoes of big-city culture. New York City bands swung and startled the Michigan town. Malcolm also met an incredible 17-year-old saxophonist, Eli "Lucky" Thompson, on his way to joining Erskine Hawkins's band, and a multitalented vibraphone player named Milt Jackson, then a high school student living in Detroit. For Malcolm, meeting these talented Black musicians was culturally vital as he struggled with the generic integration he'd been offered in white Mason.[104]

By the end of the decade, there was a racial duality to young Malcolm's life, as if he were being pulled in two directions. On one side was Mason, an illusory yet stable world where he was conditionally accepted as a "token" class president. On the other side stood West Lansing, a real but unstable world where he was unconditionally accepted as a young Black man.

Both had their drawbacks, but one sibling from Earl's first marriage, Ella Little, was on her way to Lansing. Her pivotal trip and offer helped tip the scales.

4

THE SIRENS OF ROXBURY

Mason to Charlestown

1940 to 1946

No physical move in my life has been more pivotal or profound
in its repercussions.

—Malcolm X and Alex Haley, *The Autobiography
of Malcolm X: As Told to Alex Haley*

In the early 1930s, as Malcolm dealt with hunger and a family soon to be split
apart, his half-sister Ella Little had a job interview at a department store in New
York City. They needed a "floorwalker," or someone to move about the store
and, by her mere presence, discourage customers from shoplifting. Naturally,
they wanted to hire someone intimidating, and during the interview, they
sized Ella up. At 5'9", 145 pounds, with "jet black" skin and a slight edge to her
attitude, the store stopped their search; they'd found who they were looking for.[1]

Ella's life didn't start in the North. She was born on December 13, 1913, near
Reynolds, Georgia, a rural town similar to other segregated areas in the Deep
South. In her late teens, and long after her father, Earl, had left the family,
Ella headed north to Boston to live with her mother, Daisy Mason. But since
jobs were scarce as the Depression tightened its grip over the economy, Ella
tried to find employment in the Big Apple.[2]

The floorwalker job was far from ideal. To legitimize her position, the
department store required her to wear a cleaning uniform as she walked up
and down the aisles. In between arbitrary dust swipes, Ella kept her eye on
customers. As six months passed, Ella had learned, yes, how to catch a shoplifter, but also "how to be a successful shoplifter."

Sensing no chance for promotion from her white managers, Ella quit and moved back in with her mother, who ran a general store near the corner of Lenox Street and Shawmut Avenue in Roxbury. For Ella, learning from her determined and strong-willed mother was an education in itself: "I just watched everything Ma did—how she dealt with customers, how she handled suppliers, how she dealt with competitors, and how she maneuvered around city officials. I soaked up everything."[3]

During those first few years near Boston, the top priority for Ella was to bring relatives up north from the poor farms in and around Reynolds, Georgia. As Ella helped make her mother's store a local force, she spent most of her savings on providing for newly arrived cousins who had little to nothing upon arrival. It was here that Ella had a choice: take her relatives through a welfare system full of red tape and prejudice or use the business skills she'd learned from her mother and, when circumstances grew dire, at the New York City department store.

To Ella, the choice was more about survival: "If it was a choice between our being hungry and insufficiently clothed for the cold weather and shoplifting, I shoplifted without hesitation as a common-sense response to a desperate situation."[4]

By choosing the more dangerous option, Ella was arrested quite often over the years, once even spending a month in a local jail for breaking and entering. Despite her constant brushes with the law, Ella never regretted her decision, telling her son years later that stealing "was better than going on welfare and opening up your whole life to state officials. . . . I still believe [decades later] it was the right choice."[5]

Though Ella struggled to come up with enough money to support incoming family members, she was able to amass enough from her mother's store to begin purchasing property. Most important was her relentless pursuit of a now-historic Roxbury home located at 72 Dale Street. The latest tenants, a white family whose mortgage was eventually foreclosed by Eliot Savings Bank on January 11, 1937, hoped to settle their debts by signing over their deed to another buyer. Ella seized on the opportunity and knocked on their door, offering "six hundred dollars cash and payment of overdue taxes." The white family said no, even though Ella had offered a hundred dollars more than what they had wanted.[6]

Unrattled, Ella plowed through the potential discrimination and went directly to the bank. Interestingly, the couple now wanted $900. Again, Ella offered the asked-for amount, showing the bank proof of income. Again, the owners said no.

According to Ella's son Rodnell Collins, an entire year passed, and the Dale Street home stayed on the market, accruing more and more debt. Ella once more approached the owners and again offered the $900 fee for the deed. Again, they said no, upping the number to $1,200. Ella, however, was prepared for this, and she brought out a printed agreement. If they signed, Ella would give them the $900 today and then within 24 hours provide them with the extra $300. If she didn't come back by then, they could keep the $900. Believing Ella to be foolish, they took the deal and signed. Ella then brought the signed document and the rest of the money directly to Eliot Savings Bank. Fatigued by how long the home had been on the market, the bank pressured the white family to "stick to the agreement." They did, and Ella had her house.[7]

As Ella acquired the foreclosed property, she wrote to her relatives back in Reynolds, Georgia, and also in Lansing, Michigan. When she heard that Louise had been committed to a mental hospital, Ella started to write to Hilda and Wilfred about her plan to travel to Lansing and see what she could do to help.

Back in Lansing, the family had been thoroughly divided into various homes, and their times of trauma had mainly been buried. Yvonne Little, Malcolm's younger sister, revealed only a half-century later the anguish she felt during the years before Ella's visit: "I put on a strong front. The tears were inside. Because I can remember being petrified. I didn't know how to live around anyone else. I don't think any of my family ever dealt with the others and their own pain. You're suddenly spread apart. I know [my brothers and sisters] have feelings, but [even 50 years later] we have never gotten together and talked about our pain. I know how strong it was. And I know they had it."[8]

In late November 1939, 26-year-old Ella Little arrived in Lansing, Michigan, and some of the unspoken family pain Yvonne referred to was momentarily lifted. Ella remembered 14-year-old Malcolm Little's honest reaction: "When Malcolm first saw me, I was pulling up in a taxi in front of their house. Malcolm and his brothers and sisters had stayed up all night waiting for me. He hugged me and he cried and he cried. He said, 'I can't help it. I can't help it.'"[9]

From Malcolm's perspective, meeting Ella for the first time was revelatory: "She was the first really proud black woman I had ever seen in my life. She was plainly proud of her very dark skin. This was unheard of among Negroes in those days, especially in Lansing."[10]

When Ella first laid eyes on Malcolm, she was "taken aback by how much lighter-skinned he was than the other children." Still, she quickly sensed how "bright, intelligent, and inquisitive" young Malcolm was compared to, say, the hard-edged and competitive Philbert. After the initial euphoria of her visit wore off, Ella's strong will was quickly challenged. "When I asked Philbert to do a chore," Ella said later, "he responded with back talk. I wasn't about to take such talk from [someone] I considered a child, so I popped him with a frying pan, forgetting that he was also an emerging amateur boxer. He popped me right back. After that neither of us gave the other any trouble."[11]

It became evident rather quickly that Ella favored Malcolm over the other children. There was a connection between the two. "The first time he had ever seen me, we got to talking and we talked all night," Ella recalled. "He was saying what he was going to do for me and what we were going to do for each other."[12]

Malcolm, meanwhile, was awestruck by Ella's overall character. "The way she sat, moved, talked, did everything, bespoke somebody who did and got exactly what they wanted. . . . I had never been so impressed with anybody."[13]

At this point in his life, Malcolm had finally reached solid ground and had started to showcase his academic potential. Ella knew that his grades were stellar and that he had been voted class president, but what irked her the most was how disconnected he'd become from his local Black community. An emergency intervention was required. "One major reason [I favored Malcolm over the others]," said Ella, "was his having been sent to live with [the Swerleins]. I was livid when I heard about that. It was absurd and demeaning for Michigan public officials to place Malcolm with a white family. If they had put the same kind of effort and money into getting the children to us in Boston, things might have turned out differently for all of us."[14]

During her visit, Ella told Malcolm all about the Boston and Roxbury visit that awaited him when he had a chance to visit. After traveling to see Louise at the Kalamazoo Mental Hospital on November 28, Ella personally invited Malcolm to visit her during the summer.[15]

Malcolm wanted to visit his other family in the Boston area, but an uneasy trust had settled into his life courtesy of his white classmates in Mason. He was well-liked, the president, and for once, it seemed as if he had a stable community around him.

Around April 1940, at Mason High School, 31-year-old Latin and English teacher Richard A. Kaminska was alone in a classroom with Malcolm. Kaminska, a "burly" and "bulky" white man with a "thick mustache," was considered by his colleagues to be a "decent fellow." A decade prior, he'd been a college football player, nicknamed "The Bear." Now his peers called him "Kammy," and students knew that when they came to talk to Kammy, they'd be receiving a bit of pat-on-the-back life advice.

"Malcolm," he said while seated, "you ought to be thinking about a career. Have you been giving it thought?"

The tall and gangly 14-year-old nodded. "Well, yes, sir. I've been thinking I'd like to be a lawyer."

It was then, soon after he "leaned back in his chair and clasped his hands behind his head," that Kaminska decided he knew Malcolm well enough to give the young man some of that life advice he'd given to other students. But there was one question to ask: How well did Richard Kaminska *really know* Malcolm Little?[16]

Did Kaminska know the details of the November 8, 1929, fire that burned down Malcolm's home? Had he heard that Malcolm had lost his father late Monday night on September 28, 1931? Malcolm, currently 14 miles south of where his father was killed, still, along with his family, harbored feelings of injustice and anger, questioning what really occurred. Had he been pushed, the family wondered? They were never fully convinced it was an accident, even after an investigation.[17]

And yet, after losing his mother to a mental hospital and despite being treated by his foster family as if he was some kind of "fine colt" and not being given "credit for having the same sensitivity, intellect, and understanding that they would have been ready and willing to recognize in a white boy in my position," Malcolm had started to excel in school. By the time he'd reached Mr. Kaminska's eighth grade English class, he'd managed to overcome the setbacks brought upon him. When he told Kaminska that he wanted to be a lawyer, there weren't any "Negro lawyers—or doctors either—in those days, to hold up an image I might have aspired to." Hadn't Malcolm already defied enough odds?

In an undated assignment around this time, Malcolm had all but laid out his own ambitions, completing a "career path" chart that reveals the way Malcolm's mind had been working while he was a student at Mason:[18]

Table 4.1. Career path chart—by Malcolm Little[19]

Basic Terminal Jobs	Supplementary Terminal Jobs	Intermediate Jobs	Training Jobs	Related Jobs
Lawyer	Banking	Clerk	Clerk	Orator
District	Real Estate	Apprentice	Apprentice	Banking
Attorney	Politics	Orator		Real Estate
Politics	Department			Trust
	of Justice			Company
				Department
				of Justice
				Capital
				View Land
				Company*
				Police
				Magistrate
				Teacher
				of Law

* This is the same company that attempted to evict Malcolm and his family weeks before their home burned down. Perhaps Malcolm included them as a way to break down barriers . . . or for revenge.

To Kaminska, Malcolm's "lawyer" dream was dangerous, and what he ended up telling Malcolm that day stayed with the young man for the rest of his life.

"Malcolm," Kaminska started, "one of life's first needs is for us to be realistic. Don't misunderstand me, now. We all here [at Mason] like you, you know that. But you've got to be realistic about being a nigger. A lawyer—that's no realistic goal for a nigger. You need to think about something you *can* be."

Kaminska continued, mentioning a skill Malcolm had learned thanks to his father's house-building abilities. "You're good with your hands—making things. Everybody admires your carpentry shop work. Why don't you plan on carpentry?"

And then, a finishing, pat-on-the-head touch: "People like you as a person—you'd get all kinds of work."

Perhaps today Kaminska's words come off as harsh, such as his use of the N-word, but Malcolm had become accustomed to hearing that term daily from his foster family, letting its derogatory power "slip off [his] back" to avoid trouble. But anger started to build within Malcolm, growing with each new slight. He couldn't let that word slide off his back anymore, nor did he choose to accept Kaminska's narrow future vision.

"I know that he probably meant well in what he happened to advise me that day. I doubt that he meant any harm. It was just in his nature as an American white man."

For Malcolm, his conversation with Kaminska marked a turning point: "It was then that I began to change—inside."[20]

As for Richard Kaminska, he soon left Mason, eventually becoming the principal of Marlette High School, ending his career as an educational psychologist. "Kammy" passed away in 1969 at the age of 61.[21]

Still, the exact words or phrasing Kaminska used that day are not as important as their general effect. By telling Malcolm not to pursue law because of his race, he was not only marginalizing Malcolm's future; he was marginalizing the pursuit of an education. How important could certain subjects be to him if he believed that, no matter how much he learned, he was still supposed to be a carpenter, a skill he learned not from a school, but from his father's own working experience? In this way, Kaminska's attempt at delivering a reality check pushed Malcolm away from completing his education. If anything, it pushed him toward the streets.

Of Mason and his education, Malcolm put it simply: "I just gave up."[22]

A CULTURAL REVELATION

It was the timing of his moment with Richard Kaminska that made it so impactful to Malcolm in his *Autobiography*. The classroom encounter was between Ella's visit and Malcolm's first summer trip to Boston, and it broke the illusion that his future had been made brighter at Mason High School. Malcolm quite literally was at the peak of his popularity—he could not have been more of a model student, and yet still, after putting forth such an effort to "integrate," he was told in a manner of speaking that his career ceiling might very well be carpentry.

Kaminska's commentary planted a seed of doubt in Malcolm and caused him to "jump at the chance" to see his family in and around the Roxbury district. "If I had stayed on in Michigan," Malcolm said, entertaining the thought years later, "I might have become one of those state capitol building shoeshine boys, or a Lansing Country Club waiter, or gotten one of the other menial jobs which, in those days, among Lansing Negroes, would have been considered 'successful'—or even become a carpenter."[23]

Setting aside Kaminska's discouraging remarks, Malcolm also had difficulties gaining the respect of Wilfred, who by April 1940 had from a distance become the de facto father of the family. Malcolm mentioned this frustration to Ella. Ever since Ella's visit, Malcolm had continued to write to her while living with the Swerleins, perhaps feeling more welcome there at the time than with Wilfred. In fact, Malcolm wanted to keep his Boston plans a secret from his oldest brother. "I won't say anything to Wilfred or any one else about your coming to Boston," Ella wrote to Malcolm in June 1940. "We will let it be a surprise. I know you are a good boy, & someday Wilfred will say so too."[24]

On May 4, Pa John Little, Malcolm's paternal grandfather, died. He was 81 years old, and Ella, in her letter to Malcolm, wanted her younger half-brother to *feel* that side of his family, describing his grandfather's final day. "I don't think you know who Pa is," she wrote. "He was supposed to leave May 9th for Boston. He had his clothes all packed, and got up, ate his breakfast and said he didn't feel so good. He got up from the chair and started to the bed & died before he got there." Ella and Wilfred had made the trip down to Georgia for the funeral.[25]

With his Michigan siblings all on their own separate pathways, Ella was offering Malcolm a chance to feel like a part of a family again. "Please be a good boy," wrote Ella, "so you can come to Boston as soon as school close[s]. (I know you will)." Then she made sure to acknowledge Ms. Swerlein, who apparently had allowed for the trip to happen. "Give my regards to Ms. Swerlein, & thank her for the very nice note."[26]

After finishing eighth grade near the top of his class, Malcolm boarded a Greyhound bus in late July 1940 with a "cardboard suitcase" and a "green suit" he was still paying off, purchased in preparation for the trip, Ella letting him know that she'd take care of the rest of the bill. Upon reflection, Malcolm confessed that "if someone had hung a sign, 'HICK,' around my neck, I couldn't have looked much more obvious." The bus traveled slowly along preinterstate country roads, and Malcolm grew annoyed at how the bus seemed to be traveling at a snail's pace. One reason for this was that the Greyhound Bus Company management, whose buses typically cruised comfortably between 40 and 45 miles per hour, had decided as early as 1939 to conserve rubber in the event that America joined the war in Europe. To do this, bus drivers were required to drive at a maximum speed of 35 miles per hour, potentially saving the rubber on tires. After "what seemed like a month," Malcolm stepped off the bus in Roxbury, Ella waiting to pick him up.[27]

The 15-year-old was gobsmacked. Roxbury's Black culture flooded his consciousness. "I didn't know the world contained as many Negroes as I saw thronging downtown Roxbury at night, especially on Saturdays." As Malcolm wandered around the neighborhood, he saw "black-white couples strolling around arm in arm." He gawked as all-Black church congregations elicited spasms of joy during Sunday service. At night, he walked down streets that smelled of "rich, greasy, down-home black cooking!" He listened to live jazz music and bonded with his half-brother, Earl Little Jr., a popular local singer who, when not in and out of jail, performed in a tuxedo under the name "Jimmy Carlton."[28]

In just two short weeks, Malcolm's life had changed. Two months ago, he was sitting in the back of Richard Kaminska's class, a Black outlier living with a white family in a juvenile home, and pushing through an all-white society. Now here he was, mingling with professional jazz musicians, a proud member of a Black community. He tried to write home to Wilfred, but the words escaped him. In a way, he'd fallen in love with "the sense of being a real part of a mass of my own kind for the first time."[29]

Ella fell in love with Malcolm's presence in her Roxbury home. Shortly after he returned to Mason, on August 17, 1940, Ella wrote to Malcolm: "We miss you so much. Don't swell up & buss but honest everything seems dead here. Lots of boys called for you . . . [Aunts] Sas & Gracie are fine & want you to come back. I would like for you to come back but under one condition: Your mind is made up. If we send your fare could you pay all your bills? Let me know real soon."[30]

The moment Malcolm stepped off the bus and back into Mason, a sense of "restlessness with being around white people" invaded his perspective. With the image of Black Roxbury resting in his mind, Malcolm had been awakened. At the Swerleins, he could no longer tolerate the word "nigger" and the patronizing way he was being discussed. Now Malcolm sent glares their way, and suddenly they wondered what had happened to his once-considerate attitude.[31]

The desire to fit in had started to fade at school as well. As a distraction, Malcolm looked to sports. Now in the ninth grade, Malcolm, standing over six feet tall, joined the high school football team as a left end. That fall, under the Friday night lights, Malcolm played only sparingly. The quarterback, Mike

Simone, recalled decades later that "we didn't make fun of him. . . . He was my friend, as an athlete, a teammate."[32]

With winter came basketball, and Malcolm mainly rode the bench as a backup center and played with the reserve team. During a close road game against local rival Charlotte High School that went down to the buzzer, Malcolm listened as the fans seated in the bleachers "'niggered' and 'cooned' [him] to death" and then cheered for joy after one of their players made the game-winning shot—final score 16–15. The heckling continued during a winning effort against Howell High School, another local rival. During Mason's 43–35 winning game, Malcolm was called "Rastus," an overly enthusiastic Black minstrel character, as he cheered his team on. The hate spewed Malcolm's way "didn't bother [his] teammates or [his] coach at all, and to tell the truth, it bothered [him] only vaguely." Malcolm had half his mind set on relocating to Roxbury.[33]

But before he did, he showed signs of discontentment. Once, while the school band was practicing in the auditorium, Malcolm, a member, grabbed the stage curtain and shook it so that it made waves, distracting Joseph Wyman, the band director. When Wyman could no longer give direction, he stopped the band and looked at Malcolm. "Why," he said in frustration, "do you insist" on moving the curtain?

Malcolm had a clever reply ready. "I'm blowing all that hot air back where it came from." Furious, Wyman kicked him out of the band.

At school dances, sometimes after home basketball games, Malcolm, hoping to break the jagged ice surrounding Black and white relationships, once asked two different white girls to join him on the dance floor. "I could feel the freeze . . . a physical barrier." Rejected, Malcolm headed over to a piano and pushed his hand down on the keys, disrupting the music.[34]

Back home with the Swerleins, Malcolm's cultural angst continued, and although he never told Mrs. Swerlein directly what was bothering him, she must have understood to a degree that it was a racial issue. In between football and basketball seasons, the Swerleins sent Malcolm to the home of Harold and Ivy Lyons, a Black couple already struggling financially with five children.

Once again, Malcolm was placed smack in the middle of a large family trying to make ends meet. The Lyonses were kind to him, but he wasn't able to properly communicate the anguish he'd been feeling ever since leaving Roxbury.

Malcolm's living situation, as a ward of the state, was still under the control of Mrs. Swerlein, who tried once more to move Malcolm to a more satisfying home. This time, Malcolm holed up with Mr. Sidney Grayson, a cousin of Mr. Lyons, over on Rogers Street. Once again, Grayson was kind, but Malcolm had had enough. He needed Ella, and he needed to belong to a place he thought was *real*.

The last recorded day Malcolm spent in Mason, Michigan, was February 7, 1941. He'd finished half of the ninth-grade school year and had continued to work as a chauffeur for Dr. Gertrude O'Sullivan. With his earnings and Ella's invitation, Malcolm stepped away from the all-white Mason High School and his carousel of homes. Wilfred, who knew Ella in a way Malcolm had yet to encounter, did meet Malcolm once more after finding out his plans. "I let him know what Ella was into, but it didn't make no difference."[35]

Malcolm wanted an entirely fresh start, away from Mason and away from an older brother who'd hoped he'd at least begrudgingly accept the societal limits put upon a young Black man in a white community. As Malcolm once again boarded a Greyhound bus, he believed he was giving himself a new beginning. "No physical move in my life," he later explained, "has been more pivotal or profound in its repercussions."[36]

ELLA, EARL JR., AND ROXBURY CULTURE

Near the end of her life, Ella Little reflected on her relationship with Malcolm. With sincerity in her eyes, she told the interviewer about how Malcolm arrived in early February 1941: "When he got on that bus in Mason, Michigan, to come and stay with me," she recalled, "he wanted me to know he was real. He said, 'I'll never do anything to hurt you, Ella. Never. If I do anything to hurt you, you tell me and then I'll get you a stick and you beat me.'"

When the interviewer followed with "Did you ever have to do that?" Ella said softly, "Oh no . . . no." After a slight pause, she added with a tinge of laughter: "I have been mad enough to do it, though."[37]

• • • • • • • •

Initially, Ella and the rest of her Roxbury relatives had high hopes for Malcolm. During his brief summer visit in 1940, Malcolm seemed to be a "quiet, totally obedient, dutiful, intelligent little brother." And for a brief time in February and March of 1941, he was. "I spent the first month in town with my mouth hanging open," he'd later recall.[38]

As Malcolm settled into his new life, two of his brothers, Reginald and Philbert, wrote him letters. On March 6, Philbert—now living with the Hackett family in Lansing—remained true to his older-brother-tough-love routine: "Hello Duck, how is everything there? Are you still going to school?" (He wasn't.) Then Philbert made sure to chide Malcolm's penmanship, tossing in yet another nickname: "Say Monkey, the next letter you write to me take your time & write so I can read it and for Gosh! sakes please read it over before you send it." Reginald's letter, addressed March 22, starts more playfully: "Dear Milky, Listen you lowdown-good-for-nothing . . . nice boy . . . are you going to school yet?" But Reginald was more concerned with scoring a girlfriend. "Say, if you can get a picture of a girl about 12–14 years old, will you send it to me[?] I want to make some of these girls in Lansing jealous . . . your brother, Reggie."[39]

Besides family, a couple of friends from Mason High School attempted to stay in touch with Malcolm. One teenage girl, Christine Hoyt, popped a letter in the mail so early that it might have been waiting for Malcolm when he arrived at his 89 Harrishof Street home, his address just before moving to 72 Dale Street: "Well how do you like it where you are? Gee I am in Seventh hour study hall with no one to talk to or anything to do but write to you." In March, a student teacher at Mason, Peter Hawryleiw, wrote to him: "How are you getting along? Everything at Mason is still running smoothly, except the basketball games . . . drop us a line, if you have time."[40]

He didn't. Perhaps the last things on his mind were slow study halls or high school basketball. Roxbury's culture had begun to wrap itself around his mind.

As he later explained, "I had never tasted a sip of liquor, never even smoked a cigarette, and here I saw little black children, ten and twelve years old, shooting craps, playing cards, fighting, getting grown-ups to put a penny or a nickel on their number for them, things like that. And these children threw around swear words I'd never heard before, even, and slang expressions that were just as new to me, such as 'stud' and 'cat' and 'chick' and 'cool' and 'hip.' Every night as I lay in bed I turned these new words over in my mind."[41]

Malcolm knew that Ella wanted him to continue in his aspiration to be a lawyer. That meant eventually heading back to school, a place far from his mind. Aunt Sas and Aunt Gracie, close to Ella, hoped Malcolm could begin going to a Baptist church and map out his future with a religious faith as his fulcrum, but he'd seen enough of Christianity in both its Black and white forms with foster families.[42]

No, Malcolm wanted to feel cool and confident, and at the time, his half-brother was the epitome of "hip."

Earl Little Jr., born in Georgia in 1912, was the oldest son of Malcolm's father. In the early 1930s, Earl Jr. made his way up to Boston and settled in with his mother, Daisy Mason, working at her general store by day and singing at bars and clubs at night. Gifted with height (6'4"), looks, and a strong baritone voice, Earl Little Jr.'s "Jimmy Carlton" persona mirrored his greatest influence, bandleader Duke Ellington.[43]

But just as the 1930s were brutal to Malcolm in Michigan, Earl Jr. had his own share of Depression-era setbacks. A thief since the age of 12 as he endured poverty in rural Georgia, Earl Jr. spent most of the '30s shuffling in and out of several Massachusetts prisons, even once going to jail to cover for Ella's own shoplifting.[44]

These spats with law enforcement didn't keep him from the stage. From 1935 to 1936, a batch of Jimmy Carlton songs played weekly on WMEX Boston radio, ranging from 5:45 to 6:15 p.m. and 9:30 to 9:45 p.m. Earl also traveled to Pennsylvania and New York, meeting countless other singers and musicians, such as Billie Holiday. "It was rumored that Earl had a thing going with her when she performed in Boston," said Ella. "One way he really impressed Malcolm was to introduce him to her."[45]

For Earl Jr., life revolved around three conflicting realities: prison, working day-long shifts at his mother's store, and forgetting it all on stage. On September 13, 1940, Jimmy Carlton took a gig at a club in Wilkes Barre, Pennsylvania. He stood on stage and delivered a rousing version of "Ol' Man River," a song made popular by Black singer Paul Robeson in the musical *Showboat*:

> Ah'm tired of livin'
> An' skeered of dyin',
> But ol' man river,
> He jes'keeps rollin' along.

After finishing to cheers, Jimmy smoothly transitioned into "Marie," an Irving Berlin–written swing number, but one newspaper writer described Jimmy's interpretation as the "hot version."[46]

Now living in the Boston area, Malcolm was brought into Earl Jr.'s world via "front row seats" and backstage passes. There, 16-year-old Malcolm soaked up the musical electricity and chatted with famous musicians coming through Boston. "To him," said one close friend at the time, "actors or dancers or musicians, they were very exciting people. He just loved them. Something that he got from being around these type[s] of people. I don't think I can find words to express it—it was like food is to a hungry body."[47]

Soon enough, Ella could see that Malcolm had caught Earl Jr.'s show-business bug. Around dinnertime, Malcolm often came through the door with a wave of energy under his feet, "popping his fingers and twisting his arms, singing 'The St. Louis Blues' and heading for the kitchen." At night, Malcolm sneaked out of the house and hung out with Earl Jr. and Ken Collins (Ella's future husband) at a variety of clubs. It angered Ella, who was trying to instill a bit of self-discipline in Malcolm. "They knew he was a minor," Ella said, "but they acted like two irresponsible teenagers themselves." But within months, Malcolm was sold. "Someday," he once announced, "I'm going to be like Earl!"[48]

Malcolm's adoration for Earl Jr.'s lifestyle reached its apex when, despite his ambivalence toward Christianity during his years in Mason, he decided to join Roxbury's Townsend Street Baptist Church choir. It was Earl Jr.'s idea, perhaps as a way for Malcolm to test out his vocal range.[49]

Sadly, however, Earl Jr.'s "strenuous" double life as an all-day worker at his mother's store and nighttime performer must have caught up with him. He started exhibiting symptoms of tuberculosis, and on June 3, 1941, Earl Little Jr. passed away before reaching 30.[50]

Earl Jr.'s death affected Malcolm deeply, and he refused to believe his big brother had died of natural causes. Malcolm had seen Earl Jr. bring a room to its feet. How, he wondered, could he have succumbed so quickly to an illness? At home with Ella, Malcolm quaked with disbelief. *He was poisoned*, he expressed to Ella. Earl Jr.'s death devastated Malcolm to such an extent that Ella feared he'd "lose his mind."[51]

RAILROAD TIME TRAVEL

As Malcolm attempted to keep himself together, he began to gravitate toward the more comfortable parts of Roxbury culture: "I felt more relaxed among Negroes who were being their natural selves and not putting on airs," Malcolm later explained. This part of town, briefly introduced to him by

Earl Jr. and Ken Collins, seemed real. Wealth and upper-class status—at least from what he'd seen from the "putting on airs" residents on the Hill—were foreign to him, those years eating backyard dandelion roots and expired bread still in his mind. Through no choice of his own, it was human struggle he related to most.[52]

Another Roxbury landmark near Malcolm at this time was Dr. Silas F. "Shag" Taylor's drugstore. Most everyone living in Roxbury's South End, including Ella, knew Shag Taylor, a businessman who most often appeared "distinguished-looking and always nattily dressed." Taylor was also very well-connected to local politicians and had once been appointed by four-time Boston mayor James M. Curley to the State Parole Board, acting as an intermediary between white and Black communities.[53]

Being an intermediary also meant juggling various desires. Taylor soon became a quid pro quo expert, transforming his drugstore into an after-hours nightspot, his bending of rules often ignored and sometimes supported. "I remember one time I went into Shag's on a Saturday night," recalled a Roxbury resident, "and the chief of police was sitting back there having a few drinks with Shag himself."[54]

Before Malcolm could even think about buying after-hours drinks with Roxbury residents, he needed money, and that meant finding a job. In June, only three weeks after his brother Earl Jr.'s death, Malcolm, with help from Ella and one of her friends, applied to work for the New Haven Railroad. Up until this point, Malcolm had been working for a time at the Townsend Drug Store as a "soda jerk," using his energetic charm to socialize with customers, such as future partner-in-crime Francis "Sonny" Brown, while serving up ice cream sodas. A stone's throw away was the Baptist church where Earl Jr. had urged Malcolm, before passing, to join the choir.[55]

But with Earl Jr. gone and Malcolm restless to travel, the railroad job was a way to see the country without having to pay the fare. So without any experience, the 16-year-old applied for a job that supposedly only hired men who'd at least turned 21. Thankfully for Malcolm, the New Haven Railroad—already strapped for cash and in bankruptcy—wasn't too strict on the requirement. In his *Autobiography*, Malcolm recalled that during his job interview, "a tired-acting old white clerk got down to the crucial point, when I came to sign up. 'Age, Little?' When I told him 'Twenty-one,' he never lifted his eyes from his pencil. I knew I had the job." On June 27, the day Malcolm completed paperwork designating his beneficiary, should anything bad happen, he listed

Ella and her Harrishof address first, followed, oddly, by his mother, Louise. Instead of listing the Kalamazoo Mental Hospital, Malcolm (or perhaps Ella) chose the address where Philbert was staying. As for his birthday, Malcolm traveled back four years and gave the date May 19, 1921. He was now a 20-year-old "fourth cook."[56]

Less than five months after moving to Roxbury, Malcolm had already broken the law.

From June 27 to September 13, 1941, Malcolm was either "helping load food requisitions onto the trains" or working as a "glorified . . . dishwasher" on the "Colonial," which the *Boston Globe* described as being "designed and decorated to honor famous Colonial patriots and early New England homes." The trip appropriately ended in Washington, DC, and Malcolm had an "overnight layover" there, or a free opportunity to sightsee.[57]

But DC back in 1941 was not what he expected. "I was astounded to find," he'd later recall to Alex Haley, "in the nation's capital, just a few blocks from Capitol Hill, thousands of Negroes living worse than any I'd ever seen in the poorest sections of Roxbury . . . such a dense concentration of stumblebums, pushers, hookers, public crap-shooters, even little kids running around at midnight begging for pennies, half-naked and barefooted."[58]

From the train, Malcolm could see hundreds of factories contributing to the war effort in Europe, churning out supplies and weapons. Especially along the Colonial's Shore Line route between New York and Boston, all Malcolm had to do was look out the window at stations in New London, Providence, and Mansfield to see giant "plants turning out materials to meet defense needs . . . between rolling landscape, here and there a town and village."[59]

Malcolm did manage to score a layover or two in New York City, and it was around this time, in the summer of 1941, when he was first introduced to Small's Paradise in Harlem. "No Negro place of business had ever impressed me so much," he recalled. "Around the big, luxurious-looking, circular bar were thirty or forty Negroes, mostly men, drinking and talking." There was a steady professionalism to what he saw at Small's. He'd seen so much posturing, or Black men in Roxbury "flashing whatever money" they had to show they were special. But in Harlem, no one was trying too hard. "Their manners seemed natural; they were not putting on any airs. I was awed. Within the first five minutes in Small's, I had left Boston and Roxbury forever."[60]

As for the way 16-year-old Malcolm appeared to his fellow railroad employees, a waiter who'd worked with him put it this way: "At that time Malcolm's energy was not directed toward hard work. He was wild. He had only an eighth-grade education. I could have predicted he would eventually get into trouble." In return, Malcolm respected the experience of the Black men around him at the time. "They grew me up real fast," he said later, "because in those days, railroad men were about the hippest people in town."[61]

GIRLS, MUSIC, AND A NEW HOME

It's true that trouble was awaiting Malcolm, but at least in late 1941, Malcolm was still simply a teenager whose thoughts revolved around girls, music, and style.

In November 1941, Ella was finally able to move in to her 72 Dale Street home in Roxbury. Malcolm went with her, and he was given a significant upgrade, a "kitchenette flat on the attic level, complete with a hot plate." After moving in, he wrote letters to a few girls in Michigan. One of them was 17-year-old Zelma Holman, a Black teenager who'd grown up in Jackson, Michigan, but had to travel to Lansing to roller skate, since the Jackson skating rinks at the time were segregated. In his letter, besides notifying her of his new address, Malcolm tried to sweet-talk her a bit: "Listen," he wrote in cursive with a pen on blue stationery, "will you send me a picture of you. I want to show the fellas out here that we have some fine girls in Michigan to[o] & I want pictures of only the finest 'no jive.'" He also made sure to let her know that he'd "already been in 23 different states," which is about right if you combine his ever-shifting childhood, the states he'd been through on the bus ride from Michigan to Massachusetts, and the train rides up and down the East Coast.[62]

Around the same time, Malcolm wrote to teenager Eloise Schack, describing his hopes to travel to warmer weather states such as Florida, Georgia, and California, all while setting up a pickup line: "I'm a northern farm boy, but I don't like cold weather. I guess that accounts for my being so 'warm' hearted."[63]

To 14-year-old Mary Jane Smith, a white dancer back in Mason, Malcolm—as he did with Zelma and Eloise—requested that she send him a photo of her and updated her on all the bands he'd been able to see, no doubt mentioning several he knew interested her: "Since I left Mason I've seen Gene Krupa, Cab Calloway, Ella Fitzgerald, Glen Miller [and] Count Basie (7 times) and I saw Tommy Dorsey and The Andrews Sisters when I was in New York last summer."[64]

Malcolm had charm to spare, but these girls were a thousand miles away. In between railroad stints—he'd head back to the New Haven Railroad on January 4, 1942—Malcolm made a few dollars working as a busboy at Boston's historic Parker House, only to spend most of it at dance halls at night. After meeting 18-year-old trumpet player Malcolm Jarvis at a Roxbury pool hall, the two young men scanned dance floors looking for girls to swing with. Malcolm, according to Jarvis, "showed [the street life] to me. The only thing I showed Malcolm . . . was where to go dancing and have a good time. . . . Any club where a big band was playing, we went in, and that's how he and I really got to be tight."[65]

A favorite of his at the time was Lionel Hampton and His Orchestra, in particular their hit instrumental foxtrot, "Flying Home." But it was the 18-member Count Basie Orchestra he'd been around the most, working as a "prop boy" whenever they were in town. As these big bands played at the Roseland State Ballroom, Malcolm soon embraced the dance floor, lindy-hopping his way through the night: "With alcohol or marijuana lightening my head, and that wild music wailing away on those portable record players, it didn't take long to loosen up the dancing instincts in my African heritage. All I remember is that during some party around this time, when nearly everyone but me was up dancing, some girl grabbed me . . . and there I was out on the floor. I was up in the jostling crowd—and suddenly, unexpectedly, I got the idea. It was as though somebody had clicked on a light. My long suppressed African instincts broke through, and loose."[66]

Malcolm danced with many girls at the Roseland, but between October 1941 and June 1942, there was one girl who grabbed his attention both on and off the dance floor—Gloria Strother. Between Gloria and Malcolm was a deep emotional connection, and they wrote to each other frequently. Here, for example, is a passage from a letter Gloria sent to 17-year-old Malcolm in June 1942: "There isn't much to tell that you don't already know, except that I love you, and you should know that by now. I'm glad to hear you haven't been drinking. I knew you just did because you wanted to. Keep yourself out of trouble and hurry home because I'm lonesome."[67]

Malcolm may have loved Gloria to an extent, but he wasn't about to follow in the footsteps of Jarvis, who'd married and had two children before turning 21. Besides, by the summer of 1942, a white dancer had captured his attention. "To Malcolm [at the time]," Jarvis later said, "white women had the money and the Black ones didn't. That's why his preference was, in those days, more to the white. They could afford to give him some of the things that he wanted and show him a good time. Now, he was very respectful of the Black women. I will say that. But he frequented the white ones because of that—money."[68]

BEATRICE, OR "SOPHIA"

Malcolm first met Beatrice Caragulian at Boston's Tic Toc Night Club on Tremont Street in 1942. At that time, Bea was an unmarried 19-year-old, 5'5", 110 lbs., semiprofessional dancer with reddish-brown hair and brown eyes. Bea was born in Watertown, Massachusetts, on September 16, 1922. She was the oldest child of Alice Aghajanian, who'd immigrated from Armenia with her family at the age of two. Bea's mother was pushed into an arranged marriage at an early age, and by 1921, at the age of 15, she accepted the proposal of 23-year-old Armenian American engraver Leon Caragulian.[69]

Bea's childhood was like many—a mix of charm and conflict. On July 16, 1927, her younger sister, Joyce, was born, and as the years went by, Bea "was given every advantage by her parents," thanks in part to her father's steady position in the *Boston Herald-Traveler's* editorial department. At an early age, Bea embraced dancing, and in junior high school, she won a local competition. She later described her childhood as idyllic, at least on the surface. She was "well-dressed, attended school, church and community functions, was encouraged to bring friends home, and was popular." Meanwhile, Joyce seemed to shadow her older sister as a dancer and enjoyed taking her cat to local pet shows.[70]

Both daughters felt the stress of their parents' tumultuous marriage. At least once, Bea's father was accused of domestic violence only to be found "not guilty." There was an obvious "lack of affection" between her parents, and Bea's mother clung to her, soon becoming "overprotective." In June 1940, Bea graduated from Watertown High School. Opting to not go to college, Bea sought a career as a professional dancer. She was well-suited for it. Besides her figure, people close to her described Bea as having a "naturally light and sunny disposition (other jealous types saying 'superficial')." By the time Malcolm walked up to her at the Tic Toc in 1942, Bea still lived at home and was looking for work at clubs in Boston and, if possible, New York City.[71]

Bea did have a serious boyfriend—Martin Mehran Bazarian, a fellow aspiring dancer and waiter who'd hoped Bea would be his wife and wait for him as he entered the US Army in June 1942 to fight in the Pacific. Martin had "courted" Bea for at least one year, but the earliest he could return was February 1944, and being an Armenian immigrant, he had yet to become an official US citizen.

After Martin left, Beatrice did her part to support the war, working a clerical job at the Watertown Arsenal, earning a weekly wage of $35, the plant a 10-minute walk from her home. She also frequented clubs in the Boston area and took gigs as a dancer. It was during this time that Malcolm came into her life.[72]

"She didn't dance well," Malcolm explained later in his *Autobiography*, "at least not by Negro standards." Beatrice didn't mind the "staring eyes" as she talked with Malcolm. A white woman dancing with a Black man was controversial in 1946, when fewer than 4 percent of the population approved of interracial marriage. At the Roseland ballroom, the two hit it off, especially one night, after Malcolm had chosen Beatrice over a young Black woman he'd later call "Laura." By the time Malcolm had taken Laura home and grabbed a taxi back to Roseland, Beatrice was standing just outside. She and Malcolm walked toward her "low convertible," parked "about five blocks down." To the 17-year-old Malcolm, this older white woman "knew where she was going."

Beatrice drove until they were outside the Boston area. Then "she pulled off into a side road, and then off that into a deserted lane." Beatrice "turned off everything but the radio."

With Martin fighting as an Army private in the middle of the Pacific, Beatrice, for at least "several months," continued to see Malcolm. Beatrice "would pick me up downtown, and I'd take her to dances, and to the bars around Roxbury. We drove all over. Sometimes it would be nearly daylight when she let me out in front of Ella's."

Having Beatrice hanging off his arm gave Malcolm status around Roxbury bars and clubs. "I paraded her," he admitted. Because of Malcolm's job working for a railroad company, Beatrice believed Malcolm was at least "draft-age." During the years Martin Bazarian was off fighting, Beatrice and Malcolm maintained an off-and-on again relationship, frequenting bars and dance clubs around Boston and New York City.[73]

DETROIT RED

I was the Roamer . . . roaming in darkness (smile).

—Malcolm X, Letter to Brother Raymond

By July 1942, Malcolm had started traveling at such a rate that his family had trouble keeping track: "I received your card last Saturday," wrote Hilda. "What are or were you doing in Phil? Do you still work on the train? . . . Why do you have to tell my business to everyone in Boston? How long are you going to stay in Boston if you haven't already gone?" Reginald, on the other hand, wasn't too concerned about Malcolm's whereabouts, since he was getting into his own trouble, writing to Malcolm about fighting a "sailor" near Lake Michigan and boasting about how he "knocked him clear across the sidewalk into the weeds." Reginald made sure to end his letter, addressed "Dear Fella," with a request: "Say if you have about $5 you could spare it would come in handy."[74]

Hilda was also worried about the influence Malcolm was starting to have over Reginald, and in the same month, she wrote to Malcolm's younger brother: "Are you planning on going back to school this fall? I know that if you go to Boston you won't go to school. That is, if you associate with Ella or Malcolm." Hilda had been infuriated with Ella in 1942, when Ella traveled to Lansing to assess Louise's property. Hilda was comfortable enough with Reginald to let out her frustrations and also tried to get Reginald to see the other side of their half-sister: "Ella really showed me herself when she was here," Hilda wrote. "She isn't worth spittin' on. She also told everyone here that she owned the place (she's trying to get it) and now people come out & look it over and everything. I wish I had the money I'd fence it off & have a gate so that people can't come in anytime they feel like it."[75]

By this time, Malcolm's family had splintered, with Philbert working for a defense plant in Connecticut and Wilfred employed in Ohio, so it was up to Hilda to take care of the home their mother had raised them in. But Ella—whom Hilda had nicknamed "Elephant" in a letter to Malcolm—apparently wasn't interested in helping the "Michigan Littles" to remain in Lansing.

In the same July letter, Hilda also wrote to Reginald about how stingy Malcolm had been about money: "I wrote to Malcolm almost two weeks ago & I even sent word by Ella but I haven't heard from him yet," wrote Hilda. "I didn't expect to. When he was here and after he got a job he always had some excuse for not lending me a nick[el] or so. He did give me 50 cents before he left. That's the first time in his life that he's ever given me anything. He really owed me that. He used to steal my money & everything else all the time."[76]

At 17, Malcolm had changed a great deal from the "Harpy" who ran for president less than three years earlier. He had an older white girlfriend, his night attire leaned toward the zoot suit, and he had an off-and-on railroad job that allowed him to make contacts in DC and Harlem. He was able to see the hottest bands and had learned quite a few moves on the dance floor. So whenever he returned to Lansing, he made sure to flaunt his style to people he assumed only dreamed of visiting New York City.

Yvonne, then a middle school student, remembered hearing about her hip older brother more than actually seeing him. "In Lansing," she recalled decades later, "some kids would come to school and say, 'You know, we were downtown today and we saw this man.' They'd tell about this man with this big hat and his red hair and his gold chain and these pants this wide, and I'd laugh. I'd say, 'Oh, really.' You see, I never told them that was my brother."[77]

By December 1942, Malcolm had had enough of his old home scene. He left his brothers and sisters behind and headed to Harlem. Without question, he'd already made contacts at bars and restaurants in the past while working for the railroad during his overnight layovers, but it's unknown how Malcolm chose Jimmy's Chicken Shack as his main place of employment. Still, for almost two years, the restaurant building became Malcolm's New York City crash pad.[78]

In 1936, then-21-year-old James M. Bacon opened Jimmy's Chicken Shack at 763 St. Nicholas Avenue. To give his restaurant/bar a way to stand out, he purchased a large sign in the shape of a giant red chicken that hovered over passersby on the sidewalk. At night, lights outlined the chicken's figure, and the Shack was eventually advertised as a place "where celebrities meet," best known for its "steaks and chops," its lobby walls painted dark blue with red roses and a happily "colored butterfly toying at a bud." Over time, one writer commented that the Shack was "the spot on the Hill where you can eat to your heart's content, and still have enough to pay the rent." Bacon, whose wife, Margaret, and daughter helped run the restaurant, kept the Shack open daily from noon until six in the morning. The bar kept a steady supply of "beer, wines, liquors and mixed drinks," as music, cigarette smoke, laughter, and applause filled the restaurant. Later, Malcolm said, "A jam-packed four-thirty AM crowd at Jimmy's Chicken Shack . . . might have such jam-session entertainment as Hazel Scott playing the piano for Billie Holiday singing the blues."[79]

In 1939, 30-year-old jazz pianist Art Tatum enthralled Shack patrons nightly with new music. As he played, a young dishwasher and aspiring saxophonist named Charlie Parker listened to Tatum's "God"-like melodic improvisations, making 88 keys sound like a thousand. For three months, Parker, not yet 20 and shy, allowed his dish pile to add up and took a crash course in "harmonic theory" from Tatum, whose near-blindness in no way prevented him from becoming one of the greatest pianists of the twentieth century.[80]

Malcolm loved music, but he wasn't a musician. In a figurative way, Malcolm's "music" lay in language and the way he could persuasively lead someone, anyone, to a conclusion before they themselves had reached it. Still not yet 18, this skill was only beginning to flourish. But Harlem was filled with charismatic personalities, and the art of the hustle became the rhythm Malcolm learned the quickest. "He was just wild, man," remembered Clarence Atkins, a friend of Malcolm's at the time. "He didn't give a shit about nothing. Whatever he thought was the thing for him to do at that particular time, that's what he would do."[81]

From 1943 to late 1944, Jimmy's Chicken Shack was Malcolm's base for food, money, shelter, and friendship. Atkins, an aspiring jazz musician at the time, "spent many a night drinking and talking at the La Marr-Cherie," a restaurant not far from the Shack, at 721 St. Nicholas Avenue. Atkins, talking to a biographer decades later, remembered how vital the Shack was to Malcolm's life and how Malcolm used it to begin a variety of hustles. "He was flunking for Jimmy [Bacon] . . . doing anything, like washing dishes, mopping floors, or whatever, you know . . . because he could eat, and Jimmy had a place upstairs over the place where he could sleep."[82]

In Harlem—a city suffering from racial tension to a point that, as Malcolm put it, "one could almost smell trouble about to break out"—he told Atkins about how Mr. Kaminska's dismissal of Malcolm's dream of becoming a lawyer still gnawed at him. "You know," said Atkins, "that had to have some kind of impact on his thinking for him to be constantly speaking on this in our presence." But perhaps far more, Malcolm brought up his family's struggles growing up. "He would talk often about how his father used to get brutalized and beat up on the corner selling Marcus Garvey's paper and he would talk a lot about Garvey's concepts in terms of how they could benefit us as a people. . . . He was always political, even in the midst of all that street hustling and everything else he was doing, he was political."[83]

One Sunday night, August 1, 1943, an incident occurred at the Hotel Braddock, located a mile south of the Shack. It started at 7:00 p.m. with a woman, Marjorie Polite, who was unsatisfied with the available rooms and asked for a refund. She was given one, but when she asked the elevator opera-tor for her one dollar tip back, the operator shrugged her off, claiming he never received one. Polite became very angry and was eventually arrested by an officer. A mother and son saw Polite's arrest and demanded she be freed. Words were exchanged, escalating to the point that the son, Robert Bandy, a Black soldier on leave, hit the officer and then ran, resulting in the officer shooting Bandy.[84]

Word traveled fast, and soon the words were twisted enough that many believed the officer had *killed* Bandy. But it didn't take much for a citywide protest to start. Frustration in Harlem had been mounting over the direction of the country, and many in the Black community felt torn between "hope for future equality and despair over existing injustice," not to mention being directed toward risking their lives to fight in a war while being treated as second-class citizens.[85]

It's not clear how involved Malcolm was in the riot, which, 12 hours after Bandy was shot, left six people dead, dozens injured, and two million dollars of property destroyed. "I was walking down St. Nicholas Avenue [when it hap-pened]"; he explained in the *Autobiography*. "I saw all of these Negroes hollering and running north from 125th Street. Some of them were loaded down with armfuls of stuff. I remember it was the bandleader Fletcher Henderson's nephew 'Shorty' Henderson who told me what had happened. Negroes were smashing store windows, and taking everything they could grab and carry—furniture, food, jewelry, clothes, whisky."[86]

As *Invisible Man* novelist Ralph Ellison put it, the riot was "the poorer element's way of blowing off steam."[87] Ellison, like Malcolm, was walking outside when the riot broke out and had exited the subway at 137th Street when he saw the frustrated crowd.[88]

The riot tightened police security across Harlem, but Malcolm wasn't simply working at the Shack and sleeping upstairs. Through unknown con-nections, his brother Wilfred recalled, Malcolm had started dealing mari-juana, traveling across the country and up and down the East Coast. Wilfred remembered Malcolm heading "out to California or wherever they would send him and come back with two of the biggest suitcases you ever saw, full of that stuff . . . marijuana pressed into bricks, you know . . . but they would pay him a thousand dollars a trip." In California, Florida, and of course New York and Boston, Malcolm walked the streets, as Jarvis recalled, "with marijuana sewed into the lining of that big, heavy overcoat he used to wear." Once, when Malcolm returned to Roxbury, Jarvis watched Malcolm take "a needle and break the lining open and take stuff out. Sometimes he had as much as a quarter and a half pound of it, and then he would package it up himself, roll it up into joints and sell them for a dollar apiece." After being fired by the railroad company, Malcolm used his "voided railroad pass" to ride for free. "I could jive any train conductor into letting me on," Malcolm confessed later. "I had a jungle mind and everything I did was done by instinct to survive."[89]

But in Harlem, Malcolm mainly connected with residents and patrons around the intersection of 147th and St. Nicholas Avenue. And back at the Shack, Malcolm hung out with a broke 22-year-old dishwasher named John Elroy Sanford, later famously known as *Sanford and Son* comedian Redd Foxx. Malcolm "was a sweetheart," Foxx said later, "the nicest guy you wanted to know." Contrary to the friendship Malcolm had struck up with Atkins, Foxx and Malcolm kept their talks free and easy while drumming up their own brand of trouble. "Malcolm was a different person in those days. Wasn't saying any of the things he was saying later," Foxx told a reporter many years later. "What was going on in America wasn't on Malcolm's mind or mine."[90]

Money was the main concern for both Shack employees. The wage Bacon paid them was a pittance compared to what they made from the side-hustles they had going off the clock. The two young men first met in a pool hall across the street from 707 St. Nicholas Avenue. Soon after becoming friends, others around them saw their "red hair and mariney complexions" and decided to give them the nicknames "Chicago Red" (where Foxx had spent some of his younger years) and "Detroit Red" (Malcolm preferred Lansing, but no one knew Lansing enough for it to catch on). "Malcolm didn't have the showbiz talent," said Foxx, "so he didn't give a damn what he got into. He'd take on anything to get some dough. He was a little bit more aggressive [than me], but I'd rather be sleeping with a broad and go somewhere and do fifteen minutes of comedy."[91]

One side-hustle not mentioned in Malcolm's *Autobiography* involved a female dry-cleaning employee who liked Foxx enough that she sometimes "forgot" to properly lock up after the store closed. The two Reds capitalized on this by slipping through a partially opened window and stealing "around one hundred suits." The thieves took the suits up to the 707 St. Nicholas Avenue rooftop and started to offload them for a price. "We'd sell one or two of them a day off the roof," Foxx told a magazine journalist decades later. "We never got caught for that." On that same roof, Foxx and Malcolm crashed some nights, sleeping on stacks of undelivered newspapers. "We had about 500 pounds of newspaper up there. Newspapers is some of the warmest stuff going."[92]

Small's Paradise had also at least been a brief part of Malcolm's life in Harlem. After growing accustomed to the place during his layover nights while employed with the railroad, in early 1943, Malcolm worked briefly as an off-the-books waiter for Edwin and Charles A. Small, who launched Small's off the corner of 7th Avenue and 135th Street in 1924. About a 20-minute walk south from Jimmy's Chicken Shack, Small's had become one of the best-known night spots in New York City, and one of their aims was to be "a red hot show in a cool place, where you are greeted with Southern Hospitality." Live shows went on three times a night in the early 1940s, starting at 10:30 p.m., then 12:30 a.m., and one for the road at around 3:00 a.m. The space inside was immense, with themed seating areas, such as the Dine and Dance Clover Room, the elegant Paradise Room, and the newly constructed Orchid Room. Malcolm often brought Bea, who "would come in on a late afternoon train." Depending on the room they chose, the cost to enter was between six to seven dollars.[93]

BEATRICE'S PREGNANCY

By February 1944, Malcolm had become entrenched in Harlem, avoiding the war and continuing his relationship with then-21-year-old Beatrice Caragulian.[94] Since late November 1943, Beatrice had been working as a clerk for Bachrach's Studio—a long-established portrait photography business—making $25 a week as she continued to live with her parents and younger sister, Joyce, at their 121 Dexter Avenue home in Watertown. But in February, Bea's other boyfriend, 22-year-old Martin Bazarian, returned from fighting in the Pacific. Relieved to be back in Boston, Martin filed the paperwork necessary to become an American citizen. Then, on February 22, 1944, he married Beatrice in a church ceremony in Boston.[95]

Bea broke the news to Malcolm over the phone.

Bea's news bothered Malcolm, but his good friend in Harlem, Sammy McKnight, or "Sammy the Pimp," helped him process the way Bea—and some young white American women in the 1940s—made choices:

> Sammy said that white women were very practical; he had heard so many of them express how they felt. They knew that the black man had all the strikes against him, that the white man kept the black man down, under his heel, unable to get anywhere, really. The white woman wanted to be comfortable, she wanted to be looked upon with favor by her own kind, but also she wanted to have her pleasure. So some of them just married a white man for convenience and security, and kept right on going with a Negro. It wasn't that they were necessarily in love with the Negro, but they were in love with lust—particularly "taboo" lust.[96]

According to Malcolm's account, Bea didn't want her marriage to Martin to affect their "forbidden" relationship. And Malcolm also mentioned in his *Autobiography* that Martin Bazarian "had been home on leave" when they married "and he had just gone back." It remains unknown if Malcolm meant that Martin had been on a furlough and had gone back into the US Army—the Spring of 1944 was quite volatile in both Europe and the Pacific—to complete his two years of duty.[97]

As her prison file shows, around April 1944, Beatrice became pregnant. If Martin did indeed head back to the army after marrying Beatrice, it leaves open the question of who the actual father was. A look into Martin's military record reveals that he wasn't officially discharged from the army until September 15, 1944, and had two documented stays at an army hospital, in June and August of 1944.[98]

During Bea's pregnancy, Malcolm continued to reside in Harlem, but an April 14, 1944, *Boston Globe* ad does show that "Rhythm Red—Smart Entertainer" was set to perform at the Old Howard, "Rhythm Red" being Malcolm's stage name at the time. Between July and September 1944, Malcolm, in addition to staying at the Shack, took on another job working as an "entertainer" for Abe Goldstein, the owner of a restaurant called Lobster Pond. Waiting tables, emceeing, and dealing pot, Malcolm stayed busy while with Goldstein, who later recalled Malcolm as being "a bit unstable and neurotic but under proper guidance, a good boy."[99]

But Bea's pregnancy sheds new light on Malcolm's actions starting in October 1944. By October 20, Malcolm had left Jimmy's Chicken Shack and moved back to Roxbury, choosing to take an oddly conventional job, given the side-hustles and nightclub lifestyle he'd grown accustomed to in Harlem. For $29 a week, Malcolm worked as a "warehouseman" for Sears Roebuck on Brookline Avenue, a few miles away from Bea's parent's house. By this point, Bea was six months pregnant, and Martin was no longer overseas.[100]

One can only imagine Malcolm's thought process at this time. Had Bea told him that he "might" be the father? Had Malcolm, by moving back to Roxbury, been attempting to show Bea that he could work a standard job and be a provider? Or did Bea keep the pregnancy a secret from him? Were they even communicating at this time?

Malcolm didn't have a mentor or role model to turn to. After he returned to Roxbury, Ella had become startled at how "atheist" Harlem made him. Malcolm did at times talk with Rev. Samuel Laviscount, pastor of St. Mark's Congregational Church, but it cannot be confirmed when Malcolm sought his guidance. As Malcolm later confessed to Laviscount, "When I was a wild youth, you often gave me some timely advice." Potentially stuck in a moral predicament, Malcolm could have used some advice from his parents, if he'd had them.[101]

Bea and Martin's first two years of marriage were anything but smooth. Later, in an interview with prison officials while Bea was in jail, Martin, careful to not evoke too much frustration since he wanted his wife out of prison as soon as possible, explained that their marriage had been "very satisfactory," but he "admits that they were both somewhat headstrong, [and had] ran up bills for clothes." In November and December of 1944, Beatrice's health became a concern, so she was "placed under the care of a physician because [Beatrice] expected confinement and they feared for her safety because she was always so thin."[102]

While Beatrice convalesced, Malcolm acted out. On November 10, 1944, Malcolm "walked off the job" at Sears Roebuck, angering his boss, who later told a prison official that he "would not rehire" him. And to show Malcolm's frustration even more, on November 29, he was arrested for taking a fur coat out of Ella's closet and selling it at a pawn shop for five dollars. He was given a year of probation. The famous mug shot of Malcolm with a hat on was for this crime. Ella had been the one who called the police.[103]

By the end of 1944, Malcolm was lost—directionless. During this difficult period, he started working for millionaire William Paul Lennon, Malcolm's job title being a "butler and occasional houseworker," as listed in his prison file. When later contacted by police after Malcolm had been arrested for burglary, Lennon confirmed his home address as 5 Arlington Street, a stone's throw from the Boston Common, and said to prison officials that Malcolm had been "fairly dependable" and "honest" as a "temporary" employee, being paid 75 cents an hour.[104]

Lennon maintained a double life. In the public eye, he was a hotel manager and art collector who had homes in Sandwich, Massachusetts, where he owned the Shawme Hill Farm, and Palm Beach, Florida. In 1937, he married multimillionaire socialite Jeanne Marie Scott. The couple's name often appeared in print as charitable donors to causes such as the Red Cross. Never having children, the couple was free to attend operas, host parties, and mingle with other members of the upper class in Florida, New York, and Paris, France.[105]

But in private, Lennon had a habit of paying for elaborately staged same-sex encounters with younger men, often Black. He'd hired one of Malcolm's friends, Francis "Sonny" Brown, "to undress them both, then pick up the old man like a baby, lay him on his bed, then stand over him and sprinkle him all over with talcum powder," Lennon eventually reaching "climax from that." Brown, who prison officials claimed had an "effeminate appearance and mannerisms," was just the kind of man Lennon was looking for.[106]

It was Brown who introduced Lennon to Malcolm, but what can never be fully confirmed is how involved Malcolm became in Lennon's private life. While Jarvis admitted in a letter to a biographer that Malcolm did participate in the talcum powder rubdowns described to Alex Haley in the *Autobiography*, it was mainly for financial gain, a dark side-hustle at a time in his life when not much else mattered except finding the next high.[107]

From December 1, 1944, to March 1945, Malcolm was "off grid," popping back up in April 1945 in Lansing, Michigan, as an employee for a bedding company. As for Beatrice, on January 5, 1945, at least eight months pregnant, she gave birth at a city hospital in Cambridge. In her prison file, the baby is listed as "legitimate," which meant that she had told the doctors that the child was hers and Martin's. Tragically, however, the baby was a "stillborn."[108]

After losing the baby, Beatrice, according to Martin, "had difficulty reconciling herself to this grief." She couldn't shake what had started to become an unbearable anxiety. From April to June 1945, she took a defense job at a war plant for Morse and Lockhart, but she soon grew ill and quit. In August, Beatrice suffered a miscarriage, and her spirits were low. With Martin growing more concerned, their doctor recommended a complete change of venue. And so they relocated. With Joyce and her good friend Kora (pre-robberies), they moved to Miami, Florida, in the fall of 1945, to an apartment that was a six-minute walk from South Beach. But after several weeks, Beatrice felt even worse, and the three women decided to move back to Boston. Martin, meanwhile, remained for a while in Miami, earning good money and tips as a waiter. By the time Malcolm reentered her life around November 1945, Beatrice was searching for a way to enjoy herself again—come what may . . .[109]

THE EMCEE HUSTLER

In March 1945, Malcolm once again drew the attention of the police, this time in Detroit while hanging out with 24-year-old Kenneth Pointer, a fellow Black hustler who'd had his own brushes with the law. In 1942, Pointer had been arrested for operating an illegal dice game, and in the same year, he was accused of assault after he was hit by a lead pipe during a fight in an alley. Malcolm and Pointer may have first met each other back in 1939, when both participated in activities at Lansing's Lincoln Community Center. But years on the street had changed both young men a great deal. Upon returning to Michigan, Malcolm had lost the "bounce" he'd had in years prior. No longer wearing zoot suits on a nightly basis, there was a seriousness to him now.[110]

On March 13, Malcolm, with Pointer as an accomplice, stole "clothing, [a] radio and clock" from friend Douglas Haynes's apartment in Detroit. Haynes pressed charges, and a warrant for Malcolm's arrest was issued on March 14; Malcolm was eventually arrested three days later. Pleading innocent to the charge of grand larceny, Malcolm was kept in a holding cell for eight days, his bail set at a thousand dollars.[111]

The only family member with enough money to help was Wilfred, and he did. "He knew he could count on me," Wilfred said, years later. "He would put down the worst plea down there, you had to go find something to help him out. Then when he got out, it wouldn't be long before he'd be back out in the same path again."[112]

Malcolm tried to keep on a straight path. From early April to July 5, 1945, trombonist Jimmy Williams helped find Malcolm a standard job assembling mattresses for Capitol Bedding in Lansing. At any moment during his shift, he could have daydreamed about the hundreds of dollars he made dealing marijuana in Harlem. And now, here he was, making an estimated $30 a week, grinding out his days in a city lacking the night pulse found in New York and watching Wilfred, on June 4, marry 21-year-old stenographer Bertha L. Ansley.[113]

Before the end of July, Malcolm had made his way back to Harlem, much to the dismay of Wilfred. "I tried to dissuade him from getting involved in those kind[s] of things," Wilfred said about Malcolm's general behavior at the time. "But he had made up his mind, so I backed off and let him go. He had to have the experience he had to have. And that was the route he chose."[114]

On July 28, 1945, Malcolm started a gig as an emcee at the Caribbean Club. The owner of the club had told a columnist for the *New York Age* two weeks prior that he was determined to fly to Cuba to find "native" Caribbean talent. Lo and behold, a smooth-talking showman with Grenadian roots had arrived back in Harlem. Finding "Rhythm Red" was enough for the owner to buy advertising in the weekly *Age*.[115]

The Caribbean Club billed itself as the "Home of Calypso," catering to the large population of West Indian Harlem residents who'd immigrated from islands such as Jamaica, Trinidad, Haiti, and Grenada, to name a few. Located on 7th Avenue, between 139th and 140th Streets, the club couldn't compete with more popular spots such as Small's, but it had its own niche in the nightclub scene. For at least two and a half months, Malcolm stood on stage and helped keep "The New Who-Lay Revue" clicking on all cylinders. As the emcee, Malcolm's job was focused on keeping the show moving at a quick pace, dispensing a few witticisms in between acts.[116]

First up for Malcolm to introduce was 41-year-old Lord Beginner, celebrated for helping to bring calypso music to the US. Beginner's real name was Egbert Moore, an immigrant from Trinidad. By 1945, Moore had a few radio hits under his belt, such as the fun, globe-trotting "Shake Around" and "Always Marry a Pretty Woman," a response to calypso singer Roaring Lion's "Ugly Woman." Moore became far more well-known after first returning to Trinidad and then emigrating to England in 1948, writing the 1950 anthem "Cricket, Lovely Cricket" after a West Indies cricket victory over England.[117]

After Lord Beginner's calypso set, next was Princess Minnola, billed during Malcolm's time as an "interpretative dancer," but Minnola—whose actual name has proved elusive—had delivered her act in different incarnations across North America. At one club, she was billed as a "slave dancer," the Black columnist quick to add that Minnola "really throws it around like it belongs to nobody." Other clubs labeled her a "jungle dancer" and noted that "her dance is one of the zippiest to be seen in burlesque in years."[118]

The biggest draw, however, was 42-year-old blues legend Hannah Sylvester, whom Malcolm had the pleasure of introducing to the crowd. Often called "Harlem's Mae West," Sylvester had laid down a few tracks for famed bandleader Fletcher Henderson in the 1920s and was described by the *Pittsburgh Courier* as a "tall, slim, smooth, sweet-voiced singer." One of her songs, "Midnight Blues," could have worked on one of those nights when the dance floor was empty and drinks and cigarettes mingled with late-night melancholy: "Woe and misery I can't hide / At twelve o' clock, I unlock my hate / I get the meanest kind of / Lonesome midnight blues."[119]

Malcolm had his own kind of blues. "Through all of this time in my life," he recalled later, "I really *was* dead—mentally dead. I just didn't know that I was." Malcolm's side-hustles this time around only became more dangerous. He'd started carrying a gun on him and worked as a bootlegger for Abe Goldstein, "transporting" liquor "to those spruced-up bars which he had sold to someone."[120]

Malcolm's days were not all filled with illegal activity. Contrary to what the *Autobiography* emphasizes, Malcolm was indeed reading. In late October 1945, Black author Chester Himes's debut novel, *If He Hollers Let Him Go*, was released by Doubleday, and Malcolm picked it up, connecting with what Himes himself declared "a violent, angry" tale.[121]

"I could always feel race trouble, serious trouble, never more than two feet off," writes Himes via *Hollers*'s main character, Robert "Bob" Jones. "Nobody bothered me. Nobody said a word. But I was tensed every moment to spring." Malcolm related to Jones, and the story rumbles with anger and dissatisfaction at white America, its action set over four days in Los Angeles after Pearl Harbor had been bombed. "I was tired of keeping ready to die every minute," Jones confesses in the first chapter. "It was too much strain. I had to fight hard enough each day just to keep on living. All I wanted was for the white folks to let me alone; not say anything to me; not even look at me. They could take the goddamned world and go to hell with it."[122]

There are plenty of correlations to be found between the general tone of *Hollers* and Malcolm's hard-edged life at the time. In chapter 13, one of the characters, Ben, tries to give Bob some cold truth about the nature of white people: "One thing. . . . You'll never get anything from these goddamn white people unless you fight them. They don't know anything else.

Don't listen to anything else. If you don't believe it, take any white man you know. You can beg that son of a bitch until you're blue in the face. Argue with him until you're out of breath and no matter how eloquent your plea or righteous your cause the only way you'll ever get along with that son of a bitch is to whip his ass."[123]

With *Hollers* in his back pocket, Malcolm stayed high on drugs and continued gambling, a sense of fear started to overtake him.[124] The police wanted him on a gun charge. Harlem, similar to what LA did to Bob in *Hollers*, was beginning to push back on him. By the time Jarvis, who'd been contacted by a Harlem friend about Malcolm, picked up Malcolm "on the corner [of] . . . Edgecombe and St. Nicholas Avenue," his future partner-in-crime was a nervous wreck. "He didn't even take the time to go get his clothes, he was that shaky. He got in the car and said, 'Jarvis, just the highway.' And gone. He left his clothes and everything."[125]

PART II

INSIDE

FIGURE P.2. Charlestown State Prison. Cellblock. 1940.

The will to learn, like the will to live, belongs entirely to the inmate and only he can make the choice.

—George F. Magraw, "Rebuilds Lives
of Convicts," *Boston Globe*

5
THE HELL OF CHARLESTOWN

February 27, 1946, to January 10, 1947

PROCESSING

After his arrest on breaking-and-entering charges and subsequent sentencing by Judge Buttrick, Malcolm and Jarvis were driven 12 miles south and taken into Charlestown's administration offices for processing. Since Malcolm's mug shot is dated "2/28/1946," this means that Malcolm and Jarvis didn't arrive at Charlestown until the night of February 27. Still, basic booking data was completed, and the below line of questioning, based on Charlestown's "Commitment and Booking Data" form, was followed first with Jarvis (Prison # 22842) and then with Malcolm (#22843).

Malcolm, no doubt dejected and exhausted by this point, provided answers to a clerk, who soon typed them in:

> What is your race? Negro.
> When were you born? May 19, 1925.
> How old are you? 20.
> Where were you born? Omaha, Nebraska.
> What is your religion? Protestant.
> Your civil status? Single.
> What is your occupation? Show business.

His last home address and emergency address Malcolm gave the prison clerk are redacted, but it's most likely that he gave Ella's 72 Dale Street address as his last home and Wilfred's Lansing, Michigan, address as his emergency.[1]

As for why Malcolm said "Protestant" as his faith is less clear, but so did Jarvis. Protestant, especially in 1946, was a safe and nonthreatening religion to have next to your name. At this time, Malcolm had only intermittently been exposed to Islam in its orthodox form.

But what the clerk asked Malcolm next showed the struggles he was still having with his difficult childhood. When asked to provide the names of his parents, Malcolm did say "Earl" and "Louise" and provided their birthplaces of Reynolds, Georgia, and Grenada, but he also said that they were both dead, even though Louise was still alive but struggling at the Kalamazoo Mental Hospital.

One can only offer speculation as to why Malcolm initially said this. Had he felt ashamed of the situation he was in and did not want the prison to contact or trouble her with details that could lead her to become even more stressed? In a later interview, he changes his answer and says she's alive but calls her "white." These lies must have pained Malcolm; he loved his mother, but he didn't yet know how to talk about her—especially to people outside his own family.[2]

ESCAPING "HELL"

When the construction workers finished laying the last brick on Charlestown State Prison, Thomas Jefferson had just started his second term, his relationship with slave Sally Hemmings and their children a poorly kept secret. From 1805 to 1955, Charlestown Prison jailed tens of thousands of men, only rarely undergoing renovations. As time passed, its pipes rusted and corroded, and its walls weakened and cracked, developing spores of mold. And inevitably, rats, ticks, and white lice crept through the faults in the building. By the time Malcolm and Jarvis were put behind bars, Charlestown Prison had become infested with a century and a half of nature's toxins.[3]

The size of each cell was around six-by-eight feet, and the decay surrounding both Malcolm and Jarvis was unavoidable. "In the dirty, cramped cell, I could lie on my cot and touch both walls," Malcolm recalled. "The toilet was a covered pail; I don't care how strong you are, you can't stand having to smell a whole cell row of defecation."[4]

Jarvis remembered those first few months as well: "In warm weather the stone would sweat. All you had in this little cell was a cot, a bucket, and a washbasin, all right? They didn't have toilets in there. You had to use the bucket, and every time you went to use it, you lifted the cover off. Bein' so many weeks or months old, the odor would knock you down, just like a poison gas. But you had to stomach it. If you had just gotten through eating, you would put your food all in the bucket. That's how bad it was. And bein' locked up seventeen to eighteen hours a day, that was enough to drive anybody crazy."[5]

Successful escapes from Charlestown's granite block fortress were rare and next-to-impossible unless attempted with friends or allies. On July 8, 1892, a group of nine men creatively coordinated an escape using the prison's underground sewage system. After gaining knowledge of the pipelines, the men (nicknamed "The Sewer Gang") entered a small wooden hut designated for two men to dry off after washing out the same kind of pail or bucket Malcolm was now using as his toilet. The floorboards for this hut had been loosened over time, and the nine men dug a two-and-a-half-foot tunnel underground, using one of the floorboard planks as cover. From there, their tunnel placed them onto a clogged and narrow kitchen sewer passageway. For about 15 feet, the men snake-crawled through slushy waters filled with urine, excrement, vomit, and dank, decades-old wood—the *Boston Globe* used the phrase "nauseating effluvia"—before finally crawling out of the 20 inch by 16 inch sluiceway. Covered in waste, the men then used a smuggled hacksaw and sawed through iron bars, eventually entering the much roomier main sewer passageway.[6]

More recently, on February 25, 1946, two days before Malcolm arrived, Edward W. Greenman, a 28-year-old convicted burglar, put together a "make-shift ladder" by piling together broken pieces of wood. During his shift working in the loud and archaic foundry, Greenman managed to scale the wall using the pile of wood as a stepping stool. He was caught 36 hours later, after a five-mile car chase on icy roads ended with an officer's "flying tackle" in an open field.[7]

Malcolm did harbor and even expressed dreams of making a historic prison break, but in those early days at Charlestown, he had zero allies, nor did he have any in-depth architectural insights into the now more tightly secured facility. He first needed to learn about his surroundings.[8]

The standard routine for each Charlestown prisoner, which will be described more specifically later, was mind-numbingly mundane. For at least 17 hours each day, Malcolm was forced to remain inside his cell. For 6 of the remaining 7 hours, Malcolm worked in one of the prison's industrial departments. The monotone was somewhat relieved with a 30–45-minute walk around the prison yard. The remaining 15 minutes were spent walking to a filtration room and emptying your own "slop bucket"—or personal effluvia.

PROTESTS AND DRUGS

On February 28, 1946, the exact same day that Malcolm's mug shot was taken, the 566 men locked up on four floors of cell blocks "revolted" against the prison administration, demanding they address "issues of improper food, unfair parole procedure, and wages." Several groups staged a sit-in near their workstations while others refused to go back to their cells. The correctional commissioner, J. Paul Doyle, performed a minor miracle by calming a "rebellion . . . that could have ended in disastrous results."[9]

The men had every right to protest. Malcolm's first dinner at the state prison was nothing more than a snack. As was customary, men were led from their cells to the outdated kitchen to take their meal. Malcolm was given "four cream of tartar biscuits and [a] cup of tea." Warden Francis J. W. Lanagan admitted that the kitchen manager had needed to serve the bite-sized meal, telling the press that it was "an example of the occasional light meal we are forced to serve because of food shortages."[10]

There were other difficulties. Malcolm was only allowed one six-minute shower a week and could only send out one letter per week. As for visitors, he could only have two visits every two weeks. Also, Malcolm and Jarvis's cell was near the foundry, where metal casings were forged. The foundry had become so old and volatile that, when its machines were functioning, cell blocks would "vibrate."[11]

But what really derailed Malcolm's mind was the deafening sound of metal bars closing on him. Seventeen years later, he admitted to Alex Haley how they haunted him: "Any person who claims to have deep feeling for other human beings should think a long, long time before he votes to have other men kept behind bars—caged. I am not saying there shouldn't be prisons, but there shouldn't be bars. Behind bars, a man never reforms. He will never forget. He never will get completely over the memory of the bars."

Given Malcolm's current circumstances, Commissioner Doyle may have sympathized with Malcolm's doubts about reform. "It is impossible," the commissioner told the *Boston Globe* the day after Malcolm arrived, "to attempt any kind of rehabilitation program under [the] conditions that exist here."[12]

To cope, Malcolm, "physically miserable," went back into drugs. During the weeks leading up to the February 27 trial, Malcolm was kept in a holding cell. Without much of a prison population around him, Malcolm's drug use had all but stopped, but now that he was in Charlestown, surrounded by hundreds of men dealing with the same dose of misery, finding a high wouldn't be too difficult.

"I first got high in Charlestown on nutmeg," Malcolm explained. "My cellmate was among at least a hundred nutmeg men who, for money or cigarettes, bought from kitchen-worker inmates penny matchboxes full of stolen nutmeg. I grabbed a box as though it were a pound of heavy drugs. Stirred into a glass of cold water, a penny matchbox full of nutmeg had the kick of three or four reefers." It's doubtful that Malcolm had a cellmate in an already suffocating six-by-eight prison cell, but he may have been referring to someone on his cell block. Still, nutmeg (and later harder drugs) was Malcolm's drug of choice as he hazily navigated Charlestown in those first few months.[13]

WORK DUTY AND JARVIS'S WORLD

In early March, Malcolm was assigned to the Auto Plate Shop. This department, like most others at the prison, was falling apart. On March 1, the condition of its presses was examined by Doyle, and he found that "one of the presses in the number plate shop showed signs of falling through the floor. When the concrete flooring was probed, the crowbar dropped out of sight." As Malcolm grew acquainted with stamping, painting, and sorting Massachusetts license plates for cars, trucks, farm tractors, and motorcycles, there was a perpetual storm of "paint dust in the air and noise all around" from the presses teetering on cracked concrete floors—the sewer tunnels far below.[14]

Jarvis, meanwhile, was assigned to the print shop as a job press feeder. Now divided, Jarvis and Malcolm only saw each other during the 45 minutes they were outside walking around the yard or the 15 minutes they were emptying their slop buckets. To Jarvis, it was for the best, since he was hoping to be transferred as soon as possible.

On March 6, Jarvis was interviewed by Officer Donohue, with the information being used to weigh whether a transfer to a better prison, such as Norfolk Prison Colony, would be beneficial. The 26-part interview covered family, education, employment, past residences, economic history, previous criminal charges, and habits or interests.

Donohue learned a great deal about Jarvis, part of which was how the trumpet player partially blamed Malcolm's domineering personality for the reason he was in prison.

It appears that Donohue sided with Jarvis. Here are the officer's general remarks, which he included at the end of the interview.

> Loquacious, polite and cooperative, [Jarvis] in a frank and disconsolate manner admits his culpability but attempts to minimize it by saying he was forced into participation by the threats of his accomplice. He does not appear to be the type that would deliberately choose a life of crime, but his gullibility and pliability makes him an easy tool for the machinations of others. His despondency after receiving what he considers to be an excessive sentence for the small financial gain accruing to him from the crimes, is deepened because he believes that after pleading guilty, he was not allowed to tell his version because he had associated with white girls and that the sentence indicates racial prejudice.[15]

Malcolm Louis Jarvis was born on September 11, 1923, in Boston. Jarvis's parents were "very congenial" but also "strict in discipline." Also having two other siblings, Jarvis's family remained on somewhat solid ground thanks to Jarvis's father's salary as a sheet metal worker for the Somerville Tinning Company and a musician at Scollay Square's Hotel Imperial.[16]

For most of his childhood, Jarvis stayed out of trouble, but on July 4, 1935, tragedy struck the family. Jarvis's older brother, Clifford, was at a holiday Boy Scout picnic near Houghton Pond in Milton, Massachusetts. Clifford decided to go for a swim, but, as Jarvis recalled, he "was caught up in a whirlpool undercurrent that took him to the bottom where he drowned." Jarvis admitted that he wasn't too close to his brother, but the sudden shock of death, and to a member of the family so close to his age, would "haunt" him for decades and may have nudged him toward misbehavior.[17]

In 1936, Jarvis had his first brush with the law after he stole a bicycle and was given a year of probation. Jarvis's father, no doubt still devastated by his namesake son's death, now focused his attention on Jarvis, the next oldest.

Jarvis begged his father to let him play the saxophone, but he instead received a different instrument and a stern message. Mr. Jarvis had been a professional trumpet player for many years and had gifted his own trumpet to Clifford several years before his death. Now, however, circumstances had changed, and Mr. Jarvis "shoved my [late] brother's trumpet and his own beginner's book into my hands, saying, 'If you desire to play music at all, then stay in the house and practice instead of playing and bike riding.'"[18]

So he did. "I . . . practiced my horn long and hard for hours a day." He also took a job as a "grocery boy" at a First National Store, earning four dollars a week taking shifts after school and on the weekends. But it was during his days in the classroom that his life started to change. He'd met a girl.[19]

Her name was Hazel M. Register, a junior high school classmate. Quickly, she "became my steady girlfriend." Almost every Saturday, they'd go see a film together at the local theater, Jarvis digging into his grocer's wages to pay for their tickets. Soon, they fell in love, and on April 26, 1940, they went ahead and married. Jarvis was 16. Two baby boys soon followed. As Jarvis later wrote, somewhat acknowledging how surprising his quick trip to adulthood might sound, "For a young couple to be married and to have two children before either of them was 20 years old is, in my opinion, accepting big responsibilities very early in life."[20]

In their first year of marriage, the young couple lived with Jarvis's parents. Jarvis took jobs as a porter at a Howard Johnson hotel and then later at Wilbur Restaurant on Charles Street, earning a paltry $15 a week. But in August 1941, Jarvis was hired as a "shoeshine boy" at the South Street Boston Terminal. By the time young Malcolm Little entered his life, he was a father of two, shining shoes for at least $50 a week (not including tips), shooting pool and playing the trumpet whenever he had a chance. Hazel, however, had left him soon after their marriage started after he accused her of cheating on him. As he later told a prison official, Jarvis had "jealousy" issues, and his paranoia was one reason why Hazel moved to New York City.[21]

Still, he wanted her back. He wanted to provide for his two sons. He wanted to improve his trumpet-playing abilities and write musical compositions. He wanted . . . to be a better man. And Jarvis knew that Charlestown State Prison in 1946 was not the place to do these things. With all this in mind, Jarvis hoped he could be transferred to the Norfolk Prison Colony. As he'd continue to write to his wife, hoping to regain a connection, he'd work on improving himself, and he could be given a bit of distance from the man he believed was responsible for his imprisonment.

THE FATALIST

Two days after Jarvis spoke with Officer Donohue, Malcolm was interviewed. His behavior only confirmed the conclusions Donohue had made regarding Jarvis being pushed into the robberies by a much stronger personality. Malcolm went into great detail about his drug use, telling the interviewer that he first tried marijuana when he was around 17 years old—his use increasing from once a week to once a day to the point that the effect would wear off after only a few hours. Malcolm also described how he had used cocaine and opium (and 2Yensy—the act of "scraping an opium bowl" and "dropping" it into a drink) at parties in New York "with theatrical people" but never (conveniently) in Massachusetts.[22] If Malcolm had admitted to illegal drug use in the state in which he was incarcerated, he'd be putting himself in line for another charge.

After hearing all this, along with his family, work, and school history, the interviewer's left these general remarks about Malcolm:

> [Malcolm] is a light complexioned mulatto and served [as] calculating and cautious throughout the interview. He has fatalistic views, is moody, cynical, and has a sardonic smile which seems to be affected because of his sensitiveness to his color. To offset this he seems to assume a nonchalant, complacent, superior attitude. He is worldly-wily and amoral and states "I've been heading here a long time." He further says that prior to accepting a life of crime he had weighed the penalty (of what he though[t] would be a three yr. sentence) against what he hoped to gain. He again says that had he anticipated the 8–10 yrs. sentence that he would have gone in for armed robbery instead of burglary.[23]

The interviewer had no way of knowing *how* Malcolm had become so cynical. Had it been from the dual tragedies of losing his father before having a chance to consciously embrace him and then watching the slow deterioration of his mother's mind as she faded from his life? Had it been the hunger he felt as a child and the constant struggle for food? Had it been his mother emphasizing self-reliance over accepting charity? When Malcolm told the interviewer that he'd been heading to prison for a long time, he meant it. But only a part of 20-year-old Malcolm blamed himself. The other part was waging war with a relentlessly oppressive system and a God that seemed to have his arms crossed, looking the other way.

TEARS IN HIS EYES

Malcolm survived March inside what a former warden of Sing Sing prison, Lewis E. Lawes, called "a crumbling, antiquated heap of stone not fit for men of any kind." With a new prison chef and former navy man John E. Kallaugher providing better meals, the general atmosphere of the prison started to return to normal after the February 28 protest. Still, at 4:00 p.m. on March 19, while Malcolm and Jarvis were in the yard, three men attempted to escape. One of them, again, was Edward Greenman, his new nickname "Screwball." Along with two other young men from the underwear shop, Greenman walked about 15 feet behind an engineer. Once the engineer unlocked a door to a guard room, the three men attacked, using a hammer they'd taken from a workstation and hitting the engineer over the head. They were eventually tackled to the ground and put in the oldest and most run-down cell block—Cherry Hill. It was in Cherry Hill where men on death row waited, the electric chair room a short walk down the corridor.[24]

Malcolm's first visitor was Ella, who'd driven seven miles north across the Charles River to meet her half-brother in the visiting room, where armed guards were along the walls. Malcolm, in his "faded dungarees, stenciled" with 22843, was in no mood to be gracious. As Ella recalled, "Malcolm was as jive-talking, cocky and unrepentant as ever. He showed no remorse or concern about family anxiety and seemed to believe that his only problem was being caught, that the next time he would be a smarter hustler. When I left after that visit, I was as upset as I had ever been with him." Malcolm "wished she hadn't come at all."[25]

In April, Malcolm's cynicism deepened. On April 2, he and Jarvis were taken in handcuffs and driven a mile and a half south to the Appellate Division of the Suffolk County Courthouse in Pemberton Square. They were joined in the courtroom by Beatrice and Joyce, who'd been serving their time at Framingham's Reformatory for Women. It had been a little over a month since their initial sentencing, and now the discordant quartet hoped the three judges in front of them would reconsider the sentences decided on by Judge Buttrick.

The two sisters had been waiting desperately for this moment, and they had worked with their lawyer, Walter McLaughlin, to do whatever it took to have their sentences suspended and be released on probation. According to the *Boston Globe*, it had been the first time in Framingham Reformatory history that a woman had "applied for [a] reduction" of her sentence.[26]

Right outside the courtroom was their mother, Alice, there to show her support, and Beatrice's husband, Martin, who made sure to tell the *Boston Globe* reporter that he spent two years fighting in the Pacific. Their actual presence helped confirm that, if released, the sisters had family waiting.

Joyce had the strongest case for probation. Making sure to maximize her youthfulness, she wore "yellow bobby sox" and a "white hair ribbon." As McLaughlin made a "frank" plea for the sisters, he made sure to point directly at Joyce and ask the court to see her as a "very innocent girl," telling the three judges, "Why, she's barely out of her mother's arms." Joyce was given an opportunity to speak for herself, and said, through tears, "I hope you three men will see some justice . . ."[27]

As if that had not been hard enough for Malcolm and Jarvis to stomach, next came Beatrice. "Extremely nervous," Beatrice provided a statement "with reference to how they had become involved and appealed for consideration for release on probation."

Their statements, reiterated by McLaughlin to the judges, had been expertly crafted so that all blame fell on Malcolm's shoulders. Joyce had only joined the group out of concern for her sister's nervous well-being, then she "accompanied her sister and [K]ora to an outside automobile. There she found three colored men, Malcolm Little, Malcolm Jarvis, and Francis Brown, whom they referred to as Sonny. The men told the girls . . . they had better keep still in the future and accompany them without question." They "were so frightened that they did not dare to make known to either parents or police what was happening."

Beatrice, meanwhile, said that in 1942, it was Kora who had introduced Malcolm to her. During that time, Malcolm "had been represented as an entertainer who had excellent contacts in New York with the professional dancing classes." When Malcolm called her on December 12, 1945, with "an excellent proposition . . . a dancing part in a new show that was opening in New York," Beatrice agreed to meet him but "reminded him that she had married and her husband was then in Florida." Later, she said that since their first meeting in 1942, "this was the first actual contact with him."[28]

Both Malcolm and Jarvis knew what was happening—they were being made into predatorial monsters, and the two sisters were helpless in their struggle. By April 5, their appeal had been dismissed and their sentence remained 8–10 years. For Beatrice and Joyce, their own appeal was "taken into consideration."

Salt was added to Malcolm's wounds one week later. On April 10, Malcolm and Jarvis were once again taken out of Charlestown and driven 20 minutes to the Norfolk County Superior Court in Dedham. Joining them, for the last time, were all three women—Kora, Beatrice, and Joyce. Behind the gavel this time was 68-year-old judge Walter L. Collins, a graduate of Harvard Law School and considered by one peer to be "friendly and companionable."[29]

Each member had different charges put against them. In Malcolm's case, he was being charged on three counts of B&E&L in Milton (12/5), Brookline (12/15), and Walpole (1/10). Since Malcolm robbed the Milton home with Brown only, Jarvis was only on the hook for Brookline and Walpole, and the three young women were being charged for breaking and entering into the Brookline home. No matter what, Malcolm and Jarvis both knew they were about to hear once again that dreaded "concurrent" echo. The only question was how many years.

There was a bit of drama to the proceedings. Captain Mahoney, who back in January had questioned Malcolm about the Brookline break-in, told a worker of the court that he felt "intimate relations had occurred between" Malcolm and Bea and that Malcolm "had intimated that such was true, but [Beatrice] had always denied this." Mahoney also questioned Bea's mother, saying "she was not as innocent as she would like to have appeared." In the end, Mahoney concluded that Beatrice "was more responsible than either of the two female codefendants because she was older than the other two girls, was married and should have exerted a good influence upon the girls, but had failed to do so."[30]

It all led to Walter McLaughlin calling for Beatrice to take the stand and defend her actions. Malcolm's cousin, J. C. Little, was at the hearing, and he could see how the attorney carefully led Bea toward delivering the "right" answer.

Now, Mrs. Bazarian, please tell the court why you really participated in these crimes.

I was intimidated. I was under pressure . . .

At this moment, Malcolm, according to J. C. Little, was at his wit's end. "Tears streamed down his face," and he shouted at the district attorney, "I might have known you'd brainwash her." When the attorney asked Beatrice if she "loved" Malcolm, she said no, not ever. Again, Malcolm couldn't hold back from calling out her lies: "If you didn't love me, why did you come to my place alone? Why did you bring your clothes? I didn't hold a gun on you then." J. C. then watched as Malcolm stood up, defying court rules, and "pointed his finger at Bea's father." Mr. Caragulian was seated in the back. "You told me you hated your father and mother," Malcolm said in a rage, "and wanted nothing to do with them anymore."[31]

In the end, Judge Collins tacked on three more concurrent sentences of 6–8 years for Malcolm. Jarvis, continuing to bear the brunt of being associated with Malcolm, was given 6–8 as well for his two charges. Joyce's bobby-socked plea on April 2 allowed her to walk free on April 26, but she remained on probation for two more years, as did Kora.[32]

Beatrice, however, had been exposed. Due in large part to Captain Mahoney's comments, she was given an indefinite sentence but remained imprisoned. Beatrice would have to endure another five months at the Framingham Women's Reformatory, her prison number 17977, surrounded by 400 other incarcerated women, some of whom had committed crimes of larceny, assault, and public lewdness. They were all watched over by 59-year-old progressive superintendent Miriam Van Waters and were only allowed "two one half hour visits monthly . . . spaced two weeks apart."[33]

BEA'S HUSBAND TO THE RESCUE

Bea's months at the Reformatory were quite different from Malcolm's at Charlestown. Back in 1946, most of the vocational offerings were centered around helping women become better homemakers. After being given a series of physical, psychological, and aptitude tests, women were assigned a vocation that "might be agricultural, [taking] care of children, clerical work, library work, or sewing." For a time, Bea spent several hours each day in the knitting room but found it tedious and dull and asked to be transferred to the clerical division, where she worked as a typist and completed secretarial tasks, such as "filing, fingerprinting and photography." There were also psychological evaluations. One prison worker, remarking about Beatrice's cognitive abilities, said that "she has a vital, appealing personality" and "becomes extremely rattled by failure." In addition, "her impulsiveness" scored "in the extreme" of the Porteus Maze test.[34]

Fortunately for Bea, she had an extreme husband waiting for her, loyal as ever. "To begin with," he wrote to her on April 31, three weeks after Malcolm's outburst and Captain Mahoney's testimony, "I won't rest a minute until you're out. I'm going to start from the bottom of the ladder and work up. If things don't click, don't think for a single minute that I'm going to quit right there." Martin was furious, and in his letter, he blamed Kora, the state government, and especially the probation officer for their predicament: "I hope she never eats in peace and from the bottom of my heart, I hope she suffers for the rest of her life." But he did acknowledge that taking part in the crimes was on her. "We all know you made a big mistake, your first one at that. We also know what the penalty for such a mistake would be, or we thought we did."[35]

Having a passionate and supportive husband helped show prison officials and the parole board that Bea had a home waiting for her upon release. On September 23, 1946, Beatrice rejoined Martin, finishing her probation in 1950. The couple were married for 55 years—until Martin's death—and had one daughter. Beatrice never once spoke publicly about her relationship with Malcolm before passing away in 2012. When she was encountered by one biographer many years ago, her response was "hostile."[36]

LOSING HIS MIND

Malcolm and Jarvis stayed overnight at the Dedham courthouse, famous for being the setting of Nicola Sacco and Bartolomeo Vanzetti's 1921 court case. The two men were in no mood to appreciate history, however. They now had seven charges of B&E&L against them, with one more to come. Their hopes for a quick release had been all but dashed, and neither of them had a supportive spouse on the outside to help with their cause.

When Malcolm returned to Charlestown State Prison, he received a letter from his Aunt Sas, a Christian. His aunt was worried about his faith, but Malcolm pushed away her proselytizing words. "I got a letter from [Aunt] Sas preaching to me," Malcolm wrote to Ella on April 12, 1946. "I appreciated the letter but she can have her gospel. For the past month I've been praying like mad and if there was any sign of someone up there I asked for proof of it by some justice when I appeared before the Appellate Court [on April 2]. Heretofore you can have my share of religion. They refused to cut my sentence because of the racial mixture. Well if that's the Bible way of justice, it's not for me . . ."[37]

As time went on in Charlestown, Malcolm, like any new arrival, was studied and probed. On May 1, during a psychometric test, in which he had to complete a variety of verbal and performative tasks in order to measure his cognitive capabilities—such as hearing six numbers and saying them forward and backward—Malcolm, "unshaven," performed at a "superior" level in "abstract reasoning ability" and "range of information," and his reading ability was scored as "good," higher than his math ability, which was a "high average." The psychometrist was also impressed by Malcolm's speaking ability, remarking that prisoner 22843 had a "good vocabulary" and was "able to express himself well." Still, Malcolm did let out a bit of his ongoing frustration. One of the categories of the Wechsler–Bellevue Psychometric Test where the examiner could remark was "Self-criticism Revealed During Testing." The examiner typed, "Subject [Malcolm] expressed opinion that he is losing his mind."[38]

THE JUNE 6 SWITCH

On May 17, an officer named Peterson personally visited Ella at her Dale Street home, hoping to better understand Malcolm's background. But as Peterson reported, the interview with Ella was "entirely unsatisfactory due to her refusal to answer any questions regarding family background to any extent . . . her reason [being] that she could see no value in having innocent persons names on records in correctional institutions." Ella told Peterson that she'd seen Malcolm's mother, Louise, "only once in her life and stated that she considered her colored and not white," as Malcolm had originally told the police, perhaps hoping to avoid any more questions about her. Ella then told the officer that Malcolm "never was disciplined to any extent because of the inability of his mother to control him." By the end of the interview, Peterson concluded that Ella believed Malcolm "received a much longer sentence than he deserved and laid the blame to racial prejudices in view of the fact that he was keeping company with a white woman."[39]

Jarvis, meanwhile, spent the rest of April and May hoping for a transfer. After the April trial, Jarvis started to "cold-shoulder" Malcolm. Jarvis may not have had his spouse sending passionate letters in hopes of his release like Beatrice, but he did have two sons living with his parents in Roxbury, and he had made it clear to prison officials that he wanted to eventually provide for them. That alone put him ahead of Malcolm for a transfer to a better prison. Even though Malcolm "laughed" off Jarvis pushing him away, Jarvis "sensed the hurt in [Malcolm's] eyes."[40]

Sure enough, in early June, Jarvis was given his transfer to Norfolk Prison Colony, considered by many incarcerated men to be the "country club" of prisons. On June 6, 1946, he entered a prison vehicle and left Malcolm behind, not knowing if he'd ever see him again.[41]

On the *same exact* day, there was an older, more experienced incarcerated man being transferred from Norfolk to Charlestown. This man, named John Elton Bembry, fundamentally changed Malcolm's life. Later, Malcolm said that "Bimbi" was "the first man I met in prison who made any positive impression on me." Bembry "would prove to us, dipping into the science of human behavior, that the only difference between us and outside people was

FIGURE 5.1. John Elton Bembry. Mug shot. 1948. From prison file.

that we had been caught." It was Bembry's mind, his intellect, that caught Malcolm's attention. "What fascinated me with him most of all was that he was the first man I had ever seen command total respect . . . with his words."[42]

BIMBI'S ROAD

At around 8:30 p.m. on February 18, 1943, John Elton Bembry, a 6'0", 165 lbs., "freckle-faced mulatto," approached the front door of a home in West Springfield, Massachusetts.[43] Thirty years old at the time, Bembry rang the doorbell and hoped no one answered. After waiting briefly, he saw no lights turn on and heard no footsteps inside. He backed away from the door and walked around to the side of the house.[44]

Keeping a sharp eye on the road, Bembry took out a tool and forced open a side window. He climbed through the opening, gathered himself, and started searching for anything small and gold.

On a nearby counter or shelf, Bembry found "two gold wedding rings, one lady's gold wrist watch, one lady's gold pin, one man's gold pocket watch and one cameo ring." All of it was small enough to fit into a pocket.

But there was one small glitch in his plan. A housekeeper was in another room, listening no doubt in fear to the quiet movements of a burglar. As soon as Bembry left, the housekeeper made a call to the police: the home had been broken into.

Only a short while after sneaking out of the house, Bembry saw a police car come toward him. They wasted little time and told Bembry to get in the car. Bembry did, but not before grabbing his handful of loot and subtly tossing it into "a nearby snowbank." If he'd had a few more seconds, he could have double-checked his pockets. He'd managed to dispose of everything he'd taken except one item: the lady's gold pin.

Not knowing that he had evidence on him, Bembry denied the charges brought upon him. Once police went through his clothes, however, and discovered the pin, Bembry decided to change his tune. They drove him back to the snowbank, and Bembry showed them what he'd discarded. Less than three months later, on May 12, 1943, Bembry was sentenced to 5–7 years for breaking and entering with intent to commit larceny. He was going to prison again.

The name on his birth certificate was "James Bembry," born likely on July 25, 1912.[45] His aliases were many, mainly because of the malleable spelling of his last name: John Elton Lane, John Lane, John Bember, John Elton Bembery, and later in life, John Lee.

Born in Newport News, Virginia, to parents Joseph and Eva (who gave him his lighter complexion), soon they headed south to Edenton, North Carolina, and little James watched as his family ballooned to include six other siblings (two sisters and four brothers). Like Malcolm, Bembry's father died when he was young, but as Bembry told the police, he found his "early home life" to be "pleasant—no parental quarrels—normal discipline."[46]

Bembry also enjoyed school and graduated from St. Augustine Episcopal High School in Raleigh in 1930.[47] Bembry took a summer job as a "waiter and porter" at a tourism cottage in Virginia Beach, Virginia. After high school, he left the South and headed for New York, working for two years as a porter and assistant in a barber shop. Unsatisfied with his pay, Bembry remained on a stretch of New York's West Broadway and became a "bootblack" in a shoe repair shop. It was here, however, where the siren song of the pool hall hustle caught his attention. In the fall of 1933, with Hoovervilles surrounding the city and the economy contracting, Bembry won a load of cash in a "number pool racket." Just like that, after enduring several years of poor-paying labor, he'd made enough money to last him a good while.

So he quit fixing shoes.

Over the next couple years, as the Depression rippled across the country, Bembry moved full-time into gambling—betting on dice, more number pool, and horse racing and playing cards "in and around New York City." By 1935, however, he was homeless, and police charged him with "vagrancy." Instead of jail, he was told to leave the nearby city of New Rochelle. Bembry did and chose to head west to Southern California.

On the way there, Bembry picked up another "vagrancy" charge in Idaho Falls, Idaho, and had a choice between spending 15 days in jail or paying a $25 fine. He chose jail.

It had been a long time since he won big money in New York—bets placed and lost, cities and debt left behind—until February 19, 1937, in Los Angeles. Bembry had been broke long enough, and at around 10:40 p.m. he started to trail behind a woman walking along 5th Street, between Catalina and Berendo Streets. He was targeting her purse "under her arm." Bembry picked up speed, grabbed it, and ran "between two buildings," but not before the lady could at least see him in profile. Bembry checked the contents: "$5.00 . . . a fountain pen, house keys, dark glasses, some letters and cosmetics."

The next evening, around 9:00 p.m., near the "west side of Kenmore," Bembry ran up from behind another woman and snatched her purse. She pursued him, but other nearby police officers picked up the chase. After five minutes of running between buildings, Bembry was caught "on the corner of 4th and Catalina St. . . . walking along with some money he was putting into a brown purse."

For these two crimes, and seeing a bit of history begin to pile up on his record, the judge sentenced Bembry to 1–10 years on "grand theft." He'd serve his time at San Quentin State Prison.

At San Quentin, Bembry kept busy working as a waiter in the mess hall, a "garageman" washing cars in the auto shop, and later as a general laborer after being transferred to the "San Quentin Prison Road Camp." All told, Bembry spent three years and two months in San Quentin's prison system, keeping his record clean and studying "Business Arithmetic." He'd been told, upon release, to leave the state of California.

So the drifter headed back east.

In July 1940, within two months of his release, Bembry was picked up again by the police, this time for a minor charge of being disorderly. He spent 20 days in jail, a vacation compared to his time in San Quentin.

For about a year, and apparently being homeless, Bembry wandered about the Midwest, picking up short-term jobs here and there. He saw the inside of prison cells in San Claire, Wisconsin, and briefly in Gary, Indiana, and Allentown, Pennsylvania. By the time of his arrest near the snowbank in West Springfield, Massachusetts, Bembry's "criminal history" was 15 lines long.

At Charlestown Prison, Bembry sat down for initial interviews. Officers wanted to gauge his behavior and perhaps learn why and how he'd been in and out of jail over such an extended period. After the interview, one officer typed his remarks after speaking with Bembry, calling him "pleasant, affable, neat-appearing, mild-mannered, gentlemanly, fairly talkative, informative, frank and very co-operative. Criminal record began about 8 yrs. ago, soon after he left home for no apparent reason, to wander about the country. Since then, when not in confinement, he admittedly made his living mostly by gambling and housebreaking. A rather likeable, fairly intelligent, non-vicious, freckled-face Negro, who appears capable of living a much better life if he so desires, but prognosis is rather doubtful. Considers himself fortunate in present sentence."

Those nomadic years spent drifting "about the country" had not damaged his ability to remain kind and considerate. He knew how to talk with officers, and he knew what kind of behavior they wanted to see.

After spending a little more than a year at Charlestown working in the auto shop stamping plates, Bembry was transferred to Norfolk Prison Colony. For the next three years, he received zero visits from friends or family. He was alone, again, but now with one of the largest prison libraries in the country to help him pass the time.

In July 1944, with World War II still raging outside the prison walls, Bembry was assigned to the tailor shop, where he worked on a sewing machine as a "Navy Hat Operator." Norfolk's rehabilitation philosophy centered around introducing men to a sense of real-life normalcy, and so Bembry was able to fill out his time playing, according to officials, "checkers and domino[e]s with his colored friends in the unit." Norfolk also had a baseball team for each unit, and Bembry had "a reputation as a pitcher." On Sundays, Bembry attended "Protestant services" as well.[48]

By the fall, however, he wanted more. In October, he was reported to have started reading "biographies and good fiction." Also around this time, and as Malcolm would later on, Bembry joined the prestigious and well-respected Norfolk Debating Club. In between sewing Navy hats and domino sessions, Bembry absorbed "books, political science, etc. . . . in preparation for debates." Finally, it appeared that all the experiences he'd had traveling across the country would be given a chance for expression.

With winter weather coming in, Bembry doubled down on his reading and education, finishing a correspondence course in "Elementary English and Rhetoric, Pt. 1" that he'd started at Charlestown. He then quickly requested part 2, and by the end of the season, he'd earned an official certificate of completion.

With his already advanced education beginning to coalesce with the advanced education of the streets, Bembry soon adopted a mentor status at Norfolk. In May 1945, Bembry was voted two-to-one as the "Inmate Councillor" for Unit 3–1. He'd earned the trust of his fellow men, and one official saw from a distance that Bembry had become "a well-balanced type and well-liked in unit. He is fairly intelligent and cooperative with all, polite and fairly trust-worthy." By November, his title had been elevated to "Council Chairman." The 33-year-old who'd served time in one of the country's toughest prisons and crisscrossed the country several times as a gambling, housebreaking drifter had, through the educational refinement of Norfolk's innovative system, found his voice.

Old habits die hard, however, and around November 1945, Bembry was "suspected of gambling" with another incarcerated man. The prison official noticed a drop in Bembry's work productivity, noting that he was "merely doing time" but still "reading good books." In December, the prison official started to sense a bit of overconfidence in Bembry, stating he'd become "a little too sure of himself in his assertions. Although he 'does not seem to have many close friends, he is well liked by few.'" Also around this time, Bembry stopped attending church services but remained "keenly interested in the subject of religion." Still, by March, the prison official had become impressed enough to state that, even though he was at the time doing "nothing in a constructive way toward helping himself" except "reading good books," Bembry indeed was "quite intelligent."[49]

Then, a couple months later, an incident occurred at Norfolk that helped to bring Bembry into Malcolm's orbit at Charlestown.

On Thursday, April 25, 1946, at 1:00 p.m., Bembry and hundreds of his fellow incarcerated men had just finished another underwhelming lunch and were now to start their designated job assignments. On this day, Bembry had duties in the tailor shop, located in Norfolk's laundry building. He'd been hearing rumors that men were unsatisfied with the amount of food being served for breakfast, lunch, and dinner. Before settling into his workstation, Bembry went to use the toilet.[50]

Just after 1:00 p.m., the power was turned on for all the machines, but 20 men in the tailor shop refused to begin working. Instead, they sat on the floor, one man shouting "No food—no work." Deputy O'Brien then called on those seated to "gather around him." Reading off his checklist, he asked each man individually "whether or not he wished to work." This gave the reluctant few in the group a chance to disperse and keep themselves out of trouble. Sure enough, 5 left the group of 20 and "immediately went to their assignment and started working." Of the 15 remaining men, they were determined to protest, several saying, "I'm with the gang," or, for those perhaps less bold but loyal, "I have nothing to say."[51]

Bembry had been the second name on O'Brien's checklist and missed his name being called. When he returned from the toilet, however, he saw what had transpired. When another officer assisting Deputy O'Brien came up to him and asked "Are you with these men or not?" Bembry had to think quickly. If he said no, he'd avoid punishment but could lose face with several of his fellow men. If he said yes, Bembry risked falling out of whatever favor or trust he'd earned from the superintendent and being penalized with everyone else.

At San Quentin, Bembry had been through a similar situation before, and he recalled how messy the lives of those who avoided trouble could become. In addition, he'd already become a mentor to many of the men. Bembry made his decision without hesitation; he chose to remain with the group, regardless of punishment. He did not speak out, but instead simply moved with the group toward the deputy, who made one final question to make it official: "I understand that every man in this group does not want to work. Is that so?" The deputy waited a moment, and soon nearly half of the group said, "That is correct."[52]

Punishments were handed out. Bembry, whom O'Brien even gave the benefit of the doubt ("He was in a tough spot . . .") was given five days of only bread and water, and three months were added to his sentence. Still, even though Bembry hadn't even known the specifics of the sit-down strike, he'd decided to join the group and accepted the punishment. This act may have won him more trust among the men, but it did indeed drop him out of favor with Norfolk officials. About five weeks later, on June 6, 1946, Bembry was transferred back to the archaic, falling-apart Charlestown Prison.

The reason for the transfer showed that Norfolk officials were attempting to weed out any larger sit-down strike in the future. In Bembry's prison file, it states that he was "unfit for an open prison system," but that couldn't have been further from the truth. Norfolk had helped forge John Elton Bembry into an educated man who could be trusted and admired.

Even by a man who'd been nicknamed "Satan."[53]

BIMBI UNIVERSITY

Lacking positive guidance, the picture for the future is not hopeful as seen at this time.

—Charlestown prison official in July 1946, forecasting
Malcolm Little's future, Malcolm Little Prison File

They first met in the auto plate shop. Bembry already knew the job well. "He operated the machine that stamped out the numbers," Malcolm recalled. "I was along the conveyor belt where the numbers were painted."[54]

One of the few moments of levity came at the end of a shift. Most shifts lasted a couple of hours, but the incarcerated men knew that if they finished their required "quota" early, they could sit with each other and talk like regular men on a break. It was during these rare but still illusory moments of free time that the group of around "fifteen" workers sat near the well-traveled John Elton Bembry and picked his brain. Even white guards found themselves interested in "Bimbi's" opinions.[55]

At first, Malcolm listened from a calculated distance. Once, Bembry enthralled his group with a history of Concord, the city only a 20-mile drive northwest of Charlestown. Concord has always been at the heart of American history, ever since April 19, 1775, and the "shot heard round the world"—a phrase written by Concord poet Ralph Waldo Emerson in 1837. But Bembry was more interested in telling the men around him about Emerson's young friend and writer, Henry David Thoreau. At the age of 28, Thoreau voluntarily left society behind and constructed a "ten by fifteen feet" home near what is now called Walden Pond. It was in July 1846, while living here in isolation, that Thoreau resisted paying a poll tax and was thrown in jail for a night.

The incident rattled Thoreau, and as he sat in his home, disconnected from the thrum of a corrupt society, sentences like these came from his pencil:

> The mass of men serve the state thus, not as men mainly, but as machines, with their bodies.
>
> There are thousands who are *in opinion* opposed to slavery and to the war, who yet in effect do nothing to put an end to them; who, esteeming themselves children of Washington and Franklin, sit down with their hands in their pockets, and say that they know not what to do, and do nothing . . .
>
> Thus the State never intentionally confronts a man's sense, intellectual or moral, but only his body, his senses. It is not armed with superior wit or honesty, but with superior physical strength. I was not born to be forced.[56]

As Malcolm listened to Bembry "expound upon" Thoreau's life, he understood that this wise and experienced man was trying to make a point more directly aimed at each man in the group. Bembry "would prove to us, dipping into the science of human behavior, that the only difference between us and outside people was that we had been caught."

Bembry had a general authority that Malcolm couldn't help but admire, a commanding yet understated presence. His intellect was steady, assured.

But Bembry's wisdom wasn't entirely self-contained. Most likely due to his years as a mentor in Norfolk, he had no trouble spotting a wayward youth, and at least once during that summer of 1946 at Charlestown, Bembry headed toward Malcolm's direction. His comment was direct: *You have some brains, if you used them.* Bembry wasn't trying to provoke Malcolm. Instead, it was just a way to plant an idea. Malcolm's anger was still too strong, however: "I might have cursed another convict, but nobody cursed Bimbi."[57]

Around a month passed. Malcolm spent hours in his cell brooding, pacing—exhaustion from anger and anger from exhaustion. On July 2, his final appeal for the Norfolk court to reconsider his 8–10-year sentence was dismissed. A quick release was now a distant dream. A Charlestown prison official, after evaluating Malcolm in July, believed that his future was bleak. "Prognosis is poor," he wrote. "Lacking positive guidance, the picture for the future is not hopeful as seen at this time."[58]

And then, in the late summer of 1946, that positive guidance finally came. Between 4:00 to 4:45 p.m., Malcolm and other men got their laps in walking Charlestown's yard. Around the yard, for men not interested in participating in an enlarged version of a philosopher's walk, there were benches, some newly installed due to requests made by the prison committee back in early March. This was where Bembry hung out, playing dominoes. Malcolm, seeing Bembry's carefully balanced game from a distance, changed his walking direction and casually "bumped into Bembry," causing the dominoes to tumble onto the ground. As Bembry remembered it, Malcolm "didn't say a word . . ." and continued making his way around the circle.

This wasn't about intimidation—more than that, Malcolm wanted to test Bembry. Was this wise older man as cool and collected as he came off to others, or might a bit of irritable fire throw him off his perch?

The next time around, Malcolm stopped at Bembry's bench. Seeing Malcolm simply stand and wait, Bembry stood as well. There was quiet for a moment, interrupted once by a comment from the other domino player. Malcolm ignored him, and when he was ready, he said to Bembry, "I'm sorry about the dominoes." Bembry didn't reply. From his years talking with young, rage-fueled men, he knew this wasn't about some game that helped pass the time.

Malcolm then said, rather quickly, "Do you believe in God? God the father, God the son, God the Holy Ghost, and all that crap?"[59]

Bembry didn't, but oh, how he'd explored it.

If Bembry had a religion, it was education, and he believed that was the only way to convince Malcolm to put down the nutmeg and pick up a book.

The confrontation cooled, and so began a decades-long friendship that only ended when Malcolm was assassinated on February 21, 1965. "[Bimbi helped me] come down and get out of the fog bag I was in," Malcolm later said. "At the time, the extent of my reading was cowboy books. . . . [He] started me reading serious books—you know, books with intellectual vitamins."[60]

At Charlestown, the first book Malcolm borrowed from Bembry was the prison vet's dictionary. From February 1941 to July 1946, Malcolm Little had built his character around the fast-paced alpha-like dynamics of street life. He'd learned the art of persuasion—be it to change someone's mind, acquire something he wanted, or both—an important tool in a society enamored by confidence and charisma. But he'd acquired it without an advanced education. Now here he was, with all the time in the world to fill in the gaps of knowledge he'd kept hidden from competitors. Bembry's dictionary was the start of his way out of an arrested educational darkness.[61]

Still, he was rusty, and in the last five years, Malcolm had transformed himself so completely that every word in the dictionary held a new meaning. When he told Alex Haley that "the streets had erased everything I'd ever learned in school," he meant it. And when he said he "didn't know a verb from a house," the subtext was clear: the basic rules of grammar felt like they were learned a lifetime ago, but they were there, buried under nightclubs and drugs.

So in the summer of 1946, at 21 years of age, inside a noxious six-by-eight concrete prison cell built during the Lewis and Clark expedition, among the mutterings of killers, thieves, and cheats, Malcolm Little started to reeducate himself.

"THAT BITCH WAS NUTS"

His first step back into education was a correspondence course, formally titled as "University Extension Course in Plain English, Pt. I." There was also a small prison school he attended "for a short time." While the correspondence course helped him recapture all "the mechanics of grammar" he'd learned back in Michigan, it wasn't until he started reading the classics that his imagination received a kick start.[62]

As Bembry recalled, Malcolm started with Shakespeare, an endeavor that most definitely required a dictionary, especially without a teacher providing historical, linguistic, or dramatic context. He tried *Romeo and Juliet*, but Malcolm was in no mood to read a story about forbidden love between two powerful white families. At that time, the closest Malcolm had come to love was with Beatrice, and after her April courtroom performance, she was someone he wanted to forget. He gave up reading about the lovesick couple before their suicide scene.

Bembry also directed Malcolm toward Herman Melville's colossal tale, *Moby-Dick*. Malcolm remained intrigued enough to finish the 206,000-word novel and followed Captain Ahab and his obsession over capturing, as Malcolm put it, "a god damn white whale."[63]

But Ahab, to Malcolm, was far too "self-destructive" to relate to, an interesting comment coming from a young man who around eight months prior had allowed others around him to believe he was ready to kill himself.

Malcolm brushed away his sour experience with *Romeo and Juliet* and decided to give Shakespeare another try. He was engrossed by *Richard III*, but it was a different revenge tragedy that stayed with him.[64] One day, outside his cell, Malcolm spotted Bembry reading, fully plunged into *Macbeth*, a twisted, complex story of power and betrayal. Soon enough, Malcolm entered Shakespeare's tale, and it was the dominion Lady Macbeth held over her husband, and her spiral into insanity, that stayed with him:

> You wait on nature's mischief. Come, thick night,
> And pall thee in the dunnest smoke of hell,
> That my keen knife see not the wound it makes . . .
> —Lady Macbeth, act 1, scene 5, *Macbeth*

Days passed. In different ways, Lady Macbeth's whispering manipulations reminded Malcolm of the women in his own life. At times throughout the play, Lady Macbeth could have been Ella pushing him toward becoming a great man.

But Lady Macbeth cut even deeper, and after Malcolm had finished the story, he walked around the Charlestown prison circle "lost in himself." His life could have turned out so differently. He could have stayed in Michigan and remained a "brainwashed Christian," trapped within the rigid boundaries of white society. He could have married "Laura" and leaned on her innocence to keep him out of too much trouble. But he didn't. He threw himself into a corner, wrapped in shadow. Where had his own kind of sabotage started?

He approached Bembry shortly after in the auto plate shop. He hadn't spoken to him for several days, but the first line out of his mouth was quick, as if Bembry should have been able to read his mind.

"That bitch was nuts. That's all, just plain nuts."

Bembry took his hands off the machine for a moment, confused. "Who the heck are you talking about?"

Malcolm stayed strong and direct. "That bitch Lady Macbeth," he said. But later, Malcolm finally let his guard down. Four months after arriving in prison, Malcolm confided in Bembry what had happened to his mother. He told Bembry how Louise had been admitted to a mental hospital, how she had lost her sense of being after years of struggle. He asked Bembry a question: Did he have a part in causing it? And had her descent into insanity impacted the decisions he'd made in the future?

They were questions Bembry could not begin to answer with any specificity. Simply put, he hadn't been there, and he didn't know Malcolm's mother. But one thing Bembry could tell Malcolm with a degree of confidence was that "his mother's collapse had been due to her inability to give her children what they needed."[65] No more, no less. As for the question of how she'd affected Malcolm—that was for the young man to wrestle with.

Bembry's words calmed Malcolm. Just as important, Shakespeare's stories had grabbed him by the collar and refused to let him go. One moment in *Macbeth* remained with him for the rest of his life.

In act 1, scene 7, Macbeth, alone with his thoughts, doubts the plan he made to kill Duncan and take the throne. He rigorously goes through all that could go wrong and soon convinces himself not to go through with it.

Then, just as he has made up his mind, Lady Macbeth enters. Diabolically, line after line, she brings Macbeth back toward their original plan.

Macbeth

If we should fail?

Lady Macbeth

> We fail!
> But screw your courage to the sticking-place,
> And we'll not fail . . .

As his brother Philbert later recalled, it's the line, "screw your courage to the sticking-place" that Malcolm remembered verbatim and said aloud during times when faced with a daunting challenge.

Because of Bembry's guidance, Malcolm had discovered two new passions: language and narrative. As he sat in his cell 17 hours a day, he consumed books and started to calm down from the edgy, satanic persona he'd initially taken on.

This didn't mean he'd lost his sense of rebellion, however. In the middle of his reading at Charlestown, he told Bembry, "When I get out of this place, I'm going to be a bad nigger, but I'm going to be . . . a smart bad nigger."[66]

TWO WHITE MEN ON DEATH ROW

In August, while Malcolm re-jolted his education via correspondence courses, Melville, Shakespeare, and the dictionary, two men over on Cherry Hill's death row were facing the electric chair.

Their crumbling, century-old cells were adjacent to each other, and their room of death was a short walk down the corridor, where they'd be strapped to a chair constructed by Charlestown prisoners back in 1901. Since then, 63 men had been executed—the electrical currents fierce enough to temporarily dim kitchen lights in the homes of Charlestown residents. When it occurred, husbands and wives often looked at each other and either shook their heads or sighed. "There goes another one" was all that could be said.[67]

Although these two men were scheduled to die, one of them escaped the brass hat. Thirty-six-year-old Raphael Skopp had been in and out of prison for the last two decades and had been convicted of first-degree murder after shooting Bronislaus Petruswicz in a Dorchester liquor store. He was picked up in a Nevada prison, which he ended up in after stealing a car, his one-inch lip scar recognized off a nationally distributed photo. Petruswicz's wife, upon hearing the news that the death penalty was possible, cared not one bit for the lifelong criminal. "Even the electric chair is too good for him," she told the press. "He left me with four young children to bring up without a father."[68]

Skopp only had one person publicly fighting for clemency—his mother, who drove up from New York and cried in front of Massachusetts's Governor Tobin for 20 minutes. He was moved, but the sentence remained. On August 15, 1946, Skopp chose as his last meal fresh pears and grapes to go with his prison dinner. He spoke to his brothers and even expressed to them that he was strong enough to survive the electric chair. After chatting about the Brooklyn Dodgers, his favorite baseball team, he was taken into the "execution chamber" at exactly 12:02 a.m. With a rabbi, he prayed for nearly a half-hour, repeating various prayers: "May my death be an atonement for all the sins, iniquities and transgressions of which I have been guilty against Thee." Skopp did not panic while sitting in the chair. Rather, he'd made peace with the chaos he'd made: "I lived a life that called for this. I'm willing to pay for it." At 12:31 a.m., he uttered his last words to Warden Lanagan, "Take care of my body," and a prison guard pulled the switch. Usually, it took just two to three shockwaves to kill a man, the currents "ranging from 1800 to 2200" volts, but Skopp's body only surrendered after six jolts to his system—at 12:37 a.m. From their cells, Malcolm and Bembry saw prison lights dim as they sat in darkness.[69]

What inevitably led Skopp to his execution was not just his lifelong habit of crime but a lack of influential friends and family to vouch for his character. In the case of the other man on death row, John Noxon Jr., help was everywhere.

Noxon, 49, had a resume that rarely ended up on death row—Harvard-educated lawyer, friends with former Massachusetts governor Joseph Ely, and a married father of two living comfortably in Pittsfield. His youngest son, Lawrence, was six months old and diagnosed with Down syndrome. On September 22, 1943, one month after Noxon was told of his son's medical condition, Lawrence was electrocuted while sitting on a metal tray in a damp diaper and T-shirt, cut radio wires wrapped around his left arm and plugged into a 110-volt socket. A much-publicized trial ensued. Why, for example, had Noxon tossed the baby's diaper and T-shirt into the fire before police arrived? Why had the child been left unattended while surrounded by dangerous wires?[70]

Noxon refused a plea deal for manslaughter and claimed he was innocent of all charges. A hobby of his was fixing radios, and "he had brought in a 'trouble lamp,' with [a] long cord, from the garage, turned the large console radio out from the wall and sat on the floor to get at the new tubes which he placed alongside him on a metal tray." Worried Lawrence might fall out of the "armchair," he placed him down on the metal tray after discovering he'd wet his diaper. Noxon "feared it would spot the rug, and [he] took the tray to lay the baby in." Then he left the room for five minutes, came back, and "smelled something burning—saw the 'trouble lamp' cord was on the baby's chest . . . as I tried to pull it off [and also the burned clothes], the left arm came up with it."[71]

The jury didn't buy it. The term *mercy killing* became a matter of debate—a term Malcolm himself used to describe Noxon's crime.

As he faced the electric chair, Noxon called on resources that Skopp could have only dreamed of. Over 250 letters of support came into the governor's office. Noxon's indefatigable wife continued pleading to the press. "He is a valuable man. There is a place for him in the world that nobody else can fill." Less than a week before Skopp was executed, Governor Tobin caved to the pressure coming from the public. Noxon's sentence was changed to life, and he left Skopp and the Cherry Hill cell block behind, joining Malcolm and others in the more renovated section of the building. Warden Lanagan also gave him a job in Charlestown's prison library, since Noxon lost most of the functionality in his legs and walked with two canes.[72]

To Malcolm, the leniency Noxon received was an example of upper-class white privilege. The Harvard lawyer would be in and out of Malcolm's prison life until his release in January 1949.

In September, Malcolm wanted a change, badly. Perhaps influenced by Noxon's ability to use his connections, he wrote to a wealthy and white former employer. After hearing from Ella that someone had contacted her about him, Malcolm replied in a letter dated September 12: "The person that you said called me is a very good friend of mine," Malcolm wrote. "He's only worth some fourteen million dollars. If you read the society pages you'd know who he is. He knows where I am now because I've written and told him, but I didn't say what for. He may call and ask you. Whatever answer you give him will have to do with my entire future but I still depend on you . . ." Unfortunately, nothing ever materialized from this connection, and Malcolm instead began working on securing a transfer out of Charlestown.[73]

LONGING FOR NORFOLK

More than anywhere else, Malcolm wanted to be transferred to the Norfolk Prison Colony. If he ever had any questions about "the Colony," Bembry's experience there using the enormous library and participating on the debate team would have only encouraged him to show the transfer board that he was serious about improving his education. He'd been interviewed by the Norfolk Transportation Board around late July, but Warden Lanagan later told him that his transfer request had been denied. Malcolm, "terribly upset," asked for another chance to be interviewed. This time around, and with Bembry as his role model, Malcolm impressed the Norfolk board far more than in the first interview. Their advice to him was clear: be patient—you'll be transferred, but "keep a clean record."[74]

He tried.

For all of October, Malcolm worked outside as a "yard laborer," completing his duties without causing much trouble. Besides Ella, Hilda came for a visit. After Malcolm had been sentenced, Hilda went out of her way to move to the Roxbury area so she could visit and support her younger brother. Reginald also came at least once from New York City to check in on Malcolm. At this time, they came solely out of support and had not yet joined the Nation of Islam. His siblings' visits were supported by stop-ins from cousins and friends.[75]

Malcolm also had the Charlestown State Prison library, perhaps the only bright spot within the dungeon-like building. Labeled "first-class" by a Department of Education official back in 1929, the library had assembled a collection over the years with donations coming from "private individuals and philanthropic societies." As one incarcerated man from Charlestown put it many years before Malcolm entered, "Alone with his thoughts, bitter always, vengeful sometimes, nothing does more to bring about a healthier meditation than the reading of an interesting book . . . the intellect is his theatre of action."[76]

Charlestown's library was small compared to prisons such as Norfolk, but it still had over 8,000 books covering a wide variety of subjects. Most commonly in demand were detective novels by E. Phillips Oppenheim or westerns by Zane Grey (Malcolm's "cowboy" books)—a brief escape from a mundane existence. Censorship existed as well, however—and if a novel showed a thief getting the best of law enforcement, it was most likely taken off the shelf.

Classic authors such as Robert Louis Stevenson were still read, and books that stood "the acid test of time" were *Don Quixote* and *Robinson Crusoe*. Over 30 magazine and newspaper annual subscriptions were provided by the prison, but men were not allowed to take the copy out of the library reading room.

Besides fiction, Malcolm also had quite a few nonfiction titles to choose from. In fact, the prison library had become so well-fed of law books and Supreme Court summations that it demanded its own section, even once helping a man in 1940 to "argue his case" against a judge after he was sentenced for writing bad checks. (Judge: Where did you get your law? Defendant: "From the State Prison Library, your honor.") Perhaps an idle Malcolm momentarily revisited his teenage hopes to be a lawyer as he waited for a decision to come regarding his transfer.[77]

On November 12, 1946, his hopes for joining the Colony took a hit. Malcolm still needed to be sentenced for his December 24, 1945, B&E of Ethel Swan's home in Dorchester, so for the final time, he was taken in handcuffs to Suffolk County Superior Court, about a mile and a half away from the state prison. It was a short trip for Malcolm, but not for Jarvis, who once again rejoined him in the courtroom after a 35-mile trip from Norfolk.[78]

Their judge this time around was the Honorable Francis J. Good, a devout Catholic and married father of four sons and a daughter. Good, 54 at the time, had ruled on his share of B&E charges in his 11-year career at the Superior Court. Seeing as how the two young men before him already had been given more than a handful of concurrent sentences of at least 6 years, Good decided not to exceed that, delivering instead a 3–5-year sentence. Out of the three Superior Court trials, this was the only one that did not include Beatrice, Joyce, and Kora in the courtroom at the same time. The shorter sentence was due to the fact that there was only one burglarized house under discussion.[79]

Since it was a long drive back to Norfolk, prison officials decided to keep Jarvis overnight at Charlestown. According to his prison file, Jarvis spent at least a full day in a Charlestown prison cell and walking around the yard. There was enough time for Jarvis to give Malcolm an update about Norfolk. In five short months at the Colony, Jarvis was playing the trumpet in Norfolk's prison orchestra (yes, an orchestra), playing tunes before films or debates started in a large hall big enough to hold an audience of 800. In his free time, he walked around the expansive prison yard with other Black men or "engaged in a musical jam session" in halls and other spots around the prison.[80]

There was so much to tell Malcolm. Jarvis had his own room; he could shower several times a week, and the library! Twice the size of Charlestown's. Jarvis, if his anger at Malcolm had subsided, could have even told him that in October, he contributed an article to the *Colony*, Norfolk's prison newspaper.[81]

After the trial, Malcolm had to report to work as a sewer in the underwear shop. It's hard to imagine Malcolm being able to concentrate after seeing Jarvis again, or after finally being given a three-to-five-year mocking wink of justice by another old white judge whose head was shaped like an egg. It's unknown what exactly got to him, but his "narrow-minded" shop instructor wrote him up for "shirking" and gave him three days of "detention."

Just like that, there was now a blemish on his "clean record." Detention didn't mean solitary confinement—rather it meant that privileges were taken away, such as using the library or a reduction of time walking in the yard.

So as Jarvis left for Norfolk on the morning of November 14, Malcolm was stuck in his cell.[82]

His shirking violation did lead to a job change. After serving his three-day detention, Malcolm was placed in the loud and vibrating foundry, working as a laborer amid furnaces pouring out molten metal. He learned as he went, rated by his supervisor as "cooperative in behavior, poor in skill, [and] average in effort." Malcolm admitted to Ella that his work in the foundry was "a little harder and very much dirtier, but I don't have any of those prejudice[d], narrow-minded instructors with me now."

In between his shifts in the foundry, trips to the library, and chats with Bembry, Malcolm started writing an original story in his cold, century-old cell. On December 14, 1946, he wrote to Ella, calling it *that book*:

> *My Dear Sister,*
>
> *I'm writing this to let you know what I want for Xmas. At least I'm blunt—hu? I've worn my fountain pen completely out. That's what I need, a fountain pen and a pair of gloves (preferably mittens). You asked me two months ago what I wanted for Xmas, so don't go blowing your top, now that I've told you.*
>
> *The pen, I need, because I still intend writing that book while I'm here. I've already started on it (several times) but I've had to destroy it because I wasn't satisfied with what I had accompolished [sic].*[83]

Had Malcolm started, in December of 1946, to conceive of writing his life story, as early as 21 years of age? So much had indeed already happened to him. In the same letter, Malcolm asked Ella, "Are you still going to get me transferred to Norfolk? . . . If you get me transferred to Norfolk, I'll try and complete that whole book next year. They have a fine library down there, and one can learn so ~~much~~ many more diferent [*sic*] things. My only reason for wanting to go, is the library alone."[84]

As the holiday season came and went, Malcolm remained in Charlestown, Ella's efforts not enough. Unknown to Malcolm, Ella was in the Suffolk County Jail, also incarcerated, serving a 30-day sentence on charges of larceny, assault, and battery.

So on January 10, 1947, when Malcolm was transferred to the Massachusetts Reformatory in West Concord, Ella was in a holding cell in Boston.[85]

For Malcolm, the library at Norfolk was still 14 months away, and he was still going to need Ella's help getting there.

6

THE PURGATORY
OF CONCORD

January 10, 1947, to March 31, 1948

> We believe the State [of Massachusetts] owes it to itself and to young men who, though they have committed offences against the law, are not criminals at heart, to separate them from the professional criminals, to afford them an opportunity to learn trades and remedy the defects in their education, and to make an earnest endeavor to bring them back into good citizenship.
>
> —A Massachusetts Commissioner, "The Reformatory Prison," *Fall River Daily News*

> The greatest curse of prison life is the degrading effect of idleness.
>
> —Albert Lerer, "Study of the Education Program at the Massachusetts Reformatory"

THE YOUNG MAN'S PRISON

On paper, Malcolm was an ideal fit for the Massachusetts Reformatory in Concord (MR-Concord). Ready for use as a regular state prison in 1878, Concord was rebranded as a reformatory in 1884, attempting to be a positive counterbalance to the ever-worsening experience at Charlestown, which after nearly eight decades had already earned a reputation for housing the older, more "hardened criminals" who'd given up on the idea of reform.[1]

From 1884 on, MR-Concord decided to focus on the rehabilitation of men under the age of 30. For the next 60 years, they remained true to this principle. After being transported 21 miles east, Malcolm joined 734 other men, their average age 21.2 years old. Instead of borrowing books from a middle-aged man who'd allegedly electrocuted his own son, Malcolm was instead surrounded by young men his own age—men such as George Walls, whose wife had run away from him and gone to a friend's house. Instead of being civil, Walls set fire to the friend's house. When the judge asked why, Walls's answer via his lawyer was oddly rational: "To smoke out his wife."

There were others: 19-year-old Thomas Goode Jr., who gave his great-aunt two black eyes for giving him an allowance of 45 cents instead of his standard 55 cents. Or Arthur C. Toy, a 21-year-old who attempted to rob an egg merchant. Another young man kidnapped a young woman taking tickets at a local theatre, while two young men, described in the *Boston Globe* as "fresh hoodlums," walked up to a man and asked for a cigarette. When he said he didn't have one, they beat him up and stole his wallet, then beat up a 16-year-old crippled newspaper boy in their way. In 1947, these were the type of young men surrounding Malcolm—only a few with sentences longer than 10 years.[2]

It was a 21-mile drive from Charlestown to Concord, and while being processed, Malcolm was given a new prison number: 33428. "You never heard your name," Malcolm recalled later, "only your number. On all your clothing, every item, was your number, stenciled. It grew stenciled on your brain."[3]

BAD JOKES AND ROTATING LEADERSHIP

Malcolm was assigned to the furniture shop, and for all but one of his 14 months at Concord (he was assigned to laundry the other month), he stayed there, his shop guard, Arthur Roach, keeping tabs on him. Roach was a kidder, and he attempted to break the ice with Malcolm by giving him a nickname. Perhaps it worked better with men in their late teens, but not with Malcolm, especially when he was still stung over not being transferred to Norfolk. In between the stacks of lumber and clamps, Roach went over to Malcolm and tried to disarm the young man's edginess. "Little Malcolm," he said with a smile—Malcolm's last name first. Roach liked it, but Malcolm wanted no part of the chumminess. "There's no joking between you and me," he said to Roach.[4]

No longer did Malcolm have a warden like he did at Charlestown. Instead, since he was now in a reformatory, the man at the top was Thomas F. McCusker, a superintendent. McCusker, whose only experience had been 12 years of work as a police stenographer, had started the job on January 1, 1947, weaseling into the position thanks to Governor Tobin's recommendation. Five days after starting the job, a 19-year-old man "walked to freedom while working in the cow barn" but was caught soon after while on an "abandoned railroad track." The United Prison Association criticized McCusker, claiming he was given the position based only on being "around" incarcerated men and typing out their cases. By the middle of February, six weeks later, McCusker was reassigned to a different governmental position, leaving MR-Concord in the hands of the more experienced John C. Dolan—a bespectacled, cigar-loving WWI veteran and longtime member of the Massachusetts National Guard who'd been, in various capacities, Concord's deputy superintendent since 1934.[5]

THE LAYOUT AND FOOD

Enwrapped by a brick wall 22 feet high, MR-Concord was spread across 23 acres, compared to the suffocating 4 acres at Charlestown. Most of the acreage was devoted to farming, industry shops, and a broad playing field for sports. On the farm property next to the prison, there was a barn that contained a hen house large enough for a thousand hens, a cow and dairy farm, stables for horses, and a piggery. Some of the men who were viewed as trustworthy worked and slept within the farm property. This meant that some of them oversaw the slaughtering of the animals and/or preparing them for consumption at the prison. In 1947, "27,562 lbs. of pork was slaughtered during the year." The prison used their cows to bottle over 259,000 quarts of milk. Forty-three cows were also slaughtered and consumed by the men.[6]

This self-sustainable approach to food kept costs down and was common knowledge to the men, including Malcolm, who had his own childhood experience growing his own food back in Lansing, Michigan. At MR-Concord, Malcolm and most of the other men ate their meals—which also included farm-sourced potatoes and corn—in a large dining hall located in the middle of the institution.[7]

THE BOXER

Recreationally, MR-Concord's prison culture revolved around a year-round sports program, and motion pictures showed on Sundays and holidays. Since Malcolm entered Concord in January, he was encouraged to join the basketball, soccer, or volleyball teams, playing most of the time indoors. Time for recreation was between 3:15 and 3:45 p.m. on Monday, Tuesday, Thursday, and Friday. On Wednesdays and Saturdays, a longer time was given—2:30 p.m. to 3:45 p.m.—to complete full games or matches, with Sundays giving special attention to tournament finals, between 10:30 and 12:30 p.m.[8]

Malcolm ignored the sports just mentioned. Instead, he headed over to the gym, put on some gloves, and sparred with other incarcerated men. In a way, he was reliving the sparring sessions he'd had with older brother Philbert during his teenage years back in Michigan.

The incarcerated men at MR-Concord had organized "Monday Night Club Boxing," held periodically throughout the year but largely from January through April. The event started around 7:00 p.m. in MR-Concord's Tufts Hall, a way, prison officials believed, for men to let off some steam as crowds cheered on their favorites. Typically, six or seven three-round bouts were scheduled across weight classes.

The event had been thoughtfully organized by the men. There were two referees, a timekeeper at the bell, three judges, and an announcer. There was even an in-house reporter, 23-year-old Pennsylvania-born William Paul Williams, documenting each fight, his write-ups becoming a part of MR-Concord's prison newspaper, called *Our Paper*.

On February 3, less than a month after being transferred from Charlestown, Malcolm stepped into the Tufts Hall ring. At Charlestown, Malcolm was not given many chances to move, since he was forced to spend over 17 hours a day in his cell. Now, at Concord, he had a proper gym and equipment to use. His opponent that night was Robert D. Nash, 20 years old.[9] Nash was Black and weighed in at 180 lbs., and Malcolm weighed in at 176 lbs.

Here in full is Williams describing how the three-round fight turned out: "Nash took left jabs from Little then countered with a right that did not do any damage. Little ripped a hard right in the second then both threw light jabs. This continued throughout the final round, therefore the punches had little or no effect on the other at the bell." The winner was not reported in the paper unless a knockout or a technical knockout (three knockdowns in one round) occurred.[10]

One week later, Malcolm was back at it, his opponent Frank R. Willis, 22, white and three days away from being released.[11] Willis weighed in at 175 lbs., and Little remained at 176 lbs. for the bout, which proved more brutal than the Nash fight a week before.

Per Williams, "Willis hammered lefts and rights to the head and body of Little in the opening round. Light jabs were hitting their marks then Little connected with hard blows to the head of Willis. In the second Little caught Willis with three jabs to the head at the bell. The final saw Willis the aggressor as he fired repeated lefts and rights to the head and body. Little continued to jab until the final bell."[12]

When looking into Malcolm's prison file, medical reports show him receiving treatment for a "laceration" on the chin on February 11. Most likely, Willis landed a shot that cut Malcolm and left a half inch scar near the bottom of his chin.

Malcolm took a couple of months off after the Willis fight, but on April 28, Malcolm entered the Tufts Hall ring six pounds heavier, set to fight 21-year-old Floyd Johnston, Black, who came in at 180 lbs.[13]

The fight was by far the most punishing of the three.

According to Williams, "Johnston recovered from a slow start when in the second he unleashed savage blows at Little who went down for a count of 7 being saved by the bell. Again in the third Little was counted for 7 but recovered and went to a finish more or less in a defensive sort of a way."[14]

At least as was reported in *Our Paper*, Malcolm did not fight again on Monday nights at Concord after being knocked down twice by Johnston.

FIGHTING IDLENESS

MR-Concord did have an educational program, but it wasn't the kind of system that inspired Malcolm to join. In 1947, the prison offered "Evening School." From 6:00 p.m. to 8:00 p.m., Tuesday through Friday, men joined the class their educational background fell under.

Here are the classes MR-Concord offered during Malcolm's time there, and the number of men enrolled by the end of 1947:

Special Class for Defective Delinquents = 18
Special Class for Illiterates = 42
Third Grade = 35
Fourth Grade = 66
Fifth Grade = 94
Sixth Grade = 97
Seventh Grade = 20
Eighth Grade = 64
Arithmetic Class = 20
Drawing Class = 23
English Class = 17
Algebra Class = 21[15]

Most of these classes all took place in one "large schoolroom," but according to his prison file, Malcolm didn't participate. One very practical reason was that he had finished the eighth grade, dropping out of Mason High School midway through the ninth grade. In this way, just about all classes were nothing more than an uninspiring review of the basics—an act he could go through in his cell at his own pace.[16]

Malcolm's Concord cell was a definite upgrade from Charlestown. The bars remained, but he did have an actual toilet that flushed, and the cell itself was slightly larger. Since almost all the men at MR-Concord were in their early 20s, it had been hard for prison guards to quiet those who were bored and rowdy. So as early as 1939, each individual cell was wired and equipped with "ear phones and a connection plug." From 3:00 p.m. until lights out at 10:00 p.m., Malcolm and other men could listen to a preapproved "list of stations to be turned to at specific times" and "are sent into the guard room where a master radio set connected to all the rooms is controlled by the officer in charge." Most popular were "broadcasts of news, dramas, and baseball games." In Malcolm's case, there was one moment on April 15, 1947, about two weeks before his bout with Johnston, that was particularly special to him. "I'll never forget the prison sensation created . . . when Jackie Robinson was brought up to play with the Brooklyn Dodgers. Jackie had, then, his most fanatic fan in me. When he played, my ear was glued to the radio, and no game ended without my refiguring his average up through his last turn at bat."[17]

When Jackie wasn't playing, Malcolm spent most of his time reading. Delivered to his cell were copies of *Our Paper*, a prison newspaper printed by his fellow incarcerated men and distributed to each man weekly. From his family on the outside, he received the *Michigan Chronicle*, a weekly Black-owned newspaper that covered events across the state, including Lansing, where most of his siblings still resided. It was Wilfred and his first wife, Bertha, who made sure Malcolm had a resource that connected him back to where he grew up.[18]

As Malcolm may have expected, MR-Concord's library stock was disappointing. Containing around 6,000 volumes, the collection was even smaller than Charlestown's. Even worse, men were only allowed to check out two books a week from a chaplain-approved list "posted in the shops where he works." For Malcolm, there was no walking up and down library shelves or any kind of reading room. According to MR-Concord scholar Albert Lerer, "Books are delivered by the chaplain's helpers,—each of the six boys being assigned to deliver and collect the books from specified tiers in the wings." The term *boys* was common in the late 1930s and '40s at MR-Concord, a choice that illustrates just how young the prison population was around Malcolm, who, nearing his twenty-second birthday and with a stint at ol' Charlestown under his belt, was considered a veteran.[19]

Without a strong educational program or an immersive library experience, Malcolm mainly went through the motions at MR-Concord, pleading with Ella to help facilitate a transfer to Norfolk. "They treat you like a baby here," he told her. Sure enough, there were men as young as 16 in the same dining hall as Malcolm. At times, Concord could feel like an advanced juvenile hall.

This feeling of stagnation, or idleness, contributed to his four reported moments of misconduct. On March 6, 1947, he was written up again for "shirking, poor work." And on April 29, 1947, one day after his brutal bout with Johnston, Malcolm was written up for potentially carrying a handmade six-inch blade, or "shiv." It was indeed possible, since MR-Concord was notorious for making younger men turn aggressive, trying perhaps to out-alpha others around them. Perhaps Malcolm still had a beef with Johnston. The prison file doesn't have the full story.[20]

JOINER

Malcolm did have friends around him. One man who stayed close to Malcolm was Godfrey N. Joiner. At 27 years old, Joiner was an old man compared to other men at MR-Concord. Joiner graduated high school—a rarity at

MR-Concord—and had a supportive wife taking care of their son, Godfrey Jr. After serving overseas in the navy as a cook and barber throughout World War II, Joiner returned home to find very few job prospects and a lack of respect even though he'd given the navy seven years. Between unemployment compensation and $96 monthly base pay from the navy, Joiner tried to make ends meet, but he wanted more.[21]

Joiner, with navy friend Charles Pritchett, started breaking into automobiles in and around Boston's Back Bay—hoping to "augment a poor weekly income."[22] In late July 1946, Joiner was caught with a sack of stolen goods that he took from a car and taken by a police officer down to the local station. As they walked toward the police car, the officer, according to Joiner, tried to "roughen him up and abuse him." Angered, Joiner chose to break away from the officer and run. When he looked back and saw the officer pull out his gun, Joiner took out his own ".32 calib[er] Colt automatic with a squeeze handle." The gun "fired before he had realized it," one shot wounding the officer while two shots hit the street.

He gave himself up, hoping to soften his sentence by showing cooperation. Despite the wounded officer's provocation and full recovery, Joiner was given 10–20 years. In late October 1946, he was first sentenced to Charlestown State Prison, where he may have briefly worked with Malcolm in the auto shop and then was transferred to MR-Concord in February 1947, his work assignment "Sand papering" in the furniture shop, where Malcolm was as well.[23]

Joiner and Malcolm bonded over music. While in prison, Joiner had picked up the trumpet and was looking to improve his skill. Malcolm had plenty of Harlem jazz stories to share with the aspiring musician. Over time, Malcolm told Joiner that he "preferred" the cold solitude of Charlestown to the teenage camaraderie surrounding them at MR-Concord. In a way, Joiner's age and experience may have reminded Malcolm of his brother Wilfred, who at this same time had decided to join a religious organization, an act that would eventually change Malcolm's life.[24]

MEANWHILE . . . BACK IN MICHIGAN

By 1947, Wilfred was a 27-year-old manager of a "household furnishing" company in Detroit. "I didn't even know what a Muslim was," said Wilfred. Malcolm's oldest brother had recently married, and he was content providing for his wife. Also, due in large part to the beliefs he absorbed from Louise and Earl, Wilfred naturally stood up for Black customers who were being swindled. "Our people were coming up from the South, many of them not too well educated [and] they didn't understand business too well." Wilfred made sure to stop shopkeepers from adding "another hundred dollars" to bills. Wilfred also kept white workers from flirting too aggressively with "young, beautiful black women" who came into the store. "I want to see you respect my women the same way you want me to respect yours," he told them.[25]

Wilfred also had to stand up for the Black employees under him. Once a year, pay raises were handed out, and white employees often chastised Black workers to "make them feel that they weren't worthy of their raise." On one day in particular, a Black truck driver was being given the third degree for what Wilfred felt was no reason whatsoever. After hearing enough, Wilfred confronted the white manager and said, "Look. . . . He's one of the best truck drivers we got, he's here every day, he's on time, everything we need. There's no problems with him. . . . He deserves his raise. You give him his raise."

They backed off and "gave him his raise." And, as a surprised Wilfred later said, "They didn't fire me."

It turned out that this truck driver was a Muslim, and after thanking Wilfred for helping him, he asked if Wilfred was one as well.

Wilfred said he wasn't. "What is it about me that makes you think I'm a Muslim?"

The truck driver reeled off a list. Wilfred didn't smoke or drink, and he didn't allow "white folks" to "misuse us." In other words, the truck driver said that Wilfred "believe[d] in black people and making it better for black people."

Wilfred was surprised, and admittedly a bit naïve. "Is that what Muslims believe in?" The truck driver assured him that yes, that belief was at the core of his religion—the Nation of Islam (NOI).[26]

Soon after, Wilfred became a regular at NOI meetings. He was impressed at how the organization sought those who had been excluded, or disenfranchised from society. "They were reaching for those that nobody else wanted," Wilfred explained during a lecture given at the University of Massachusetts, Amherst. "[The] NAACP didn't have any use for them, because they didn't have anything to offer. Urban League didn't need them, nobody wanted them. They were misfits. They were reaching for those who were drunks, and dope addicts, and prostitutes. Those who were on the welfare, doing nothing. Those who just didn't fit into society, [or] had nothing to add to it."[27]

To Wilfred, it wasn't for reasons of faith that he committed himself to the NOI. He wanted to help. Firsthand, he started to see the transformation so many downtrodden Black men and women went through after joining the religion. They "cleaned up," started "wearing clean clothes," and "found employment."[28]

It wasn't long after that Wilfred spread the word about the NOI to his siblings. Philbert, also living in Detroit, bought in, and Hilda understood the impact the organization was having on those who'd been all but cast aside by the white power structure. They were also able to reach and persuade Reginald, who'd been drifting back and forth between New York and Boston, surviving in much the same way Malcolm had been before being arrested. "We all got together and decided we better let Malcolm know about this," recalled Wilfred. "Even though we had been scattered, we kept up with each other, and we tried to do things together as a family."

And as a family, they knew it would be next-to-impossible to convince Malcolm to join the Nation. As Philbert recalled, Malcolm "had [a] very low tolerance for religion." After Wilfred and Philbert failed to convince him via letter, the Little family knew their only shot at converting their imprisoned brother was to pass the baton to Reginald, the brother who best knew Malcolm's current state of mind.[29]

REJECTION

After enduring seven months of stagnation at Concord, Malcolm wondered if he'd ever be transferred to Norfolk. Without any progress on Ella's side of the fight, Malcolm went ahead and wrote the following letter to Jim Dwyer, dated July 28, 1947:

> *Mr. Dwyer,*
>
> *A year ago, while an inmate of Charlestown State Prison, I was interviewed by the Norfolk Board. I was terribly upset when the warden told me that I wasn't to be transferred so I wrote to you for consideration. I was rewarded with another interview from the Board. After re-hearing my plea they told me that I would be transferred and in the meantime to keep a clean record. Well, I've*

kept my record clean and, instead, they've sent me here at Concord. My sole purpose for wanting to go to Norfolk was the educational facilities that aren't in these other institutions. If I had completed my education I never would have been in prison today. I'm serving ten years for burglary on my first offense—my first crime. That doesn't fuirt [sic . . . hurt?] so [much] because, being a Negro, I'm used [to] heavier punishment than usual. But, I have long ago realized my mistakes and cannot see how an educated man would break into other people's houses.

Since my confinment [sic] I've already received a diploma in Elementery [sic] English through the State Correspondence Courses. I'm very much disatisfied [sic], though.[30]

The[re] are many things that I would like to learn that would be of use to me when I regain my freedom. I do know that if I prepare myself now, while I have the time, I will never have to break the law to secure a living. It does hurt, tho', to watch murders, thieves with records dating back to the cradle, and "what not" going to Norfolk every day, while I (for reasons unknown to me) want to benifit [sic] by the place and can't get there for nothing.

I've been confined for eighteen months now and my record is clean. I've been here in Concord under Mr. O'Grady for six months and can only refer you to him for any reference of my character.

All I'm asking you for is a chance to ammend [sic] my mistakes. Then, if I fail, I have no one to hate but myself.

Thank you Kindly,

Malcolm Little[31]

Despite his impassioned plea to Dwyer, Malcolm remained at Concord. And with nothing but time, Malcolm started to resort to his old, street-hustling ways. According to 23-year-old Heywood Hampton, he watched as Malcolm became the "cellblock's bookie," using a "pad and pencil" to keep track of bets on sports. Winners were awarded cigarettes or paperbound IOUs. The bets helped increase the excitement of listening to a baseball or football game on the radio. A game-winning hit may have caused a whole cell block to momentarily shout for joy, the groans of losers not far away.[32]

Like Godfrey Joiner, Hampton served in the armed forces during World War II, from 1943 to 1946, before being honorably discharged from the army. Hampton grew up poor in Worcester, Massachusetts. After his parents separated when he was 11, Hampton lived with his mother, four brothers, and two sisters as they survived on welfare and whatever funds their father could contribute. Dropping out of high school at 16, Hampton worked a few odd jobs before joining the army. After his service, he found himself back in Worcester with few opportunities.

In October 1946, Hampton was walking with two other friends down Summer Street. He had just finished having a few drinks at a "Dixie Barbeque" when a man came out of the restaurant and stopped Hampton and his two friends. The man asked them where he could find a "sporting house," since he owed someone a bit of money. When the man took out his wallet to show them, Hampton and the trio "jumped him" and took $15. Police were nearby, and after being shot at twice, Hampton was arrested on charges of robbery. A B&E charge was added for when he broke into an office building and stole two watches. After a delayed trial, Hampton was sentenced to five years.[33]

Malcolm, at 6'2", towered over Heywood, who was 5'6" and around 170 pounds. Along with Joiner, the three men must have stayed together while eating in the large dining hall. With so many men in one place, Malcolm witnessed "fights" often, causing him to miss the mundane stink hole of Charlestown as he continued to harbor hopes of eventually being transferred to Norfolk. The danger of a fight didn't stop Malcolm from "sneaking to the front of the line," perhaps to collect a reward for winning a sports bet.[34]

Malcolm also filled the time by telling Joiner and Hampton tales of his life before prison, peppered with clever turns of phrase. Once, Malcolm found himself around a group of weight lifters. Instead of feeling outmuscled, Malcolm gave Joiner and Hampton the line he used—or thought of using: *I've never lifted anything heavier than a woman's slip.*[35]

REGINALD'S VISIT

When not trading tales of love and lust in the dining room, Malcolm spent much of his time in the furniture shop crafting, assembling, or repairing tables, chairs, and benches. Evaluated by MR-Concord officials as a "poor and uncooperative worker," Malcolm still was taught how to craft a variety of items. According to Ella's son, Rodnell Collins, Malcolm learned how to craft musical jewelry boxes, at times giving them to relatives as gifts. Collins, as a child, came on occasion with Ella to MR-Concord, whose visitation rules were more flexible than those at Charlestown: "I remember his putting me on his knee while they talked. Sometimes he would tell me stories, which became parables as I got older. I thought of Uncle Malcolm as a big brother who gave me a small table and chair that he made in the prison workshop."[36]

In the 63 weeks he spent at MR-Concord, Malcolm received 34 visitors—a high number, especially since many men (such as Bembry, for example) often received no visitors for months at a time.

Nineteen of Malcolm's thirty-four visitors were an assortment of friends, their names redacted from his prison file. Three cousins who lived in Roxbury came to see Malcolm a combined total of six times. The remaining eight visits were likely from Ella (five times) and Reginald (three times), since "Sister" and "Roxbury" are not redacted, and Reginald was the only "Brother" whose address at the time was in New York.[37]

Indeed, it was Reginald who brought Malcolm one step closer to the Nation of Islam. Hilda's letters may have also helped legitimize the idea. Since Hilda was often a steadying presence during his childhood, her supportive words and maturity helped keep Malcolm from believing that the men in the family hadn't been taken by some kind of scheme.

Each brother had tried in their own way to convince Malcolm that they'd found "the natural religion for the black man." But Malcolm's skepticism wouldn't allow Wilfred or especially Philbert to convince him otherwise. To Malcolm, his older brothers were too easily taken by a movement, and he was determined to remain his own man. But when a letter from Reginald arrived for him, Malcolm's eyes opened. "Reginald's letter was newsy," he recalled, "and also it contained this instruction: 'Malcolm, don't eat any more pork, and don't smoke any more cigarettes. I'll show you how to get out of prison.'"[38]

Reginald's command startled Malcolm. For so much of their relationship, Malcolm had been the leader, the streetwise older brother who helped Reginald grow into a man of strength. But here Reginald was, *showing* Malcolm that he could help him.

The thoughts of quitting smoking and pork haunted Malcolm as his prison time ticked away. He needed an unbiased voice—someone whose strength had come not from religious belief but from undiluted humanism: "I wanted, in the worst way, to consult with Bimbi about it. But something big, instinct said, you spilled to nobody."[39]

So he let it stew. It's unknown if Reginald backed up his "no pork or cigarettes" letter with one of his three visits to MR-Concord, but it may not have been necessary. Malcolm finished off his last pack of cigarettes and said sayonara to the habit. If Reginald's get-out-of-jail promise had any semblance of truth to it, Malcolm didn't want to "fluff it."

His rejection of pork, however, had a ripple effect through the younger MR-Concord prison population. As other men knew, most of their pork was raised, killed, and served in prison. Once, in the dining hall at noon during lunch, Malcolm was served a "meat platter." It had been several days since Reginald's resonating letter, and as Malcolm stood in line, his younger brother's words came to him in "flashes." Perhaps his mother's rejection of Mr. Doane's two pigs flashed across his mind as well. Regardless, he passed the platter down the prison line. When someone gave him a look of confusion, Malcolm spoke four words, the sentence pushing him toward a new path: "I don't eat pork."[40]

ELLA AND SHAG

This was just the start of Malcolm's religious journey, the formation of a snowball that would soon cause an avalanche. But in MR-Concord in early 1948, Malcolm was still very determined to pursue his educational interests. As both Godfrey Joiner and Heywood Hampton recalled, at no point during his time at MR-Concord did they see Malcolm undergo any kind of "religious conversion." Rather, Malcolm continued to write to Ella, hoping she could use her local connections and have him transferred to Norfolk.[41]

After many months, Ella finally found someone who could help Malcolm. His name was Silas F. Taylor, or "Shag," the 60-year-old owner of the Lincoln Drug Store on the South End of Roxbury. "Shag Taylor could get your street cleaned, fix a pothole, get a vacant lot cleared, garbage collected, an abandoned car removed," remarked one established Boston resident. "If you needed someone released from jail, needed a job—whatever. Nobody had any question he was the premier man, he was *the* person, he was the machine's man, and his power came from the machine."[42]

Yes, Shag had connections—not just with the local police who allowed him to sell late-night liquor but also with judges and on up to Boston mayor James

Michael Curley. It was Curley who, as governor of Massachusetts back in the mid-1930s, appointed Shag to the State Board of Parole. For decades, Shag was an active Democrat, and he made history by becoming the "first president of the Massachusetts League of Colored Voters." In short, Shag was just the right kind of man who could help Ella nudge Malcolm toward Norfolk.[43]

Shag was receptive when Ella met him. All he needed "was cold cash." The bribe from Ella could then be split between Shag and a short "heavyset" white judge, who'd help to prioritize Malcolm's name or, put another way, move him up the list.[44]

Even if Ella hadn't intervened, Malcolm may have eventually been transferred anyway. According to a 1948 report completed by superintendent John C. Dolan, both MR-Concord and Charlestown State Prison were hoping to "relieve overcrowding." Instead of simply transferring hundreds of men to Norfolk, the three prisons took a triangular approach to the initiative. At first, over a hundred men were transferred from Charlestown to MR-Concord. Now overcrowded, MR-Concord's transfer board spent 1948 reviewing a total of "421 cases," Malcolm's being one of them. Out of those, a total of 215 men were transferred to Norfolk,[45] more than 50 percent.[46]

Though, even with the high percentage, Malcolm may have needed all the help he could get. His prison record wasn't stellar. From being a "poor and uncooperative" worker to having four instances of "shirking," Malcolm wasn't exactly a model Norfolk prospect.

On March 25, 1948, Malcolm was interviewed by the Norfolk transfer representative. Three days later, he wrote to Ella, expressing his doubts: "I really don't think I'll be transferred but one never can tell. I want to go down there pretty badly, and I have long learned that the things one wants most just never come. I don't know whether it would help if you were to appear at the state house this week in my behalf, but it certainly wouldn't do any harm."[47]

Unknown to Malcolm, Ella's bribery offer to Shag Taylor and subsequently to a local judge helped expedite his transfer.

Years later, Malcolm gave his half-sister all the credit: "In other prisons, convicts often said that if you had the right money, or connections, you could get transferred to [Norfolk,] whose penal policies sounded almost too good to be true. Somehow, Ella's efforts in my behalf were successful . . . and I was transferred to Norfolk."[48]

Finally, after two hard years of prison, Malcolm Little, cigarette-free and pork-free, was going to finish his education.

FIGURE 7.1. Norfolk Prison Colony. 1951. Photo found in Henry Wooldredge's unpublished undergraduate thesis at Dartmouth.

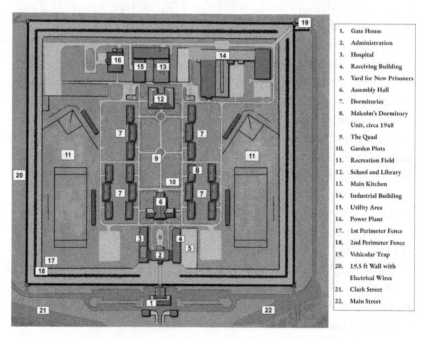

1.	Gate House
2.	Administration
3.	Hospital
4.	Receiving Building
5.	Yard for New Prisoners
6.	Assembly Hall
7.	Dormitories
8.	Malcolm's Dormitory Unit, circa 1948
9.	The Quad
10.	Garden Plots
11.	Recreation Field
12.	School and Library
13.	Main Kitchen
14.	Industrial Building
15.	Utility Area
16.	Power Plant
17.	1st Perimeter Fence
18.	2nd Perimeter Fence
19.	Vehicular Trap
20.	19.5 ft Wall with Electrical Wires
21.	Clark Street
22.	Main Street

FIGURE 7.2. Layout of Norfolk Prison Colony with key. 1940s.[1]
Malcolm's prison room was in the dormitory unit 2–3,
"behind [the] Receiving Building."[2]

7

THE PARADISE OF NORFOLK

March 1948 to January 1949

He who lights a candle in the wilderness may set the very heavens aflame.

—Tagore, as quoted in "Orientation of New Men," *The Colony*

ORIENTATION

On March 31, 1948—a 50-degree day with a clear sky—Malcolm Little entered a prison vehicle at the Massachusetts Reformatory in Concord and was transported 40 miles south to Norfolk Prison Colony.

Prison guards led Malcolm into the gatehouse. The gatehouse was where many of the guards lived, their weapons arsenal and shooting range in the basement and their living, dining and exercise rooms on the upper floors. Upon moving through the front doors of the gatehouse, Malcolm saw to his left visitor benches and glass cases holding "nick-nacks" for sale, such as ties and wood-carved figurines. Straight ahead was a "massive steel door" and a 25-foot-long "bullet-proof glass enclosure," behind which guards worked at desks. The prison guard traveling with Malcolm then walked up to the glass enclosure and spoke through a tiny porthole just wide enough to accept a human voice. Paperwork was then handed over.[3]

A guard behind the bulletproof glass enclosure pulled a lever, and the steel door opened.

Malcolm was taken directly through to a corridor that led out the back side of the building and through to an 8-by-10 tunnel. As Malcolm walked down this tunnel, he noticed several vents along the side walls. Harmless looking on the surface, the vents were capable of spewing "tear, sneezing or nauseating gas" in the event of an escape. Reaching the end of the tunnel, the steel door was opened by a guard standing in a tower above them, who'd been given a signal via mirror from the downstairs guard.[4]

Once through these doors, Malcolm was officially inside the colony of Norfolk. If he looked back, he'd have seen an inmate-built 19.5-foot wall made of reinforced concrete with a metal core. Atop this wall were three lines of electrical wires that hovered diagonally. If Malcolm were to attempt an escape over the wall, he'd have been electrocuted by a current of either 2,300 volts (during the day) or up to 4,400 (at night), both numbers high enough to at least triple the power of any defibrillator. Above the entrance he'd come through was an octagonal-shaped watch tower.[5]

As Malcolm continued moving toward the Administration Building, to his left and right was yet another escape deterrent—an 11.5-foot metal fence surrounding the entire perimeter of the colony. Placed 70 feet away from the wall, it was next to impossible for Malcolm to escape over these two enclosures. Even the wilder idea of secretly digging underneath the wall was nothing more than an irrational fantasy, since the wall's base was between 4.5 feet to 18 feet underground, given "the nature of the land."[6]

About a hundred feet away from the wall was a redbrick, C-shaped building. The guards brought Malcolm into the entryway of the Administration section of the building. It's here that Malcolm was fingerprinted, given a new prison number (8077), and outfitted—his new attire black pants, a white T-shirt, and a work uniform. Once processed, Malcolm was taken to one of the 66 rooms in the Receiving Building, connected to Administration.[7]

Compared to what he'd later experience, the Receiving Building was far from a warm and welcoming place. Malcolm's room had a steel door with steel walls. The floor was concrete, and his lone window had horizontal bars lined on the outside that couldn't "be cut with a hacksaw, nor broken by a stroke of the sledge hammer." Once again, escape was nearly unimaginable.[8]

Still, men did scheme. In July 1947, 9 months before Malcolm's arrival, 37-year-old Abraham Goldenberg, 15 years into a life sentence for murdering his girlfriend "because she would not marry him," had been at Norfolk for 4 years when guards searched his room and "found a wooden ladder, a rope scaling ladder, two knives and a dummy automatic pistol made out of plaster." Goldenberg had been waiting for "foggy weather" before attempting his escape over the walls. To complete the plot, Goldenberg had even constructed a life-size dummy of himself that he'd put under the sheets of his cot before risking an escape. For his punishment, he was taken from his Norfolk dormitory and placed in one of the maximum-security cells located on the top floor of the Receiving Building. Given how elaborate the plot was, Goldenberg may have still been in the same building when Malcolm arrived, his outdoor exposure relegated to walking on the fenced-in roof, the fence put in place to prevent suicides.[9]

Malcolm had far more flexibility than Goldenberg. On that first day, he was given a set of linens and told how to make his bed to avoid any trouble. Instead of joining the "desperate criminals and disciplinary cases" on the roof of the Receiving Building, Malcolm and other new fish could exercise in a fenced-in yard next to the building. It was here where Malcolm first laid eyes on Norfolk's "campus." Looking past the fence in one direction, Malcolm saw part of the rec- reation field, where Norfolk fielded a football team that played an eight-game fall schedule against other local teams. In another direction, Malcolm saw the side of one of the six dormitories he'd soon be transferred to. In front of that dormitory was a courtyard, or "the Quad" to Norfolk regulars. Bordered by at least 300 four-by-six garden plots, this was where, starting around May 1, men planted fruit and vegetable seeds. More commonly, the Quad was the social nexus of the colony, where men gathered to talk or compete over checkers and dominoes.[10]

Still, on his first day, Malcolm was taken back into the Receiving Building and served dinner in a small dining room with other new arrivals. One incar- cerated writer summed up this surreal experience of prison congeniality: "At supper [the new man] is surprised; this place isn't so bad after all. He has a table with three other men who he knows, or if he doesn't, he soon will. We all have a different tune when it comes to soup, etc. He thinks he will like it here, [and] it is the beginning of a feeling that perhaps there is hope left after all."[11]

It's unknown who Malcolm came into Norfolk with, or even whether he felt as hopeful as the writer suggests, but the act of being around men in a similar situation, sharing stories of what they'd heard of Norfolk (*They've even got a Glee Club!*) compared to where they'd done "bits" may have calmed Malcolm. And if Malcolm had any intimate knowledge of Norfolk's inner workings to share, it was Bembry's and Jarvis's own experiences he relayed.

After that first day, Malcolm was taken back across the Administration Building and to the connected hospital. He was given a medical and dental examination "as thorough as anywhere." Once cleared, Malcolm began to learn all about this new prison, a place he later said "represented the most enlightened form of prison that I have ever heard of."[12]

A BRIEF HISTORY OF NORFOLK PRISON COLONY

> One thing we [as citizens] are apt to forget is that unless a man
> is in [prison] for life, he goes out again and what you make him
> in prison is what he is when he gets out.
>
> —Howard B. Gill, *Boston Sunday Globe*, as quoted
> in Henry L. Wooldredge, "Inside the Wall of the
> Norfolk Prison Colony at Norfolk, Massachusetts"

Norfolk's creation and progressive prison philosophy was mainly the doing of Howard Belding Gill, a Harvard-educated economist. Gill, along with his mentor, penologist Sanford Bates, abhorred the treatment men were receiving at Charlestown (and to a lesser extent, MR-Concord) and believed it was a waste of time and taxpayer money to not try to reform a man properly. As Gill put it, "The ultimate aim of prisons is to return the individual to society better fitted to meet the normal demands of that society."

And, as Gill later admitted, "this is not a new principle."[13]

Indeed, it wasn't—at least not on the surface. While shaping his vision for Norfolk, Gill immersed himself in the history of America's prison systems. In particular, he mentioned the early Pennsylvania Quakers, who first decided to isolate a man so that "they might have the opportunity to contemplate their past and prepare for the future." But this forced solitude caused most men to lose their sense of "reason." Isolation protected society from the individual but not the individual from the society he was soon to rejoin.[14]

Over time, this problem was eventually identified, and a new theory of prison reform was created, called the Auburn System. Men couldn't just think and reflect all day—they needed to be put to use. In Auburn, New York, prison warden William Brittin helped to create this new system, in which men had their own cells and also a workstation. Not only did the men appreciate having a project to complete, but the prisons themselves benefited economically from their labor. From 1825 to around Malcolm's time at Norfolk, the Auburn System, after a few degrees of modification, was the national choice when designing a prison.[15]

Norfolk, however, would be different.

In his *Autobiography*, Malcolm and Haley described Norfolk as an "experimental rehabilitation" prison facility, and it was. In plain terms, Howard Gill's vision was to simulate a closed society—a microcosm of the world that awaited each man upon their release. Put another way, Gill wanted "reality" behind a wall.

It was bumpy going at first. Gill had a vision, but he wasn't a multimillionaire, nor did he have much political clout. Fortunately, he found an ally in Lewis Parkhurst, a Massachusetts senator disgusted with the continued existence of Charlestown State Prison. Parkhurst presented a bill in 1922 to build a new prison and shut down Charlestown, but he lost the vote, 19 against, 3 for, and 18 abstentions. Determined to awaken a reaction, Parkhurst lobbied among members of his own party, but "they were not interested." Prison issues always seemed to be of secondary importance. As Parkhurst continued his solo pursuit, he clung to words spoken by a bishop: "When will the dungeon fit only for the Middle Ages, the State Prison, be razed and the men who are the wreckage of society be given a house, not of despair, but of hope?"[16]

Without any political allies, Parkhurst went to the press. He composed a "letter setting forth the conditions at Charlestown and the need of a new prison in as vigorous language as [he] could command." Out of the 33 newspapers that received Parkhurst's letter, only one small local newspaper published it. So much for making waves.

Now that he was absent political support and lacked press coverage, it appeared Parkhurst's mission was about to end. And it would have for most. But Parkhurst had money, so he bought "one quarter page in each of the leading newspapers of the State."[17]

The headline read,

Massachusetts Needs a New State Prison

Whatever of strength or time or income I can possibly spare for public service will be devoted hereafter to this cause until this disgrace now attached to our Commonwealth is removed.[18]

The ad worked. Parkhurst received responses from all over Massachusetts. Local community leaders invited him to speak at public events. He did so, and after leaving office, he continued from 1923 to 1927 to raise the issue to the public and politicians willing to listen.

With the election of Governor Alvan T. Fuller and the supportive groundwork laid out by Parkhurst, the idea for a new prison finally appeared in early 1927. Governor Fuller utilized 880 acres in Norfolk owned by the state government. Fuller started modestly, approving only "a beginning" amount of $100,000 to clear the land and build the wall.[19]

What Fuller approved was, indeed, Howard Gill's vision for Norfolk Prison Colony. But the amount budgeted was miniscule, and Gill knew it'd be a constant struggle to receive state funding. He also knew he needed to keep costs not just low but eye-poppingly cheap.

Free prison labor was his best option.

Construction officially began on June 1, 1927, when 12 men from Charlestown State Prison were transferred to 10 crudely built wooden buildings near the Norfolk site. These buildings, placed in an oval, were left over from an abandoned project. Back in 1912, the land was purchased in hopes of building a mental hospital, but that was never completed. After World War I, the buildings were used as recovery centers for soldiers suffering from wounds and trauma. When Gill, his chief engineer Maurice Winslow, guards, and incarcerated men arrived, these same buildings were "ready to collapse." Swiftly, they transformed them into a construction camp complete with a main kitchen, a dining room, and living quarters. For the next five years, a circulation of around 700 incarcerated men lived at "The Oval" and built Norfolk. Of these men, 35 couldn't resist the open door of nature and attempted to run away. As Gill later reported, 5 returned voluntarily, 1 passed away, and 23 were recaught. Only 6 were able to elude capture.[20]

It's worth noting that Gill had not spent years plotting Norfolk's design. It was only after officially becoming the superintendent of Norfolk in November 1927 that he saw the plan Sanford Bates and the Department of Correction had concocted that he turned toward a progressive mindset. "They had plans for a high-rise, what I call 'medieval, monolithic, monkey-cage monstrosity' and I said so." Bates trusted Gill's opinion ever since, back in 1926, Gill refused to manipulate the data in one of his prison industries papers to benefit a cotton manufacturing business. When Bates saw how disappointed Gill was in Norfolk's preliminary design, he put the ball in Gill's court: "Bates asked me what I would propose as an alternative. I said, 'I don't know.' They gave me a couple of architects and we came up with a plan in six weeks for what was to become . . . the Norfolk Prison Colony."[21]

By the end of 1932, most of the Colony had been constructed, and by 1934, the six dormitories were complete. By the time Malcolm arrived in 1948, there were nearly 800 men around him, divided into groups of 50 and spread across five of the six dormitories. About 60 of the men were serving life sentences.

Each dormitory building was divided into three units. So if you were a new arrival, as Malcolm was, you were assigned a dormitory number and then the unit number within the building, such as 3–1, 4–2, and so on. As Gill later admitted, his design "borrowed heavily" from the Lorton Reformatory, a progressively minded prison project in Virginia spearheaded by the Roosevelt administration, designed by Snowden Ashford, and built largely by incarcerated men. "That seemed a good idea for Norfolk," Gill said, "I proposed a similar design and, to my great amazement, they accepted my plan."[22]

Gill's design owed quite a bit to the Lorton Reformatory, but his vision for rehabilitation would be far more original.

THE NORFOLK PLAN

A day or so after his examinations in the hospital, Malcolm met with Mr. Chamberlain, the senior community officer, and an orientation committee consisting of incarcerated men who'd been a part of Norfolk culture for quite a while. Their message to Malcolm was clear: no matter what you choose to do with your time here, maintain "communal harmony."[23]

This harmony was cultivated by a five-pronged approach to each man, developed by Gill and perpetuated by post-1934 superintendent Maurice Winslow:

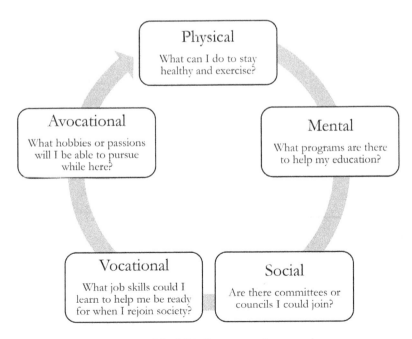

CHART 7.1. Norfolk's five-pronged approach.

Table 7.1. Vocational departments at Norfolk Prison Colony, 1948–50

Departments	Duties
Clothing and tailoring	"Make double-breasted suits, overcoats, topcoats, mackinaws, caps, baseball uniforms, coveralls, hospital and kitchen uniforms . . ."
Shoe	Sixty-one incarcerated men and four supervisors. Carts of leather are wheeled into the cutting room and then the stitching room. They also help repair beaten-up football cleats.
Metal	Two divisions. Metal 2 workers make basic wastebaskets, trash barrels, water buckets, drinking cups, water pitchers, pie plates, and metal bowls. All ends up at the painting booth. Metal 1 workers make stainless steel sinks and learn the craft of drafting, running a punch press, and power brake as well as sheet metal work.
Concrete	Men help to produce guardrail posts, anchor blocks, concrete pipes, surveying bounds, garden furniture, curbing, and cemetery vaults, many of which are sent across the state. In future years, incarcerated men would help with future highway construction.
Laundry *Malcolm's assignment*	Responsible for, among other things, washing and drying clothing and hospital staff uniforms.
Woodworking	Make, among other things, venetian blinds and brush blocks and duck nesting houses. Also make basic furniture repairs to tables, benches, and chairs.
Tobacco	Tobacco comes in 1,000-pound hogsheads, then is broken down, weighed, mixed with light flue and dark barley, then separated, blonded, and steamed. The men also make "Bull Durham."
Print Shop	Create *The Colony*, an 8- to 16-page newspaper sent out to Norfolk's gen pop but also anyone "on the outside." Rates were $1 a year for the general public and 35 cents for men at different prisons.[*]
Maintenance	General repairs and assistance across various departments.

[*] Description comes straight across numerous issues of the *Colony* in 1948 to 1949. The *Colony* was usually published the first and fifteenth of each month, and its issues can now be found via the Harvard Law School library.

Within a few days of his arrival, Malcolm was extensively interviewed by prison officials. They asked him to explain his situation at home, the vocation he hoped to pursue while at Norfolk, potential hobbies or avocational pursuits, and interests in recreation for his health. A category for "personal" was reserved for the interviewer to take notes analyzing Malcolm's personality.[24]

Sadly, official accounts do not exist of what Malcolm said during his interviews with Norfolk prison officials. It's safe to say, however, that Malcolm emphasized his immense desire to use the library. As for jobs, he was assigned to the laundry, due in part to his month of experience back at MR-Concord.

LAUNDRY AT THE COLONY

On Friday, April 9, Malcolm was finally allowed out of the Receiving Building and was walked down a sidewalk to the laundry, his vocational assignment. On his way there, Malcolm passed the Assembly Building on his left, where movie nights, debates, concerts, and other performances were held. Still on his left was the Quad, the social center point for the entire colony. It was here where many of the men worked in their gardens or sat at picnic benches playing dominoes, checkers, chess, or cribbage. Much to the annoyance of the men, playing cards were not allowed due to gambling temptations.

On Malcolm's right were the dormitories he'd soon be joining, and behind them were the baseball and football fields. Just before reaching the doors to the laundry, Malcolm passed the school building—its classes and library soon to have an enormous impact on him.

Each vocational department had its own challenges, and the laundry division was no different. The three-floor building was connected to the larger industrial structure where a high percentage of Norfolk men worked, unpaid.[25]

The issue of labor wages was tense and ongoing during Malcolm's Norfolk stint. Men incarcerated in Massachusetts had been receiving some kind of wage (a pittance, really) until 1942, when the wages stopped to support the war effort. In 1946, a law was passed in Massachusetts allowing men to once again be paid for their labor, but only on paper. Malcolm, along with all the men at Norfolk, never received a government penny for his work in prison.[26]

Almost all the laundry work was completed on the first floor of the building, with the second and third floors reserved for general workshop space.

As with Bembry and others in the auto shop back at Charlestown, and to a lesser extent Heywood Hampton and Godfrey Joiner in Concord's furniture department, Malcolm soon bonded with his fellow laundry workers simply because of how much time he needed to spend there. First, however, he needed to learn how the department worked.[27]

One man, Lester Wilkins, who worked alongside Malcolm, wrote in detail how the laundry division went about its business, focusing on a typical "early Monday morning," when, under the instruction of a "Mr. Driggers," the biggest amount was delivered.

At "about 8:30," wrote Wilkins in the *Colony* newspaper, "the truck rolls up and drops perhaps twenty-seven to thirty baskets which are then weighed in and taken to the sorting table where the clothing is sorted and checked and put into wheeled baskets." In his first few weeks on the job, Malcolm joined the rest of the workers in sorting out the articles of clothing, such as bedsheets, towels, pillowcases, shirts, pants, and "underclothing." Once separated, "John Sylvia" started the washing machines with help from a man nicknamed "Ruf" Royal. Wilkins records these names in his article, but it should be noted that some men did not want to have their actual name published in the *Colony*, since people on the outside did subscribe to it.[28]

Once the washing cycle was finished, the clumps of wet clothes were taken to the extractors and "spun damp dry." After the extractors did their job (thanks to "Johnnie Martin and Johnnie Perry"), the men's prison attire and underwear were taken to "the dry tumbler" while towels and bedding were taken to "the mangle," a machine that flattens and presses articles using dual rollers.

Once finished and dried, this again was where Malcolm and the rest of the staff joined in and helped. "Each inmate," wrote Wilkins, "has an individual box over which is his name and laundry number." This meant that in a back room were at least 800 boxes with labels such as "Little—8077." In his early days learning the laundry routine, Malcolm spent many hours sorting and folding clothes and placing them in the correct box. On Thursday, these boxes were hauled to all the dormitories, where the men picked up their clean outfits.[29]

Laundry wasn't only responsible for incarcerated men's clothing and bedding. Clothing from the Colony hospital came in separately, such as "nurses' uniforms, doctor's coats, pants, caps, etc." Any potentially infected articles were taken over to the steam sterilizer, its operation maintained by a man named Adelard Quinter.

Since hospital attire needed more attention than regular clothes, care was taken with each uniform. As Wilkins wrote, "These [uniforms, coats, pants, and caps] are sent to the hand finishers where we find 'Red' Little and Jimmie Ang who put in the pleats and finish off the collars and cuffs."

Wilkins's article came out in the February 15, 1949, edition of the *Colony*, meaning Malcolm—setting aside one month working in the kitchen, which we'll get to later—had grown comfortable enough with the group to reveal his street name on the outside, and he hadn't yet fully suppressed his last name.

The job may sound easy, but Wilkins made sure to let the reader know that the group kept busy: "In the month of December 1948, we handled twenty-five and one half tons of washing, or 77,774 pieces, from all sources, which includes the Colony and Pondville hospitals, the Oval, Farm, Gate House, Industries and the Main Colony, without a single loss. That, we think, is something to crow about."[30]

MOVING IN

We entered prison as boys. We exited prison as men.

—Malcolm Jarvis, *The Other Malcolm*

Around late April 1948, Malcolm was transferred from the Receiving Building to dormitory unit 2–3. Waiting for him was Malcolm Jarvis. It had been about 16 months since they'd last seen each other back at Charlestown, and Norfolk officials, exercising the initial trust they attempted to give all new arrivals, allowed the two former partners-in-crime to be reunited again, "across the hall" from each other.[31]

Although it had been just over two years since the burglaries, both young men were already undergoing transformations of character. In Jarvis's case, his time at Norfolk before Malcolm's arrival was a mix of ups and downs. Two weeks after his transfer from Charlestown in June 1946, he was written up for "quarreling" with an officer. Without anyone to help him, unlike Bembry for Malcolm back in Charlestown, Jarvis kept his head down and worked in the clothing department as a piece presser. He went through the motions there, interrupted by a brief two-month stint in the print shop before heading back to clothing, where he settled into a job working the sewing machine and stitching buttons to suit coats. A year passed until he was transferred to the medical division, working as a janitor. It was while here, however, that the fear of death startled him. While mopping hallways and floors, Jarvis often worked in and around the basement morgue. A "phobia" came over him, and soon after he expressed to prison officials a deep fear of contracting a disease on the fourth floor, where tuberculosis patients had been isolated and treated. Jarvis didn't mind the custodial work, but he requested a transfer out of the hospital. In February 1948, he got his wish, moving to the kitchen to work as a "garbageman." By the time Malcolm moved into unit 2–3, this was Jarvis's job.[32]

Far more important than his vocational assignment was his music, and here Jarvis had become deeply immersed in playing the trumpet and writing compositions. In fact, on April 6, 1948, Jarvis received from Boston University's Extension School the fifth section of a correspondence course he was completing in harmony and counterpoint. Also at that time, Jarvis had been a part of the prison orchestra that played on special occasions, such as movie nights (usually Friday) before the film started and as warm-up and intermission music during debates. Jarvis was the second-best trumpet player behind a professional named Al Miller, and the leader of the orchestra, Eddie McHarg, believed Jarvis was a virtuoso. In his memoirs, Jarvis remembered one confidence-boosting moment when he brought an original composition to McHarg, who went ahead and played it out on the piano. After finishing, McHarg "sat still while staring into space, deep in contemplation with a faraway look in his eyes." After a moment or two, he told Jarvis, "This isn't an ordinary piece of music. It is something much more than that. It's so beautiful and expresses so many feelings."[33]

Compared to Malcolm, Jarvis had had a two-year head-start at Norfolk, so in those early months, it was Jarvis who showed Malcolm around.

As Malcolm recalled in his *Autobiography*, "The Colony was, comparatively (to Charlestown and Concord), a heaven, in many respects. It had flushing toilets; there were no bars, only walls—and within the walls, you had far more freedom. There was plenty of fresh air, it was not in a city. . . . Each 'house' [unit] had three floors and, greatest blessing of all, each inmate his own room."[34]

Norfolk assigned Malcolm to a single room on either the second or third floor of "house" 2–3. Each man's room had a connecting cubicle, while each floor, except for the basement, had a toilet and shower room. The common (or recreation) room was on the first floor, as well as a cafeteria with a dining room. The basement, meanwhile, was a place where men could spread out and create a workspace for their avocational passions. It was also a great place to play Ping-Pong, Jarvis recalled.

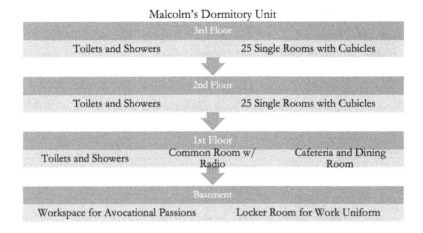

Malcolm's Dormitory Unit

3rd Floor	
Toilets and Showers	25 Single Rooms with Cubicles

2nd Floor	
Toilets and Showers	25 Single Rooms with Cubicles

1st Floor		
Toilets and Showers	Common Room w/ Radio	Cafeteria and Dining Room

Basement	
Workspace for Avocational Passions	Locker Room for Work Uniform

CHART 7.2. Malcolm's dormitory unit at Norfolk.

MALCOLM'S DORMITORY UNIT

Men were free to roam the floors of their units. If they left the building, however, they needed to pin a note to a bulletin board so that one of the two house officers knew where they were at all times. Tracking Malcolm's movements and his progress were house officers Horace Dow and George Power.[35]

For the most part, the men respected and appreciated the freedom they were given. Jarvis used the common room to sit near the radio and listen to music in the hopes of being inspired to write a new composition. Malcolm, meanwhile, was more interested in following Jackie Robinson's second Major League Baseball season with the Brooklyn Dodgers.

Food at Norfolk was prepared in the central kitchen and "then transferred in trucks through tunnels to the various dining rooms in the different buildings." In Malcolm's case, his breakfast, lunch, and dinner were transferred via dumbwaiter from the underground tunnel entrance to his unit kitchen, then presented on a "heated table" in the dining room, and served with plenty of gravy on a round ceramic plate. The dining room was a tight space of two lines of seven wooden booths built by past incarcerated Norfolk men.[36]

Malcolm had tried to stop eating pork before arriving at Norfolk, still inspired by Reginald's promise to get him out of prison. Pork at Norfolk, however, was not just a piece of meat to be discarded. It was used in a variety of ways.

Here, for example, is a list of Norfolk's daily supply of food, including the amount brought into the colony and the price for each. This was the necessary amount to serve around 800 men.

Table 7.2. One average day's supply of food—Norfolk Prison Colony

Ingredients	Amount	Price
Clams	15 gallons	3.33 per gallon = $49.95
Fish	275 pounds	0.27 per pound = 74.25
Lard	48 pounds	0.30 per pound = 14.40
Macaroni	160 pounds	0.11 per pound = 17.60
Doughnut Mix	100 pounds	0.13 per pound = 13.00
Cereal	38 packages	0.14 per package = 5.32
Milk	1158 pounds	0.05 per pound = 57.90
Sugar	200 pounds	0.09 per pound = 18.00
Onions	190 pounds	0.02 per pound = 3.80
Miscellaneous Vegetables	N/A (Seasonal choices)	29.18
Dried Peaches	50 pounds	0.14 per pound = 7.00
Black Pepper	10 pounds	0.50 per pound = 5.00
Salt	100 pounds	0.02 per pound = 2.00
Coffee	100 pounds	0.36 per pound = 36.00
Eggs	30 dozen	0.40 per dozen = 12.00
		Total: $345.40
		0.37 spent per man (on average)
		792 men as of 10/1/1948[*]

* "The Kitchen Situation," *Colony*, October 1, 1948, 13.

The ingredient to focus on is lard, which is rendered from fatty pig tissue. Especially back in 1948, lard was used to sauté fish and vegetables, and even to make bread. Malcolm's intentions may have been sincere, but it was next to impossible to avoid any semblance of pork in his meals.

EDUCATION

Norfolk's maximum-security walls and minimum-security community comforted Malcolm. Later he wrote to a friend that in a way, he felt freer than he'd ever been in the past. "Do not picture us as being in prison," Malcolm wrote. "I was in prison before entering here. . . . the solitude, the long moments of meditative contemplation, have given me the key to my freedom." In Norfolk, Malcolm had found the safest home he'd ever known. As a child, he endured poverty, starvation, and a splintering family. As a foster teen, he suffered through the indignity of being called a "nigger" by his white host family while simultaneously feeling like an outsider at school, no matter how well he performed in class. In Roxbury and New York, he let the ruthlessness of the streets define his troubled soul, but its vicious underground nearly killed him.[37]

Even in Charlestown, the conditions had been too brutal for Malcolm to thrive, and Bembry's example saved him from going mad. At MR-Concord, Malcolm suffered from a lack of opportunities, and a dangerously uninspired prison population kept him from reaching his full potential. Recalling his days living in unit 2–3, he continued, "In place of the atmosphere of malicious gossip, perversion, grafting, hateful guards, there was more relative 'culture' [at Norfolk], as 'culture' is interpreted in prisons."[38]

In Malcolm's case, Norfolk's culture started with the library, and now that he had a library card, he was allowed—after notifying his house officer or leaving a note on the bulletin board—to walk outside through the Quad to the school building, purposely located in the center of the Norfolk campus. The library was on the first floor, and compared to Charlestown and Concord, Malcolm marveled at the degree of freedom he'd been given. He could "walk up and down shelves and pick books. There were hundreds of old volumes, some of them probably quite rare. I read aimlessly, until I learned to read selectively, with a purpose."[39]

The Norfolk Prison Library had humble beginnings. As early as 1932, books for Norfolk men were delivered via a "small portable school house" located within the walls. With the Massachusetts government now invested in Norfolk's completion (and success), Edith Kathleen Jones, an employee of the State Department of Education, led a book drive and was able to secure the first thousand volumes and put in place a "modern system of cataloging."[40]

For several years, this portable library remained until the School Building was completed. Once it was, there were empty shelves to fill. Once again, longtime advocate and investor Lewis Parkhurst stepped in. While on a visit to Norfolk in 1935, Parkhurst said this: "I want to see this library completed. I intend to see that it has books, appliances and equipment the best in the country."[41]

He meant it. Pushing 80 years old at the time of this quote, Parkhurst had been Norfolk's leading private donor, and some of the long-term incarcerated men and prison officials even dubbed him the "Father of Norfolk." Nearing the end of his life, Parkhurst may have considered Norfolk's success as a part of the legacy he wanted to leave behind. Even Malcolm, somewhat dismissively, credited Parkhurst in his *Autobiography*: "Norfolk Prison Colony's library was one of its outstanding features. A millionaire named Parkhurst had willed his library there; he had probably been interested in the rehabilitation program."[42]

Quite. In January 1936, the library as Malcolm discovered it finally opened inside the school building. By February, Parkhurst had delivered over a thousand books along with a large globe and wall maps of the world. He also provided the materials and equipment necessary to set up a bookbinding area so that "worn and damaged books" could be "repaired, renovated and rebound."

The question now stands strong: Who *exactly* was Lewis Parkhurst? Was he, as Malcolm's tone alludes to, just another white millionaire throwing his money around in the hopes of not being forgotten? Why did Parkhurst turn so strongly to prison reform during his years as a senator until his death? These are valid questions, since the books in Norfolk's library eventually transform Malcolm's life, and nearly the entire collection (around 15,000 volumes) can be directly or indirectly traced back to this man.[43]

Parkhurst wasn't a stereotypical millionaire, meaning he didn't receive his fortune from his parents or aggressively pursue wealth and power ala Carnegie, Morgan, or Rockefeller. After graduating from Dartmouth College in 1878, Parkhurst became a high school principal, eventually joining Ginn and Company, a publisher of textbooks. After advancing into a partner role, Parkhurst worked as the company's treasurer for the next quarter-century. His daily thoughts were dominated by publishing a wide range of textbooks and balancing the company's budget. In the underregulated era of the Gilded Age, Parkhurst amassed his fortune simply by selling books within a rapidly expanding network of schools and colleges, and also through sound money management.[44]

By 1904, Parkhurst was married and a father of three children. His oldest, Wilder, was all set to follow in his father's footsteps. The 18-year-old had been the editor of his high school newspaper and had enrolled at Dartmouth. By the start of his sophomore year, Wilder was a "popular" student on campus, and his future seemed bright.

On September 17, 1904, however, Wilder, after "attending a performance at a Boston theatre," became ill. His appendix ruptured, and surgery was completed to remove it. Though it had seemed the worst was behind him, Wilder became sick again a week later and died.[45]

The Parkhursts were devastated. Six years later, Parkhurst gave $50,000 to Dartmouth toward a new administration building. The gift was in honor of his son, and the building was named Parkhurst Hall.

In 1912, Parkhurst; his wife, Emma; and his son, Richard, traveled to Egypt, or as he called it, "the land of the Pharaohs." His reason for taking the trip was simple: "Having been twenty-five years in the publishing business, I determined to take a good long vacation." The trip would be revelatory.[46]

On a visit to the University of Cairo, Parkhurst witnessed what he deemed the "center of Mohammedan teaching and fanaticism for the whole Eastern world." A Christian unitarian, Parkhurst still wanted to feel the pulse of other cultures and religions. Walking onto the Cairo campus, Parkhurst described what he saw in a letter to a friend: "There are ten thousand pupils here, and hundreds of teachers, all squatted on the ground in groups. It was a wonderful sight—young men and middle-aged from all parts of Africa and Asia, each nation by itself, languages and costumes strange and most picturesque; men of all shades of color."[47]

It hadn't been easy entering this sacred space of learning. Tensions had been raised due to the Italo-Turkish War being fought. As Parkhurst "looked into the room where the Turks were," he was "hissed" at several times, "and one or two sp[a]t at us as we passed." Parkhurst didn't take their anger too personally, writing that "all white men look alike to them."

Despite the friction, Parkhurst gained a wider educational perspective after visiting Arabic schools in the area, finding that the subjects taught—language, law, logic, rhetoric, and poetry—were all centered around the Qur'ān. He admired how devoted the students were, but while visiting Greece and reflecting on the classic, ancient battles led by Xerxes and the Persian empire, Parkhurst couldn't help but imagine the ramifications of a Western world dominated by the East: "Had [Xerxes been successful], there might have been no western world; and if America had been discovered by the Mohammedans, which is doubtful, instead of Harvard College and the Athenaeum Press at Cambridge there might have been a lot of fanatical priests squatted on the ground as at Cairo, trying to prove that the Koran of the fourth century contained all the law, philosophy, and religion necessary for us of the twentieth."[48]

To Parkhurst, it was wrong to have the education of the next generation bound too rigidly to the past. Still, he had a deep fascination for world culture, and by the end of his trip, he'd purchased a portion of a rare Coptic translation of the book of Luke, written in 884 CE. Upon leaving Egypt, he described the impact the country had on him: "Six weeks and three days, and every one of them sunny and pleasant, and every one full of interesting experiences. I never expect to have such a restful and interesting and instructive season again, as I certainly never have before."[49]

Parkhurst was still alive when Malcolm first entered the prison library in spring 1948. As you can probably now imagine, his book collection had been molded by a lifetime of experience. "History and religions were his special interests," Malcolm explained. When Parkhurst passed away on March 28, 1949, nearly his entire library had been shipped to Norfolk. Malcolm later wrote that "thousands of his books were on the shelves, and in the back were boxes and crates full, for which there wasn't space on the shelves."[50]

Table 7.3. Norfolk Prison Library genres from 1948 to 1950

Accounting	Economics	Food Service	Pottery
Advertising	Education	Geography	Radio
Aeronautics	Electricity	Horse Breeding	Religion
Ancient History	Engineering	Mathematics	Salesmanship
Biography	English	Mechanical	Science
Business Law	Composition	Drawing	Short Story Writing
Business Practice	Exploration	Model Making	Theology
Carpentry	Fiction and	Modern History	Travel*
Chess	Literature—*Balzac,*	Music	
Civil Rights	*Chaucer, Dickens,*	Philosophy	
Cow and Dairy	*Dos Passos,*	Photography	
Running	*Dostoevsky, Elliot,*	Park Production	
Debating	*Goethe, Gogol,*		
Drama	*Huxley, Koestler,*		
	O'Casey, O'Neil,		
	Poe, Roberts,		
	Shakespeare,		
	Stearne, Tolstoy,		
	Wilde, among		
	others.		

* For the majority of this list, see "Library Column," *Colony,* June 15, 1948, 13. Other *Colony* articles were used as well.

Back in Mason, Malcolm had access to a small school library, and in Roxbury and New York, he'd decided to submerge any educational priorities in favor of gaining respect with fellow street hustlers. For the next 22 months, this superior library became his second home.

Upon entering, and besides the wall maps and large globe, Malcolm saw something very similar to the following description written by a *Colony* writer in 1948: "The library is located in the School Building, on the first floor in a large spacious room, the beamed ceiling is high and lofty, the walls are adorned with large paintings done in oils. The lighting is excellent. The furnishings are appropriate, massive oak library tables and chairs are installed."[51]

The bookshelves lined the walls of the library, the books organized in accordance with the Dewey decimal system and maintained by George F. Magraw, Norfolk's head librarian and educational director. If a man wanted anything related to higher learning, Magraw, a graduate of the Massachusetts Institute of Technology, was their man. "When the prison gate becomes locked on a man his head is filled with rushing emotions," Magraw said several years later. "They are confused, bitter and bewildered. This is the time when they need help and need it badly. Here then is where the reconstruction program begins."[52]

Although Malcolm had started improving his grammar and handwriting as far back as Charlestown, he was still unsatisfied with the letters he wrote. When it came to street slang, he could write for pages, but he'd started to take a more serious communicative turn in his correspondence. While family members continued to write to him about Elijah Muhammad and the benefits of joining the Nation of Islam, Malcolm had started completing Elementary English and Rhetoric assignments given to him by Magraw:

> Many who today hear me somewhere in person, or on television, or those who read something I've said, will think I went to school far beyond the eighth grade. This impression is due entirely to my prison studies.
>
> It had really begun back in the Charlestown Prison, when Bimbi first made me feel envy of his stock of knowledge. Bimbi had always taken charge of any conversation he was in, and I had tried to emulate him. But every book I picked up had few sentences which didn't contain anywhere from one to nearly all

of the words that might as well have been in Chinese. When I just skipped those words, of course, I really ended up with little idea of what the book said. So I had come to the Norfolk Prison Colony still going through only book-reading motions. Pretty soon, I would have quit even these motions, unless I had received the motivation that I did.

I saw that the best thing I could do was get hold of a dictionary—to study, to learn some words. I was lucky enough to reason also that I should try to improve my penmanship. It was sad. I couldn't even write in a straight line. It was both ideas together that moved me to request a dictionary along with some tablets and pencils from the Norfolk Prison Colony school.

I spent two days just riffling uncertainly through the dictionary's pages. I'd never realized so many words existed! I didn't know *which* words I needed to learn. Finally, just to start some kind of action, I began copying.

In my slow, painstaking, ragged handwriting, I copied into my tablet everything printed on that first page, down to the punctuation marks.

I believe it took me a day. Then, aloud, I read back, to myself, everything I'd written on the tablet. Over and over, aloud, to myself, I read my own handwriting.[53]

A decade and a half later, Malcolm said this to an audience: "I finished the eighth grade in Mason, Michigan. My high school was the black ghetto of Roxbury. My college was the streets of Harlem. And my master's was taken in prison."[54]

Indeed, prison was his graduate degree, and his advanced studies were just beginning.

ONE MORE HUSTLE

In May, as Malcolm settled into his vocabulary-building exercises, Jarvis dealt with some heavy news. His wife, Hazel Register, had passed away on May 6, 1948, leaving his two sons without a mother and their father still stuck in prison. Norfolk adhered to the common prison "next of kin" standard, so

Jarvis was able to leave Norfolk in a vehicle and was taken to the funeral ceremony where he saw his two boys, who were living with his parents in Roxbury. Hazel's passing must have affected Jarvis, especially after he spent so many years agonizing over her mental health (she'd been diagnosed with a form of schizophrenia). In February 1947, Jarvis had sent an emotional letter to Hazel, "telling her that he is not dependable," according to Norfolk prison officials who opened the letter before sending it out, "and for her to get a divorce from him as she is still young enough and beautiful enough to re-marry and enjoy the good things in life which he was unable to give her." Having also attended one funeral while in prison for a grandfather he'd loved dearly, Jarvis felt the clock of mortality ticking.[55]

At Norfolk, an intensity to *improve themselves* dominated the prison lives of both Jarvis and Malcolm. In one room, as Malcolm worked on his assignments, pacing back and forth as he reread and recited the dictionary, Jarvis threw himself into music, creating musical scores and entering songwriting contests. "For three years," he'd later write to his mother, "I have slaved to study and I have written music until my fingers were about to drop off."[56]

They didn't spend all their time studying, however. For exercise, they chose the gym, and in late May and early June, there were plans being made to put together a boxing event. Both men were interested in helping out.

Malcolm had mainly dismissed the idea of team sports. Norfolk's predominantly white football and baseball teams didn't appeal to him. Boxing, however, had been a part of his life ever since he sparred with Philbert back in Michigan, helping his brother prepare for fights in his Golden Gloves tournaments, not to mention Malcolm's three bouts back at MR-Concord. After spending long stints filling in his tablets and working on his "word-base," Malcolm needed some exercise. Punching bags and jumping rope worked as an outlet. "Malcolm was a fighter from the word go," Jarvis said, referring not so much to their Norfolk days but instead to their time together before prison. "Contrary to popular opinion, Malcolm was a very good boxer. In a minute flat, he could deck the average street thug."[57]

The best boxer in Norfolk at the time was Boise Phillips, 23, a Black 5'5", 160 lbs. former sailor on the back end of a 10-year armed robbery sentence. In the early morning in October 1943, Phillips, then 18 and needing money to get home, attacked a man with a brick while drunk, taking what was in the man's pockets. Police caught him a short time later, and he pleaded guilty, serving a short stint in Charlestown and then MR-Concord before being transferred to Norfolk in 1946.[58]

Respected by aspiring fighters for his boxing skills, Phillips was a headache for prison officials. One Norfolk guard described Phillips as "a self-centered, thoughtless, sleepy acting individual who seems to have an utter disregard for the rules of this institution. One who requires constant supervision and is untrustworthy." Indeed, Phillip's prison file is filled with infractions and disciplinary reports of fighting and insubordination.[59]

Still, his skill in the ring had other aspiring prison boxers hoping to someday go three rounds with him. As the fight card was being assembled, it became clear that whoever ended up going against Phillips would be considered the Main Bout.

According to Jarvis, there was a racial undercurrent to this event in particular. Phillips was not generally hated—he was actually helping to train anyone in the gym hoping to improve—but there was a desire to show that a white man could compete with a Black man in the ring. This was amplified by the lack of a strong white boxing champion at the heavyweight level. On June 26, the "Brown Bomber" Joe Louis was set to defend his heavyweight championship against "Jersey" Joe Walcott in a rematch in front of 42,000 fans in New York's Yankee Stadium. Malcolm, who followed Joe Louis just as much as he did Jackie Robinson, would have made sure the radio in the common room was tuned in to the fight.[60]

Even though Boise Phillips was not at the same level as the Brown Bomber, the men were excited to have an actual professional-level fighter at Norfolk. With the Joe Louis fight stoking everyone's interest, fight card organizer Jimmy Madeiros decided to turn the event into a miniature simulation of Yankee Stadium's. On July 5, the boxing ring was brought out onto the football field, giving the entire prison population a chance to watch the fight. Even tuberculosis patients could view the contest from an enclosure on the hospital roof.[61]

The white incarcerated men chose 24-year-old Warren Dewan as their best contender against Phillips. Dewan had come to Norfolk after being arrested for robbing a Forge Village mill office with three other men back in January 1947. Described by a fellow Norfolk man as a "husky" fighter, Dewan trained using the V-step footwork of Willie Pep, a professional lightweight champion. His "white team" did what they could to get him ready for Phillips.[62]

Malcolm and Jarvis soon became Phillip's Black training team, joining him in the gym and lending their support as Boise, according to one Jarvis interviewer, "chugged around the makeshift track that encircled the ball field." On June 12, Malcolm was transferred to the kitchen for his vocational assignment. The timing is interesting, since the move allowed Malcolm to work side-by-side with Jarvis. Malcolm's official job title was "kettleman," while Jarvis was still taking out the garbage. During the weeks leading up to the fight, Malcolm, charged with tasks such as boiling eggs, handed a few extra eggs to Jarvis, who smuggled them out of the back room and gave them to Boise. Since April, Boise had been training extra hard to change his "excess fat into muscle," so the protein from the eggs (which he ate raw) helped with energy and recovery.[63]

Indeed, Malcolm was deeply committed to the July 5 boxing event. In fact, on July 1, less than a week after Joe Louis knocked out Jersey Joe Walcott in the eleventh round, the Colony rushed to publish the official fight card, "subject to change . . . ," with a familiar family name in the Preliminary section.

FIGHT CARD

Norfolk Prison Colony—July 5, 1948

MAIN BOUT

Phillips—161 Pounds vs. Dewan—164 Pounds

SEMI FINAL

Lupo—155 Pounds vs. Hawkins—161 Pounds

PRELIMINARY BOUTS

Little vs. Hoynoski
Benfield vs. McDermott J.
Paul vs. Sordillo
Dean vs. Cavanaugh
Gauthier vs. D'Autiuel
Goyette vs. Bobick
Robichaud vs. Giorior

As it stood on July 1, Malcolm Little was set to go three rounds with Chester Hoynoski, a white 25-year-old veteran of World War II. Malcolm's scheduled opponent had arrived at Norfolk in November 1947. Chester, or "Chet," was an "all-around athlete" and "worked out like a cyclone" in the gym, according to two Norfolk writers. Hoynoski had been on parole back in 1942 when he was drafted into the army. He served in England, France, and Germany, returning home two years later to his wife and three children. He was angered, however, that he'd have to return to the status of a parolee. The news stung him. In July 1947, he and his older brother, Louis, had stolen a safe from a Ford Auto Sales office. While attempting to open it with a sledgehammer, a police officer nearby heard the noise and arrested them.[64]

Hoynoski was a difficult matchup for Malcolm, but here's the thing: the fight didn't happen. On July 15, the *Colony* recapped all the fights, and each bout is given at least a mention, but not Little vs. Hoynoski.

Looking into Chet's and Malcolm's prison files, the match-up seems inappropriate from a measurement standpoint. Chet, at 5'8" and 196 lbs., was much heavier than Malcolm, so Madeiros may have squashed the fight since the men were in different weight classes. One flaw to this idea is that, according to the *Colony*, the weigh-ins had been happening over one week, although they admitted that "because of a lack of space in this issue and the lateness of the weigh-ins we can not cover the possibility of other bouts or speak of other fighters in detail."[65]

If the reason wasn't as practical as weight difference, one could also argue that it was Malcolm choosing to practice his growing degree of restraint and discipline. It's easy to imagine a preprison Malcolm defying the weight discrepancy and pushing Madeiros and Hoynoski to move ahead with it, risk be damned. But the bout was no doubt a high-risk, low-reward situation. If Malcolm won, he'd still be stuck in the same acre of space as a then-aggravated Hoynoski, no doubt hoping for a rematch. If he lost, however, he risked humiliation. With his self-education plan finally beginning to unveil itself, it would have been a mistake to relive his ego-driven street-tough days in prison. Better, he may have thought, to save that mental strength and fight the etymology of "aardvark" instead of an experienced war veteran.

As for Boise, July 5 was a good day. With 750 incarcerated men, as well as guards, hospital workers, and patients, surrounding the outdoor ring, Phillips put his "camp reputation" on the line and gave Malcolm, Jarvis, and other Black men a reason to cheer and many others a moment to temporarily forget that they were behind a 19.5-foot concrete wall with electrical wiring.

The bout was so well-attended and memorable that Joel Winslow, the son of the superintendent Maurice Winslow, remembered heading up to the prison hospital's X-ray room to watch from behind a window. "It was a slugfest," he said.[66]

Colony writer Willie Roach summed up the fight: "Game but unable to stop the two-fisted attacks of his opponent, Dewan picked himself up from the canvas twice in the first round at the count of nine. Later in the second heat, a sizzling right to the mid-section by Phillips while Dewan was on the ropes, led to the final knockdown which came seconds later. On his knees Dewan attempted to rise, but couldn't quite make it as Referee Red Chapman tolled the fatal ten."[67]

After the July 5 field events, which included sprints, horseshoes, baseball pitching contests, and a "horse back race" (won by Hoynoski), Malcolm's prison life went back to a more normal routine. On July 7, he signed up for plaster work, helping to spread mortar over brick that had started to wear down. Most men liked plaster work because it gave them a chance to work outside. For Malcolm (and Jarvis, who joined later), the summer sun and clear days were a welcome break from being stuck in the industries building all week.[68]

On July 12, Malcolm was transferred back to the laundry. Now that he had accomplished his food-smuggling goal of helping Boise, there was no reason to remain in the kitchen—the most complained about department, since it carried the responsibility of feeding all 800 men. Still, in the month he spent in the kitchen, Malcolm had a firsthand view of how the food was prepared, perhaps even picking the brains of a few cooks and asking them how they incorporated pork into the meals.

The months of July and August rolled by without too much trouble. Malcolm continued to complete his English and Rhetoric correspondence course assignments (7 out of 10), and he made sure to fill out his tablets with new dictionary words, his penmanship improving with each new page. Trips to the library and writing to family and friends filled out his days.[69]

In the early summer, Malcolm received a "preachy" letter from Philbert. In it, Philbert wrote that the family was "happy to own [Malcolm] as a brother." The word *own* offended Malcolm. In his reply, Malcolm scolded Philbert, using his dictionary and rephrasing a famous quote from poet Alexander Pope to get his older brother to stop his proselytizing tone:

> Phil, I love all my brothers and sisters. In fact, they are the only ones in the world I love or have. However, never say "we are happy to own you as a brother" to me. That sounds like tolerance, which is: allowing something that cannot be helped or wholly improved. "To err is divine, to forgive, human." That makes sense to me both ways. Under no circumstances don't ever preach to me. I mean the way enclosed [in] your letters. That sounds . . . phony. All people who talk like that sound phony to me because I know that is all it is; just talk.[70]

Philbert was already attempting to bring Malcolm into the fold of the NOI at this time. Malcolm hadn't yet been moved further by Reginald, but he was beginning to distance himself from his past preprison life. "I have forgotten mostly everything that occurred before I came here," Malcolm wrote in the same letter. "What I do remember only comes back during fleeting moments."[71]

About four to five months later, on November 28, 1948, a Tuesday morning, Malcolm wrote to Philbert. The first line of his letter reads, "In the name of 'Allah,' the Beneficent the Merciful, the Great God of the Universe . . ."[72]

What changed?

During these many months, Malcolm experienced an educational and religious awakening so profound it changed his life.

SCHOOL AND TEACHERS

On September 7, 1948, Malcolm joined the prison school educational program. His timing was fortunate. George Magraw had been looking to set down a more organized and high-level school program, one that benefited men just as much as the more attended and properly funded industrial program. Malcolm, being 23, enrolled voluntarily; if he had been under 21, the prison would have required him to take the classes.[73]

At the start of the school year, there were an estimated 124 students divided into five categories. The first and most introductory level was the "Americanization" class, reserved primarily for immigrants and/or second language students and taught by two incarcerated men. Basic citizenship rules and survival English made up most of the curriculum. In May 1948, a Norfolk reporter wrote that there were "15 men in the school with one common interest: the desire to learn; this has molded the whole class into a friendly, interested group."[74]

The next two sections may have been lumped together due to a lack of faculty or enrollment. "Elementary" served men who'd completed school up to the fourth grade, and "Intermediate" meant the student had completed either the fifth or sixth grade. Topics such as history, English, and basic math were covered. The math class, taught by Dr. Hester, was described by a *Colony* writer this way: "Wandered into the mathematics class in the School Building where Dr. Hester was attempting to clarify the common denominator situation and succeeding very well for most of the class. The class distinctly divided itself into sections: The men who were working along with the Doc in an attempt at reaching an answer . . . the men who were coasting along but assimilating the knowledge . . . and the men who didn't much care about common denominators. Now it's a funny thing about fractions . . . you can't ignore them and expect to live a sane life."[75]

The final two sections were Malcolm's territory. "Junior" consisted of men who'd completed the seventh, eighth, or ninth grade, with "Senior" covering the tenth and eleventh. Seeing as how Malcolm had left Mason, Michigan, midway through the ninth grade, he was assigned to the Junior High section, with classes ranging between 6 and 10 students.[76]

Magraw had organized the schedule so that there were morning and afternoon classes, the morning ones being the most attended. From Monday to Friday, Malcolm attended class from 8:00 a.m. to 12:15 p.m. Subjects taught were history, literature, and civics, with math as an option. During breaks, students were allowed to step outside and have a smoke, cigarettes being available for purchase from the Gate House store.

It's important to know how deeply committed Magraw was to improving an incarcerated man's educational life. "Working with inmates," he said in 1955, "is the most satisfying work in the world. These are men who have literally run out of friends. Many of them have nowhere to turn. They are always looking for a straw at which to grasp. If you can show them a way to rearrange their lives so they can begin [again] and have a secure future[,] they're most sincere in their desire to try."[77]

From September to late December 1948, Malcolm was ready to try, and his prison schedule was now packed. At 6:30 a.m., a morning bell rang loudly throughout the dormitories. Men were given 15 minutes to use the bathroom, put on their clothes, and be seated in the dining room for breakfast. Tables were individually called up to where the warm food was served. The first time around, men were given similar portions of bread, eggs, and coffee. After everyone had been served, and if there was enough food left, house officers offered seconds.

After breakfast, Malcolm headed to the school building, walking up a flight of stairs to the second floor, where classes were held in rooms with "blackboards of the latest design and chair-desks." Since Malcolm had stopped smoking ever since talking to Reginald at MR-Concord, he had time to peruse the library aisles for something interesting. Over in the Assembly Building was the prison store, where men could purchase "ice cream, candy and cigarettes," the transaction recorded on slips of orange paper and later charged to their accounts.[78]

Malcolm mainly had two male teachers, and their innovative approach to class time proved to be very important for his educational development. The first was Richard W. Nash, 27, who taught English and literature. Nash served in the US Army, loved baseball, and often called Malcolm "Brother Little" in class, according to his son. "[Malcolm] was certainly one of his most ambitious students."[79]

An article in the *Colony* newspaper shows that Nash was well-respected and delivered useful and engaging classes. During Malcolm's time in school, one *Colony* writer popped in on a literature class taught by Nash, and he described it this way:

> [I'm] in the school room which Mr. Nash so ably controls the atmosphere tingled with mental alertness. Mr. Nash is obviously an able teacher and what is more that *rara avis*, a teacher who can talk and capture the interest of the entire class. There was no fidgeting here. Each man was interested in what the teacher was saying. The subject was the use of that contrary item; an apostrophe. From the apostrophe Mr. Nash took the class through some very interesting verbal experiences covering contracts, written and otherwise. It was good practical stuff and it made the apostrophe much more interesting to survey in its relation to every day life. A good manner of teaching, and it went over. There was no day dreaming in this class, thanks to Mr. Nash.[80]

Nash also created activities built around the concepts of critical thinking. Once, his son recalled, Nash brought into Malcolm's class two articles that covered the same topic. They were "written by different people with totally different slants." Nash emphasized the importance of perspective and bias. "After Malcolm read them," his son recalled, "he and my father discussed when you read something, always remember the source."[81]

Working side-by-side with Nash was Malcolm's second teacher, John A. O'Connell, a Dartmouth grad who'd served in the navy. O'Connell was more hands-on than Nash when helping Magraw create this new five-level class structure. Both teachers worked hard to engage their students, but the contents of their classes were of secondary importance to Malcolm, who preferred self-studying and coming to his own conclusions. In Nash's, Malcolm may have asked questions about Shakespeare's plays, since he'd been grappling with the Bard's works since his time with Bembry and *Macbeth* at Charlestown. O'Connell, meanwhile, was a source of contemporary governmental knowledge as well as history.

O'Connell shared memories of having Malcolm as a student. "He didn't think [Malcolm] was supposed to be there," remarked his son. In Malcolm, O'Connell saw "a man who had a great future" ahead of him. The 24-year-old Ivy League grad could see rather quickly that Malcolm was "extremely bright" and "always looking to learn more." O'Connell had earned his master's degree from Teacher's College and often expressed to his children that "a lot of problems in the world" were simply from a lack of education.[82]

Most importantly, Malcolm's two teachers wanted to challenge their students more directly. Lecturing about the apostrophe or discussing the aftermath of World War II may have been interesting enough to kill some time, but the two teachers—O'Connell especially—wanted to give the men more authority over their own education.

CLASSMATES

So who were the men surrounding Malcolm? By cross-checking last names in the *Colony* with the *Boston Globe*, we can piece together at least three students who participated in the same "Junior" level morning class as Malcolm, all of whom were white.

To start with, there was 48-year-old Frank Kearney. Back in 1941, Kearney was caught close to "the Mexican border" after "eluding authorities" for 17 years. Back on New Year's Eve in 1924, Kearney "and a companion" held up a tailor shop. Kearney attempted to hit the tailor, Harry Hamberg, over the head with his gun, but it "accidentally discharged" as he struck him. The tragic blunder turned Kearney into a global hobo, as he evaded capture by traveling to "Europe, South America and Mexico."[83]

Also around Malcolm was 28-year-old Nathaniel Cavagnaro, who was serving time after being charged with 10 counts of B&E&L. A part of a local gang, Cavagnaro was caught after taking $32 off a taxi driver. Eventually admitting to a series of breaks, Cavagnaro pleaded guilty, and Judge Allan Buttrick, only three months after sentencing Malcolm and Jarvis to 8–10 years, gave Cavagnaro 3–5 years.[84]

Then there was Stephen Antosz, 28, a former "brush shop" worker. One night, while out celebrating with a friend who'd just become a father, the pair, both married, offered to drive a 21-year-old woman home when she was waiting at the bus stop. She accepted the ride. After making a brief stop for drinks, the three went back into the car, but the woman began resisting both men. Antosz and his friend assaulted the girl and then threw her out of their car in the middle of the night. For this, Antosz and his friend were given 7–10 years for assault with intent to rape.[85]

It's unknown how well Malcolm knew these men and the crimes they committed. Perhaps he didn't want to know. But in that classroom, each man hoped to turn the page and start anew, and there was one activity all of them had in common. As their teachers soon discovered, the men wanted to debate. So, on Fridays, Nash and O'Connell began to work with the Norfolk Debating Society and incorporated debates into their curriculum.

THE NORFOLK DEBATING SOCIETY

Malcolm may have first heard about the nationally recognized Norfolk Debating Society from Bembry, since his first prison mentor had been an active member back in 1944. But the debate club's immense reputation had been clear to Malcolm from the moment he picked up an issue of the prison newspaper. In the April 1, 1948, edition of the *Colony*, there on page one is an editorial from an incarcerated man venting about a heckler who interrupted a recent debate against a local university. In that same issue was a note stating that the debating team was mentioned in the March 8 issue of *Time* magazine. By the time Malcolm arrived at Norfolk, the debating team had made national headlines. To each of the 800 men at Norfolk Prison Colony, the debating team's success was a way of showing the general public the importance and potential of educational development behind prison walls.[86]

There had been a debating team at Norfolk Prison Colony ever since 1931. In those early years, two individuals were fundamental toward its founding and development—Cerise Carmen Jack and Albert J. Farnsworth.

Ms. Jack should be given credit for the debating club's creation. Cerise, or C.C., was married to a Harvard environmental professor, and had made newspaper headlines as a progressively minded critic of Woodrow Wilson and as a vice president of the Birth Control League of Massachusetts, a forerunner to Planned Parenthood. But what attracted Cerise toward prison reform was the controversial 1921 Sacco-Vanzetti murder trial. Believing the two Italian Americans were innocent, Ms. Jack contributed a hundred dollars to their legal counsel. While they were incarcerated, Ms. Jack also visited the men and sent them fruit baskets and letters of support before they were executed amid proclamations that as immigrants they were being treated unfairly.[87]

Ms. Jack became involved with the Norfolk Prison Colony during Howard Gill's tenure as superintendent, and she, according to former Norfolk debater and scholar Thomas Vigrolio, "wanted to encourage prisoners in their educational pursuits."[88]

One of the first Norfolk prison debaters to create headlines was 33-year-old John H. Robinson, who'd been the chairman of the debating club in 1935. Two years into a five-year sentence for writing bad checks, Robinson had learned the art of debate and studied law behind bars to such a point that he chose to be his own lawyer during his appeal. He lost, but his "eloquence" impressed the judge and the press covering the trial.[89]

Ms. Jack's death in 1935 left the club to Mr. Farnsworth, a life insurance executive who'd been volunteering his time at Norfolk one day a week ever since 1932. With skilled debaters such as Robinson, Farnsworth helped to arrange debates with local organizations, the first being the Young Men's Hebrew Association (YMHA) in June of 1936. Losing by a thin margin, word started to travel to colleges that the prison had a competitive debate team looking for challengers. Soon, MIT and Harvard decided to enter the prison. One can imagine why—for young men looking to strengthen their character and overcome fear, there was no better place to do so than on a stage with a well-educated convicted felon.[90]

By 1948, the debating team had gone up against Suffolk University, Boston University, Brown, Princeton, and Holy Cross, to name a few. Eventually, debating teams from England's Cambridge and Oxford University sent young men to the prison, only for them to come away with a loss and a newfound sense of humility.

There was one young female debater from Boston University who braved the potentially hostile crowd and competed against Norfolk. Her name was Bernadette Martocchio, and for three years in a row, 1946, '47, and '48, she competed against Murdo Margeson, the chairman of the team. Norfolk won each time, and Martocchio, a law student, endured "unfavorable comments" made by several of the 700 men in attendance. But by the end, one *Colony* writer revealed how impressed he was with the young woman, describing her argumentation skills as "sharp and to the point. . . . Miss Martocchio . . . has given us some interesting moments as the leading debater of her team."[91]

Malcolm Little entered Norfolk just after Martocchio's final debate, and the list of expert prison debaters in front of him was long. By the fall of 1948, there were at least two men in their early thirties who had several years more experience than anyone else at the colony. In his *Autobiography*, Malcolm called them "walking encyclopedias."[92]

NOS. 1 AND 2 ON THE DEBATE TEAM

At the top making the decisions was Murdo Margeson, born on August 1, 1918. Murdo had been getting into trouble ever since he was eight years old, when he was fined for "malicious mischief" in Nova Scotia. In school, he made it to the seventh grade before "failing" all his classes and dropping out. Soon he dropped into gang life, and after being arrested for a B&E&L in the nighttime at 15, Murdo was sent to the Shirley Industrial School, where he joined other "juvies" as they learned different trades such as plumbing and carpentry. But Murdo wasn't interested. He frequently ran away, briefly stealing cars, only to be returned to the school.[93]

But on October 28, Murdo, now 17, once more ran from the Shirley Industrial School, hopping onto a moving train that ended up in Vermont.

He hitchhiked back home, but he didn't stay long. With a friend, Murdo wanted to secure enough funds to rent an apartment far from his home and Shirley. At 7:00 p.m., Murdo and his friend climbed up onto the roof of a liquor store and forced open a skylight. They hopped down to the floor and grabbed "five quarts of wine and some pennies" that added up to around seven dollars. Not exactly the haul they were looking for.

Trips in and out of trouble continued, until August 5, 1937. Murdo, along with an accomplice, robbed three Chinese-owned laundromats. The judge, seeing the long record of the 19-year-old, gave him 8–10 years in Charlestown. "Holding up people to get money," an interviewer wrote in Margeson's prison file, "gives him a thrill which no other activity seems to afford."[94]

Murdo's sentence was doubled when, eight months later, after being transferred to MR-Concord, he attempted an escape in the middle of the night. Two other men concocted the scheme while staying in the hospital. One of them went to the toilet and acted as if he passed out. The officer on duty, William Searle, went to check on him in the stall, but Murdo and another man came at Searle with a shiv in Margeson's pocket, a "scrubbing brush," and a "porcelain mug" from the dining hall. For 10 minutes, the three men and Searle fought each other, and the men eventually overwhelmed the officer, tying his hands and feet and taping his mouth shut. They attempted to file the bars, but they didn't have enough time. Other officers came, and Margeson went back to his bed, attempting to play dumb. Unfortunately for him, Officer Searle, despite suffering "nine scalp wounds . . . [that required] fifty stitches" and head trauma that lasted the rest of his natural life, still had the mental faculty to recall who assaulted him. Just like that, Murdo's sentence was now 16–20 years.[95]

Perhaps it was the undeniable fact that he could no longer escape the institution, or that he was to spend at least the next decade in prison, but Murdo turned toward self-improvement and education. He took correspondence courses, learned welding and Spanish and in 1944 was transferred to Norfolk Prison Colony. He became a voracious reader, soon taking on the editor position for the *Colony* newspaper.[96]

And yes, he debated. In a way, he'd been debating his position most of his life. He had a loving mother and a father who managed his own business but kept himself emotionally distant from Murdo. In his 137-page prison file, it's unclear why Murdo developed such violent tendencies. Murdo had even been sent briefly to Bridgewater (the "nuthouse," as Malcolm knew it) to see if he suffered from psychopathic tendencies. But nothing stuck. For Murdo, the one strength he knew he had was debating. In one day, he could convince one guard that he was polite and considerate while another guard called him a "master at killing time." Murdo could place a debate crowd in the palm of his hand, "holding them up" in awe of his persuasion.[97]

The other member of the debating society that Malcolm needed to impress was 34-year-old Russell B. Noble, a good friend of Murdo's and possibly one of the most self-educated men at Norfolk.

In February 1931, Noble, an orphan, was an upstanding 17-year-old honor student. He attended Sunday school, delivered newspapers, and had a part-time job as a florist. Noble's plan was to save enough money for tuition to attend a local college. He had looks—many compared him to bright-eyed teen idol singer Rudy Vallee—but he may have placed too much pressure on himself to be a "model student." At school, he'd overseen collecting funds from students to make a class book, and he also needed a bit of money to pay for his own class pictures. Instead of touching the $150 in his bank account set aside for college, Noble (his older brothers perhaps egging him on) had the idea to break into one of the rich Haverhill homes he'd been delivering newspapers to for the last six years. One stuck out—the home of 39-year-old widow and socialite Clara Clement Ellis.[98]

Russell took a different approach to his break-in than Malcolm. First, Russell went to the library and read a *Back Bay Murder* Mystery book. The story helped him form a vague plan. First, he took shears from the floral shop he worked at, then he grabbed a hammer and flashlight from his aunt's basement. Believing Ellis would be asleep, Noble came in through an unlocked parlor door at around 1:00 a.m. He wanted something expensive he could sell to cover his two school expenses. He walked through rooms silently, then opened the door to Ms. Ellis's room. She was sitting up in her bed with a lamp light on when he entered. Ellis, shocked, threw the lamp at Noble, striking him and causing the room to go dark. She stood up to confront him, but all it took were two strikes of his hammer, and Ellis fell to the floor, unconscious. Russell left, grabbing a "white gold wrist watch" on his way out. As for Ellis, her maid discovered her the next morning, still unconscious. Two days later she was dead.[99]

The *Boston Globe* published the details of the wristwatch. A day or so after the robbery, Noble was identified as having Mrs. Ellis's watch in his possession.

Like Malcolm, a watch had been his undoing.

It took three hours of questioning, but Noble, especially after learning of Ellis's death, pleaded guilty to second-degree murder. If he hadn't, he'd have been charged with first-degree murder, the electric chair a possibility.

Noble was given a life sentence and taken to Charlestown, one of the youngest lifers in Massachusetts history. The case grabbed headlines in the *New York Times* and shocked the Haverhill community.

For the rest of the decade, Noble stayed at Charlestown. If he didn't end up being the model student, he did become a model prisoner. By 1933, he'd started working on a book that argued against the idea of capital punishment, asking friends and relatives to bring him research to support his opinion. Over the years, he completed the equivalent of five degrees via correspondence courses. When a popular prison chaplain, William Whitney, retired after 25 years, it was Noble who pooled together enough funds from other incarcerated men to give him a gift. "When you go home, Mr. Whitney," Noble said in the Charlestown chapel, "you will find a nice studio couch as a token of our affection for you and deep appreciation of your help."[100]

By the time Malcolm met Noble at Norfolk, the "lifer" had served 17 years in prison and had been debating for at least the last 3 years. He'd learned how to be a printer and spent most of his time reading in the library and repairing book bindings. It's unknown if any *Back Bay Murder Mystery* books made their way into his hands again.

MALCOLM WATCHES HIS FIRST PRISON DEBATE

On October 7, 1948, Malcolm and 30 other men crammed into the Council Room for the first meeting of the Norfolk Debating Society. Murdo Margeson announced to the group that there would be 15 club meetings "every other Thursday night." Murdo hoped for at least four outside debates, with the Norfolk team to be chosen "from the inside members."[101]

For the newbies in the crowd lacking public speaking confidence, Murdo emphasized that "no member has to talk at all if he doesn't care to." Members could help the chosen debaters with "research" and at each meeting provide "constructive criticism."[102]

With that out of the way, a debate had already been organized and prepped so new members such as Malcolm could watch and comment on it. The debate topic was an issue everyone in the Council Room could relate to:

Do you agree or disagree:
Society provides ample opportunity for the released inmate to
make good.

Two men—Joseph "Mo" Mahoney and Rupert "Russ" Newhall—took the
affirmative while Alan Locke and Roland Bradbury were given the negative. In
place of scoring or judges, the audience decided who was the most convincing.

Mahoney was the most experienced debater, and perhaps because of this,
he was given the Sisyphean task of defending a society that had decided
through its imperfect system to put every man in front of him in prison.
Still, Mahoney tried, using his wit and popularity as an adequate joke-teller
and kitchen manager to make his case, drawing no doubt from his practice
in previous debates. His partner, Russ Newhall, was a first-timer, doomed to
hang out behind Mahoney's veteran shadow.[103]

On the other side, Bradbury, 30, was known for his "immense vitality" on
the football and baseball fields, but that did not necessarily translate to the
debate stage, where verbal conviction was the key to victory. His partner, Alan
Locke, had been recruited to the Debating Society after delivering a "soap
box oration" among a crowd outside the yard after the state government had
passed a "Good Work Time Bill" that benefited the men.[104]

For Malcolm, seeing this live debate was a revelation. For several months,
he'd lived a "hermit"-like existence, reading books, listening to classroom lectures
from Nash and O'Connell, and writing letters to friends and family. As he'd
later admit, "My reading had my mind under like steam under pressure." As he
watched Mahoney struggle to debate the affirmative (*Parole offers the ex-convict
many advantages . . .*) in front of a groaning audience and then Locke attempt
to bring the crowd to his side (*They give us 10 bucks, a suit, and kick us out of
here. . .*), he grew more convinced that he could hold his own up on that stage.[105]

After it was over, Malcolm and 24 other men signed up to participate in
the next debate. Out of the group, Murdo chose eight, four on each side—
Malcolm being one of them. The topic was a hot one, given that the 1948
presidential election was only a month away. One side was assigned the
Democratic party platform (Harry Truman), while the other would argue in
favor of the Republican platform (Thomas Dewey).

Malcolm was given the Republican side. Originally scheduled for
October 21, the official debate ended up being one week later. Malcolm had
three weeks to research and prepare his case.[106]

Out of the three other members on his team, Malcolm knew one of them from his time back in Charlestown: John Noxon, the Harvard-educated lawyer who'd survived a close call on death row by calling on his connections with men of influence. Since then, Noxon had his sentence reduced multiple times. In fact, Noxon would soon be released from prison in January 1949. From death row to a free man in four and a half years.[107]

In his *Autobiography*, Malcolm explained Noxon this way: "A celebrity among the Norfolk Prison Colony inmates was a rich, older fellow, a paralytic, called John. He had killed his baby, one of those 'mercy' killings. He was a proud, big-shot type, always reminding everyone that he was a 33rd-degree Mason, and what powers Masons had—that only Masons ever had been U. S. Presidents, that Masons in distress could secretly signal to judges and other Masons in powerful positions."[108]

Malcolm must have shaken his head at the trajectory of Noxon's prison time. But as for this debate topic, the politically active and well-connected lawyer was the ideal partner.

REGINALD OPENS HIS EYES

It was around this time when Malcolm was visited in the afternoon by Reginald, now 20 years old. Malcolm's younger brother appeared somewhat changed. He hadn't seen him since his transfer from MR-Concord, but Malcolm had continued to resist cigarettes and pork as much as he could. After receiving countless letters from Philbert, Wilfred, and Hilda asking that he begin his commitment to the Nation of Islam, Malcolm "was really keyed up to hear the hype he was going to explain."

Of all his siblings, it was always Reginald who knew Malcolm the most. They'd shared long and hungry walks to bakeries during their childhood, dodged trouble using their "street-hustler" mindset in New York and Boston, and endured the pain of a police system stacked against them.

But on this day, Reginald seemed in Malcolm's eyes to be "carefully groomed." His demeanor had changed, and at the start of his visit, he pushed his older brother into a state of impatience, sharing small talk about "family" and "what was happening in Detroit [and] Harlem."[109]

Most pressing to Malcolm, however, was the pork and cigarettes. What was the story behind Reginald telling him to quit them?

Reginald stopped speaking in an "offhand" manner. Then, as Malcolm later put it, "he said, finally, as though it had just happened to come into his mind: 'Malcolm, if a man knew every imaginable thing that there is to know, who would he be?'"

Ah, this "indirection." Malcolm had seen this approach before from "Reg." Whereas Malcolm preferred to be strong and "direct," Reginald had learned how to gain Malcolm's attention more through rhetorical curveballs. Reginald's style "often irritated" Malcolm, but at the moment, he had nowhere to go, so he played along. "Well, he would have to be some kind of a god."

"There's a man," Reginald said, "who knows everything."

"Who is that?"

Reginald continued. "God is a man. His real name is Allah."

Immediately, Malcolm remembered one of Philbert's "preachy" letters that mentioned the name "Allah." Instead, however, "I just listened." This wasn't Philbert being overbearing and judgmental, or Wilfred giving paternal advice, or Hilda imploring Malcolm to listen more closely. This was Reg . . . his closest brother, and he was "putting me onto something."

Reginald started with a number: 360, or "the sum total of knowledge." God, in a way.

But there was a force against God, a devil. As Reginald explained, "The devil has only thirty-three degrees of knowledge—known as Masonry." Within these limits of power, "the devil uses this Masonry to rule other people."

Malcolm sat confused, but he waited as Reginald unraveled his abstract tale.

Reginald mentioned a man, an American named Elijah, "a black man, just like us." God had spoken to Elijah. The message was direct: "The devil's time was up."

Then Reginald started to come back onto Malcolm's radar. "The devil is also a man."

Malcolm reacted. "What do you mean?"

It was at this point, as Malcolm retold the moment years later, that Reginald, "with a slight movement of his head," turned Malcolm's attention toward other men at Norfolk talking with friends or family. It's possible Malcolm knew their names, even what sports they played or what clubs they'd joined.

"Them," Reginald said to Malcolm. "The white man is the devil."

The profundity of that sentence left Malcolm gobsmacked. Of course, he'd often been angry or ambivalent toward white people, but they hadn't all been devils.

"Without any exception?" he asked Reginald.

"Without any exception."[110]

The social welfare workers in Michigan. Mrs. Swerlein and her casual use of "nigger." Mr. Kaminska telling him he couldn't be a lawyer. Beatrice and Joyce throwing him under the bus. Judge Allan Buttrick (a thirty-second degree Mason) giving Malcolm and Jarvis 10-year sentences. Their faces flashed across his mind.

Several days later, Reginald spent another afternoon with Malcolm, talking "for two solid hours about the 'devil white man' and 'the brainwashed black man.'" The seed had been planted. Reginald had shown Malcolm a new way of looking at the American system that had pushed him toward jail. Reginald, knowing he had Malcolm's full attention, became more direct. "You don't even know who you are. You don't even know, the white devil has hidden it from you, that you are of a race of people of ancient civilizations, and riches in gold and kings. You don't even know your true family name, you wouldn't recognize your true language if you heard it. You have been cut off by the devil white man from all true knowledge of your own kind. You have been a victim of the evil of the devil white man ever since he murdered and raped and stole you from your native land in the seeds of your forefathers . . ."[111]

Many years later, Malcolm wrote to journalist Peter Goldman about this revelatory moment: "[Reginald was] able to convert me in five minutes. Despite my many experiences with whites, the fact that I had grown up with whites and was reared by whites and had socialized with whites in every form of their life, and even though I was in prison, I still respected whites. But when my brother told me that God had taught Mr. Elijah Muhammad that the white race was a race of Devils, my eyes came open on the spot."[112]

Interestingly, in the *Autobiography*, after talking to Reginald the first time, Malcolm went to see John Noxon, who was comfortably passing time in a "soft job" in the education building. At this same time, Malcolm may have been listening to Noxon's Republican debate points. Noxon, meanwhile, had been very frank about his status as a high-level Mason. With his mind firing on all cylinders, Malcolm recalled the following conversation:

"John," I said, "how many degrees in a circle?"

He said, "Three hundred and sixty."

I drew a square. "How many degrees in that?" He said three hundred and sixty.

I asked him was three hundred and sixty degrees, then, the maximum of degrees in anything?

He said "Yes."

I said, "Well, why is it that Masons go only to thirty-three degrees?"

He had no satisfactory answer.

Throughout October, Malcolm, Noxon, Ingalls, and Sampson studied the Republican party platform. Newspapers, books, magazine articles—Malcolm used what he could to build his case: "Whichever side of the selected subject was assigned to me, I'd track down and study everything I could find on it. I'd put myself in my opponent's place and decide how I'd try to win if I had the other side; and then I'd figure a way to knock down those points." Now that Reginald had taken his mind for a trip, Malcolm kept his own agenda to himself as he studied: "If there was any way in the world, I'd work into my speech the devilishness of the white man."[113]

MALCOLM DEBATES

In Norfolk during the fall of 1948, there was a studious hum around the School Building and dormitories. One *Colony* writer tried to describe it, stating that some of the men "are curious, for perhaps the first time, about a million items." He encouraged others to "walk around through the units and observe the men who used to run around aimlessly [but are] now in their rooms reading . . . and slightly irritated if they are interrupted." Even their manners had become more formal. "They walk up to you now with questions and opinions . . . rather than disconnected wise cracks."[114]

In October, Malcolm was in the middle of a spiritual and intellectual awakening. In the mornings, he attended classes and at night he prepared for debates. In between those dry spaces of time, Reginald's words filled his mind, and joining the Nation of Islam, back then a religious haven for disenfranchised African Americans, started to become more of a reality. In the library, Malcolm walked up and down the aisles, searching for books in some way related to *his* history—something real and undiluted. Whether it was J. A. Rogers's *Sex and Race*, or Frederik Bodmer's *The Loom of Language*, or one of the 51 volumes in the Harvard Classics set, Malcolm checked them out and went back to his 2–3 dormitory unit. "I read more in my room than in the library itself," he explained later. "An inmate who was known to read a lot could check out more than the permitted maximum number of books. I preferred reading in the total isolation of my own room."[115]

WEEKDAY PRISON SCHEDULE—
TIMES ARE ESTIMATES

Malcolm Little, Unit 2–3—September to December 1948[116]

6:30 a.m.

House officer wakes men with morning bell.

6:45 to 7:00 a.m.

Breakfast in the first-floor dining hall.

7:00 to 7:45 a.m.

Return to rooms, make beds, stand for inspection.

7:53 a.m.

Work/school whistle sounds.

8:00 a.m.–12:15 p.m.

Classes in the School Building (history, literature, math).

12:15–1:00 p.m.

Lunch back at the dining hall.

1:00–4:30 p.m.

Laundry shift; visiting hours.

4:30–5:00 p.m.

Council meetings in each dormitory unit, or recreation.

5:00–5:30 p.m.

Dinner in the dining hall.

5:30–9:00 p.m.

Library, prepare for debate, organized activities, be in dorm room by 9:00 p.m.

9:00–9:30 p.m.

Standing count by guards.

10:00 p.m.

Lights out.

*Norfolk Population, as of October 1948:
792 men, 58 serving a life term

During these months, as class topics, religion, and debate swirled through his mind, Malcolm became a voracious reader. As the guard yelled "lights out" at 10:00 p.m., he was frustrated. The guard's call "always seemed to catch me right in the middle of something engrossing."

Instead of sleeping, like most of the men around him, Malcolm went ahead and sacrificed his "20/20 vision" by clinging to the one hallway light kept on. "Fortunately," Malcolm recalled with great accuracy, "right outside my door was a corridor light that cast a glow into my room. The glow was enough to read by, once my eyes adjusted to it. So when 'lights out' came, I would sit on the floor where I could continue reading in that glow."[117]

The house officers did their leisurely checks once an hour. They were able to check through a window and see a man's entire bedroom area. If they weren't in their bed, there'd be trouble. "Each time I heard the approaching footsteps, I jumped into bed and feigned sleep. And as soon as the guard passed, I got back out of bed onto the floor area of that light-glow, where I would read for another fifty-eight minutes—until the guard approached again. That went on until three or four every morning. Three or four hours of sleep a night was enough for me."[118]

It was in these quiet, early morning hours that Malcolm connected with books. In prison, the stories he read took him out of his enclosed space. He traveled back in time, wrestling with John Milton's epic poem *Paradise Lost*, pushing through the ethereal forests of Shakespeare's words, and falling deeply into the fascinating life of Dutch-Canadian Pierre van Paassen, whose memoir had been recommended by a *Colony* writer in the October 15, 1948, issue. Reading had awakened him. As he explained later, "I certainly wasn't seeking any degree, the way a college confers a status symbol upon its students. My homemade education gave me, with every additional book that I read, a little bit more sensitivity to the deafness, dumbness, and blindness that was afflicting the black race in America."[119]

Malcolm also wanted to better understand religion. To do this, he read the Bible "continuously," hoping to find his own path to salvation.[120]

On a Friday in the middle of October, one of Malcolm's teachers, John A. O'Connell, collaborated with Murdo and organized an in-class debate. Malcolm was already preparing his argument for the Republican platform panel discussion on October 28, so he welcomed the extra opportunity to hone his public speaking skills.

Since this was outside of the Norfolk Debating Society committee, the debate was an exhibition and stands as the first time (at least on record) that Malcolm Little stood in front of a room and formally debated.

This was the topic:

> Do you agree or disagree:
> Heredity is more effective than environment.[121]

For Murdo, it was a chance to see up close the new talent who'd signed up. The idea of "nature" being more important than "nurture" was already quite broad. To add to the broadness, Murdo and O'Connell agreed that there should be "no restrictions, no qualifications, no concessions," just practice. In a way, it was a trap. By creating such a rule-free debate, Murdo was baiting the new debaters into fouling. Although the foul wouldn't be counted, Murdo would know it was a foul, and his estimation of the debater could then be privately noted. *Nope . . . that wouldn't work*, he'd think.

There were three judges designated for the debate: Murdo, Russell Noble, and Roland T. Bradbury. Mr. O'Connell assumed the responsibilities of chairman.

Malcolm had been assigned the negative, meaning that he was set to argue that a man's environment had more of an impact than his ancestry. He had two debaters on his team—Cavagnaro and Antosz—and they argued against Kearney and two other men.[122]

The debate was set: Three men on one side of the room, three on the other, three judges sitting in front, and the rest of the class listening intently as a volunteer kept time with a stopwatch, Mr. O'Connell watching the arguments unfold, hoping to learn more about his students.

Unfortunately, Malcolm's responses were never recorded, but now that we know he was the only Black debater of the six and that the issue of race was on his mind due in part to Reginald's visit, perhaps it's safe to assume that Malcolm spoke from his heart and without fear.

Malcolm's team lost—it didn't help that he'd been stuck with an inexperienced Antosz and a forgettable Cavagnaro—but Malcolm impressed Murdo, who wrote in the *Colony*, "The decision was given to the affirmative [heredity] by a close margin but [Malcolm] Little gave them a rough time of it all the way."[123]

One wonders, just *how* could Malcolm have given his three opponents—white men who were arguing that their hereditary nature was more "effective" than the nurturing of their environment—such "a rough time"?

One can only look at the books Malcolm had around him. In the first chapter of *Sex and Race*, Rogers quotes a white University of Berlin professor, who stated that "we now know that color of skin and hair are only the effect of environment and that we are fair only because our ancestors lived for thousands, or probably tens of thousands of years, in sunless and foggy countries."[124]

Regardless of what books he used to make his argument, the experience was something he'd never forget: "I will tell you that, right there, in the prison, debating, speaking to a crowd, was as exhilarating to me as the discovery of knowledge through reading had been. Standing up there, the faces looking up at me, things in my head coming out of my mouth, while my brain searched for the next best thing to follow what I was saying, and if I could sway them to my side by handling it right, then I had won the debate—once my feet got wet, I was gone on debating."[125]

On October 28, Malcolm sat with three other white men—John Noxon, *Colony* editor Ray Sampson, and E. Ingalls, who worked in the tobacco department and acted in skits—at the Republican table for a political panel discussion. This was the second official debate society meeting, so the crowd was far more inclusive. The presidential election between Democrat Harry Truman and Republican Thomas E. Dewey was only five days away, and national polls strongly favored Dewey, the governor of New York, who, coincidentally, was campaigning in and around the Boston area on that very day.[126]

There had, inevitably, been some discussion regarding the two major presidential candidates, but Murdo had decided to localize the talk. Officially, Malcolm and the seven other prison debaters discussed "the merits and shortcomings of the *state* Democratic candidates for office . . . and their platform as opposed to the Republicans and their platform."[127]

This meant, in Malcolm's case, that he'd need to learn the views of the current Republican governor, Robert F. Bradford, and the state's two US senators, Henry Cabot Lodge Jr. and Leverett Saltonstall, all of whom, like John Noxon, were Harvard graduates.

As much as Malcolm may have prepared for this discussion, this was more Noxon's moment to kiss the governor's feet. Back in September, Governor Bradford had mentioned to the press that he hadn't yet "made up [his] mind to act favorable" toward Noxon's petition requesting a pardon. It wouldn't have taken much for Malcolm to see the potential hobnobbing. One white Harvard graduate prisoner was about to be freed by another white Harvard graduate governor. Sure enough, Bradford did pardon Noxon, and the "mercy killer" walked out of Norfolk 10 weeks after this debate, on January 4, 1949.[128]

As for the debate discussion in general, one *Colony* writer who attended summed it up this way: "The Republicans were represented by Noxon, Ingalls, Little and Sampson who stressed their opinions in all sincerity towards their party. The meeting was very successful and a number of laughs were enjoyed by the members. . . . No vote was taken to decide who won this discussion but there is no doubt that the vast majority of the audience are democrats." In the end, Massachusetts did vote in a new governor, Democrat Paul Dever, and Truman, who Malcolm attempted to write to directly in June 1950, defeated Dewey—surprising many pollsters.[129]

On Thursday, November 4, the Norfolk Debating Society held another meeting in the Council Room. Once again, Malcolm had been chosen to debate, but this time he only had a week to prepare, and there were stakes. The winning duo from this debate would go on to face Clark University, a private college 40 miles west in Worcester. The Clark debate would also be held in the 800-seat Assembly Hall. Now that the debating society had made its way into *Time* magazine, they had a reputation to protect, and thanks mainly to Murdo and Russell Noble, the team had been riding a three-year winning streak, their most recent victory in late October 1948 against Holy Cross College. Winning streak or not, Murdo was determined to allow some new blood to take a shot at their prison's biggest stage.[130]

Malcolm's topic was, circa 1948, timely:

> Do you agree or disagree?
> The U.S. Government should permit unlimited immigration
>   of professionally trained Europeans.[131]

Malcolm and Frank Kearney were assigned the negative—no, the government should *not* allow all highly skilled Europeans to enter the country. Their opponents, J. O'Dell and Fred Roberts, were to argue that, yes, all "professionally trained" Europeans should be accepted by the US.

With Norfolk's debate-winning streak and newly respectable image on the line, Murdo, Noble, and other veteran debaters would have been extremely critical in evaluating the four men standing at the front of the Council Room. Were their arguments cogent? Were they delivered in a professional, palatable manner? How often did they foul?

As the *Colony* writer who attended the event described it, the atmosphere inside the Council Room was "red hot," with the debaters and audience members locked in and showing "real spirit."[132]

Malcolm and Kearney could not have had more different debate styles. Kearney was "the more serious type," and during the debate, he may have borrowed heavily from his decade and a half on the run from the police. In these years as a fugitive, Kearney had traveled extensively throughout Europe, fighting in the Spanish Civil War on the side of the "loyalists" (or "reds" to the opponents). He'd even spent time pre-1941 as a prisoner in internment camps in France and Germany. In a very hands-on way, Kearney *knew* Europe, and the *Colony* reporter wrote that he "really went to town and had plenty of logic in his argument."[133]

With the older and experienced Kearney setting a stoic tone, Malcolm offered the exact opposite. Although in his *Autobiography* Malcolm downplayed his experiences as an emcee at clubs in Harlem, Boston, and Lansing, he had brought with him to prison the ability to entertain a crowd. In his prior debates, Malcolm had often used humor to deliver his argument. The *Colony* writer in attendance that day remembered Malcolm's style and wrote that "Little as usual gave the audience a number of laughs by telling his experiences with refugees during the war years." One can imagine Malcolm recounting his days as a waiter in Harlem's Small's Paradise or at Abe Goldstein's Lobster Pond. Certainly, he had served his share of "professionally trained" but corrupt Europeans who'd fled their country during the war. *Not all Europeans are angels*, he may have expressed. *And what is so wrong with a professionally trained African?*[134]

Kearney and Malcolm's performance did not impress Murdo and the judges enough. Instead, they complimented J. O'Dell and Fred Roberts for being "well-prepared" and having an "excellent" delivery of the issue. The largest fault that Malcolm and Kearney had, according to the judges, was that they "gave their opponents plenty of grounds for action at the rostrum." If Malcolm had brought the question of race into the debate, that would have been deemed "out of bounds" by the judges, and if Kearney had been too dry in his delivery, that would mean he lacked the ability to persuade a larger audience and the three guest judges.[135]

Ten days later, on November 14, O'Dell and Roberts faced off against Clark University. It's unknown if Malcolm watched the competition in person, but the Assembly Hall was "crowded," and the Colony orchestra played music at the beginning and intermission of the debate. Earl Bartlett, a singer, "cleverly entertained the audience with his own arrangements of some popular numbers in the form of stirring vocals." O'Dell and Roberts got off to a slow start, perhaps due to a small bout of stage fright. The three judges—Boston lawyer Wendell Colson, public relations employee for the United Prison Association John Bond, and Walpole High School principal Harold A. Strout—voted for Clark University, 173 to 158.[136]

On November 26, a Friday morning, John O'Connell and, to a lesser extent, Richard Nash decided once again to collaborate with Murdo and put the Junior and Senior classes together and hold a four-on-four debate. The Junior class was represented by Malcolm, Kearney, Stephen Antosz, and one other debater named F. Lucas. The same judges—Murdo, Noble, and Bradbury—volunteered their time, scored the debate, and called fouls when necessary.

Unlike the hereditary versus environment debate, there were now established rules. Each debater "was given a ten-minute presentation period and seven minutes for rebuttal." With eight debaters and a bit of calculation, this turned out to be a long, 136-minute contest.

It was also a debate Malcolm remembered for the rest of his life.

As he explained to Alex Haley 15 years later, "'Compulsory Military Training—Or None?' That's one good chance I got unexpectedly, I remember."[137]

Indeed, that was the topic. The exact wording was, according to a *Colony* reporter, "that compulsory military training be adopted by Congress." Malcolm and his other three Junior class debaters were given the negative.

The topic was controversial. On the "outside," in June 1948, as the Cold War between Russia grew more troublesome and tensions remained high along the border of North and South Korea, US armed forces had seen a drop-off in military enrollment. Not wanting to show the Soviet Union any signs of weakness, a Selective Service Act was passed by Congress, targeting men between the ages of 18 to 26. Soon after, President Truman—troubled by the disrespectful treatment and abuse of Black war veteran, Sgt. Isaac Woodard—signed Executive Order 9981, ending racial segregation in the armed forces.[138]

During this contentious prison debate, one of the Senior class debaters brought up the Second Italo-Ethiopian War (1935–37) to support his stance that military training was necessary. During this war, Italy, under the Fascist regime implemented by Benito Mussolini, attacked Ethiopia with advanced military weaponry, including the illegal use of mustard gas, a violation of the Geneva Protocols. Ethiopia's armed forces could not withstand such an attack. As Malcolm put it, "My opponent flailed the air about the Ethiopians throwing rocks and spears at Italian airplanes, 'proving' that compulsory military training was needed."

His opponent had been trying to make a simple point. If Ethiopians had the proper arsenal and been trained in modern weaponry, they could have defended themselves more effectively.

But that wasn't what bothered Malcolm. Especially now that Reginald had given him a sense of racial clarity, Malcolm didn't want his opponent to get away with such a simplistic view of Ethiopians.

"I said [to my opponent that] the Ethiopians' black flesh had been spattered against trees by bombs the Pope in Rome had blessed, and the Ethiopians would have thrown even their bare bodies at the airplanes because they had seen that they were fighting the devil incarnate."

One of the judges—most likely Murdo—"yelled 'foul.'" Malcolm had committed a logical fallacy—something akin to a hasty generalization (as had his opponent)—by making it a "race issue." But he'd made his point. To Malcolm, the white man had always sent mixed messages, simultaneously blessing themselves while destroying others, and this hypocritical madness was something Ethiopians wanted no part of.[139]

To support his claim, Malcolm told everyone to head downstairs to the library and read Paassen's *Days of Our Years*. Sure enough, his argument did indeed have proof. In chapter 7, titled "Ethiopian Interlude," Paassen describes how the Ethiopians were victims not only of Mussolini's fascist takeover but also of France's and England's complicity after promising, via guidelines connected to the League of Nations, that they would defend Ethiopia and the Coptic Church. One passage supports Malcolm's statement. "The Pope even went so far as to recall the French Catholic missions who had worked in Ethiopia for three-quarters of a century. Thus the Vatican's complete subservience to the policy of Fascist imperialism was completely demonstrated." Indeed, the Pope had, figuratively speaking, blessed the bombs that fell, a Catholic-sanctioned attack. To Ethiopia, it was a betrayal. As Emperor Haile Selassie told Paassen, "If Mussolini were permitted to attack Ethiopia with impunity a precedent would be set up which would destroy the moral basis of international relationships and pave the way for a series of bloody wars."[140]

Malcolm may have fouled in the judges' eyes, but his side ended up winning the debate with a score of 453 to 417. The judges later wrote that "each man delivered his material with good poise and sound logic, although a few men were a little nervous when first standing at the rostrum, but they soon overcame it as they went along." On the same day, Malcolm went back to the library to check and see if Paassen's memoir was still there. As Malcolm remembered, "That book, right after the debate, disappeared from the prison library."[141]

One Black Norfolk incarcerated man, Stanley Jones, remembered Malcolm's times in front of a prison crowd and the effect his delivery had on the listeners: "I don't care what side of a debate Malcolm was on, he did an excellent job. The way he used to talk, he got a standing ovation, all the time. People listened—the issue was not whether they bought what he said or not; the fact was, he was able to get people's attention."[142]

PRAYER

Two days after the debate, on November 28, Malcolm wrote to his brother Philbert. In the last few months, he'd absorbed dozens of books, debated in front of crowds, studied the intricacies of language, and been spiritually awakened by Reginald. The letter is the first instance, as of this book's printing, that Malcolm writes of Allah.

The letter begins with an opening salve or prayer, using language that Philbert or Wilfred may have sent him in previous letters: "In the name of the 'Allah,' the Beneficent the Merciful, the Great God of the Universe . . . and in the Name of His Holy Servant and Apostle, the Honorable Mr. Elijah Mohammad. All praise is due 'Allah.'"

There is an undeniable positivity to Malcolm in this letter, a renewed appreciation for his brothers and sisters. "If you could only realize the blissful happiness bestowed upon me by the arrival of your previous letter you would write to me continuously forever," writes Malcolm. "All praise to Allah for the moisture of your letter . . . moisture that cools the dust from my thirsty soul . . . drops of Dew from that ever-flowing Spring. Please, my Brother. . . . Accept my most humble thanks."

Malcolm wrote to Philbert that he'll be attending "bible classes in here starting tonight." Already committing the Bible's stories to memory each night, Malcolm planned to "attend to let their conversations familiarize my mind with biblical incidents . . . but I [will] shout out their conclusions."

Malcolm also wrote to Philbert about the "negro mason" and "360" degrees, topics similar to the ones he brought up with John Noxon. It was a conundrum that gnawed at him. What if a Black man sells out to the white man, choosing the path of a mason, whose purpose was to prioritize individual consciousness over any kind of religious faith and favor status over helping those who'd been left behind? "I know the devils but what of those 'negroes' who call themselves masons?" Malcolm wrote. "Once they become that, isn't it impossible for them to become of the flock of sheep again? I hear they have to curse God, and once one curses God, he automatically loses his 'birth right' . . . thus a 'negro mason' ceases to be or have the rights of a black man? So wouldn't that make the darkest of the masons actually white?" For a moment, Malcolm recalls his mother Louise's reluctance to accept help from a corrupt system: "Now I can see why Mom always instructed us against the Truth . . . and she was consistent in her practices of it."

But it was the Bible that enraptured Malcolm at this point in time. Not able to send the letter out on November 28, Malcolm continued adding to it on the night of November 29 and urged his brother "to try and write more often, and remember I love to hear all you have to say, especially concerning the Bible."[143]

Norfolk made an effort to bring the Christmas holiday into the prison. The Salvation Army gave each man a gift basket, and holiday decorations were placed around the dormitories as the snow piled up. In almost every unit, a Christmas party was thrown. In unit 3–2, band leader Eddie McHarg put together a few holiday numbers with several other orchestra members. Some units celebrated with a bit of "group singing" of folk songs and Christmas carols. Some even tried a poor man's Fred Astaire dance routine.

As for Malcolm's dormitory unit, 2–3, "it was like the Western Front," wrote a *Colony* reporter, "all quiet, but the boys made a nice gesture, they donated $19.00 in candy, etc . . . for the Catholic Orphanage in Franklin, MA."[144]

By late December 1948, Malcolm wasn't interested in celebrating Christmas. Through his continuing correspondence with his siblings in Michigan, and most likely Elijah Muhammad, the religion of Islam was on his mind, and as the new year arrived, Malcolm was poised to use his second year at Norfolk to better understand his newfound faith.

But before he could devote himself to the Islamic faith, before he could put his life in the hands of Allah, he needed to commit to the act of prayer. As he'd later explain in his *Autobiography*, "The hardest test I ever faced in my life was praying. . . . Bending my knees to pray . . . that took me a week. I had to force myself to bend my knees. And waves of shame and embarrassment would force me back up."[145]

Malcolm, despite the progress he'd made in prison, the books he'd read, the classes and debate, still felt conflicted about his past. Enough time had passed, enough solitary contemplation, for Malcolm to believe that he no longer wanted to be the street hustler he once was. But could he be *better*? What kind of man did he hope to become? He'd seen flashes of a role model in Bembry, but Malcolm knew that his old Charlestown friend wasn't interested in Islam. Malcolm had been awakened by Reginald and his brothers and sisters to a religion that purposely built itself away from the American white man's oppressive system. The Nation of Islam was for the forgotten, the cast aside, the downtrodden. But for Malcolm, it was more than that. It was a *world*—a way for him to believe in himself without feeling manipulated or corrupt.

It was a second chance. "For evil to bend its knees, admitting its guilt, to implore the forgiveness of God, is the hardest thing in the world," Malcolm explained. "Again, again, I would force myself back down into the praying-to-Allah posture. When finally I was able to make myself stay down— I didn't know what to say to Allah."[146]

He would, in time. And Norfolk's library and debate, along with Philbert, Wilfred, Hilda, Reginald, and Elijah Muhammad, helped him find his voice.

The Muslim prayer involves a series of steps meant to pull you away from the society around you and into a purer state of mind. First, Malcolm needed to complete *Wudu*, or washing his hands and feet, and if possible, wear clothing deemed in his heart as uncorrupted and prepare a clean space using a rug or, perhaps, since he was in prison, a towel. Once he had prepared himself, he'd begin to offer *Salah*. To do this, as Malcolm was taught through letters and visits from his siblings, first he'd need to raise his hands, his palms facing outward and close to his ears. At this point, Malcolm's mind was still "above" his heart, so he was still in the process of intellectualizing the prayer. Malcolm would next say, "Allahu Akbar" (Allah is the Greatest). Then he'd place his right hand on top of his left and put them atop his heart. A message is spoken here softly, under his breath: "O Allah, how perfect You are and praise be to You. Blessed is Your name, and exalted is Your majesty. There is no god but You."

There were many prayers to be learned here. One line, however—"*A'udhu billahi minash shaitanir rajim*," or "I seek shelter in Allah from the rejected Satan"—was important for him to absorb as he sought to move on from his past self.

Next, Malcolm bowed, his hands on his knees, his head (intellect) along the same line as his heart (emotion). As he bowed, he said, *Allahu Akbar, Subhana Rabbiyal Adhim*, or "How Perfect is my Lord, the Supreme." He stared at the place on the ground where he'd rest his head. Before kneeling, he'd rise back up and say, "Allah hears those who praise Him . . . Our Lord, praise be to You."

Then came the difficult part. Malcolm Little—Harpy, Detroit Red, Jack Carlton, Rhythm Red, Satan, 23 years old, without a father and without his mother's attention—kneeled, his "forehead, nose, palms of both hands . . . knees, and toes all touching the floor." Three times, in this position, Malcolm's mind now *under* his heart, he'd say, "How Perfect is my Lord, the Highest."[147]

Malcolm had submitted himself to Allah, to a force greater than himself. His spiritual journey into Islam was set to begin.

8

THE FALL OF LITTLE

January 1949 to March 1950

I don't have to familiarize you with the background of my case. You know what I'm here for. It's my own fault I'm here because if I'm dumb enough to mess with those kind[s] of people, [then I] belong in here. They don't have to put any rope around my neck in order to wake me up . . . as it is, they lynched me with time.

—Malcolm to Philbert, February 1949

THE SUPERINTENDENT ENGINEER

Norfolk Prison Colony may have been Howard B. Gill's dream, but it was Malcolm's superintendent, Maurice N. Winslow, who made it into a reality.[1] After 21 years of building, maintaining, repairing, and governing Norfolk, Winslow was set to call it quits at the end of 1949. "The politics," he'd later mention on his resume, "was getting too much for me to stomach."[2]

Far more than the high-minded and idealistic Gill, it was Winslow who could relate to the men at the Colony, most of whom had come from a poor upbringing. "Nothing was ever handed to me," he'd told his wife and two sons, David and Joel. "I lost my teeth to malnutrition while working my way through college, and I know what it's like to be hungry and down."[3]

Physically, Winslow did not come off as intimidating; at 5'8", 158 lbs., and white, he resembled most of the prison population. But when necessary, and when "angered," Winslow could speak in a "salty" language the men understood. He did it not just to command their respect but also "because I want them to know where I've come from."[4]

Winslow was born on a farm in Falmouth, Maine, on April 28, 1903, the "youngest of nine children." Early on he showed an ability to put things together, and by 1925, he'd earned his degree in civil engineering from Tufts. Work as a draftsman and expeditor followed, as did marriage to Alice Harrington in 1927. Then around this time, Howard Gill's prison project came calling. Beginning in the summer of 1928, Gill placed Winslow in charge of the wall's construction as well as the supervision of all prison labor. By the time 1934 rolled in and Gill hit some trouble with the media for being too soft and laid back, Winslow had already established a solid rapport with the men and was named the superintendent.[5]

As his son David recalled, "My father . . . continued polices he considered sound and changed those he felt had contributed to Gill's demise—particularly in the area of uniforms [which were changed to variations of standard Black pants and white shirts]." Gill had even allowed men to have dogs in the colony, but that privilege began to backfire when men used them "to attack guards." Winslow banned dogs, and once the general public unrest began to die down (Gill had been well-respected as an intellectual and progressive), Winslow was left with a prison he knew inside and out and a 250-acre farm surrounding it. "They grew most of everything they ate, essentially," said Joel Winslow. "They had 120 milkers. Pigs. Chickens. They grew hay and alfalfa to feed the livestock. Garbage for the hogs was no problem; that came right from the prison. They grew peas, beans, corn, potatoes—all kinds of vegetables."[6]

It's astounding to imagine how much Winslow knew about Norfolk by the time Malcolm arrived. If, for example, Winslow saw a man who somehow had hopped the first perimeter fence and was digging a hole next to the wall, Winslow knew from his work as an engineer how deep the man needed to dig to get under the wall. If a man figured out how to cut the electricity to the prison, Winslow knew that backup generators would kick in, making escape over the wall impossible.

Winslow had supervised the digging of wells on the farmland around the prison, the wells being the source of the men's drinking water and, to a smaller extent, the town of Norfolk's. He also outlined the construction for the tunnels underground that were wide enough for vehicles to move through, transporting meals to each dormitory unit dining room via a dumbwaiter.[7]

You name it, Winslow had a hand in its creation.

But Winslow wasn't just interested in the structural integrity of the prison. He did believe in Gill's initial vision and considered each man's overall experience. Going further than Gill, Winslow believed it was up to a man's own "self-initiative" to reform his character. After all, as Winslow was fond of saying, "reformation constitutes a one-man revolution."[8]

In an interview he gave to a *Colony* reporter in April 1948, Winslow was asked what he believed were "the greatest benefits to the inmates" at Norfolk.

Staying true to his logical and pragmatic personality, Winslow responded in an a, b, c structure. He believed that Norfolk offered each man . . .

> An opportunity for individual initiative to develop.
>
> An opportunity for a prisoner to live as near a community life as possible to that on the outside.
>
> An opportunity to learn a trade or receive an education. The success of this depends on the individual desire.
>
> A better chance for the type that gets into trouble under a more strict regime.
>
> An opportunity to maintain family relationships and contacts under a more wholesome environment.
>
> An opportunity to maintain better contact with the outside world rather than being isolated and out of touch when released.[9]

In different ways, Malcolm benefited from all six of Winslow's points. With the library, school, and debate, Malcolm did indeed develop his "individual initiative" and "education" while being part of a "community." Charlestown and Concord were both "stricter" than Norfolk, and it was only through Winslow's system that Malcolm could finally have enough space to go after intellectual pursuits. Also, through longer visits with Reginald and Hilda, Malcolm grew much closer to his brothers and sisters as they kept him informed of life on the outside.

But religion at Norfolk was a different story.

Compared to Charlestown and MR-Concord, Norfolk, under Winslow's supervision, offered a wider variety of religious services. In 1949, Malcolm was now one of around 873 incarcerated men on average at Norfolk. From this number, 240 attended the weekly Sunday Catholic mass at 8:30 a.m. in the Assembly Hall. Nearby in the chapel, 75 men took a seat in pews for a Protestant service at the same time. After the Protestants vacated the chapel, in came the Christian Scientists, 14 on average, to listen each week at 10:10 a.m.

to a service that emphasized healing through prayer and the belief in a more human-centric Christ.[10]

On the first Thursday of every month, Jewish services were held at 10:45 a.m., an average of 17 men attending. For those in between the beliefs of Protestants and Catholics, there were Episcopalian services once a season, with 20 Anglicans taking the time to listen to a priest who *can* be married deliver a message of peace. Rounding out the list were two services a year for the Greek Orthodox Church and one service for the Russian Orthodox believers, around 18 attending.[11]

Islamic services were never offered, nor mentioned.

MALCOLM'S POETIC NERVE

At the beginning of 1949, Malcolm, now with a shaved head and a sprouting chin beard, had started to move away from most of the programs Norfolk had to offer, such as debate (he'd soon return) and school. In his prison file, Malcolm is recorded as leaving the school program on January 15, the reason being that he'd become a "disturbing influence."[12]

The wording implies that a teacher may have spoken to prison administration. While it was not reported as to how exactly Malcolm had disturbed the class, one reported disruption came from Harvey Williams, who was in Malcolm's class. During one period, the two men were discussing the politics of Black singer and activist Paul Robeson. In May 1948, Robeson spoke before the Senate against the Mundt-Nixon Bill, which would have forced members of the Communist party to, among other controversial aspects, publicly register their party status. Robeson had also campaigned for Progressive Party candidate Henry Wallace, a politician whose views Malcolm may have studied in preparation for his panel discussion debate back in October.[13]

Robeson, considered one of the most famous Black Americans in the '30s and '40s due to numerous film and stage performances, watched as the general public vilified him as a Communist sympathizer. By 1950, Robeson had been blacklisted by the US government, an eventual victim of McCarthy-era politics.[14]

In class, Malcolm defended Robeson's political views, changing the way Williams had thought of the actor. If Malcolm had alluded to communism as superior in any way to capitalism, then the teacher, given the tense "red" atmosphere of the late 1940s, could have labeled his ideas as "disturbing" and asked him to either change his views or leave class.

Malcolm left.

With his mornings now freer, Malcolm went more deeply into his study of Islam. He began committing to memory certain prayers that Wilfred or Philbert sent to him. In January and February, he fell into the literary worlds of three Persian philosophers—Saadi Shīrāzī, Omar Khayyam, and Hafiz. With Shīrāzī, it was his epic poem, *The Gulistan*, written in the middle of the thirteenth century, that captivated Malcolm. In a letter to Philbert, he quotes without explanation from the Norfolk library's English language edition:

> He is no friend who in thine hour of pride
> Brags of his love and calls himself thy kin,
> He is a friend who hales his fellow in,
> And clangs the door upon the wolf outside.[15]

In the same letter to Philbert, Malcolm quotes from Hafiz's most famous book of poems, *The Rubá'iyát of Hafiz*, originally written in Persian in the fourteenth century:

> O time of broken bows that none would mend[!]
> The bitter foe was once a faithful friend.
> So to the skirts of solitude I cling,
> Lest friendship lure me to an evil end.[16]

So much has already been said about Malcolm's conversion to Islam, his political views, and his outspoken nature, but it was here, at Norfolk, where Malcolm found his true love—language. Whether memorizing vocabulary from the dictionary, absorbing etymological principles from Bodmer's *The Loom of Language*, or reading and writing poetry from ancient Persian poets, Malcolm had an insatiable desire for the written word. But it was poetry that affected him the most. As he described to Philbert, "I'm a real bug for poetry. When you think back over all of our past lives, only poetry could best fit into the vast emptiness created by man."[17]

Malcolm may have been swimming in quatrains and metaphor, but with Philbert, he made sure to remain transparent, confessing at the end of his letter that "most of the time I put down poetry to take up space so it will look like I'm writing a long letter so I can receive a long one in return."[18]

JARVIS'S BLUES

By the end of January 1949, Malcolm had found some meaningful self-direction. Jarvis, however, was contemplating suicide.

During the time Malcolm was in school and debating, Jarvis continued to write musical compositions in his room, sending them off to record companies in the hopes that they would sell. They didn't, but he kept trying, and he continued to complete higher level correspondence courses in harmony and counterpoint to improve his songwriting skills. He remained the "garbageman" in the kitchen, performing at an "average" level. Whenever able, he tried to gain control of the radio in the common room and tune in to a music show or practice his trumpet in his room (often annoying several men nearby) and also in the basement. On November 18, 1948, Jarvis was a part of an "Inmates Variety Show," performing a "trumpet solo," his act wedged between a singer and a skit by a group called the "Hill Billies."[19]

But Jarvis often struggled to find meaning. While at Norfolk, he'd attended the funerals of both his grandfather and Hazel Register, his first wife, and his two sons were growing up with their grandparents, in a situation more stable than anything he alone could give. "Please take under consideration," Jarvis wrote to his mother on January 30, 1949, "that there comes a time in every man and woman's life, when they reach the cross roads of life. The road that goes to the left is bad and that to the right leads to good. At the present time I find myself at that cross road."[20]

Jarvis justified his devotion to music as a way to escape the confinement of prison, hoping his skill would translate to a reliable profession he could hang his hat on after being released. But after so much effort and failure, he wondered what use he was to his family or society: "I think now that all these three years [in prison] were spent trying and batting my head against a stone wall. Now the question might arise. Why don't I think of my two children? Well, I'll answer that by putting it this way. Hazel wanted to do things for them, and often thought of them. But now she's lying six feet deep. On the other hand, she probably is doing them more good, by being where she is, than I could ever do being in prison. I have often thought I would much rather keep her company than to give these people two or three more years of my life."

There was desperation in Jarvis's letter to his mother: "And on top of that two more years to go just because my skin is black (which was no fault of mine). Every man in prison realizes he has committed a crime against society, and must pay for such. But what does society pay for its crimes against man?"[21]

Jarvis, through newspapers carried by the library, had been keeping track of 22-year-old Robert Faulk, a Black Roxbury resident who'd made headlines after committing a series of crimes (assault, B&E, attempted murder) over a stretch of one week in the Boston area, ending in Faulk shooting himself in the head, surviving but losing his eyesight. "I know [Faulk] and his entire case better than I know my own family. . . . I understand why he did what he did," Jarvis wrote to his mother.[22]

Above all, what angered Jarvis the most about the Faulk case was how "exaggerated" the press coverage had been, the *Boston Globe* calling him a "drug-crazed desperado" and a madman, even publishing a picture of Faulk after he'd shot himself, shirt off, wrists tied by rope to a stretcher. To Jarvis, Faulk had entered prison at the age of 18 and was more a victim of a rigged system, similar to Jarvis's racially biased case.[23] "That kid," Jarvis wrote, "is a good example of what too much [jail] time can do to a man. . . . I have been in here for three years now, and I am beginning to get disgusted with this whole affair. I am making an e[a]rnest plea to my family and people. To get me out of this place before I change in heart and soul."[24]

Nearly all letters coming out of Norfolk were reviewed and/or censored. Sure enough, Jarvis's letter to his mother was flagged, typed up, and given most likely to Winslow, who decided to assign Jarvis a psychiatrist for two months. To show how close Jarvis and Malcolm (and Reginald, at this time) were, Malcolm reported the news in a February letter to Philbert: "Tell Reg that Jarvis was examined by the psychiatrist (I murdered that spelling yesterday[)]. It all stemmed from a letter he wrote to his family to try and interest them in speeding up his release."[25]

Faulk, while awaiting sentencing, recovered from his head wound as a patient in Norfolk's hospital. For the next year, Winslow allowed Faulk a Braille instructor. As a result of his attempt to rehabilitate, Faulk avoided a life sentence and was instead given 25–30 years for his crimes—sentenced by Malcolm's judge, Allan Buttrick. One wonders if Malcolm or Jarvis made any attempts to communicate with him.[26]

Jarvis was in trouble, and Malcolm, along with Heywood Hampton—who'd transferred to Norfolk shortly after Malcolm—were his closest friends at the time. At the end of his letter to his mother, Jarvis asked her if he could "borrow that <u>big Bible</u> from home for a few weeks." Religion was on his mind, and his friend across the hallway was ready to show him a more hopeful path.[27]

When Jarvis's parents and two sons came to visit him, Malcolm often joined him, both seated on a "wooden bench." Decades later, Jarvis's son, Malcolm L. Jarvis Jr., recalled seeing his father "in his powder-blue prison shirt and striped black-and-white pants," this other very serious man seated next to him.

Jarvis Jr. was just a "tyke" at the time, but "for some reason, that other man terrified me. He seemed to have such a mean face. I never talked to him until one day when he asked me, 'Do you like school?' I said, 'Yes.'" Malcolm then said, "Always listen to, and obey, your grandparents."[28]

HAPPENINGS AROUND THE COLONY

February, March, and April rolled by as Norfolk's prison population hovered around 900. Many men had, like Malcolm, found their passions and were given the time and space to pursue them. One incarcerated man, Art Whitney, had built an eight-foot model yacht from materials he'd scrounged together from different departments, eventually showing it off in the library.

Whitney's feat was impressive, but another man, Gregory Feodoroff, had him beat. From a dormitory basement, he carved a five-foot-high figure of Christ on the cross from wood, its intricate design so professional that a local Catholic priest agreed to showcase it at the front of his metropolitan church, thousands kneeling before what the priest called "the prisoner's cross."[29]

Russell Noble, meanwhile, wrote nuanced editorials in the *Colony*, building a case to adjust the possibility of parole for men serving a life sentence. As a part of the debate team, he and Joseph Mahoney agreed to debate two local Haverhill attorneys for WHAV, a local radio station, winning easily. Mahoney and another debater greeted Boston University for their annual debate, winning for the fourth year in a row.[30]

But by March, many, including Malcolm, had lost interest in the Debating Society, now with only 9 or 10 active members—down from nearly 60 at the beginning of fall. The men had grown frustrated that the "walking encyclopedias" at the top were taking all the new opportunities that came with being recognized by *Time* magazine. The debate club, one *Colony* writer reported, "should be used for something else besides individual gains for a few." With the 1948–49 season rolling to a close, this was a problem Murdo, Noble, Mahoney, and Bradbury needed to address the next season.[31]

Other more general issues among the Norfolk population had to do with how money was allocated from the Gate House store. The lifers, around 60 in total, and other men with long sentences wanted funds set aside for larger goals, such as getting radios in each room. Meanwhile, the short-term incarcerated men, who made up around 75 percent of the population (those serving 10 years or less) were more interested in voting for updates in sports equipment and bringing in special events and films. One complaint had to do with the debate club being allotted money for study materials and "refreshments" for the opposing team, the number matching the orchestra's entire annual budget.[32]

At this point, Malcolm's world revolved around the library, a few friends, and reading and writing letters. His prison life had shrunk, but in a deeper, more intense way. His only continuing vocational obligation was the laundry, and he was rated as being a poor worker "who washed the pants in the laundry," one *Colony* writer complained, "like washing your feet without removing your socks."[33]

Safe to say, becoming a skilled laundry worker was not high on Malcolm's to-do list.

A PATCHWORK RELIGIOUS EDUCATION

Wilfred is going to dictate a lengthy letter to Hilda for me . . . and I'm awaiting it most anxiously. Knowing that Islam is the Truth, makes the lack of it even more noticeable. I know nothing yet I'm ahead of those by whom I'm surrounded . . . and night after night I beg Allah to let me be his humble servant. . . . to let his light shine within me so all will know whom I serve . . . and all are aware, believe me.

—Malcolm to Philbert, August 9, 1949

Malcolm wanted more.

He wanted to meet an imam, to go to a mosque, to read the Qur'ān, but Winslow, in his final year, had no plan to devote space and time to a religion very few in the prison believed in at the time. Knowing this, Malcolm knew it was on him to dig up whatever available resources he could find about Islam.

He absorbed Sa'di's *Gulistan* and both Hafiz's and Khayyam's *Rubaiyat*, but they weren't nearly enough. He was reading the King James Version of the Bible (possibly the "big Bible" that Jarvis had asked his parents to bring), but he wasn't sure if the conclusions he reached were even slightly accurate. "What I read from the Bible I try to do with my own mind," he wrote to Philbert in June of 1949, "and not from the views of those 'popular' conceptions. I find I make many interesting conclusions, but they are violently contrary to popular belief."[34]

He needed someone to bounce ideas off of. Without a guide, Malcolm tried to use his etymological passion for words to find a deeper truth: "Jesus Christ has a 'popular' meaning, and concept among the average people," he wrote in the same letter. "That is, in the 'English sense.' But the words themselves must surely have a definite meaning, and make clearer reading in their original language. In Hebrew or Arabic I have found Christ's title to be: Yus Asaph Masah, or the Anointed (Masah) Traveler (Masih or Siahat) and Gatherer (Asaph) Yus (Jesus). This doesn't have to mean one person, but could mean those 'select' group who are chosen by God's 'representatives' to gather in his children. Because they have been so widely scattered by the forces of Satan, it takes traveling to reach them."[35]

Malcolm not only wrote to his siblings. As early as November 1948, and only after being urged by Hilda, he had started writing to Elijah Muhammad. None of these early letters have survived, but it may have been Elijah Muhammad's idea that Malcolm reach out to the Watchtower Bible and Tract Society, now better known as Jehovah's Witnesses. Early in the 1930s, when the Nation of Islam was beginning to formulate its mission and philosophy, there were surface commonalities—refusal to take inoculations, to fight in a nonholy war—between the two religions, most likely due to Muhammad's fondness for the Watchtower's second president, Joseph F. Rutherford. When Muhammad took over the leadership of the NOI from Wallace D. Fard, he encouraged many of his early followers to read and listen to Rutherford's lectures.[36]

Malcolm wasn't interested in becoming a Jehovah's Witness. Rather, he wanted to discuss with an expert the similarities and differences between the Christian perspective of Jesus against the Islamic perspective. He also wanted to know how Christians felt about the prophet Muhammad.

It's worth noting that Malcolm did not (at least on record) approach John A. Samuelson, Norfolk's chaplain, a Protestant minister, *and* the director of the debating society. Although the Jehovah's Witness was in many ways a Christian religion, its intense beliefs kept the Protestants, Catholics, Episcopalians, Church Scientists, and Orthodox believers at arm's length. As one Protestant minister of 40 years put it, "One is either a Witness or one is lost." This no-middle-ground attitude was similar to the beliefs the NOI had formulated. In this way, Malcolm could have a more productive discussion with a Jehovah's Witness—two religious absolutists debating the weaknesses of those in between.[37]

Malcolm asked a prison official, possibly Winslow or Magraw, if he could discuss his newfound religion with a local Jehovah's Witness. Living near the prison with his wife and son was 43-year-old J. Prescott Adams, a Jehovah's Witness who agreed to meet with Malcolm over a span of "several months." Their discussions mainly revolved around various viewpoints and "similarities between" Jesus and Muhammad. Adams was "struck" by Malcolm's general curiosity toward Jesus, yet he couldn't help but feel that Malcolm had some kind of hidden agenda. Adams could tell that Malcolm wanted to believe, but he also felt that Malcolm was more concerned with preparing for a fight. "He had a great ego that he was feeding," Adams wrote to a biographer.[38]

MALCOLM THE POET

Prior to prison, Jarvis had been exposed to a different, more established denomination of Islam. While living in Roxbury in the mid-1940s, Jarvis struck up a friendship with Abdul Hameed, who told Jarvis that he was an Ahmadiyyan Muslim. The Ahmadiyyan movement started in Punjab, India, near the end of the nineteenth century. Similar to the Nation of Islam's belief in extending the adoring title of "prophet" to its current leaders, the Ahmadi's beliefs were "in violent opposition to orthodox Islam."[39]

Religion wasn't what brought Jarvis into Hameed's path; rather it was the way he carried himself: "[Hameed] was a very distinguished-looking man; well built and weighing about 220 pounds, he wore a black fez with a long black tassel and a neatly trimmed beard." It was the confidence and authority that Hameed exuded, walking around Roxbury without caring what others thought. When Jarvis introduced himself, the trumpet player soon learned that Hameed was a classical pianist. "He owned an eight-foot Mason Hammond concert grand piano. All my life I had never heard a finer quality sound from a piano."[40]

Jarvis, after some arm-twisting, was able to bring "Rhythm Red" Malcolm to meet Hameed, but Malcolm wasn't interested at the time. Now, however, was a different story. At Norfolk, Jarvis corresponded regularly with Hameed. One important July 1949 letter Jarvis wrote shows the connection he'd developed with Hameed and the level of respect Malcolm had for him.

The letter begins with a poem, written by Malcolm, who used the name "Red Little." By this point in time, Malcolm knew that Hameed was a classical pianist, so he—while absorbing ancient Persian poetry—decided to write a poem that interconnected Hameed's love for music and Islam:

Music

By "Red Little"

Music is not created
It is always here
surrounding us
like the infinite particles that constitute life, it cannot be seen
    but can only be felt
Like Allah
like life.
No tis not created, but like the never dying soul, permeat[e]s the
    air with its pr[e]sence
ever waiting for its Master
The Lordly Musician
The Wielder of the souls
to come and give it an earthly body
making it into a song.
Music with out the Musician is like life with out <u>Allah</u>
both in desperate need of a home
a body
the completed song and it[s] creator.[41]

In the letter, Jarvis relayed to Hameed how happy he was to hear that his two sons attended a religious service. Jarvis's entire family had visited him on Sunday, July 31, and his two sons "were so excited today, both of them trying to tell me all about [the church service, called 'Jew Ma'] at the same time."

The letter also implies that Jarvis had indeed devoted himself to Islam and that this commitment, with Malcolm's help, had helped rescue him from the despair he'd been feeling months ago. "Your prayers for Brother Malcolm Little and I were certainly answered this week. Little has taught me a few of the prayers, those I couldn't quite get at first I'm still working on."

Jarvis also shared an incident that happened while he was working in the kitchen: "I was working on my job and silently saying to my self . . . Al-Hamdulli la [Alhamdulillah, 'praise be to Allah'] when I was approached by Satan. A fellow cursed me for no good reason." Jarvis's anger grew. "I stood still and watched him. He ordered me to move, [and] when I didn't he threw a bucket of water on me. I was about to strike him and froze in my tracks. I later found out if I had hit him I would have gotten in serious trouble, because, my skin is black and his is white. No body saw him [throw] water on me but every body would have seen me hit him." He credited Islam for helping him hold back his anger. "Allah was with me, because he would not let me strike, and I thus avoided a lot of trouble."[42]

Hameed did visit Jarvis and Malcolm, helping them along their pursuit for answers to Islam, and was partly responsible for bringing to them an English-language version of the Qur'ān, translated by Indian Muslim author Abdullah Yusuf Ali in 1937. "One of the other Brothers here obtained the Yusuf Ali Quran," Malcolm wrote to Philbert. "I'm reading it, along with many other subjects Wilfred mentioned in his recent letter."[43]

But the summer of 1949, Malcolm was mainly listening to himself, as he considered the changes soon to come in his life. One passage to Philbert, written in August 1949, shows how his study of language, religion, and poetry had started to reshape the way he saw the world. "I sat here at the window one evening," he wrote, describing the view of the Quad from his dormitory room, "gazing out into the yard at the fellows congregated here and there . . . in little groups . . . listening to the thunder overheard. The thunder roared louder and nearer . . . still, they remained outside. Suddenly the clouds did burst, and before they could reach their rooms . . . all were wet."

To Malcolm, there was symbolism here. "Now, that started me to thinking, and wondering, Allah always warns before there is a change. I did wonder if everyone would be the same way in the End . . . seeing, and hearing the signs of the inevitable all around them . . . but taking no heed till it was too late . . . and becoming caught in the Final Disaster."[44]

His ruminations were still abstract, but one thing was clear—he had a future waiting for him, and when the thunder came, he'd be one of the first to hear the rumble.

A NEW RECRUIT AND AVOIDING PORK

Naturally, Malcolm and Jarvis started recruiting within the prison, but they were met with general resistance. Godfrey Joiner, who'd transferred to Norfolk on April 7, 1949, and joined the orchestra as a trumpet player, heard Malcolm's NOI pitch but wasn't interested. "Malcolm suggested I get a Qur'an. I said, 'I don't need a Qur'an.' We still remained friends. . . . But I think he resented [my] not accepting Islam."[45]

Malcolm also tried to convert his former classmate Harvey Williams, but Williams had his doubts: "What turned me off was that he was talking about white people as devils. But he and Jarvis were in there for messing around with white girls. If a white man is a devil, so's a white woman."[46]

One man who did buy in was 26-year-old Osborne Greene Thaxton, who worked in the concrete department. Like Malcolm, Thaxton was in on a B&E&L charge (five to seven years) and had endured stints at Charlestown, Concord, and now, as of September 9, 1949, Norfolk. According to his prison file, the 5'11", 185 lbs. Thaxton was described as a "lone wolf" but also "polite and cooperative . . . one who knows his way around. He is well institutionalized."[47]

Thaxton was born on September 13, 1923, and raised in Springfield, Massachusetts—the third oldest of nine siblings. Money was tight, and the family accepted social welfare. Thaxton dropped out of school after finishing the eighth grade and started to work in factories, first as a machine operator and then as a welder. Later he served domestically in the armed forces as an army private.

Poverty had a stranglehold on Thaxton's young adult years; he also had to absorb the blow of losing his mother in 1945, attending her funeral while serving time at MR-Concord. Starting from 1939 (for stealing a bicycle) to 1948, Thaxton was charged with a crime eight times, all B&E, with the exception of one 1947 incident, when he was out one evening after having a few drinks and was "arrested for being drunk late at night and creating a disturbance with loud talking." This charge, while Thaxton was on parole, returned him to MR-Concord, where he was put to work on the farm driving a tractor. In the dining hall, Thaxton could have run into a not-yet-converted Malcolm Little. One wonders if Malcolm, after hearing Thaxton's story, shook his head in disbelief: *So you're back in here for being a loud drunk?*[48]

At Norfolk, Thaxton found structure and discipline. After leaving the Receiving Building and moving into dormitory unit 3–2 in early November, Thaxton soon fully understood that drinking had been at the root of his misbehavior. He'd naturally been frustrated financially, but it was liquor that sparked his impulse to take what wasn't his.

Thaxton started walking the Quad with Malcolm and Jarvis. He used the library and ordered a correspondence course, hoping to improve his Gregg shorthand, a form of pen stenography meant to quicken the act of note-taking. With family far away, Thaxton only received one visitor, Harold Wheeler—a 36-year-old

FIGURE 8.1. Osborne Thaxton. Mug shot. 1952. From prison file.

Jehovah's Witness. Interestingly, Wheeler, a year before meeting Thaxton, had also been arrested for disturbing the peace, but not at night and not while drunk. Wheeler and another JW associate had attempted to hold an outdoor religious service at a public park—their loudspeaker being heard a quarter-mile away. The judge let Wheeler go, citing the right to religious freedom.[49]

Malcolm, Thaxton, and Jarvis were also free to practice their Muslim faith at Norfolk, as long as it did not disrupt Norfolk's routine. Thaxton, meanwhile, committed himself to a disciplined routine. No longer would he desire pork, alcohol, or cigarettes. Instead, he read Watchtower material from Wheeler and followed Malcolm's self-disciplined lead. By restricting his wants, Thaxton believed he could become a better man.

It was very difficult to avoid eating pork, however. As previously described, the Norfolk cooks used lard in just about all their dishes. Fortunately, Jarvis worked in the kitchen and was able to help Malcolm avoid pork on days when it was served. Later, after he left prison and married Betty Shabazz, Malcolm let her know how he and Jarvis kept from starving. "[Malcolm] had very strict eating habits," said Mrs. Shabazz. "While he was in prison he had become a Muslim and had stopped eating pork. In order to harass him, knowing his feelings about pork, the cooks used to always dip the serving spoon in some pork substance [like lard] before serving him anything. To get around this, he had a friend [Jarvis at Norfolk] who worked in the kitchen to toast a loaf of bread which he would then eat with cheese that he had bought in the commissary. This was his main diet during his last few years in prison."[50]

Malcolm, Jarvis, and Thaxton took this restriction seriously and refused to help other men, most of whom felt that their meals were too small. "The Muslims were so strong about the pork, they wouldn't even get it for you on the chow line," said incarcerated man Stanley Jones. "It caused problems sometimes, because a lot of brothers couldn't understand, you know, why you won't get the pork for me. 'You don't have to eat it, don't put it on your tray, just tell 'em to put it on my tray.'"[51]

SCHOOL AND GREAT BOOKS

Starting in September, Malcolm, despite being a "disturbing influence" back in January, was allowed back into the prison school program. He was even allowed to enter the "Senior" level, which meant taking classes in "History,

English and Literature, Public Speaking, Spanish and Current Events," taught by Mr. O'Connell and Mr. Nash. New to the curriculum were the regular use of "sound films to supplement instruction" and public speaking—due to the success of last year's lively debates.[52]

It may have been during his public speaking class that Malcolm first debated his fellow incarcerated men on topics such as "the identity of Shakespeare." Malcolm had been reading the King James Version of the Bible as well as a few of Shakespeare's plays—bits of *Macbeth* repeating in his mind—and started to sense a similarity in the language. "They say that from 1604 to 1611, King James got poets to translate, to write the Bible," Malcolm explained. "Well, if Shakespeare existed, he was then the top poet around. But Shakespeare is nowhere reported connected with the Bible. If he existed, why didn't King James use him?" Against his fellow prison school debater, Malcolm attempted to convince the class that Shakespeare was, indeed, King James, and that it was this man "who poetically 'fixed' the Bible—which in itself and its present King James version has enslaved the world."[53]

Also during the fall and into the winter, Malcolm supplemented his prison school classes by joining a Great Books Foundation discussion course, which met in a council room at least biweekly a total of 17 times. Malcolm attended 15 of them. Jarvis (7 times) and Thaxton (2 times) also gave it a try. Even the "walking encyclopedias," Murdo and Russ Noble, were frequent participants.[54]

At Norfolk, Malcolm's Great Books classes were conducted by Dr. Edward Meshorer, a 35-year-old Harvard-educated medical doctor with underlying interests in education and psychiatry. By Meshorer's side was Leonard Tucker, a 28-year-old Dartmouth graduate and civil engineer. Meshorer wanted the course to have a strong impact on those who participated. "This course," Meshorer explained to the *Colony* writer, "is meant to disturb you. In fact, the more disturbed in mind you become, the more successful the meeting." No matter what, "the course will teach you to think if you can't and better if you can."[55]

Going as far back as 1927, the idea of having a Great Books Foundation started with Dr. Mortimer Adler, who in New York started 15 public courses that used the Socratic method to discuss great works of primarily Western civilization. In 1930, the University of Chicago took Adler's idea and introduced it into their curriculum as "seminars." Not wanting to only be for the college student, the Great Books Foundation started "adult discussion groups" in communities across the country. Especially after World War II, with so many historic European cities in rubble and governments looking for clear direction, there was an intense desire across the country to reconnect with classic works by Plato and Aristotle, to name a few.[56] For the discussions to have a significant impact, it was required for moderators to first receive training.[57]

During these training sessions, both Meshorer and Tucker were taught to "start arguments" and keep the conversation "moving" from idea to idea as they remained an objective guide. This assertive style of discourse, promoted strongly by the University of Chicago's Robert Maynard Hutchins, was meant to break away from the rigid "pragmatism" pushed by educator John Dewey. "Truth," as Hutchins put it, "is the moral application of the idea." Malcolm, given his religious beliefs, may have agreed.

As one *Colony* writer explained, "These [Great Books] discussions are particularly pertinent to the inmates of Norfolk. The doctrines of 'Justice, Law, Truth and Liberty' that are discussed and verbally pulled apart at these meetings are 'made to order' subjects for Norfolk inmates. We inmates are first order referents of these abstractions. We live what outsiders merely discuss as abstract concepts."[58]

The Great Books Foundation, a nonprofit, kept itself in business through donations and by selling cheap reprints of classic works. Norfolk, by agreeing to run a course, purchased those reprints and distributed them to the men who signed up. In this way, Malcolm was given at least 15 copies of classic literature while at Norfolk, and after reading each one, he had a chance to discuss the books with Ivy League–educated moderators.[59]

One book discussed during Malcolm's time at Norfolk was Niccolo Machiavelli's *The Prince*. Dr. Meshorer's wife sat in, and after the discussion ended, she was stunned by the group's overall intellect. "The meeting was dynamic!" she reported. "I was greatly surprised by the intense interest displayed by the men. The group surpasses by far many Great Books groups on the outside." Another local reverend who also comoderated agreed. "The group was intellectually above the majority of outside Great Books groups."[60]

As for Malcolm, there exists in his prison file one short comment about his participation in the Great Books discussion: "Had his own ideas, but was O.K."[61]

DEBATE AND A RADIO DEBUT

On October 4, 1949, 26 members of the Norfolk Debating Society met for the first meeting of the new season. The number was much lower than in the past, perhaps due to the society appearing more elitist and intimidating now that it had a national reputation. But Murdo, as well as Rev. John A. Samuelson, had an exciting new opportunity to announce.

The United Prison Association (UPA) in Massachusetts decided to sponsor "a series of radio programs to be broadcast over a state-wide network of stations." The program they had in mind was called *The Prisoner Speaks*, a half-hour program that combined "discussion of penological subjects . . . with music by [the] inmate glee club and orchestra."[62]

Reverend Samuelson, attempting to give more of the debating members a chance at some spotlight, told the group that they "were expected to take part in the club's activities, Forum [on the Radio] or Debating, and that a club Board of Directors will select the men for the Collegiate debates."

By instituting a vague "Board of Directors" requirement, the debating society had given up some of its own autonomy and become less about a man's individual experience and more an opportunity to receive favorable press and showcase the success of Norfolk's progressive plan. The college versus Norfolk debates had for over a decade and a half been a badge of honor for each Norfolk debater who participated. Now, it seemed, the expectation to show Norfolk off in a positive and respectable light superseded the need to have each man mature as a thinker.[63]

Regardless of the debating society's new professional direction, Malcolm accepted a spot speaking on the radio. On November 17, he was the second of four speakers (Murdo being the first) to support the idea that, yes, "capital punishment should be abolished." The UPA supplied the tape recorder, and the four speakers were given a few minutes each to state their case. Once finished, their recordings were sent to the radio station.

The Prisoner Speaks debuted on Station WMEX (AM 1510) on January 5, 1950, and aired weekly a planned 13 times from 8:30 a.m. to 9:00 p.m. The show began with a "round table" discussion topic addressed by Norfolk debaters, followed by music from either the glee club or orchestra.[64]

Malcolm had five weeks to research capital punishment before the day of the recording. It's clear, when one reads all four responses, that Malcolm must have worked together with Murdo, John McDermott (third), and H. P. Haskins (fourth) to create a sense of cohesion. Murdo's response, for example, gives the listener a brief overview of the history of capital punishment in the US: "Up until the latter part of the 18th century," Murdo explained, "capital punishment by drowning, hanging in chains, burning and other quaint forms of doubtful retribution were extensively applied in this country." Eventually, a "limitation of the forms of execution" meant only "the noose and the bullet." Murdo then credited Ohio (a territory in 1788) with "limiting . . . the death penalty to the crime of murder." Pennsylvania qualified this action in 1794 by stating that only "murder in the 1st degree" counted as a crime that brought the possibility of an execution. By 1900, Murdo explains, "all states had . . . abolished public executions."[65]

Eventually, Murdo argued, the death penalty would be abolished in the US. It was only a matter of time. "Conclusions can be drawn from the history of capital punishment, that it is unacceptable to the American people."[66]

Next was Malcolm, who used Murdo's setup and argued against the concept of deterrence theory—the idea that the fear of a punishment, such as death, can keep a man or woman from killing before they do.

Had Malcolm worried about the death penalty when he robbed those eight homes? Hardly; he'd pointed a gun to his own head. Malcolm did not fear death as a punishment back then.

But that, in prison years, was a lifetime ago. Here he was, older and wiser, his eyesight a far cry from 20/20 after devoting thousands of hours to reading small print in darkened places. Here he was, a changed man, ready to speak to the local community.

On February 2, 1950, at 8:30 p.m., WMEX 1510 aired *The Prisoner Speaks*. For the first time, the voice of Malcolm Little reached thousands of listeners. One wonders . . . did he tell Ella to tune in? Was Hilda still in the Boston area at the time? Had Reginald caught his brother's commanding voice? Had Beatrice, now living with her husband in the Boston area, inadvertently had her radio dial on 1510 and recognized Malcolm's voice?[67]

We'll never know. But we do know what he said:

> The whole history of penology is a refutation of the deterrence theory, yet this theory, that murder by the state can repress murder by individuals, is the eternal war cry for the retention of Capital Punishment.
>
> Granting that murder is the worst crime and that the punishment should fit the crime, is the death penalty the most appropriate punishment? The answer to that question based on his observation of hundreds of murderers, has been written by the late Lewis E. Lawes, warden of Sing Sing Prison in

an address. Warden Lawes observed that life imprisonment is a greater punishment and is often dreaded more than death. Mr. Lawes knew a number of men who sincerely pleaded that the customary appeal for a commutation should not be made. Further demonstration that men do not fear death as much as is generally assumed is found to be in the fact that it is necessary to watch the condemned closely to prevent them from taking their own lives.[68]

The experience of the Rev. T. Roberts of England further proves the ineffectiveness of Capital Punishment as a deterrent. Rev. Roberts inquired of 167 capital offenders as to whether they had ever seen a public execution and was answered in the affirmative in all save but six cases. Therefore there were 161 instances of the failure of the deterrence theory. That is not an isolated set of figures. Such instances are quite in accord with the principles of social psychology. It is a well known fact that pickpockets in England would ply their trade with great success at the execution of one of their members.[69]

Another factor refuting the deterrence theory is the fact that murder is the very crime where the fear of the penalty is the least likely to be present. The murderer is often mentally incapacitated to such a degree that he does not understand the consequence of his action and if competent may be so blinded by the passion of the moment that all thoughts of the future have been expelled by his unreasoning fury. He may, however, be a person who kills deliberately in the act of committing some other crime and who feels immune from punishment because of his own cleverness or because of "influence." In the case of the first mentioned class the deterrent effect will be nil. In the case of those last mentioned it could undoubtedly be great. If the professional or architect of the so-called "perfect" murder knew that he would almost certainly be executed we would have fewer murders of a certain type. But such actual deterrence can only result from mandatory death penalties, [which would require] almost perfect detective forces, incorruptible police and judiciary, juries unswayed by human emotions and a stern pardoning power.[70]

These unobtainables would result in such a large number of executions that the defenders of the death penalty would stand aghast.[71]

JARVIS, JOINER, AND RACISM IN THE ORCHESTRA

In November, while Malcolm went to school, discussed great books, and prepared to make his debate radio debut, Jarvis continued to be a part of the prison orchestra. There always seemed to be some kind of event for the orchestra to help bring a bit of energy to the incarcerated men. Headed by trumpet player Eddie McHarg, there were 18 members—five on trumpets, three on saxophones, two playing trombones, one playing a baritone horn, a violinist, a pianist, a guitar player, two on drums, and two singers. Often, the orchestra warmed up the crowd with a few tunes before a film started, such as the 1948 Esther Williams romance *On an Island with You* (shown at Norfolk on October 23), the Ronald Reagan comedy *John Loves Mary* (November 13), or the Bill Elliott western *The Last Bandit* (November 19).[72]

The orchestra was racially mixed, with at least seven of the members being Black. Back in the fall of 1949, the Black band members gravitated toward hits churned out by Duke Ellington, Dizzy Gillespie, and Miles Davis, while the white players preferred Tommy Dorsey, Woody Herman, and Artie Shaw. In Jarvis's case, he was written up this way by a *Colony* writer: "Mal Jarvis—the hot licks kid and arranger. Played professionally and plans on continuing soon. Has written quite a few numbers and is a Dizzy Gil disciple. Favorite band: The Diz and trumpet, the same."[73]

Still, there were tiffs. Godfrey Joiner, who'd picked up the trumpet back in MR-Concord and had, according to his wife, "20 months" of experience, was third chair in the trumpet section. His mentor, Jarvis, was second chair (Al Miller, who'd been a professional for many years, was first). On November 9, during a practice, Jarvis went into a trumpet solo. Joiner, hoping to improve quickly, "appeared to be playing along with [Jarvis], and . . . he continued to do so after [McHarg] had told him to stop playing." Instead of stopping, Joiner "held his trumpet to his mouth and acted as if he were playing" and would "mouth and finger his instrument" as he followed Jarvis's line. This act annoyed McHarg, and McHarg's annoyance annoyed Joiner. How was he supposed to learn "if he didn't go through the motions while Jarvis was playing"?[74]

McHarg had had enough of Joiner. His resentment toward the aspiring trumpeter had been building, and he kicked him out of the band. The next day, Joiner went to the senior community officer (SCO) and told him he was being "unfairly treated" and felt McHarg was racially prejudiced in the way he treated Joiner. Angered, Joiner also went to Herbert E. Tucker, the chairman of the Boston NAACP.

The SCO interviewed half of the band, especially other Black members (but not Jarvis). They, however, backed the well-respected McHarg. Al Miller even went so far as to say "that when [Miller] had a band . . . the musicians did as they were told, or they were fired. He said that whoever was leader must be a leader in fact, and not in name only."[75]

Joiner never was allowed to return to the band, turning instead to piano as he attempted to rally support for a new orchestra. His love of music continued for the rest of his life. After being released from prison in the early 1950s, Joiner moved back south to segregated Shreveport, Louisiana, where he became the band director at Booker T. Washington High School and with his wife and son built their own home. In 1987, near the end of his life, with their neighborhood soon to be bulldozed for a new highway to be made, Joiner told the newspaper how he felt about the matter. "There's no need worrying about tomorrow when it's not promised to you," he said to the reporter. "I just take it one day at a time. . . . I've always been able to accept the inevitable and not let anything bother me."[76]

LITTLE NO MORE

> Too much water will kill most plants . . . but most plants aren't fortunate enough to be where I am with the precious time to absorb the Truth . . . so let your Spring flow freely . . . and if I begin to drown I will sing out.
>
> —Malcolm to Philbert, December 12, 1949

On Sunday, January 29, 1950, Malcolm started a letter to his brother Philbert. Two weeks earlier, he'd once again chosen to drop out of morning school classes to focus more on the realizations he was coming to on his own. For George Magraw, who'd witnessed Malcolm's educational ambitions escalate in the last two years as he managed the library and School Building, he was a bit disappointed: "I would have liked him to stay in school."[77]

What continued to consume Malcolm was the Bible. Relying on help from J. Prescott Adams, prison Bible school classes, letters from Elijah Muhammad, letters from his siblings, and his own reading, Malcolm wanted no less than to master God's text. To do this, he had his own reading process. "Studying the bible," Malcolm wrote, "I used to read in the Old Testament till I got tired of it, then I'd go to the 'New,' then to 'Rev.' . . . and so on like that to keep any one subject from preying too heavily upon my mind. . . . It was a help."

In Philbert's previous letter, he'd given Malcolm an update on the "current events" happening outside Norfolk. Four years had passed since Malcolm had been a "free" man on the outside, but with his newfound faith, it seemed all the "devils" were moving in response to a "fear of the unknown."[78]

During this time, President Truman and the American military were considering adding the hydrogen bomb to the country's arsenal, mainly "in view of the belief that Russia has the theory of it too." Fear and uncertainty sat in the minds of many American politicians. One US senator sought to explain the need to add a bomb 1,000 times stronger than the atomic bomb: "We must remain strong. We want to preserve the peace of the world and the hydrogen bomb will serve that cause just as the atomic bomb has done since it ended the war and gave us peace."[79]

Being away from society's maddening cycles of war and peace allowed Malcolm time to reflect. Since he lived in a Christian nation, mastering the Bible more than the average Christian would be an advantage in almost any argument once he left prison. And, as he'd been doing for the last several years, Malcolm applied etymological principles to his studies.

On this chilly night, the letter *X* was on his mind, as on other nights in the past . . .

In Dayton, Ohio, on April 22, 1948, a man named Charles Lee Oliver was arrested by the FBI after attempting to steal a pouch from a "bank messenger." When he was taken in front of a commissioner, a US marshal, and a district attorney, they read over his paperwork and noticed that Mr. Oliver had not written his last name.

"Your name," the commissioner said, "is Charles Fivex. . . . ?"

"Yes sir, that's my name. I have another name, Charles Lee Oliver. But I don't recognize that name. That's my slave name."

There was a look of confusion on both their faces. "How old are you?" the commissioner asked.

"I don't know."

"Well, are you 20?"

"I don't know."

The district attorney jumped in. "Would you say you were 30?"

"I couldn't say."

More confusion. The district attorney touched Charles's arm, questioning his existence. "You're here, aren't you? You're not a phantom. And you're not an infant. You're over 21, aren't you?"

"Perhaps."

That was enough for the marshal. On the official record sheet, the marshal rounded up and wrote 25. The paperwork complications continued during fingerprinting, and after he'd finished, Charles wrote, "5X."[80]

The clerk wasn't amused. They wanted an explanation. Charles gave it to him. The reporter, who was as flabbergasted as the rest, paraphrased Charles's explanation this way: "[Charles] is a member of the nation of Islam, the religion of Mohammed. He is affiliated with Temple No. 4 in Washington, D.C. In that temple, he was given the name Charles 5 X because he is the fifth man named Charles to join."

Charles 5X went on to explain that his "plantation owner master" had been named "Lee Oliver." As for his age, well, records weren't kept from his birth.

Eventually, he was given five years, but the "X" name change made local Dayton news . . .[81]

Malcolm knew from his NOI-converted siblings that his slave name "Little" would soon be history. Officially it couldn't be dropped until after he was released from prison. For now, as he sat in Norfolk, he tried to grow accustomed to that *X*. "I've been thinking of something else," Malcolm wrote to Philbert that January evening. "'Christmas' is often contracted and spelled 'Xmas' . . . so if X can replace the word 'Christ' they both must mean the same thing."

Throughout his letters to Philbert, Malcolm was comfortable showing his brother how he was considering a thought or a theory. His letters often knocked around several thoughts without reaching a conclusion. In this way, he was asking Philbert for help but also processing his own realizations. "The surname of the Tribe of Judah, the City of David, the temple of Solomon, Bethlehem, Jerusalem, (which are all the same, and composed of the same thing . . . Jesus . . . the Saabas) . . . must have been 'X' and signed like that. Our old people still make it. I thought it was because they couldn't write. But it must have been their real name. It shows how adept the devils are at confusing."

Malcolm continued, adding an illustration of a compass to try to make his point clearer: "Jesus was the Foundation of the world, so he must also have been the Four Corners. I used to wonder how this could be, but. Was looking usually in the wrong directions. . . . so I now look inward. Where the Four Corners meet [Malcolm draws the *X* like a compass pointing north/south/east/west] . . . is all in all . . . over 360 degrees . . . and four corners must have 360 degrees. No wonder we were born on the square . . . and 'X' really does mark the Spot . . . (and algebraically represents the . . . Unknown.)"[82]

The history of the symbol/letter *X* is also quite unknown. From hieroglyphics to the Phoenician alphabet to the Greek *khi*, then finally entering the Roman alphabet as well as becoming the Roman numeral for 10, the letter *X* has felt its share of languages. As for religious symbolism, the *X* has also been identified as a saltire, or a diagonal cross, ever since Saint Andrew's crucifixion in Patras, Greece, in 60 AD. Saint Andrew, a disciple of Christ, asked not to be placed on a standard cross as Jesus was 27 years before. Instead, Saint Andrew's hands and legs were tied to two *X*-shaped tree trunks, where he survived for three days before passing away.

Yet the most frustrating aspect for Malcolm was that this history had all been comfortably altered by Western Christian perspectives. Saint Andrew's crucifixion was an incredibly important moment, but was there not an entire continent south of Greece that held truths long buried by Christianity's shovel?

Malcolm searched. In his *Autobiography*, he settled on explaining his *X* to Alex Haley this way: "For me, my 'X' replaced the white slavemaster name of 'Little' which some blue-eyed devil named Little had imposed upon my paternal forebears. The receipt of my 'X' meant that forever after in the nation of Islam, I would be known as Malcolm X. Mr. Muhammad taught that we would keep this 'X' until God Himself returned and gave us a Holy Name from His own mouth."[83]

On January 29, 1950, Malcolm finished his letter to Philbert. As far as we have on record, it was the first time he signed "Malcolm X."

Soon after, Malcolm began signing most of his letters with the *X*. In March, he wrote to "Brother Raymond" several times, hoping to recruit him and other jazz musicians into the Nation of Islam. His letters never sound like sales pitches—rather, Malcolm's words brim with empathy, compassion, and a strong sense of direction. "Another Brother here is going to write you," Malcolm wrote to Raymond at the end of a six-page letter:

> *I hope you don't think I am burdening you, but I do believe it is best this day for all of us to be in constant touch with each other. . . . We have been separated for so long. Until I hear from you again, I keep you firmly within my heart, and include you in all of my prayers. May the Almighty Allah guide you and bless you always in the Name of his Holy Servant, the Honorable Elijah Mohammed.*
>
> *As Salaam Alaikum*
>
> *Sincerely*
>
> *Your Brother Malcolm X*[84]

LEAVING PARADISE

The Muslims demanded respect and they got respect, and I think that was the important thing in any prison population. But the administration was more scared of 'em than anybody else.

—Stanley Jones, incarcerated during Malcolm's time, as quoted in William Strickland, *Malcolm X: Make It Plain*

"The more of Islam I grasp," Malcolm wrote to Philbert, "the more I wish to be alone where I can meditate upon the Richness of Allah's Great Manifestations that are being brought to Light before our eye each day."[85]

It was hard to meditate and pray at Norfolk, a prison whose layout and philosophy urged the men to feel they were a part of a community—as they would be upon their release. In the dormitory's common room, for example, it was usually the "first man" back from the dining hall who grabbed control of the only radio in the common area of unit 2–3. Once secured, he'd turn the volume up loud and, depending on the day, listen to shows such as *The Lone Ranger*, *Superman*, or *Jack Armstrong, the All-American Boy*. If a music lover grabbed the radio, then bebop, boogie woogie, or "hillbilly tunes" blared from the speakers. For those who didn't mind and simply wanted to listen to anything, games of dominoes and checkers went on around the room until lights out took everyone to their rooms.[86]

Unlike Charlestown and MR-Concord, Norfolk had yet to invest in earphones for each man, fearing both the expense and the lack of camaraderie that would inevitably occur from men retreating to their rooms to listen to their chosen radio shows. To add to Malcolm's discomfort, the dormitory units lacked heat during a bitterly cold March, with "high winds" pushing blocks of snow and ice off the roof slopes of dormitory units, some men dodging mini-avalanches as they pushed through the entrance.[87]

But Norfolk's communal atmosphere wasn't really what aggravated Malcolm; it was how the community—and the administration—acted toward Islam. Having the freedom to move around each day, Malcolm was able to communicate his NOI message to many of the other Black incarcerated men. As he wrote to Philbert in March, he'd been encouraged by how the younger Black men listened to him, but the Norfolk guards and possibly other men criticized the religion. "They not only ridiculed the Truth," Malcolm wrote, "but with expertly concocted and perpetuated lies they made the youths even fear to be seen with me."[88]

Norfolk was without doubt a cozier form of prison, but only if the men followed the rules and rehabilitated in a way that fit the institution's vision of reform. Islam, especially a form of Islam that emphasized the Black race over the white race, had not been accepted in Norfolk's world. So it's no surprise that Malcolm felt that his persuasive arguments were being undercut by the prison system's own brand of persuasion.

It's also important to note that Malcolm, after nearly two years, may have already been in touch with most of Norfolk's Black prison population and wanted a different audience. According to 1950 census record counts conducted from April to May of that year, Norfolk had a general population of 984 men, but only 89 were Black. The average age of those Black incarcerated men hovered around 32 years old. As for Charlestown State Prison, out of 597 men, 74 were listed as Black. Malcolm wanted to talk to these men, even though only a few were "ideal" candidates, meaning single and in their 20s.

If Malcolm had simply wanted to reach this kind of man, he may have considered being transferred back to MR-Concord, where most of the men were still young and single.[89]

But the solitude to meditate was Malcolm's top priority.

TYPHOID

In Malcolm's prison file, one March 1950 comment in particular shows how Malcolm had been viewed by several Norfolk prison guards and officials: "Subject is reported to be a shrewd and cunning individual. One who complains about prejudice of officers and interference with his religious beliefs (Moslem). He appears unnecessarily race conscious and is outspoken about the superiority of his race."[90]

As Malcolm stewed, Jarvis grew closer to his friend. After a March 2 "insolence" violation—Jarvis argued too aggressively for a prison guard's tastes—Jarvis was transferred to laundry, where Malcolm had remained. In his prison file, Jarvis's spare time activities around March included "reading, studying the Moslem faith, writing musical scores," and playing in the orchestra. His "numerous correspondence" mainly described "musical scores," being a Muslim, and the "care and teaching" of his two sons. Jarvis was now a year removed from his thoughts of suicide, and thanks in part to Malcolm, he'd been given a positive direction.[91]

Prison officials weren't impressed. In a March 1950 report, they gave a summation of Jarvis's character: "At first [in 1946] he was egotistical, self-centered but studious and well behaved and [had a] good attitude." But after four years, Jarvis now had a "race prejudice" and came off as "superior and critical of [the] institution."[92]

Osborne Thaxton stayed close with Malcolm and Jarvis, making lamps and reading fiction in his spare time. Two years into his sentence, a prison official asked Thaxton why he didn't attend any religious services offered. Thaxton's reply was clear. "[I have] my own religion."[93]

In January 1950, he'd heard that his younger brother, Leroy Thaxton, had been sentenced to Charlestown State Prison. Thaxton was concerned for his brother, since Leroy's reading ability was low and Charlestown was, well,

Charlestown. Prison officials looked more favorably upon Thaxton than Jarvis and Malcolm, stating that he'd "conformed fairly well to institutional routine," but in the middle of March, he, along with his two friends, prepared to leave Norfolk behind for good.[94]

Norfolk mainly used a network of water wells around the prison facility. This, coupled with their tunnel transportation and sewage systems, meant that there was a chance that wells could be contaminated with typhoid bacillus. Typhoid outbreaks were a strong concern, especially for closed communities such as prisons, when the disease could be spread not only through sewage but also through food, milk, and flies and by "human carriers" who showed no symptoms but could pass on the disease through unwashed hands.[95]

At both MR-Concord and Norfolk, men were required to receive a typhoid vaccination. This meant that all 980 men at Norfolk were, annually, "injected . . . with dead typhoid fever germs . . . under the skin in the upper part of the arm, in three doses usually at weekly intervals."

Prior to joining the Nation of Islam, both Malcolm and Thaxton had been given the inoculation at MR-Concord (and Thaxton during his time in the military). Jarvis and Malcolm had also been vaccinated at Norfolk as recently as the prior year. But now their priorities had changed. The NOI, partly out of governmental distrust stemming in part from the highly controversial Tuskegee Syphilis Study, forbade its members from receiving vaccines. In addition, vaccines also included gelatin, which contained elements of pig flesh. Consuming any form of pork was strictly forbidden in the Qur'ān. If Malcolm, Jarvis, and Thaxton agreed to the vaccination, they'd be going against their religion's beliefs. So they had a choice: take the shots and stay at Norfolk, or resist and face the consequences.[96]

Around March 18, the three men made their decision together. They knew that by resisting the vaccination, Norfolk administration would not allow them to remain in the prison. The only prison that had "treated" water was Charlestown. If they refused the shot, that 145-year-old dungeon was their future—17 hours inside a cell; cold, lifeless iron bars; and, of course, those waste-filled buckets.

Malcolm was determined to stay true to his beliefs. On March 18, a day after talking to Reginald about Islam, he composed an eight-page letter to

Brother Raymond, a Harlem musician, and his words reflect a man devoted to his own religious worldview: "The most beautiful thing in the world, and is a beauty that forever attracts, is that which is read in the depths of ones eyes . . . therein lies the essence of ones Soul . . . the Book of Allah . . . for it is this deep unfathomable work of Nature that forever leaves the onlooker mute with silent admiration." Malcolm went on, describing his ideal mindset: "People who possess this look of far-awayness are very deep thinkers . . . and are often classed as 'Dreamers.' The Dreamers are never sad, for they remain not in this wicked world of sadness . . . they live in the 'within' . . . they can climb to the 'Heights,' and abode in Worlds of their own . . ."[97]

On March 19, on the same day Boston University came for its annual debate against Norfolk, Malcolm talked to his corrections officer, Horace Dow, and told him his thoughts: He'd refuse the vaccine on religious grounds. Dow accepted Malcolm's decision and told him that he needed to be interviewed by the assistant deputy warden at the time, Jeremiah Dacey. Malcolm told Dacey, according to Dacey's report, that he "anticipated we would soon be given typhoid inoculations and that he had recently found out that this was against his religion." The *recently* word choice was how Malcolm justified accepting last year's vaccination. Dacey, not exactly thrilled at having this kind of disruption to his routine, told Malcolm that "it was mandatory that every inmate at this institution be inoculated and that should they refuse they are returned to the institution from which they came." Malcolm knew this, and since MR-Concord meant the same vaccine dilemma, he told Dacey that he "did not mind being sent back to State Prison." Dacey, without question in disbelief that a man would "not mind" being sent back to one of the worst prisons in the country, reported the matter to Superintendent Edward Grennan, who was new enough on the job that he was still using Maurice Winslow's letterhead as paper. Grennan, on the same day as Malcolm's interview with Dacey, typed up a report to Commissioner Elliott E. McDowell and "requested" that Malcolm be "returned" to Charlestown.[98]

Just like that—from corrections officer to assistant deputy to deputy and finally to state commissioner—Malcolm's transfer was approved three days later.

Thaxton was next. On the morning of March 21, 1950, Thaxton let his house officer know that he wasn't going to take the upcoming vaccination because it was "against his faith to allow anything to be taken from or put into his body." In came Dacey again, reminding Thaxton of his time in the military and at Concord. *Why now?* Thaxton was resolute. That was "before he had taken his faith seriously and he did not know what he was doing [back then]." Dacey once again performed the same routine as he did with Malcolm, telling Thaxton that "it was necessary at all state institutions not having treated water to immunize against a possible typhoid epidemic." Thaxton knew. Of course he knew. And he kept private the fact that he'd be reunited with his brother Leroy—a fact that may have only complicated administrative matters.[99]

Up the ladder went Thaxton's request, and on March 23, Malcolm and Thaxton were in the same prison vehicle headed toward Charlestown, which, despite having treated water, was stated by then-Massachusetts governor Paul Dever "as the most antiquated and unsanitary institution of its kind in the entire United States. Its continued use by the Commonwealth is little short of disgraceful."[100]

Jarvis was the last to meet with Dacey, and once again, Dacey made him aware of why they needed to transfer him to Charlestown if he refused the inoculation. Jarvis told Dacey that "it was against his Moslem faith . . ." and that was that. Because he was last, Jarvis had to wait a week (March 30) to be transferred to Charlestown.

Jarvis had been at Norfolk for almost four years. He'd had a garden, played in the orchestra, written dozens of musical compositions, and he'd endured emotional setbacks such as the loss of his wife and sister and suffered through depression and suicidal thoughts—only to be saved by a newfound faith in Allah.[101]

That final week at Norfolk was a song with a melody only he understood.

9
THE RISE OF X

March 1950 to September 1952

My time, my whole Life at present, is lived within the letters I write and receive . . . for the beautiful words from my beloved Brothers and Sisters create an atmosphere for me that no devil can destroy.

—Malcolm X, March 9, 1950

In early 1950, Massachusetts Gov. Paul Dever announced that, finally, Charlestown State Prison was to be demolished, and a new maximum-security prison would soon be built in Walpole. Once completed, this $3.4 million prison would receive most of the men at Charlestown. On the day they broke ground, Dever reminded the public that this new building was necessary, saying that "the ancient bastille of Charlestown" had been "condemned as unfit for humans 70 years ago."[1]

This *would* have been good news for Malcolm, Jarvis, and the two Thaxton brothers, but new prisons aren't built overnight. In fact, Charlestown continued to function until 1955, when a new prison (MCI-Walpole) was finally completed.

This meant that Malcolm and his fellow "humans" had to serve out the remainder of their sentence inside "the oldest prison still in use in the United States or England." Even worse, Charlestown State Prison's infrastructure was slowly beginning to shut down—closed work departments, staff and administration laid off or transferred, new equipment orders denied, annual budgets sliced—pushing Malcolm and the 590 or so other men around him into a state of survival, as they continued to urinate and defecate in small pails, emptying them out each day, porous concrete walls and rusted iron bars surrounding their cells.[2]

Charlestown's "library," meanwhile, had seen better days. In 1950, men were permitted on Tuesday and Thursday afternoons to peruse the creaky shelves of what one *Mentor* writer described as "old and slightly outmoded" books. Gone was any semblance of Norfolk's diverse library offerings, and with no bindery and a nonexistent budget, Malcolm was stuck reading from badly tattered books.[3]

On Saturday, March 25, Ella came to Charlestown to visit Malcolm. She arrived "late," and they only had a few minutes to talk, time limits being enforced far more strongly than at Norfolk. "Ella wants to try and get me out," Malcolm wrote to Philbert a day later. "Previously when she has asked me if I wanted out I have said, 'not particularly.'" This time was different, however. "I told her to do whatever she can."

This was not the same Malcolm who entered Charlestown in 1946, back when the isolation of an old cell drove his embittered mind toward madness. He may have told Ella to try to do whatever she could, but Malcolm was far more prepared mentally for this new stretch. "Here we are in our cells for seventeen of the twenty-four hours each day . . . and what more could one desire who wished to meditate upon the Truth." Inside a decaying, soon-to-be-demolished jail cell, Malcolm now had the discipline and religious faith necessary to transcend his dire situation. "Prison, thanks to Islam, has ceased to be prison . . . for I have learned to love the pricelessness of Pure Solitude."[4]

MAKING HEADLINES

Malcolm wanted more than solitude, however. He wanted to begin spreading the message of the NOI to other Black men at Charlestown. The earliest convert was Osborne's younger brother, Leroy, who only finished the second grade before dropping out, was labeled by prison officials as illiterate, and suffered from "stuttering." He was serving a 10–12-year sentence for assault with intent to rape a white woman, but a psychiatrist's report stated that "doctors found no signs of rape after examining" the woman, and that Leroy "strenuously denies this offense." Still, there was little doubt of the assault; Leroy had attempted to steal the woman's purse and overpowered her after she had just stepped off the bus.[5]

Even though Leroy could not "read or write and [could] not do the simplest problems with figures," he could listen, and as soon as he made Malcolm's acquaintance, he committed himself to Malcolm and the NOI. He wanted to be better.

With belief came confidence. Eight months after first meeting Malcolm, Leroy was written up by a prison guard for being "out of place." Where was he? In "room 86 Extension . . . standing in the middle of the room praying." When the guard said he could pray any time, just not "out of place," Leroy talked back to him, saying he'd been given approval by a different prison guard. "Who's the bigger man around here," Leroy said, "you or [Deputy Warden] Blaney?"[6]

Praying toward Mecca was one of Malcolm's concerns upon arriving back at Charlestown, and he made this and other religious demands known to 58-year-old warden John J. O'Brien. The bespectacled Charlestown warden—a married father of three who'd gained years of experience as an assistant superintendent under mentor and friend Maurice Winslow—had heard from Norfolk about the three Muslims.[7] Now they were four, and Malcolm, their spokesman, had a few requests:

> Cells facing east toward Mecca.
> No pork in their meals.
> Work assignments in shops quiet enough to pray during breaks.

For O'Brien, it was a difficult spot to be in. If he denied their requests, he'd be denying their religious freedom—a well-known American right and an attractive media subject. At first, he was apprehensive, but Malcolm knew he had him. During their brief negotiations, Malcolm made sure to let O'Brien know that an Egyptian Consulate member was one phone call away from coming to the prison to help their cause. "He'll appreciate our position. He'll tell you that our religious freedom is being interfered with unless we get cells facing East—and Mecca."[8]

These words are not directly attributed to Malcolm, but they sound like a man who'd spent his time learning the art of debate and argumentation with a high-quality debate team.

O'Brien gave in to their "cells facing east" demand. This unique concession, a maximum-security prison warden acquiescing to a group of Black Muslims, was discovered by a reporter and picked up by the United Press newswire. Soon, an account of the conflict was published in newspapers as far away as Kentucky. "The four grew beards and mustaches," a journalist wrote, "and won a battle against being forced to eat pork—which they said was prohibited by their new religion."[9]

The wording of the newspaper is not entirely correct. They could eat it or not, but just like Norfolk, lard was used as an ingredient when preparing food, so it was next to impossible to avoid it completely. Still, the awareness that Muslims did not want pork was made loud and clear by Malcolm and the rest of the group.[10]

As for the work assignments, some newspaper articles state that three of the men had secured transfers from the foundry because it was too noisy, but this is not true either. Here are the job assignments of the four men according to their prison files:

Table 9.1. Charlestown State Prison—work assignments

Malcolm Little	Malcolm Jarvis	Osborne Thaxton	Leroy Thaxton
3/24/1950—Auto 4	3/30/1950—Auto 1	3/24/1950—Auto 4	1950—Yard
3/25/1950—Auto 1	11/18/1950—Print	4/5/1950—Foundry	—Kitchen
4/5/1950—Yard		8/16/1951—Foundry	—Clothing
6/15/1950—Auto 2			—Carpenter
8/31/1950—Laundry			—Laundry-Dates Unknown

Only Osborne Thaxton chose to work in the foundry. It's possible that Malcolm told Warden O'Brien that the environment of their work assignment needed to take into account prayers during breaks. This O'Brien could allow, as long as prayers did not affect their output or disrupt the workforce.

Still, the men's efforts were published in local newspapers such as the *Springfield Union* and *Boston Herald*. Malcolm was causing trouble again—the good kind.[11]

"MINISTER" MALCOLM AND COMMISSIONER McDOWELL

Malcolm hadn't yet been officially deemed an NOI minister, but he was already looking to help in any way he could.

The power a minister had to change the minds of authorities was on display at Charlestown. One Black incarcerated man, 34-year-old dishwasher Edward H. Lee, had been charged with the murder of a 57-year-old man during a clothing store hold up and was sentenced to death. In March 1950, with his execution date coming soon, Lee—in the same Cherry Hill death row cell block as John Noxon and Raphael Skopp had once been—started to meet with Charlestown's prison chaplain, Rev. Howard P. Kellett. The minister met daily with Lee, listening to his story. Kellett had been in this position for the last 10 years, hearing the desperate pleas of men not wanting to die, but his visits with Lee felt different. Kellett became "convinced" that Lee was innocent. Over time, he learned that Lee had been beaten by police officers after the arrest and during the abusive interrogation made three different confessions in 12 hours. Kellett, telling the warden and Governor Dever that this was the "first time [he] ever felt this way," recommended that Lee's life be spared. Kellett's words were enough, and on April 12, 1950, Lee's sentence was commuted to life, all thanks to the words of a minister.[12]

Granted, Malcolm was not a white Protestant minister like Kellett, but if the Nation of Islam could grow to such a point that their religion would be just as respected, perhaps he could one day exert just as much influence over injustice as Kellett.

On April 18, two days before his "cells facing east" victory was published in newspapers, Malcolm continued to try to help his fellow Muslims. He wrote a letter to the Massachusetts commissioner of corrections, Elliott E. McDowell. The tone of the letter is religious, direct, and confident. It was written regarding a Black man back at Norfolk whose name is unknown.

Many of Malcolm's prison letters postconversion (October 1948 and on) begin with an introductory prayer or preamble—an invocation to Allah. For any non-Muslim, such as McDowell, to open this kind of letter meant being alarmed by its apocalyptic tone. One assumes that Malcolm did this not only to show the intensity of his faith but also, in this case, to grab the commissioner's attention. *You are to take my words seriously. Listen to me . . .*

In the name of Allah, the All-Wise True and Living God, the Almighty Master of This Final Day of Judgment . . . and in the Name of His Holy Apostle whom He came to this Bottomless Pit to Raise from this Level of Death to a Live Perpendicular to Be the

First Begotten of the Original Squares, the Honorable Mr. Elijah Mohammed.

As Salaam Alaikum

Commissioner MacDowell [sic],

One of my Muslim Brothers is being held in solitary confinement at the Norfolk Prison Colony. Because of his sincere desire to rid himself of the intellectual and spiritual bondage which had him enslaved, he whole heartedly embraced Islam . . . and by doing this he incurred the wrath of Mr. [redacted]. Because the Brother wishes to be <u>Black</u> (instead of negro or colored), because of his desire to be a good Muslim, and because he is supposedly without friends or relatives to call upon he is being maliciously persecuted.[13]

The letter flips between prophetic language and a practical request. In short, Malcolm wants McDowell to review the reasons why this man was still being punished. "Brother [deleted] has been in solitary now nearly four months. He is locked up for reasons that flow from the warped minds of biased men whose ignorance has filled their hearts with racial and religious prejudice. I do not believe you are familiar with the circumstances in the case; if you were the situation would be altered."

It's unknown if McDowell resolved the situation, but he did send the letter to Norfolk superintendent Grennan, and made sure to inform Malcolm a week later through an intermediary that he did indeed read the letter.

But Malcolm and McDowell were just getting started.

On June 6, Malcolm wrote to the commissioner again. This time it concerned matters involving Leroy and Osborne Thaxton. After a shortened religious invocation, Malcolm got right to the point:

We, the Muslims at Charlestown prison, keep to ourselves, we mind our own business, and we have never broken any regulations of this institution. We spend all our own time studying, thinking, and speaking with each other about our own people, the Black people. We are seeking the Truth about ourselves, our

God, and the devil. Is this against the law? If so, whose law? The Law of Almighty Allah; or the law of "mitey" devil? If our present endeavors are wrong we should be punished outright; if we are insane we belong in Bridgewater; if our Quest is in Truth we should be left in Peace.

One of the Muslims [Leroy] is illiterate; his flesh-and-blood Brother [Osborne] requested of the deputy that they be placed in work-shops together so that he could teach and assist him in acquiring an education during their spare moments between tasks. The deputy refused their request without hesitation; he actually refuses to allow two Brothers to rehabilitate themselves . . . yet, the homosexual perverts in here can get job-changes whenever they wish to change or acquire new "husbands." You figure that one out![14]

For Malcolm, this was all about winning the moral argument, and McDowell's very public debate with Dr. Miriam Van Waters, the superintendent of Beatrice's former prison, Framingham Women's Reformatory, was headline news in the papers. McDowell had wanted Van Waters dismissed based on a number of charges, one of which was her "failure to prevent or recognize the existence of associations which have," according to Van Water's attorney, "resulted in homosexual practices among the inmates of the reformatory." By using the phrase "homosexual perverts," Malcolm was attempting to use examples to provoke a reaction from McDowell.[15]

Malcolm continued his letter, complaining of how disappointing Charlestown's prison library was. "In our earnest attempt to learn something about our own people we set out to purchase some books on Black History. The books were authored by J. A. Rogers (historian, anthropologist, Egyptologist, etc), a noted member of the Pittsburg[h] Courier's editorial staff. We were also refused this request, and were informed that it was against the law for us to have them or to delve into 'things of that nature' (the speaker evidently forgot himself). Is it actually against the 'law' for a Black man to read about himself? (let me laugh!)."

The aspiring minister of justice also noted how the guards were fanning the flame of racial tension: "The deputy [Charlestown warden] has also personally threatened some of the younger fellows, telling them that he would make it tough for them if they associated with us or if they took an interest in the Truth. [The deputy] concocts lies, speaking unwisely of things that are beyond his knowledge and over his head, things that he has not the capacity to understand. He unwisely discusses us with the white inmates, an act that increases racial tension and ill-feeling."

Malcolm then described to the commissioner a close call involving an incarcerated Black Muslim and a prison guard working under the deputy: "One of [the deputy's] 'white tools' recently nearly hurried the Day of Judgement by getting near one of the Muslims and starting a loud conversation about 'black bastards.' Smelling a rat, [the Muslim] ignored the remark; he was seeking Peace. He explained the incident to the deputy, requesting a transfer from the shop in order to avoid unnecessary 'excitement' . . . the deputy told him to come back and see him the next day; when [the Muslim] came [back], the deputy laughed in his face and refused the request."

Again, it's unknown whether Malcolm's request on behalf of Leroy and Osborne was granted. Most likely, the guards didn't want Leroy to join Osborne in the foundry—a dangerous and unpredictable place to work—because supervisors were concerned Leroy was not mentally capable of protecting himself in such a volatile work environment. It *is* possible that Malcolm was granted the right to request the purchase of the works of J. A. Rogers, whose books he'd already devoured back at Norfolk.

There was one request Malcolm made that can be verified through prison files as being approved. "I am well aware," Malcolm wrote, "that you [McDowell] have records there and in Washington D.C. showing that all of my Brothers in Detroit are Teachers of Islam, one [Wilfred or Philbert] being the minister and secretary of the Temple there. The Muslims here [at Charlestown] have not been allowed to write to them, on the pretext 'that inmates can't write to relatives of inmates.' I'm certain that you have acquired enough [Masonic] degrees to know that all Muslims are Brothers in Truth. Knowing you are familiar with Islam (to a degree[16]), I'll not elucidate. Never deter or attempt to prevent a Muslim from Seeking his Light! Have you not been taught this? Will you go against your own knowledge?"[17]

Malcolm's words were strong, and it appears that McDowell bent somewhat on this matter, since Osborne Thaxton and Malcolm Jarvis are on record as having been contacted or visited by Malcolm's brothers—Osborne wrote to Philbert "Shah," and Jarvis met Wilfred at Charlestown.

Still, during this back and forth with McDowell, Malcolm had the wherewithal to understand how his letters were incidentally portraying Warden

O'Brien. Shouldn't Malcolm be addressing these matters with him instead of going over him to the commissioner? Perhaps he did, and perhaps O'Brien recommended to Malcolm that the religious issues mentioned should be brought to McDowell's attention. Regardless of the direction, the warden, at least in Malcolm's letters, was beginning to look pretty bad.

Leave it to Malcolm to attempt to smooth over the situation in a letter addressed to O'Brien on June 26, 1950:

> *Warden O'brien,*
>
> *Dear Sir, One of the main factors of doing time is the friendliness and understanding of the Warden and officers of the prison.*
>
> *I believe in giving credit where it is due, and I'd like to say on behalf of my buddies that we greatly appreciate the kindness of you, the deputies, and all the officers and [personnel]. Although they fully uphold the position they must fill, they always are willin[g] to answer with a smile, any question we want to ask.*
>
> *There is always a pleasant answer to our questions, and it[']s a good feeling to know that each of these men is in a sense a swell guy. As for you and the deputies Sir, every man here refers to them as a man with a heart.*
>
> *Aside from what I[']ve written, this letter has no other purpose other than to say that we are glad to be under the rule of such a staff. Thanks.*[18]

It was an oddly worded letter. Was Malcolm being sarcastic? "Answer with a smile" and "a pleasant answer" sound purposely neutral and could be taken several ways. What *kind* of smile was it? Was it pleasant to Malcolm because it amused him? Or was Malcolm sincere because he'd been granted some kind of privilege and wanted to show his appreciation? Or, as one biographer hypothesized, perhaps Malcolm knew that June 26 was "exactly one year before" his parole meeting, and this letter was simply trying to butter someone up.[19]

Warden O'Brien believed Malcolm had somewhat good intentions. Three days later, the warden wrote to McDowell, asking for the letter to be included in Malcolm's file: "It would be nice to have in his folder for future reference."[20]

HANGING ON

These epistolary arguments helped pass the time, but Malcolm was still faced with 17 hours of solitude in a decrepit prison on the verge of closing. To make matters worse, in August, Paul W. Foster, a columnist for the *Berkshire Eagle*, heard from a source that Charlestown's prison staff was suffering from "low morale." The root cause was from well-behaved men being "beaten" by other men who'd been deemed "favorites" by guards. Ever since 1946—when Malcolm first entered Charlestown—a few of the men were selected as "trust-ees," which meant they had the responsibility of making decisions for the entire prison population. While this system may have helped quell riots in the past, it was vulnerable to a few bad apples. As Foster put it, "Some of the complaint from the staff includes claims of favoritism toward particular prisoners. Some of them chosen as trust[e]es are said to be among the men with the worst records before the confinement. They have reportedly been engaged [in July and August] in knifing escapades in which the prison guards have been the victims."[21]

In other words, Malcolm's short time walking in the prison yard was fraught with men carrying around shivs who had enough authority to stab a prison guard and get away with it. Low morale indeed. And with the new prison not set to begin construction until early 1951, Malcolm would indeed be stuck for the remainder of his sentence inside an entropic prison system and a building that existed even before his great-great-grandfather Hajja had been pushed onto American shores. Even Jarvis felt the age of the prison, titling one of his musical compositions *The Bastille Concerto*, "Bastille," the term used for a French fortress during the 1789 revolution, being one of many nicknames given to Charlestown's crumbling façade.[22]

The conditions were brutal enough that, on October 3, Malcolm sent a letter to Warden O'Brien to see if it was possible to be transferred *back* to Norfolk. O'Brien, however, dictated to an intermediary that he believed a transfer request was "inadvisable."[23]

Make no mistake, a sense of desperation emanated from Charlestown. One Roxbury man, 35-year-old Martin F. Feeney, exemplified the mood for many on the inside. On October 16, 1950, Feeney, serving 15 years for armed robbery, plotted an escape attempt with another incarcerated man, John Kerrigan. Feeney waited for the day that Warden O'Brien would be gone. Sure enough, October 16 was the same day the warden would be attending a groundbreaking ceremony over at the construction site for the new prison. Feeney, in Charlestown less than a year, "attempted to crash through the inner gate" of the visiting room while waiting for an unknown visitor. He and Kerrigan "hurled themselves at the gate hoping it would spring open." It did not. A year before, Kerrigan had tried to escape by "concealing" himself in a packing case on a truck. Five minutes later, the truck was checked, and Kerrigan was back in prison.[24]

Seventeen and a half hours a day inside a 150-year-old 6-by-12 cell in an underfunded prison with a pail for a toilet . . . this would break many men, and Feeney had had enough. Four days after his botched visiting room escape, he purposely broke his eyeglasses, picked up a shard, and cut his left wrist twice. Nearby, a guard saw Feeney bleeding and managed to stop him from finishing the job.[25]

Purpose. A greater good. These concepts are thrown around quite a bit, but for incarcerated men, they are the difference between hanging on or caving in. Feeney had not found his purpose, just like Malcolm during his first year at Charlestown, when his future teetered between life and death. But here Malcolm was now, a man committed to a message he needed to share with the world. In October, he wrote to his new sister-in-law, Henrietta, Philbert's wife: "The tears of joy will roll down my cheeks as I see the Black Man throughout the World coming together in true brotherhood." It was Allah who would save the American Black man from the sharp claws of a white-favored American society, and Malcolm needed to hold on to help this dream become a reality. This was *his* greater good—a cause larger than the prison that held him.[26]

It helped that he had support. Near the end of 1950, Malcolm had made his way back to the laundry department, but once per day, he and the rest of the prison population—in phases—made their loops around the yard. It was here where he'd have a chance to talk with Jarvis and the Thaxton brothers. The group occupied their time by testing each other mentally. "We experimented with sending mental messages to each other," Jarvis wrote in his memoir. "The following day, we would discuss who sent whom what message and if it were received. Several times we were successful, hitting the nail right on the head. It scared us . . . [and] forced us to give this process our deepest respect." Jarvis called it the practice of "mental telepathy and clairvoyance."[27]

But after enduring eight months of Charlestown's hell-like conditions, Malcolm's health had started to decline. "I have ulcers or something," he wrote to Philbert in December, "but I've had my 'fill' of hospitals since being in here. Ole man, think I'm actually falling apart physically. Nothing more physically wrecks a man than a steady prison diet . . . and I've had [it] for years . . . now." By trying to avoid pork, Malcolm had made prison life even harder to survive. His diet largely consisted of bread and cheese bought from the consignment shop, and without enough movement or exercise, stomach aches and constipation were inevitable.[28]

Even reading, his favorite activity, had become more difficult. "I had come to prison with 20/20 vision," he explained in his *Autobiography*, "but when I got sent back to Charlestown, I had read so much by the lights-out glow in my room at the Norfolk Prison Colony that I had [an] astigmatism and [was given] the first pair of the eyeglasses that I have worn ever since."[29]

FAMILY VERSUS BELIEF

A bit of hope arrived in early December 1950, when several family members came from Detroit to visit him over the holidays. While in prison, Malcolm had often spoken warmly of his large family, showing pictures to other incarcerated men. "Someone [in Charlestown] remarked of the picture of you and Hilda," Malcolm wrote to Philbert in December, "that you were a fine looking couple. When I said you were my Brother and Sister they were surprised . . . because my ugliness just didn't coincide with your handsomeness and her loveliness."

Philbert was back in Detroit, on trial for assault after a run-in with police officers outside his Detroit Temple, leaving Wilfred and Hilda to visit Malcolm.[30]

For Wilfred, it was one of those big-brother visits. He had a few things he needed Malcolm to understand, and since Malcolm's first attempt at parole was five months away, this was a perfect time to see if he'd listen. Wilfred had heard how Malcolm was successful in his "cells facing east" request, but Wilfred knew that attitude wasn't going to get him out of prison. As the family sat with Malcolm in the Charlestown visiting room, Wilfred was direct. "You've been causing too much trouble in here," he told him. "[You're] always challenging the guards and challenging everybody who was in authority." To Wilfred, this part of Malcolm, always "challenging authority," had never changed.[31]

Authority *needed* challenging. Wilfred understood this—*but not all the time*. Malcolm's parole was coming up. If he didn't change his attitude, Wilfred believed, they wouldn't let him out. "So I told him, 'Look, there's a book you need to read that will do you more good than the Bible in here.'" Malcolm was surprised. For the last few months, he'd been reading the King James Version of the Bible constantly, paying close attention to a passage in Matthew 26, verses 33–34, when Jesus predicts the betrayal of Peter: "Jesus said unto him, Verily I say unto thee, That this night, before the cock crow, thou shalt deny me thrice." Around the time Wilfred and family had come to visit, Malcolm was attempting to understand the differences in betrayal between Peter and Judas, even wondering to Philbert, "Was Peter Judas? Could this describe the story of Peter[']s denial and Judas['s] betrayal?"[32]

Malcolm was deep within his own self-study of the Bible, but now Wilfred wanted him to go in a different direction, so his oldest brother handed him a copy of Dale Carnegie's 1936 bestseller, *How to Win Friends and Influence People*. Malcolm listened to Wilfred's explanation of the self-help book, then shook his head. "He looked at me like I was crazy," Wilfred said. "He wouldn't read it!"[33]

Also in the visiting room was Jarvis. As Wilfred remembered it, Hilda had asked Charlestown guards to allow Jarvis to join them. Jarvis was also up for parole soon, and he told Malcolm's family sure, he'd read it; anything that could help him get out sooner.

The visit stuck with Malcolm, as did Wilfred's subsequent letters. Paired with similar pleas for Malcolm to comply more with authorities, Malcolm's mind was taken on a "long sojourn out in space." His religious studies cooled, and he began to reflect on who he'd been.[34]

In a letter dated January 9, 1951, and possibly sent to Elijah Muhammad, Malcolm laid into himself, chastising his past behavior: "I was guided by hate, envy and the craving for revenge . . . deluded by my own vanity and self-esteem; I was blinded with my own ignorance and false sense of reasoning. In my effort to justify my many self-inflicted wrongs I placed the blame upon everyone except the one who was mainly responsible for all of my troubles . . . myself."[35]

Malcolm mentioned "an enlightening visit from my family in Detroit" and how his "many past errors were then made known to me. I am not, and never shall be, too proud to admit when I am wrong . . . and with great remorse I now think of the hate and revenge that I have been preaching in the past. But from here on in my words shall all be of Love and Justice."[36]

Malcolm sounded certain here, his solitary thoughts moving toward asceticism. How seriously was he going to take himself? And how seriously should he hold others accountable for their weaknesses? Yes, he had friends around him—Jarvis, the Thaxton brothers—and he had his brothers and sisters writing to him, but the men he most admired were in the pages he read for hours a day. Twelfth-century Persian poets, biblical legends, ancient African historical figures, and self-proclaimed living prophets such as Elijah Muhammad. *These* were great men—their flaws shrouded by their own mythic potential. In many ways while imprisoned, Malcolm related to the intensity of these men more than Wilfred's laid-back humanity. *Dale Carnegie? Really?*

These were difficult times for Malcolm, and his ever-strengthening ideal-ism was severely put to the test when his brother Reginald started to show up to Charlestown appearing more and more downtrodden. Then one day, he started to criticize Elijah Muhammad, and it was as if Reginald had stabbed his older brother. "It caught me totally unprepared," Malcolm wrote later of Reginald's act of forsakenness. "It threw me into a state of confusion. My blood brother, Reginald, in whom I had so much confidence, for whom I had so much respect, the one who had introduced me to the Nation of Islam. I couldn't believe it! And now Islam meant more to me than anything I ever had known in my life. Islam and Mr. Elijah Muhammad had changed my whole world."[37]

For Reginald, the past year or so had been filled with highs and lows. After joining the Nation of Islam in 1948, Elijah Muhammad promoted him to the position of "chief minister at Harlem Temple No.7." For a while, Reginald had a bit of stability. But after Reginald started an affair with his married secretary, Elijah Muhammad chose to suspend him from his position. In June and July of 1950, Reginald was hospitalized in New York for a physical ailment. And in December of the same year, Malcolm wrote to Philbert that "Reginald hasn't written for over a month. See if you can ascertain his whereabouts and well-being."[38]

Reginald wasn't well. His life had started to fall apart, and he blamed Elijah Muhammad for banishing him from the NOI. For his Charlestown visits, Reginald's appearance deteriorated, and now Malcolm was concerned. "When he had been a Muslim, he had been immaculate in his attire. But now, he wore things like a T-shirt, shabby-looking trousers, and sneakers. I could see him on the way down. When he spoke, I heard him coldly. But I would listen. He was my blood brother."[39]

That *blood* devotion, so important to Malcolm, was set against his beliefs. He wrote Elijah Muhammad, pleading to his mentor to be more lenient toward

Reginald. And then, in a memorable scene described in the *Autobiography*, Malcolm had a vision:

> It was the next night, as I lay on my bed, I suddenly, with a start, became aware of a man sitting beside me in my chair. He had on a dark suit. I remember. I could see him as plainly as I see anyone I look at. He wasn't black, and he wasn't white. He was light-brown-skinned, an Asiatic cast of countenance, and he had oily black hair.
>
> I looked right into his face.
>
> I didn't get frightened. I knew I wasn't dreaming. I couldn't move, I didn't speak, and he didn't. I couldn't place him racially—other than that I knew he was a non-European. I had no idea whatsoever who he was. He just sat there. Then, suddenly as he had come, he was gone.[40]

In these lonely times—spending 120 hours a week alone inside a small, decrepit prison cell—it's not too surprising that Malcolm began to have these kinds of visions, but what is interesting is that Malcolm, while constructing his *Autobiography* with Alex Haley, had chosen to place this moment at the same time he was between forgiving or dismissing Reginald.

There's a reason for this.

In a June 11, 1952, letter to Sister Beatrice Clomax, Malcolm wrote of the same moment but described it differently: "Allah has talked to me before and once He sat beside my bed and let me know that Elijah Muhammad was His messenger. . . . I saw him with my own eyes when my mind was being torn between following Reginald or The messenger. In my moment of doubt, Allah, Himself came and removed the doubt so today I will devote my life to the work of His messenger."[41]

Soon after the vision, Malcolm, after writing in the hopes of reinstating Reginald, heard back from Elijah Muhammad: "If you once believed in the truth, and now you are beginning to doubt the truth, you didn't believe the truth in the first place. What could make you doubt the truth other than your own weak self?"[42]

This absolutist approach was just the kind of clarity Malcolm needed to continue his righteous path, but Elijah Muhammad's words all but ended the unconditional love Malcolm had for Reginald. "From that day on, as far as I am concerned, everything that my brother Reginald has done is wrong," Malcolm explained. This decision, to side with belief over family, tormented Malcolm to the point of regret—especially when he later found out that Elijah Muhammad had a series of affairs with his office secretaries, the same offense that had doomed Malcolm's brother.[43]

As for Reginald, his mind unraveled. In a *Boston Globe* article dated October 22, 1951, it's reported that Reginald Little was "wanted on a charge of violation of the Selective Service Act." With the military using the draft to recruit men to fight in the Korean War, Reginald "came up to the Boston FBI office two weeks ago, [and] said he was a Moslem and that it was against his military beliefs to go into military service." Malcolm's younger brother, without the full support of his NOI family, turned to Ella for support. "I heard no more about Reginald until one day, weeks later, Ella visited me; she told me that Reginald was at her home in Roxbury, sleeping. Ella said she had heard a knock, she had gone to the door, and there was Reginald, looking terrible. Ella said she had asked, 'Where did you come from?' And Reginald had told her he came from Detroit. She said she asked him, 'How did you get here?' And he had told her, 'I walked.'"[44]

Malcolm "believed he had walked." But no matter how hard Reginald's life became, Malcolm could not summon enough sympathy to forgive him. In Malcolm's ascetically rigid mind, Allah had punished his brother, and Reginald only had himself to blame.

But the guilt remained sharp as ever for Malcolm, who years later confessed that it wasn't Allah that had driven Reginald into a mental institution "but the pain [Reginald] felt when his own family totally rejected him for Elijah Muhammad, and this hurt made Reginald turn insanely upon Elijah Muhammad."[45]

JARVIS INFLUENCES PEOPLE

Dear Mother,

All I can say now is I have been as close to death as one man can get without actually dying. . . . I would much rather be dead than to give these people another five years of my life. This is truly the way I

*feel, so I sincerely hope you and the family will get together and do
what you can to free me from the clutches of these evil forces which
have me imprisoned behind bars. Your Son . . .*

—*Malcolm Jarvis*[46]

In May 1951, Malcolm and Jarvis were up for their first chance at parole. It
was clear from the start that Jarvis had a better chance of being released. As his
prison file shows, Jarvis's family—meaning his mother and father, two brothers,
two aunts, two cousins, and a step-brother—had visited him at Charlestown.
All of these family visits were documented and placed in each parole board
member's folder. The more visits by an invested family "on the outside" meant
the better chance an incarcerated man has of convincing the parole board to
give him an early release.

As Malcolm told Jarvis directly, "You don't have to worry about convincing
the parole board that someone is interested. You have a mother and a father!"[47]

True, but Jarvis also needed to accept responsibility for what he did,
and in a way that was particularly convincing to the board. For example,
Jarvis couldn't simply walk up to the parole board, his family ready to receive
him, and say, *Yep. My fault. Shouldn't have done it.*

There was an art form to this admission, and Jarvis had some useful advice to
absorb from Wilfred's copy of Dale Carnegie's *How to Win Friends and Influence
People*. In chapter 1 of the 1943 edition of the book, Carnegie describes how
famous criminals—Al Capone, Dutch Schultz, and "Two Gun" Crowley—never
"blamed themselves for anything." Carnegie even corresponded with former
Sing Sing warden Lewis Lawes, the same warden who toured Charlestown
State Prison at the beginning of Malcolm and Jarvis's sentence. In the book,
Carnegie quotes Lawes as stating that "few of the criminals in Sing Sing regard
themselves as bad men. They are just as human as you and I. So they rational-
ize, they explain. They can tell you why they had to crack a safe or be quick on
the trigger. Most of them attempt by a form of reasoning, fallacious or
logical, to justify their anti-social acts even to themselves, consequently stoutly
maintaining that they should never have been imprisoned at all."[48]

When Jarvis faced the parole board members, he owned up to his mistakes.
The parole board committee's comments show this: "[Jarvis] is not anti-social
and bears no animosity toward the sentencing judge [Allan Buttrick], the

District Attorney, or the arresting officer. He attributes his present offense to his own stupidity, and gives no reason for his prior criminality."[49]

As for religion, Jarvis told the committee the truth, since it showed on his record that he had not attended any of the Christian services provided at Norfolk or Charlestown. "[Jarvis] claims to be a member of the Moslem Faith. He read the Bible, the dictionary, books on philosophy and history, played in the orchestra, and did some plaster work at SPC." On top of completing six assignments for an Elementary Latin correspondence course, working without difficulties in Charlestown's print shop as a "type storage man," and his continued work writing musical compositions, it was clear to the parole board that Jarvis had been making active efforts to improve himself.[50]

The parole board committee considered as much as they could from the data given to them. They knew how much Jarvis had in his bank account— 48 cents—but knew that, since Jarvis told the committee that he'd be living with his parents in Roxbury, the low amount was not too much of a concern. As for his plan to work, Jarvis was "leaving it up to his family to get him a job."[51]

But what may have been the most convincing reason for the parole board to grant Jarvis his release was who he had lost and neglected. From 1946 to 1951, Jarvis attended three funerals during his prison years—his grandfather's in June 1947, his estranged wife Hazel's in 1948, and his sister Elsie's in November 1950. On top of these difficult losses, Jarvis had no choice but to watch his

FIGURE 9.1. Malcolm Jarvis. Mug shots. February 1946 (L)
and when he left in June 1951 (R).

two boys grow up without a father, visiting him only intermittently while in prison. This inability to be a father gnawed at him. In his memoir, Jarvis remembered how hard he prayed in 1946 while awaiting his 8–10-year sentence: "Oh Lord, oh Lord, please hear my sad and humble plea . . . please send me home. Please give me this one and only chance to prove to everybody that I am not bad, but good—with a good heart. Please, oh Lord, send me home for the sake of my two baby sons who would really be the ones to suffer if I am kept in prison."[52]

They weren't babies anymore, but they were waiting for him. On June 26, 1951, after spending 65 months in jail, Malcolm L. Jarvis was given a suit, a $20 bill, and his freedom. His family drove him back to their home in Roxbury, seven miles away.[53]

There was one certain valuable still waiting for Jarvis when he arrived at his parent's house: a diamond ring. "When I got sent to prison," Jarvis confessed 40 years later, "that ring was at my house all during the 5½ years I was at prison." Now the ring had a heavy symbolic value—a painful but necessary reminder of the mistakes he'd made. "It cost me 5½ years of my life, and I'll always keep it."[54]

MALCOLM CONFUSES PEOPLE

Malcolm's case for parole in May 1951 was never very strong. If released, one tentative plan was to remain in the Boston area and live with Ella, but a glance at Ella's criminal record and Malcolm's prison file shows several potential problems. To start with, Ella had Malcolm arrested for stealing her fur coat back in November 1944. Ella also had her own long list of infractions with the law and had been to court at least 10 times for a variety of alleged crimes.[55]

No, Ella was not an option, and even if she were, she may not have wanted to sponsor Malcolm. According to Jarvis, who postrelease visited Ella to talk about why Malcolm was denied parole, Ella was worried that Malcolm might marry one woman, Jackie Massey, who had expressed interest but had a notorious reputation. As Ella later confessed to a biographer, "I'd have rather seen him dead than marry Jackie."

Ella wanted to help Malcolm but in her own way, and she may not have wanted to handle an aspiring minister for the Nation of Islam. Would he continuously try to convert her? After his visit with Ella, Jarvis was under the impression that Ella would rather Malcolm stay in prison than return to the Boston area.[56]

Another sister who had moved to the Boston area, Hilda, may have also been consulted by the parole board. In fact, a redacted document in Malcolm's prison file shows that on June 20, 1951, well after the decision was made, a parole board official did in fact visit with a "sister" of Malcolm's. Judging by Ella's reluctance, Hilda is the best guess: "Discussed [Malcolm's] case [with his sister] at great length. She was a most difficult case to begin with and most biased in [Malcolm's] behalf and against all of society. Finally she seemed to understand what the [Board] was trying to accomplish . . ." Hilda may have expected Malcolm to be released but wasn't able to sponsor him.[57]

The simple truth was that the parole board was unconvinced that Malcolm could return to society without breaking the law. Charlestown's psychiatrist, Henry M. Baker, filed a report after meeting with Malcolm on May 4, 1951. His comments show that Malcolm was still rebellious and, to non-Muslims, difficult to understand: "This twenty-six-year-old colored man from the British West Indies, has a most peculiar appearance, with his bald head, carefully trimmed beard, and general air of importance. . . . He claims to be a Mohammedan, but his conversation expressed a confused jumble of ideas which make little sense."[58]

Still, he had a chance, but Malcolm's sharp attitude came through during the parole board meeting. When asked if he felt "animosity" toward the officials who sentenced him, Malcolm said his past crimes were due to "ignorance"—an important difference compared to Jarvis's Carnegie-approved and more likable answer of "stupidity." Also, the parole board was aware that Malcolm was considered the leader of their burglary ring, and they may have wanted to avoid releasing him at the same time as Jarvis, who was on record as saying that, true or not, he'd been coerced by Malcolm into robbing houses.

The final straw, however, was that Malcolm, "due to the warrant ledged against him . . . had made no plans" regarding his future. This outstanding warrant, connected to an unresolved arrest in Detroit in 1945, had actually been dismissed on April 28, 1947—a decision Malcolm may have only been aware of on May 15, 1951, when the parole board received official notification. If true, it would have meant that Malcolm didn't have enough time to contact his family in Detroit and set up sponsorship (a job and residence). Without this, there was no hope for Malcolm to be granted parole.[59]

One more year . . .

One more year inside a 150-year-old prison, and one less friend.

If he had to be in prison, Malcolm at least wanted his favorite library back in his life. So on June 6, 1951, Malcolm sat at his desk and started writing a letter. He had a request . . .

DREAMS OF NORFOLK

In January 1951, 54-year-old Lt. Col. Maxwell B. Grossman took over as commissioner of corrections after Elliott McDowell had "asked for retirement" after three years on the job. Grossman—bald, bespectacled, and a fan of bow ties—was described by the *Boston Globe* as an "affable man" who believed religion was "the best way" for a man to rehabilitate himself. "As I see it," said Grossman, "religion is the most important thing. If you have a place of worship, even if confined behind prison bars, there is a chance of eventual rehabilitation."[60]

Grossman intentionally kept the term *religion* general. After earning his fortune as the founder of an envelope manufacturing company, Grossman donated funds toward both "Catholic and Jewish chapels" at Massachusetts prisons and hospitals. "No one is closer to an inmate of a prison than a priest, a rabbi or a minister," said Grossman. "Inmates know that they can trust these men of religion and they confide in them, knowing that they will receive good counsel."[61]

Grossman's beliefs may have given Malcolm hope as he started his letter. This time, Malcolm was not on the offensive, as he'd been with McDowell. His tone in this letter, printed in its entirety, is bereft of any threats from Allah, or accusations of discrimination. Malcolm is asking the commissioner for one simple favor—to return to Norfolk.

Commissioner Grossman,

Realizing that you are beset by many headaches of your own, with people constantly abusing your generosity, I hesitate to trouble you with my trivial problem. However, you are the only one to whom I may turn for assistance. . . . I know you can help me, if you will.

A few years ago while at Norfolk I discovered I was very much in the dark, and having become suddenly aware that I had long been dwelling in the Shallow Grave of Ignorance and of the low level to which it had kept me regulated, I vowed to use my every moment thereafter seeking to attain the maximum degree of Truth, and to take a step in no direction until I was certain it was right. . . . this of course soon led to my being returned to Charlestown.

You, being a well-traveled man wise in the ways of all the world, having withstood all tests and surmounted all obstacles in all walks of life (as your present social status will surely attest), can easily understand the precarious position in which my desire to be always right placed me, especially since I was yet unable to distinguish my left from my right.

When experience is the only available Teacher one must suffer many set-backs.

Fourteen months have passed since I was returned from Norfolk. I have not yet acquired a living knowledge, but although I am yet very much in the dark my understanding of Islam has matured to the degree wherein I can now easily adapt myself to whatever the situation demands. I know that I am able to walk in perfect accord with all rules governing Norfolk.

Having reached the stage where I can walk without fear of stumbling or being wrong, I would like to be allowed to return to Norfolk. My prison record is clean (my not having lost any "good time" will attest to this).

Norfolk's atmosphere is more balanced, and without a balanced path the journey is only made more difficult.

Thank you very kindly for taking time from your many duties to look into this.

Sincerely,

Malcolm X. Little.[62]

For Malcolm, this letter is revelatory toward his character at the time. It is not a letter of regret but more an admission that he had to act the way he did at Norfolk to make sure of his beliefs "and to take a step in no direction until [he] was certain it was right." Malcolm's religious rigidity (not submitting to typhoid inoculation) was necessary for him to understand his faith. Now he was self-confident enough in his faith to "easily adapt [him]self to whatever the situation demands."

What's also impressive about this letter is Malcolm's obvious grammatical advancement since his December 1946 letter to Ella. In this letter, Malcolm deploys a gerund-driven, Latinate style, delaying the main verb, similar at times to John Milton's *Paradise Lost* and the King James Version of the Bible, two texts that he devoted hours of time and study to while in prison. After four and a half years of writing letters and reading classic literature, Malcolm had given himself a degree in linguistics.

But Malcolm could have been Shakespeare, and it still wouldn't have changed his fate. He was stuck in Charlestown.

Grossman acknowledged receipt of the letter and reported through an intermediary that Malcolm's case would be heard soon, but nothing ever materialized. It very well could be that Malcolm's next parole hearing, scheduled in May 1952, put a stop to Malcolm's transfer request as a top priority, since Malcolm would most likely be granted parole within a year. The less movement between prisons, the better, especially when the light of a man's freedom could be seen at the end of a long, dark tunnel.[63]

All Malcolm needed to do now was follow his own advice: *Adapt myself to whatever the situation demands*. Malcolm needed to give the parole board what they wanted.

FINDING HIS SPONSOR

Months passed without much change. Besides reading and writing letters, Malcolm worked in the furniture department and began fulfilling orders for "jewel chests" made by mosques in Detroit and Chicago.

Philbert had ordered them, hoping to improve the look of his mosque—the Michigan Temple of Islam, at 1474 Frederick Street in Detroit. This was no trouble on Malcolm's end, seeing as how he had time, and the extra money left over went into his pocket.

Malcolm knew that his older brother could relate to his time in prison. On June 15, 1950, Philbert got into trouble with the law after being involved with three other Muslims in a "shooting fray with police . . . in front of the Temple." According to reports, their car was "double-parked," and when police asked them to move, the group attacked the officers, beating one officer "badly with his own night stick" and scratching and tearing off "most of" the other officer's uniform.

The police retaliated by shooting two of the Muslim men. As the scuffle went on, four Muslim women were sitting in the car "dressed in religious gowns and turbans," including Wilfred's wife, Ruth. Philbert was eventually charged with "felonious assault," and in late January 1951, he was sentenced to two months in prison, three years of probation, and "ordered to make restitution of $2,201 to [the] Receiving Hospital for treatment."[64]

When Malcolm wrote to Philbert on December 19, 1951, he wondered if his brother regretted placing the expensive jewel chest orders, and he also alluded to the time Philbert spent in jail: "We don't want you to buy from us just because we are Muslims, but we do wish all of you would help us to sell whatever we make and in this way we can provide ourselves with much needed nutritional substance. We heard the devil had you for a few months so perhaps you can more easily understand what we mean."[65]

Health was a big concern for Malcolm during this time: "Since having begun recently to make a little spending change," Malcolm wrote in the same letter, "I have been eating fairly well and have since realized that all my previous difficulty was stemming from my lack of nourishment. They feed well here but you know I can't eat pork. I see the parole board again in five months and I'm wondering If I should be saving my money so I can come out with something, or should I continue to spend it for food. Frankly, I think my health is more important than my appearance, and you know there is nothing more miserable than a 'hungry hulk . . .'"

Then Malcolm conveyed this next bit of news: "A very wealthy man, for whom I once worked, visited me today and is going to try and get me a reconsideration from the parole board (*Insha Allah*). The Will of Allah will be done. By the way, he's not an original. However, he can give me a home and a job, which is something I lacked when I saw them before."

Who this mysterious wealthy man was is uncertain. One biographer believed it was Paul Lennon, who Malcolm worked for as a "butler and occasional house worker" back in 1944. Indeed, Lennon was wealthy, but it's very hard to believe that Malcolm gave serious thought to moving into Lennon's home, especially after he'd been through such a transformation of character. Perhaps Lennon offered Malcolm a hefty sum of money or a donation to the Nation of Islam. Or, perhaps Malcolm was reminded of how John Noxon managed to shortcut his way out of prison using high-level connections and considered using Lennon simply as a fast way out of Charlestown's hell.[66]

Regardless, by January 15, 1952, whoever this wealthy man had been didn't matter. The day after a visit with Hilda, Malcolm decided on how to find a sponsor, and he wrote to Philbert—who wasn't a potential sponsor, since he was still on probation—about his future plans. "As you know, I see the parole board again in four months (May) and I may try to get paroled to Detroit," Malcolm wrote. "To do this, I must have a job and a home there and this information must be in the hands of the parole board here before I see them. Also the parole board of that state has to be willing to accept me from this one."[67]

Detroit was an excellent choice. With his record now clean in Michigan, and with several family members living there and the fact that he was raised nearby, the parole board would find this idea promising. Now it was up to the lone family member who could support him—Wilfred. "I'd made arrangements," Wilfred said years later. "I'd gone to the people that I worked with, and they agreed to give him a job, and also he could live with me and my family."[68]

While Wilfred put the plan together, Malcolm continued fulfilling orders for jewel chests. Elijah Muhammad had approved an order of 15 chests for his Chicago Mosque. It was money in Malcolm's pocket, and extra food. "You know this made us [Muslims] well pleased," Malcolm wrote to Philbert, "and we are getting set now to turn them out as fast as our finances will allow."[69]

Malcolm was eating well and on track with a plan. He was also around this time given a reminder of how life could have turned out for him had he never gone to prison. In January, Lionel Hampton's band had come to the Boston area to play a few gigs. Hampton's sextet had just released their record *Moonglow*, and Al Hayse, Hampton's trombone player, took time out of his day to visit Malcolm at Charlestown. Malcolm hadn't seen Hayse in over "six years," not since his time living in Detroit back in 1944.

The hard lifestyle Hayse had endured stayed in Malcolm's mind. "He brought me up to date on that particular life," he noted to Philbert, "and though he admits they're all dying like flies from fast living, he's still living a fast life himself. I studied him, as he talked, and learned how lucky I've been [to not go in that direction]. He's aged tremendously!"

More than others, Malcolm had an affinity for jazz musicians, perhaps because he'd been an entertainer himself and knew how difficult the lifestyle could be. Malcolm wanted to help Hayse, so he tried to tell him about the Nation of Islam. "His impression of Islam has been formed from their observations of the various Muslims (so-called) in show business who say one thing and do another," Malcolm again wrote to Philbert, "thus I didn't press the subject. But someday I shall introduce him to some real Muslims (be it Will of Allah). Hamp too."[70]

LET'S TRY THIS AGAIN

On June 11, 1952, Malcolm sat in his cell, nervous. Within the next two weeks, he was again scheduled to see the parole board. Thanks to Wilfred, his case for release was much stronger than it was a year before. Though he'd yet to receive official approval, Malcolm was set to move in with Wilfred and his wife, Ruth, at their home on 4336 Williams Street in Inkster, Michigan—about 13 miles from Detroit's city center.[71]

Still, parole boards were well-known for making unfair decisions. In 1952, one *Boston Globe* article estimated that the three members of the board oversee "more than 2000 cases" annually and rely heavily on recommendations. Without adequate time to prepare for each case, the board also couldn't help but rely on their first impressions. *Could he be trusted? Was his personality like the description in his case file?*[72]

It wasn't so much that parole boards were seeking to deny every incarcerated man. On the contrary, there were financial advantages. In 1950, it was estimated that it cost Massachusetts around $50 a year to "supervise a man on parole at the same time the man becomes a taxpayer." But for him to remain in prison "costs the state $1013 per year."[73]

None of this Malcolm could control. For the last year, he'd kept his record clean, avoided conflict with other incarcerated men and guards, and stopped writing inflammatory letters to the commissioner or warden about being unfairly treated. In a way, Malcolm had begun to embody several of the principles in Dale Carnegie's book. As Wilfred recalled many years later, after Malcolm was rejected in 1951, Malcolm "went and got that book, and he started to study it and put it into practice. You wouldn't believe the change that book made in him. In fact, they couldn't believe it in prison. They didn't know what to do with him. Here's this guy . . . always giving them a hard time and challenging everything. All of a sudden, now he's a diplomat!"[74]

A nervous diplomat. On June 11, Malcolm wrote to Sister Beatrice Clomax: "Please forgive my poor writing in this letter," he wrote, "but for some reason tonight I am not at full ease." Though Malcolm knew the parole board was coming to Charlestown "before two more weeks pass," they could actually come on any of those days. "I hear the Parole Board might be here tomorrow," so he had no choice but to wait each day out, his future on pause.[75]

Still, he always had time to dream and reflect, and it's clear from his letters to Ms. Clomax, a member of the NOI and a mother to two grown sons and a daughter, that Malcolm was comfortable sharing his thoughts. "There are many things that need to be done," Malcolm wrote of his ministerial ambitions, "but so few to do the task. I have looked around and wondered why more of our people aren't being awakened. There is no one to awaken them."

Malcolm believed the responsibility lay with him to jolt to life Black Americans who'd lost their will to push back against an oppressive system, and this inevitably meant sacrificing companionship. "There is nothing I would like more so than a beautiful Muslim wife and family," Malcolm wrote to Ms. Clomax, "but something tells me fate has chosen me to lead a lonely life, for I have the ability to speak to my people and guide them to the Apostle, and I can not go to Georgia, Alabama and into the heart of this devil's strong hold where the truth has not been heard unless I am free to travel and preach, and that is my one and only desire, to preach to my people."[76]

Unless I am free . . .

After 13 agonizing days of waiting, the parole board finally came to Charlestown on June 24, 1952. In their folders was all the updated info: Malcolm's plan to leave the state, his plan to work at the same company as Wilfred, and his plan to live with him. As he sat down with them, Principle #1 of Dale Carnegie's *How to Win Friends and Influence People* may have been circling his mind: "Don't criticize, condemn or complain." All Malcolm needed to do was keep himself in the most acceptable light during this short meeting. And as the meeting moved forward, principle #8 was useful: "Talk in terms of the other person's interest." *Prison has made me a better man.* And *I have no anger or resentment toward anyone—the judge, the prosecuting attorney, or the officers who arrested me. I deserved this.*[77]

Again, Dale Carnegie was no Bill Shakespeare, but he was the kind of thinker Malcolm needed to rescue himself from the dungeons of Charlestown. As Malcolm deployed the vernacular of a reformed diplomat, the parole board listened and considered. But they held off on voting until the next day.

For years Malcolm had been behind bars, behind walls with electrical cables, his faith in Allah and dreams of serving Him his sole motivation to keep going. "I do not want to exalt myself above my people," Malcolm wrote to Ms. Clomax, "I want to help to exalt our entire nation. This can be done only by sacrifice."[78]

Prison had been a forced and much-needed sacrifice for Malcolm, but he could now see where he fit into the fabric of America.

On June 25, the news he'd been waiting to hear for years finally came.

A RIOTOUS SEND-OFF

My Dear Sister Beatrice,

Surely Allah is the Best Knower and has finally seen fit to allow me to be released from seclusion and in His Language of Mathematics my sentence has been filled, for I have served 77 months and if I had had to serve 7 more months I would have had to complete 7 years. I love my sevens (smile).

—Malcolm X Little to Beatrice
Clomax, June 29, 1952[79]

The date for Malcolm's release was tentatively scheduled for July 22, contingent that he relocate to Detroit. This meant coordinating with the state of Michigan and running a "pre-parole investigation" to make sure that Wilfred's home and job were legitimate and that a parole officer in Detroit was available to be assigned to Malcolm.[80]

But Michigan's Department of Corrections (DOC) was slow in its response to the Massachusetts parole supervisor. Fortunately for Malcolm, he had his books, newspapers, and correspondence to keep him busy. On June 29, he wrote again to Beatrice about his resolve to remain single once released. He used his brother Wilfred's December 1950 visit to Charlestown as proof: "When Brother Wilfred was in Boston for a week, two years ago, a great number of people to whom he spoke were receptive to Islam but his family duties in Detroit made it impossible for him to return to Boston and cultivate the seeds he has sown. . . . That is why I have decided to remain single, so no one will be dependent upon me, then I can move about where ever I am needed and help my people to help themselves . . ."

Malcolm continued, admitting to Sister Beatrice how restless he'd feel if all he could be was a conventional family man: "Surely a Muslim wife and children are Allah's greatest gift to a Muslim," he wrote, "but I could never sit peacefully at home and give happiness to one while there are millions who suffer because there is no one willing to come and tell him how to relieve his suffering. Besides, my life belongs to Allah, for I was on the road to certain destruction and no one but He could have saved me so I want every second of this life to be spent serving Him, and I can serve Him only by saving others, as he saved me."[81]

Charlestown prison administration, assuming Malcolm's release would go through eventually, started moving him through the initial stages of release. On July 1, he put on a made-in-prison suit-and-tie (to be altered later) and posed for his release photo.

FIGURE 9.2. From Malcolm Little to Malcolm X. Mug shots. 1946 and 1952.

It is a staggering sight to see Malcolm's February 1946 entry photo and July 1952 release photo side-by-side. He'd entered Charlestown Prison on February 27, 1946, at 6'2", 172 lbs., and with no eye trouble. Now Malcolm was 6'3½", 185 lbs., with an astigmatism from all the late-night reading he'd done. Seventy-seven months ago, he was an atheist who'd happily dropped out of school. Now he was an aspiring Muslim minister with a library for a mind. Preprison, his friends were fellow street hustlers looking to make a quick buck. Now Malcolm had dozens of friends he'd never met—heartfelt Muslim pen pals in Boston, Harlem, and Detroit—and he wrote to them with the conviction of a man who'd survived a society that had corrupted his mind to such a point that he'd put a gun to his head.

But several weeks went by without a response from Michigan's DOC. By July 22, his original release date, Malcolm had still not heard any news. Not wanting to give Charlestown authorities any reason to keep him in prison, Malcolm had kept his record clean, completed his work assignments without trouble, and kept his head down. The wait must have been agonizing.[82]

And on the afternoon of July 22, Charlestown rioted.

In April, May, and June of 1952, there had been a reported 12 prison riots across North and South American prisons. Hunger strikes, hostages held, property destroyed, guards killed—the men at Charlestown had read all about it in newspapers.[83]

As for Charlestown itself, the prison's ever-decrepit condition, its lack of incoming resources, and lame-duck status had kept both prison guards and incarcerated men on edge. Tension was high, and tempers easily flared, many men secretly keeping self-made shivs, clubs, and blackjacks for protection, or to make threats. As well, a heat wave had hit the Boston area, causing drought and turning the prison into a humid, stench-laden furnace.[84]

The "smoldering discontent" inside Charlestown began to escalate on Monday, July 21, when a prison guard, nicknamed "Bobbins," approached an unnamed prison laundryman and asked him to wash his "trousers." The laundryman refused, and according to 29-year-old Fritz O. Swenson, guilty of murder and the ringleader of the riot, "We're not supposed to do guard's clothes." Bobbins didn't like this, and he told the men in laundry that they wouldn't be allowed to wash their own clothes.[85]

This infuriated Swenson and other laundrymen. For the rest of the afternoon, they started a sit-down strike, refusing to work. The guards did not attempt to change their minds. The shift ended, and the protesting men were given dinner and returned to their cells. But by 5:30 p.m., four of the men who protested had been taken from their cells and placed in solitary. When the guards reached Swenson's cell, however, the ringleader refused to move. As he put it, "They asked me if I was coming out peacefully. I said, 'No, you'll have to drag me out.' Then, they told me, 'We'll come in and do it,'" but Swenson was ready. "No you won't," he told the guards. "I've got two straight razors."[86]

They didn't. But by the next morning, July 22, Swenson was suffering from severe headaches and stomachaches, and after allowing a doctor to visit him in the cell, he blacked out and was eventually taken to the prison hospital.

Swenson's actions were considered by other men who'd been taken out of their cells to be long-overdue acts of defiance. Whispers of a coordinated uprising began in the detention block. One man, Robert Conlin, faked an illness, his performance convincing enough that his cell was opened. Conlin "pulled a bar which released seven other hardened prisoners." Swenson, in his hospital room, was able to see and hear a few of his friends stirring up trouble. He "grabbed up a knife with a blade a foot and a half long. Then he ran through several shops, inciting other convicts. 'They're gassing some of our guys,' Swenson shouted. A lie. 'Are we going to let 'em get away with it?'"

Malcolm was prepared to let them get away with it, even if it were true. But close to "40 prisoners rallied to" Swenson, setting fires in the paint shop and taking three guards hostage. The large group ended up "barricading" themselves in the "loft of Auto Plate Shop No. 4."

By 3:30 p.m., over 300 Boston police officers encircled Charlestown's prison wall. Dozens of tear gas grenades were thrown into the auto plate shop by prison guards. But they did not keep the rioters from holding their ground. Instead, they released one of the prison guards as a way to begin negotiations. Soon, Warden O'Brien and Commissioner Maxwell Grossman headed over to the auto plate shop, but Swenson and three others who'd assumed leadership roles desired "a Globe man" to publish their complaints and demands. By 8:00 p.m., Paul V. Craigue, a *Boston Globe* reporter, was sent into the prison and documented their grievances, some of which were "bad and insufficient food, seventeen hours of cell confinement, no pay for prison work, and poor personal sanitation" and one six-minute shower a week on Saturday.[87]

As this played out, hundreds of men, Malcolm included, were locked in their cells and hadn't yet been given dinner. Outside the prison walls, hundreds of curious bystanders could hear the rhythmic "metallic clankings of hundreds of supper trays rattl[ing] against the cell bars . . ." accompanied by dozens of men "singing for their supper."[88]

After nearly 16 hours of negotiations, the standoff ended after the incarcerated men voted to stop at 5:15 a.m. The rioters had damaged nearly $17,500 worth of prison property. This included the destruction of the dental office, burn damage, and broken windows, not to mention the toxic damage caused by prison guards hurling hundreds of tear gas grenades into the prison. The two guards taken hostage were not harmed, and 43 men were given 10 days of solitary confinement, their meals only bread and water. Malcolm and the rest of the uninvolved men were given the day off from their work assignment as the prison assessed the damage and repair.[89]

Tensions cooled, and Malcolm stayed on track. Finally, on July 29, 32-year-old Michigan parole officer Godfrey G. Agriesti submitted the final preparole investigation paperwork necessary for Malcolm to be released. After several more days of cross-state correspondence, the day finally came: August 7, 1952. Malcolm put on his tailored suit (he'd later call it a "cheap Lil' Abner suit") and tie and said his farewells to the Thaxton brothers and other Muslims. Before heading out the gate, he was given a "lecture" (*as long as you are on parole you are still under our authority*), a $20 bill—Massachusetts state law at the time—and paperwork to turn in to Agriesti when he reached Michigan.[90]

As for his time in prison, Malcolm put it this way years later: "I never looked back, but that doesn't make me any different from a million inmates who have left a prison behind them."[91]

RELEASE

Thursday, August 7, 1952, was cloudy—temperature in the mid-70s. Malcolm was taken to the front gate of Charlestown and released to Ella. It had been five days since he'd had his unfulfilling six-minute shower, and the first place he wanted Ella to take him was to a *hamam*, or Turkish bath. Malcolm didn't want a basic scrub down; he wanted a deep and thorough cleansing. A *hamam*, popular in Middle Eastern countries, is divided into three parts: First 15 minutes in a sauna, or hot room, to warm up the skin, followed by a 15-minute intense wash and scrub down, where Malcolm, lying on a hot marble floor, was doused with hot water as a professional scrubbed the dead skin off his body—a delightfully painful experience. Once finished, Malcolm's body was covered in a thick blanket of soap bubbles, a foamy balm massage to help relieve the burning skin sensation. As Malcolm put it later, "I got some of that physical feeling of prison-taint steamed off me."[92]

Malcolm stayed the night of August 7 at Ella's 72 Dale Street home in Roxbury. As long as he reported in person to Mr. Agriesti in Detroit by August 9, Malcolm wouldn't be in trouble. He and Ella must have spoken for quite a while, but Ella wasn't interested in any potential proselytizing from her younger half-brother. Ella was her own woman, and Malcolm quickly understood that "she wasn't going to become any Muslim."[93]

Malcolm met with Hilda before boarding his bus. She gave him a bit more money to go along with the $20 he'd been given by the prison. With the extra cash, he bought three items: a "better-looking pair of eyeglasses, . . . a suitcase and a wrist watch." To Malcolm, "I was preparing for what my life was about to become," but one can't help but wonder if that watch purchase caused a brief memory-flicker of the one he'd stolen six years ago.[94]

The current interstate highway system didn't exist back in 1952, so Malcolm's bus ride from Boston to Detroit was at least 16 hours long, the bus traveling at intermittent speeds below 55 mph along the now historic Route 20. Unlike the more efficient but less scenic I-90, Route 20 glides along the edges of the shore of Lake Erie, especially between Buffalo, New York, and Erie, Pennsylvania. As the bus made its way toward Detroit, Malcolm may have allowed himself a slow breath or two and absorbed his new reality.[95]

He was free—set to debate a nation. His weapon was a rhetorical style and wit that combined graduate-degree-level, self-taught "King's English" with a hard-earned, street hustler's "ghetto idiom." He planned to speak empathetically to the young Black men sleeping in alleys or dealing drugs and to the young Black women selling their bodies at night. As best he could, he'd convince them to not allow the system to get the best of them.[96]

Three weeks after that bus ride, Malcolm met Elijah Muhammad in person, his parole officer allowing him to temporarily cross state lines to attend an NOI service in Chicago. But perhaps overlooked at the time, the FBI already had special agents keeping an eye on the organization, and at least one of them had infiltrated Elijah Muhammad's Chicago Mosque. Seeing that Malcolm was going to be an active ministerial presence, a Chicago-based SA forwarded Malcolm's information to a special agent located near Norfolk, Massachusetts. Sure enough, on September 23, 1952, provocative letters written by Malcolm while he was in prison were handed over by prison authorities and used to begin the first pages of what would end up being a 13-year, 3,600-plus page FBI file.[97]

Though free from being behind bars, Malcolm was far from finished dealing with American law enforcement. After only 23 days of freedom, he was now under the surveillance of the FBI, where he would remain the rest of his life. The bureau's first memo, dated May 4, 1953, identifies its new target as Malcolm K. Little and lists his aliases as "Malachi Shabazz," "Rhythm Red," and "Detroit Red." The memo goes on to list his arrests, his potential communist ties, and his interest in "the Muslim Cult of Islam."

It is not until a memo dated August 23, 1954, that the FBI begins to recognize him as Malcolm X.[98]

EPILOGUE

FIGURE E.1. Inside Norfolk Prison Library. Circa 1992. Photo by Diane Asséo Griliches. Courtesy of William Mongelli.

It is said that no one truly knows a nation until one has been inside its jails. A nation should not be judged by how it treats its highest citizens, but its lowest ones.

—Nelson Mandela

The prison system has certainly changed since Malcolm's 77 months in Charlestown, MR-Concord, and Norfolk. To give you a sense of how much, consider that in 1948, there were a grand total of 152,564 prisoners in state, federal, and correctional/reformatory facilities in the US. By 2022, there were around 1,900,000.[1]

Perhaps this could be less of a shock if one factors in the increase in population. Well, in 1948, the US population hovered around 149 million. In 2022, it was 332 million.[2]

Put another way, in 1948, about 1 out of 1,000 people were in these kinds of facilities. Now that number is 7 out of 1,000. So according to just these statistics, an American is seven times more likely to go to prison nowadays than in 1948. A Black American male, meanwhile, is now 20 times more likely to be put behind bars, depending on the year and location.[3]

No matter how you work the numbers, America has a deeply rooted prison issue. There are many fine books and documentaries describing the current prison experience and how some prisons have become more corporatized and profit-driven, needing a certain "prisoner quota" to continue generating revenue.[4]

As of today, Norfolk is the only prison left from the time Malcolm was incarcerated. After Malcolm was released from Charlestown State Prison on August 7, 1952, the decayed and decrepit prison was finally shut down and demolished starting in 1955. Now Bunker Hill Community College rests there—a theoretical victory for education.

MR-Concord, meanwhile, has undergone a dramatic transformation in the last 70 years. Later called MCI-Concord, the site, in 1959, was largely demolished and reconstructed, instituting new policies and initiatives.

Norfolk (later renamed MCI-Norfolk) is really the only prison with a direct through-line between Malcolm's time and now. And as you now know, it was also where he chose to push away from his troubled past and become the man most of us are familiar with today.

In 1992, around when Spike Lee's *Malcolm X* film was released, Boston journalist Howard Manly visited MCI-Norfolk and interviewed a few of the men. Malcolm's legacy at the prison had remained intact. Several incarcerated men spoke to Manly and said they were attempting to rehabilitate themselves in a way similar to how Malcolm used the prison. "One of the things that Malcolm developed inside here was discipline," said 33-year-old Faheem Najee Shabazz, 15 years into a 30-year sentence for armed robbery and assault and battery. "He used the prison atmosphere like a womb and when he came out he was ready." Shabazz also wanted "people on the outside" to "not think that just because somebody is incarcerated, they should be cast aside. As a matter of fact, I would say there are many of us being formed. They can look forward to another Malcolm real soon."

Shabazz, who'd committed his crime in his late teens, believed Malcolm's story ought to be used as a teaching tool for those who feel lost and purposeless. "Young brothers, especially those that are incarcerated, should put more emphasis on what [Malcolm] did while he was in prison," said Shabazz. "I talked to a lot of guys when they first came to prison and they think that they can't do anything. I simply say, 'Look at Malcolm.' He came in like a lot of us, caught up in the streets."

Another incarcerated man, Jamaican-born Jamaal Iman—five years into a second-degree murder charge committed in his early 20s—told Manly how Malcolm's story had motivated him: "I believe Malcolm's sincerity to search for knowledge throughout his prison term has really inspired me to reconstruct my behavior." Perhaps even more importantly, Iman saw how Malcolm was able to evolve his perspective. "Malcolm had the ability to change . . . after he went to Mecca, and saw all sorts of Muslims, including Caucasians, to say that his previous 'White man is the devil' teachings were wrong. That proved his sincerity, his purity of thought."

In 1992, MCI-Norfolk was near its capacity, holding around 1,250 men— about 450 more than in Malcolm's time. Of those 1,250, Manly reported that "an estimated 100 members" were "members of the Muslim community." This commitment leads many to quit certain vices, such as smoking, and attempt to live up to the potential they see in themselves.[5]

William Mongelli worked for three decades (1991–2021) as a librarian and instructor at MCI-Norfolk, helping men further their education.

As of 2023, the MCI-Norfolk general library had nearly 16,000 items, including a mix of "Blu-ray disks, DVDs, cassettes, VHS tapes, newspapers, magazines, and books on CD." There is also, down the hall, a law library with over 1,000 "hardcover legal volumes."

Incarcerated men cannot access Wi-Fi or the internet, for obvious precautionary reasons, but they are able to complete research on a computer. For those interested in studying law, Mongelli explains. This was correspondence that "legal research content is provided via LexisNexis. Norfolk subscribes to approx. 100 'infobases' (Lexis's own term for a legal database) via a closed LAN. Men sit at one of 20 Wyse terminals, log onto the system, and access these infobases. The search function or interface is similar to doing a Google search."[6]

Men are allowed to check out four books at a time and keep them in their rooms for two weeks. The amount of time a man can stay in the library has changed a great deal since Malcolm's time, however. On most days, Malcolm had the evening hours to peruse the library and find a book. Now, an incarcerated man's time is more routinized. "During 15-minute movement periods, guys sign out to the library from their [Dormitory] Units," William Mongelli explains. "There are three of these movement periods in the AM, two in the afternoon, and two in the evenings. When I left, the library was open to population inmates on Thursday evenings only. The other nights were reserved for my classes."

So what are they reading? "Presently," Mongelli continues, "the urban fiction genre is the most popular, these being thinly-disguised soft-core porn about vampires, etc. Because of the influence of TV shows, fantasy is the biggest draw, just as in the free world. Biography has always been popular, as have mathematics and science books, books on various philosophers, literature, and self-help. As far as general fiction, inmate taste runs parallel to what you'd expect to find in the free world."[7]

As for the classrooms above the library—the same rooms where Malcolm honed his debating skills—gone are chalkboards and erasers. As of 2021, projectors, whiteboards and desk chairs fill each classroom. Men still hoping to complete their high school education have the opportunity to take classes from teachers coming in from the "outside." Per MCI-Norfolk's Orientation Guide, the prison "offers a wide range of educational programs that includes instruction from Adult Basic Education (evenings), Basic Math and English, pre-GED classes and GED classes, English as a Second Language and Special Ed/Special Needs classes."[8]

In the early 2000s, Mongelli incorporated Malcolm's *Autobiography* into a few of his classes.[9] His efforts were appreciated by the men. "Once [during class]," Mongelli recalls, "one of the inmate participants said, 'You realize that Mongelli is the only person here, staff or inmate, that gives any kind of program on Malcolm? We should be doing something.'"

But they never did. As the years went by, Mongelli notes that most of the younger generation has lost touch with Malcolm as a role model. "My experience was that the younger inmate population considers Malcolm as socially and historically irrelevant. In other words, it's OK to watch a PBS special on him, but he represents the 1960s, and not what's happening in the country now." More noteworthy to young incarcerated men is Stanley "Tookie" Williams, a cofounder of the Crips who sat on death row in San Quentin for over a decade before being executed by lethal injection in 2005. Tookie had tried valiantly to atone for his past mistakes and discourage Black youth from joining gangs.

He wrote books aimed directly at children and young adults, and he was even nominated for the Nobel Peace Prize four times for his efforts.[10]

It may be easier to envision a former gang leader as someone more relatable to modern times, but even Tookie found inspiration in Malcolm's story. In his memoir, Tookie battles doubt as years go by in prison. "Naturally," he writes, "there are other prisoners who have undergone major personal change and can appreciate what is required to uplift oneself from the bowels of wretchedness. Through experience I knew the futility of trying to subvert or to outfox these existing conditions. I would have to bend it to the will of my determination, to rise above the madness. There have been numerous prisoners who have failed, but that didn't faze me. I knew of a few Black men—one in particular, Malcolm X—who underwent a miraculous change from a seemingly permanent criminal to a reborn Black man." Tookie was not interested in Malcolm's religious conversion. Rather, he took strength from Malcolm's ability to "bend" his conditions to his favor, even while in prison.[11]

Like Malcolm, Tookie, a skilled reader before prison, took reading even more seriously while at San Quentin. In the early 1980s, he'd grown "tired of skipping over certain words, or having to stop and jot down a word to look up later on." Instead of allowing the problem to linger, Tookie acted, and he "started browsing the dictionary and became fascinated with the different words, definitions, and foreign phrases."[12]

Tookie wasn't exactly following Malcolm's model. As you'll see in the next paragraph, he learned his own way:

> In a short period I developed a style of mnemonics for memorizing long lists of words written on one side of a sheet of paper, then folding it with the definitions on the opposite side. It became clear that the more words I retained, the better I was able to understand what I read. Months earlier I had been given an old pocket-sized dictionary with most of the pages scotch-taped together or missing. I tried to hustle the prison chaplain out of a dictionary, but a few weeks later he surprised me with a large Webster's Collegiate Dictionary. After I expressed my gratitude, the chaplain said, "I know you'll put that book to good use—but use the Lord's book, too!" Shortly afterwards I asked a prison Imam for a thesaurus, which he provided. I tried Malcolm X's alphabetical technique for remembering words,

which I found to be tedious. Instead I randomly selected words from the dictionary, thesaurus, and other books. In spite of my former schoolteachers' assertion that I was ineducable, my intent was to memorize the entire dictionary.[13]

Other men have used their time behind bars to learn about injustice. Albert Woodfox spent 43 years in solitary confinement, reading hundreds of books to prove his innocence on a murder charge. "Reading was my salvation," he wrote in his memoir. Woodfox first clung to "radical" books about "politics and race" that had come to Angola State Penitentiary in Louisiana by donation, many of which had slipped through the cracks of prison censors. His conviction was eventually overturned in 2014.[14]

During those agonizing decades of isolation, Woodfox found inspiration from Malcolm's story. "Malcolm X taught me that it doesn't matter where you start out, what matters is where you end up. . . . Malcolm gave me direction. He gave me vision." But especially after hearing an audio cassette in the late '90s, Malcolm's words came to life: "I'd read Malcolm's writings in books many times before. It was something special to hear Malcolm's voice. The biggest lesson I learned from Malcolm is that change is possible, that you can transition from what society has made you as a result of your race and your economic situation, and redefine yourself."[15]

On August 10, 2023, I entered the grounds of MCI-Norfolk voluntarily. After years of staring at blueprints of its buildings, learning about its history and evolution, I wanted to feel as much of the environment as I could. Although I was not incarcerated, I wanted to share—at least for a little while—the same ground as Malcolm and see out the same windows he had.[16]

The emotional experience is something I've found difficult to put accurately into words, though I've tried. But besides feeling the air inside Norfolk's dormitories, the Assembly Hall, school, and industry building, what I did not expect was to meet so many incarcerated individuals (I've been told that they prefer "incarcerated" to "prisoners" or "inmates"). One man, Rickey "Fuquan" McGee, I met while standing in the Assembly Hall, where debates had taken place during Malcolm's time. Fuquan was 26 years into a life sentence, a victim in a mishandled trial. Rather than grow bitter, Fuquan rose above the injustice and educated himself in prison. In 2021 at Norfolk, he founded what very well could be his legacy, the Harriet Tubman Project, which meets twice a week. Its mission is to "dismantle structural racism beginning with abolishing the mental slavery that exists within the institutions, and educating the participants on their legal and moral obligations to participate in their own fight for freedom."[17]

The meeting was well attended when I saw it, with between 40–50 men sitting in the Assembly Hall seats, looking at a whiteboard set up on the side aisle of the auditorium.[18]

I often spend years of my life looking into the past, but seeing the men actively working on a specific congressional law, I felt blitzed into the present, the now of things. Yes, Malcolm was a special individual, but he was far more concerned with men in Fuquan's situation than his own. I'd needed to feel that in my bones.

There are currently around 2,000 state and federal prisons in the US. Of those, there are fewer than a thousand libraries, and of those libraries, fewer than 70 percent have designated staff. Even fewer have trained librarians creating educational programs like George Magraw did for Malcolm and William Mongelli did for thousands of incarcerated individuals.[19]

Bottom line, there is a good chance that if you call your local correctional facility today and ask them (a) if they have a library and (b) if they have a librarian, they will say no.

The issue grows even more complicated if, for example, you decided to donate this very book to a prison. As I write this, I foresee some prisons banning it on the grounds that it depicts an "escape" and may encourage "group disruption" or "anti-authority attitudes," disregarding all other potential benefits.[20] The fickle nature of American prison boards approving or rejecting books can be summed up in an evaluation of a dozen Georgia state prisons by the *Atlanta Journal-Constitution*. Besides reporting one prison as having "fewer than 2,000 books for approximately 1,000 prisoners," the newspaper's report revealed that "although nearly two-thirds of Georgia inmates are black, more than half of libraries have no books on Martin Luther King Jr., [born in Atlanta, GA] and two-thirds of them don't have anything on Malcolm X [father born in Reynolds, GA]."[21]

Malcolm may always be remembered more for converting to Islam while in prison and shaping his message, but it was his dedication to reading that transformed his mindset. To put it as plainly as I can, without Norfolk's system and extensive library, we might not ever have heard of Malcolm X. Without a well-stocked library in a prison, there is little-to-no hope for a man's educational awakening.

FIGURE E.2. Norfolk Prison Colony display case next to library. January 26, 2011. Organized in part by former MCI-Norfolk prison librarian William Mongelli, who provided the picture.

In a world where 70 percent of an estimated 11 million incarcerated individuals are deemed "functionally illiterate," perhaps it's time to take a much stronger look at prioritizing literacy rates, the rewards being less crime and more cultural understanding. As Malcolm put it, "I have often reflected upon the new vistas that reading opened to me. I knew right there in prison that reading had changed forever the course of my life. As I see it today, the ability to read awoke inside me some long dormant craving to be mentally alive."[22]

ACKNOWLEDGMENTS

I was driving down a four-lane highway for no reason on a snowy night in the middle of December. It was 2003, and I had the music cranked up. Neil Young was my teacher back then, and as "Like a Hurricane" blew out of my speakers, for a brief moment, the confusion about who I was, what I wanted to be, and where I was going, dissipated. I was 22.

That night in December I will remember for the rest of my life.

I was in the middle lane, going 60 mph, a snowstorm blowing in. The roads seemed safe enough, so I decided midtrip to end up at a bookstore in Akron, Ohio, a couple miles down. But during one of Neil Young's long guitar solos, I suddenly lost control of the car. I started to skid, and I made the mistake of twitching the steering wheel to my left. It was all that was needed to put me into a spin.

I'd slowed by then, and the 360-degree spin felt like an eternity. In the middle of the spin, I saw two semi-trucks no more than 30 yards away. They were in the middle two lanes, side by side. They were coming right toward me, and there was nothing I could do about it.

I put my hands up (as if that was going to stop them), but when I stopped squinting for a moment, I saw both trucks, at the last second, shift over one lane and zoom past me. I remember hearing a shrieking metal vibration from how close they were to hitting my '91 Buick Regal.

No other cars were around, thankfully. I'd stopped moving on the highway, and the spin had brought me back around to the direction I was supposed to go. I turned down the music and coughed once, my heart pounding so hard I could feel it in my throat.

I started back down the road and made it to the bookstore, but I couldn't focus. I stared at the books all around me and at the workers behind counters, and I had never felt so disconnected from the world.

After enough time passed, I grabbed a book and sat down in a chair next to an escalator. I opened to the first page, but all I could do was read an imaginary line, over and over again.

You should be dead . . . you should be dead.

The book was Malcolm X's *Autobiography*. I bought that copy, a paperback, and still own it today. Now, after 20 years, I understand why the book appealed to me then. At 22, I was angry, frustrated, confused, and directionless but driven to change who I was. When I looked at that book cover and saw Malcolm's glaring eyes, it was as if he was saying "enough." I'd had enough . . . of what? I wasn't sure, but the certainty of his words gave me a sense of self-worth. In a way, I'd placed myself in my own kind of prison, and only purpose and determination could release me.

During the next 10 years, I moved to Japan, got married, came back to the US, became an ESL college instructor, worked in Switzerland, and then moved back to the US, and in December 2012, I found myself car-free at a public library in Bellevue, Washington. I had an idea for a book: 40 biographical portraits of historical figures struggling at the age of 22. Malcolm was at the top of the list, but after rereading the *Autobiography*, I was unsatisfied by the lack of primary source work done on his years in prison; hadn't anyone looked deeply into prison files or prison newspapers?

From that point on, my wife, Yuka, and I discussed two men—Dr. King, whose seminary years are the subject of my first book, and Malcolm. I made it my mission to find out as much as I could about Malcolm's prison years.

I had a lot of help along the way . . .

A large portion of this book's content was created using prison files, archival letters, prison newspapers, correspondence, and site visits.

I'd like to first thank MA-DOC's Jamie M. Joyce for answering all my prison file requests. This book would look quite different without Jamie's help and patience. Also, Caitlin Ramos, reference archivist over at UMass Boston's Massachusetts Archives, helped with many of the prison files as well. I couldn't have finished the book without their help. After looking at over 1,200 pages of prison files . . . my eyes will never be the same.

Sofia Caballero Stafford was a massive help at the NYPL's Schomburg Research Center. The Schomburg holds most of Malcolm's prison letters, but there were others, as well as many from his teenage years, over at the Charles H. Wright Museum of African American History in Detroit. For those, database manager Melissa Samson and archivist Michelle McKinney were vital in giving me access. I strongly recommend that anyone in the Harlem or Detroit areas stop by these research centers and check out their collections.

I must say, reading Norfolk Prison Colony's newspaper, the *Colony*, was an absolute revelation. Each issue brought me closer to Malcolm's day-to-day prison existence, and for this, I must thank Lesley Schoenfeld and her digitizing team at Harvard Law Library. Lesley also provided access to Charlestown State Prison's newspaper, the *Mentor*, which shed new light on what incarcerated individuals were concerned with during those postwar years. For the 1950 issues of the *Colony*, John Hannigan over at Massachusetts Archives gave me access to what they had. Caitlin Ramos once again came to my rescue when I needed access to MR-Concord's *Our Paper*, and it was there, at the Massachusetts Archives building in August 2023, that I discovered Malcolm's time boxing. For their help, I am deeply grateful.

In August 2023, thanks to financial assistance provided by Lakeland University—a special thanks to Beth Borgen and Joshua Kutney and the Massachusetts Historical Society—I was able to fly from Tokyo to the Boston area and complete research at Harvard (Zoe Hill at the Houghton Library), Boston College (Andrew Isidoro at the John J. Burns Library), and UMass Boston. Also a special thanks to Morgan R. Swan at Dartmouth's Rauner Special Collections for helping with several important files and Lauren Stark at the NYPL's Schomburg Center for Research in Black Culture.

Also during this trip, I toured MCI-Norfolk, an experience I briefly describe in the epilogue but that remains too personal for me to adequately express. Still, thank you to Superintendent Nelson Alves and his team for allowing me to tour the grounds and ask very specific questions about a prison that *remains* focused on rehabilitation.

Geri Tasker, chairman of the Norfolk Historical Commission, helped navigate me through some of the rare documents within their collection. Thank you, Geri!

Still, despite all this support, you wouldn't be reading this book without the help of Matt Becker, the UMass Press editor who took a chance on an expat living in Japan writing about Malcolm X. Matt has been a joy to work with. Special thanks as well to marketing manager Chelsey Harris, EDP manager Sally Nichols, production editor Ben Kimball, and Brianna Blackburn and the team at Scribe for helping to put this book together.

So many others . . . Ilyasah Shabazz, Rafael Monserrate, Dan Winslow, Paul Eckstein, David Garrow, Jonathan Eig, Keith Miller, W. Jason Miller,

Abdur-Rahman Muhammad, Louis DeCaro, Nancy Hughes, William Mongelli, John and Greg O'Connell, Rick Nash, Ruth Lionberger, David Learoyd, Mark Feeley, Ben Stubbings, Megha Wadhwa, Carin Wolfe, Ryan Rashotte, Charles Laurier, Roger Grabowski, Jessica McDonald (who designed the Norfolk Prison Colony map), Wayne Watson, Mark Winston, Arthur O'Keefe, Anna Husson Isozaki, Mark Marino, Allan Harley, Simon Park, Mike Frank, Sean Parr, and Joseph Parr have either supported me as experts, early readers, researchers, friends, family or all of the above. I can't thank them enough. During my August research trip, both my mother, Heather Joy Frank Parr, and my father, Gary Paul Parr, supported my efforts.

And of course, Yuka, *mon amour. Tu es mon soleil et ma lune . . . merci.*

NOTES

NOTE TO THE READER

1 Julius Lester, "The Angry Children of Malcolm X," *Sing Out* 16, no. 5 (October/November 1966): 21–25. Insan, also named Robert S. Preston, wrote this poem in 1971 while serving three life sentences at Norfolk Prison Colony and is published in Elma Lewis's *Who Took the Weight?*, 49–50.

CHAPTER 1

1 Haley and X, *Autobiography*, 159.
2 Malcolm Jarvis Prison File. Jarvis mentioned Brown's spousal situation in his own "version" of what happened. Also mentioned in Malcolm Little Prison File, "Subject's Version of the Present Offense."
3 Malcolm Little Prison File, "Subject's Version of Present Offense."
4 Malcolm Little Prison File, "Subject's Version of Present Offense"; "The Caribbean Club," *New York Age*, July 28, 1945, 11. The *Age* ad runs with the name "Rhythm Red" until October 6, 1945. In his prison file, Malcolm mentioned that he did some dancing under the name "Rhythm Red."
5 Haley and X, "Bathroom," in *Autobiography*, 166. December 5 is in Malcolm Little's prison file. He mentions in the file that they first went to Belmont; however, the Brush Hill Road address was in Milton.
6 Address in Malcolm Little Prison File. An advertisement on Zillow for this home listed it as being built in 1920. The name of the owner was either redacted or not included in any of the prison files I checked.
7 The 1940 Census lists "Francis E. Brown" as a 17-year-old "inmate" at the Norfolk Prison Colony. Malcolm Jarvis's prison file describes Jarvis's confession and how they were "not friends."
8 In Perry's *Malcolm*, Perry describes Sonny as being "built like Jersey Joe Walcott" (95). This would have been based on his interview with Malcolm Jarvis.

9   Malcolm Little Prison File. Malcolm mentioned that Brown was always the one who went to the back door or storm window to enter the house before he let Malcolm in. Also, as Jarvis told Bruce Perry, Malcolm didn't "know how to pick a lock." Perry, *Malcolm*, 95.

10 Malcolm Little Prison File, "Additional Sentences / Indictment Statements."

11 Kora M. "Parker" Mardirosian Parcauskas. Her maiden name was spelled "Marderosian" in prison files as well as in the 1940 Census. Kora was born on April 26, 1924, had two brothers and sisters, and graduated from South Boston High School in 1942. She remained in the Boston area most of her life, becoming a "multigraph supervisor at Harvard . . . and Boston University alumni offices." The hard time with her parents was mentioned in the Beatrice Bazarian Prison File. See also "Kora M. 'Parker' Mardirosian Parcauskas," Find a Grave, https://www.findagrave.com/memorial/141599376/kora-m_-parcauskas/photo#source.

12 Malcolm Jarvis Prison File; Beatrice Bazarian Prison File.

13 The address 248 Gray Street was found in "Mrs. Nora Eberhardt," *Boston Globe*, October 25, 1947, 3. Eberhardt's name was in Beatrice Bazarian's prison file. Also in Beatrice Bazarian's prison file was the quote about "thrill and excitement'" (Dr. Rak's Report on Beatrice Bazarian RW 17977). Zillow states that the house is a four-bedroom home built in 1904. "It looks like a good deal" was a quote by Malcolm, mentioned in Malcolm Jarvis's prison file.

14 The address was found after discovering Rollin Hoyt's name in Beatrice Bazarian's prison file and then finding the obituary of Rollin Hoyt. "Rollin W. Hoyt, Business Executive," *Boston Globe*, September 1, 1960, 12. The process of breaking into Hoyt's home was found in Malcolm Little's prison file, after comparing the materials taken from the home with Bazarian's prison file. Nowhere does it explicitly say that Brown was the one who broke in, but since Jarvis admitted that Malcolm couldn't pick a lock, it's evident that Brown was the man. Malcolm also said in his prison file that the process of breaking into the homes was always the same.

15 Malcolm Jarvis Prison File.

16 Malcolm Little Prison File, "Official Version." The document has been heavily redacted; however, names can be confidently assumed based on cross-checking Jarvis's, Beatrice's, and Joyce's prison files with Malcolm's. Kora, who did not have to serve prison time, does not have a prison file; however, she was questioned by Arlington police and told them about how the group placed all the loot on a table in most likely Jarvis's apartment.

17 Haley and X, *Autobiography*, 156.

18 Beatrice Bazarian Prison File.

19 Joyce Caragulian Prison File.

20 Cunningham and Golden, "Malcolm," 28.

21 Haley and X, *Autobiography*, 156.

22 Beatrice Bazarian Prison File.

23 Malcolm Little Prison File; Joyce Caragulian Prison File; and Beatrice Bazarian Prison File.

24 Malcolm Little Prison File; Joyce Caragulian Prison File; and Beatrice Bazarian Prison File.

25 "Deaths and Funerals: Robert F. Estabrook,'" *Boston Globe*, December 29, 1958, 16. Address found in "Cambridge Sisters Arrested; Loot Found in Homes," *Boston Globe*, January 16, 1946, 2.

26 Malcolm Little Prison File; Malcolm Jarvis Prison File. There is a picture of Jarvis's ring in Bill Cunningham and Daniel Golden's *Boston Globe* article "Malcolm" that shows the ring's design. It looks very much like the one described to the police by the Estabrooks. "It cost me 5½ years of my life, and I'll always keep it." The ring had been at his parent's house when he was arrested.

27 The Estabrook haul was put together using the Malcolm Jarvis, Malcolm Little, and Beatrice Bazarian prison files.

28 Malcolm Jarvis Prison File; Malcolm Little Prison File; Beatrice Bazarian Prison File.

29 Hotel Victoria information could be found in an advertisement in the *Brooklyn Daily Eagle*, December 28, 1945, 8. The floor information is on the back of a 1945 linen postcard with the hotel's image on the front.

30 Joyce Caragulian Prison File.

31 Police went over to the Estabrooks at around 10:00 a.m. on December 17. Malcolm Little Prison File; Beatrice Bazarian Prison File; Joyce Caragulian Prison File. In Perry's *Malcolm*, Malcolm Jarvis mentions two cars heading down Merritt Parkway and Malcolm Little playfully shooting at Jarvis's Buick out of Bea's convertible (98). It's hard to fully believe either side. Jarvis, in interviews, does at times sensationalize tales, while the girls were most likely trying to separate themselves from the boys in their prison files to make them look less guilty.

32 Malcolm Jarvis Prison File, "Subject's Version of Present Offense." The name "Little" was redacted, but when comparing prison files and timelines, it's clear that Jarvis was talking about Little and not Francis Brown. Also in the prison file there is mention of Jarvis and Little breaking into a home on December 24.

33 Malcolm Jarvis Prison File, "Additional Sentence Data." The next page, "Additional Sentences," lists Ethel F. Swan. The address for Swan's home may have been 1058 Adams Street, according to her June 9, 1964, obituary in the *Boston Globe* on page 48.

34 Malcolm Jarvis Prison File.

35 Malcolm Little Prison File; Malcolm Jarvis Prison File. It's mentioned that when Jarvis was arrested on January 17, he had on the same tan topcoat. See also "Cambridge Sisters Arrested; Loot Found in Homes," *Boston Globe*, January 16, 1946, 2.

36 "Roxbury Man, 20, Arrested at Gunpoint for Series of Breaks," *Boston Globe*, January 13, 1946, 10. The reporter mistakenly named the Brookline

man "Stanley Miller" when in Beatrice's and Joyce's prison file, it is "Charles Miller."

37 Leave 19 Summer Street, West Roxbury, to be exact, according to a *Boston Globe* article on June 25, 1936. An October 26, 1950, *Boston Globe* article shows a picture of Detective Slack, his face away from the camera.

38 "Roxbury Man"; Haley and X, *Autobiography*, 171–72.

39 For the wedding band information, see Perry, *Malcolm*, 99–100.

40 Haley and X, *Autobiography*, 162; "Roxbury Man." Also Malcolm Little Prison File.

41 Malcolm Jarvis Prison File, "Employment History," lists him working for the railroad company starting December 1945 and contracted until June 1946. Similar to Malcolm's experience, the railroad jobs were typically six-month contracts. Jarvis would be arrested on January 15, 1946.

42 Haley and X, *Autobiography*, 162. It's possible that Brown ended up in South Carolina. See "Several Sentenced," *Greenville News*, October 29, 1946, 3. A "Francis E. Brown," listed as age 25, was sentenced to three years for housebreaking and larceny. I contacted the South Carolina DOC but was told that they don't keep prison files longer than 20 years, so Brown's file has been destroyed.

43 Malcolm Little Prison File, "Subject's Version of Present Offense.'"

44 Malcolm Little Prison File, "Criminal Record.'" Also see Collins with Bailey, *Seventh Child*, for more information about Ella Little.

45 Malcolm Little Prison File, "Subject's Version of Present Offense."

46 Malcolm Little Prison File, "Roxbury Dist. Ct."

47 Beatrice Bazarian Prison File, "'Outside Investigation Sheet': Interview with Subject's Husband: Mr. Martin Bazarian." Martin told the interviewer that Beatrice called him one day before being arrested, so perhaps January 14. A different account in Beatrice's prison file says two days before, which could also mean that Beatrice did in fact read that January 13 *Boston Globe* article.

48 Beatrice Bazarian Prison File. Martin also called Kora a "bum," the paragraph earlier. It's possible but unlikely that "the other party" was Jarvis only because Martin does not refer once to Malcolm, Jarvis, or Shorty in his angry letter.

49 Jarvis with Nichols, *The Other Malcolm*, 52–53. Jarvis mentioned Framingham as where the police apprehended him, but it's reported as "Newtonville" in his prison file.

50 Malcolm Little Prison File, "Official Version." Jarvis's name was redacted, but through process of elimination and pronoun usage, it can be safely assumed the officers were referring to Jarvis.

51 "3 Girls, 2 Men Held in Series of House Breaks," *Boston Globe*, February 8, 1946, 20. Kora is pictured.

52 Haley and X, *Autobiography*, 173. For Ella's quote, see Collins with Bailey, *Seventh Child*, 47. Collins is Ella's son, and he quotes her often in the memoir.

53 Jarvis with Nichols, *The Other Malcolm*, 61–62; Haley and X, *Autobiography*, 173.

54 "Allan G. Buttrick," obituary, *Boston Globe*, November 30, 1954, 20; November 29, 1954, 25. A picture of Buttrick can be seen in the *Boston Globe*, March 24, 1939, 27. The 1940 Census lists Buttrick's family. His daughter, Virginia, worked as a secretary in 1940.

55 Joyce Caragulian Prison File. Kora does not have a prison file, but her updated sentence was included in the April 10, 1946, report in Joyce's Prison File.

56 Joyce Caragulian Prison File. Although she was given the same amount of time as her sister, she would eventually be released from Framingham Reformatory on April 26, 1946.

57 Beatrice Bazarian Prison File.

58 Jarvis with Nichols, *The Other Malcolm*, 61; Malcolm Jarvis Prison File.

59 Pricilla King, interview by Blackside, Inc., September 9, 1992, 14, transcript archived at Washington University, St. Louis.

60 Jarvis with Nichols, *The Other Malcolm*, 61; Malcolm Little Prison File.

CHAPTER 2

1 Ned Sublette and Constance Sublette, *The American Slave Coast: A History of the Slave-Breeding Industry* (Chicago: Chicago Review Press, 2015), 13.

2 Information originally collected by the Emory University Trans-Atlantic Slave Trade Database, and reprinted by the International African American Museum (IAAM).

3 The treaty was published in full in the *Weekly Raleigh Register*, February 24, 1815, 3.

4 Mia Sogoba, "History of the Bambara: Segou and Kaarta," *Cultures of West Africa*, April 21, 2018. According to Sogoba, *ban* means to "end" or "refuse," and *mana* means "masters."

5 According to David M. Robertson's excellent biography, *Denmark Vesey*, "commercial vessels swore that on a calm sea they could smell a slave ship five miles away, before it became visible" (32). As for the amount of time it took, I used *The Autobiography of Omar ibn Said*, a short document written by Said describing his capture by Africans in 1807: "Then there came to our place a large army, who killed many men, and took me, and brought me to the great sea, and sold me into the hands of the Christians, who bound me and sent me on board great ship and we sailed upon the great sea a month and a half, when we came to a place called Charleston in the Christian language. There they sold me to a small, weak, and wicked man, called Johnson, a complete infidel, who had no fear of God at all." Tabish

Khair et al., ed., *Other Routes: 1500 Years of African and Asian Travel Writing* (Oxford: Signal, 2006), 219.

6 "Ajar" is the name given to him by Charleston officials. Since names were very often misheard or purposely altered, there is a chance, according to Malcolm's half-sister Ella Little, that Hajja's official African name may have been closer to "Haja," more closely linked to the Islamic faith prevalent near Hajja's region. Ilyasah Shabazz and Tiffany Jackson more accurately spell it as Hajja in their novel, *The Awakening of Malcolm X.*

7 Robertson, *Denmark Vesey,* 34.

8 Robertson, 35.

9 Robertson, 51. Vesey's story is truly remarkable and, in a poetic way, foreshadows the influence of Martin Luther King Jr. and Malcolm X. As Vesey rallied support for his rebellion, around 1817, an African Methodist Episcopal Church was built in Charleston, and many of those executed (thirty-five by hanging) belonged to the church. Vesey, while not a minister, still used religious methods, such as quoting scripture, to persuade slaves to join his cause. Likewise, Vesey, who in the years before his planned revolt refused to bow "courteously," demanded that Black slaves take control of their own destinies and not wait around for someone else to fix their plight.

10 Robertson, 134.

11 Collins with Bailey, *Seventh Child,* 6.

12 The dates 1840 and, later, 1847 were assumptions I made after discovering two newspaper articles. In the *Edgefield Advertiser* (SC), on December 25, 1839, page 3, it was reported that "Allen Little" had married a "Miss Susan Berry," thus formally starting his life as an adult provider, which meant he'd soon be acquiring property and slaves. Again, in the *Edgefield Advertiser,* on November 10, 1847, page 3, an "Allen Little" placed a "Notice" in the paper for anyone interested in acquiring a "valuable tract of land, containing 690 acres, situate[d] in Edgefield District, on Burnets Creek, near Red Bank." By placing two important announcements in this newspaper, this most likely meant that Tony and Clarrie lived in the Edgefield area of South Carolina after being sold to the Littles.

13 Collins with Bailey, *Seventh Child,* 7.

14 Collins with Bailey, 7.

15 Collins with Bailey, 7; "Notice," *Edgefield Advertiser,* November 10, 1847, 3. Little mentions that he is "intending to change his residence."

16 Collins with Bailey, 9. Malcolm's words come from during an interview on the television show *City Desk* on March 17, 1963, WMAQ-TV Channel 5, Chicago, IL.

17 According to Malcolm's daughter Ilyasah Shabazz, their ancestry may be traced back to Yoruba.

18 McDuffie, "Diasporic Journeys of Louise Little." McDuffie's groundbreaking article included research trips to La Digue, Grenada, Louise Little's birthplace, and interviews.

19 Henry B. Lovejoy's 2010 article in *African Economic History*, 38, cited in McDuffie, 152.

20 McDuffie, 152.

21 McDuffie, 151–53.

22 John Angus Martin, *A–Z of Grenada Heritage* (Oxford: Macmillan Caribbean 2007); McDuffie, 152.

23 Haley and X, *Autobiography*, 5.

24 Perry, *Malcolm*, 385n.

25 Perry, 3.

26 Collins with Bailey, *Seventh Child*, 9. The date of Pa John's death was communicated to Malcolm via a letter written by Ella in June 1940. In it she states that Pa John passed on May 9, 1940, the day he was supposed to leave for a trip up to Boston.

27 Collins with Bailey, *Seventh Child*, 25. For the 1940 date, see the letter from Ella Little (Johnson's) to Malcolm, May 1940, the original of which is located at the Charles H. Wright Museum of African American History in Detroit, Michigan (hereafter Wright Museum).

28 "Bishop Turner Talks," *Atlanta Constitution*, July 14, 1890, 5.

29 Haley and X, *Autobiography*, 4.

30 *Journal and Tribune* (Tenn.), August 17, 1890, 5.

31 *Atlanta Constitution*, July 14, 1890, 2.

32 Amy Louise Wood, *Lynching and Spectacle: Witnessing Racial Violence in America, 1890–1940* (Chapel Hill: University of North Carolina Press, 2009), 31–32.

33 Strickland, *Malcolm X*, 15.

34 1920 Census; Collins with Bailey, *Seventh Child*, despite having Ella as a source, does not list the proper order of children born (33, 36).

35 Sarah A. Soule, "Populism and Black Lynching in Georgia, 1890–1900," *Social Forces* 71, no. 2 (1992): 431–49. For more information on the 1906 Atlanta Race Massacre, I recommend *Veiled Visions*, by David Fort Godshalk (Chapel Hill: University of North Carolina Press, 2005). Godshalk estimates in his introduction the number of African Americans killed across several days to be "at least twenty."

36 "The Atlanta Crimes," *Brooklyn Times*, September 24, 1906, 8. The Bialystok Pogrom (located in what is now northeastern Poland) occurred over three days in June 1906, and over 80 people were killed.

37 Booker T. Washington, speech, September 18, 1895, during the opening of the Atlanta Exposition. Washington, *An Autobiography: The Story of My Life and Work* (Naperville, IL: J. L. Nichols, 1901), 138.

38 *Marcus Garvey: Look for Me in the Whirlwind*, produced and directed by Stanley Nelson, written by Marcia Smith, aired February 12, 2001, on PBS. Around the 16- or 17-minute mark is the advertisement for Garvey's "Big Mass Meeting: A Call to the Colored Citizens."

39 Perry, *Malcolm*, 24n. To Perry, it's unclear if this was Malcolm's father.

40 Jan Carew, "Malcolm X's Mother in Montreal: A Pioneering Educator," chap. 3 of *Re/visioning: Canadian Perspectives on the Education of Africans in the Late 20th Century* (Ontario, Canada: Captus, 1998), 18–24. The chapter is excerpted from Carew's book, *Ghosts in Our Blood*.

41 Eric Williams, *From Columbus to Castro: The History of the Caribbean, 1492–1969* (New York: Random House, 1970), 95, 105. When France had control, Williams states that the ratio hovered around 1 to 10. During the Revolutionary War, the French momentarily took back control over Grenada, handing it back to the British in 1784. See Tessa Murphy, "A Reassertion of Rights: Fedon's Rebellion, Grenada, 1795–96," *The French Revolution*, no. 14 (June 18, 2018): 1–26, https://doi.org/10.4000/lrf.2017.

42 Murphy, 1.

43 Murphy, 17.

44 Carew, "Malcolm X's Mother." The quotation used is Wilfred Little, Louise's firstborn, during an interview with Carew.

45 Perry, *Malcolm*, 22, 394n. Louise's quote comes from Bruce Perry's interview with Louise. The exact phrasing Mr. Perry used was "Laughing softly as she recalled the pain, Mrs. Little told me, 'When the teacher lashed me . . .'" Unfortunately, Perry's records are not available until 2041, so I cannot verify the interview. I have, however, in the course of working on this book, independently verified dozens of Bruce Perry's facts that came from interviews. Perry's prose delivery—direct and muscular—and armchair child psychology conclusions have caused some Malcolm X scholars to write that Perry had some kind of vendetta against Malcolm. A closer reading (accompanied by fact-checking) reveals that Perry completed profoundly important work and reported without fear the stories his interviewees shared. This should be commended, but the stories the interviewees shared can of course be put into question. I chose to use Perry's Louise quote without knowing the context of the interview because, well, there just aren't many quotes of Louise's in existence. When 2041 rolls around, I'll have a listen to the interview and modify the text if necessary.

46 Perhaps due to the limit in opportunities, Carew, in his "Malcolm X's Mother" chapter, mentioned that "emigration from Grenada had been a necessity in the past and remains so to this day" (21). The "1,000 acres" is actually "1,000 cane acres," as given in Williams's *From Columbus to Castro*, 368.

47 Perry, *Malcolm*, 3; McDuffie, "Diasporic Journeys of Louise Little," 154. The date's discovery was made by independent scholar Jessica Russell, whom McDuffie thanks and credits in his paper. Russell's book, *The Life of Louise Norton Little*, presents official passport documents showing that Louise's trip from Grenada started on May 22, 1917. Also, as is later explained, Edgerton Langdon, according to Carew, first heard Marcus Garvey speak in New York in 1916. Carew, "Malcolm X's Mother," 22.

48 Haley and X, *Autobiography*, 9.

49 *Marcus Garvey: Look for Me.*

50 As quoted in Grant, *Negro with a Hat*, 49.

51 Grant, 79–80. Before his debut, Garvey attempted to get W. E. B. Du Bois to introduce him, but the Black scholar declined. The two men would end up as rivals, with Du Bois believing in the "Talented Tenth," an elite Black community to help lead the rest.

52 Marcus Garvey, speech, July 8, 1917, Harlem, in Hill, *Marcus Garvey*, 213.

53 Paul-Andre Linteau, *The History of Montreal: The Story of a Great North American City* (Montreal: Baraka, 2013), 119.

54 Carew, "Malcolm X's Mother."

55 Carew, *Ghosts in Our Blood*, 131. Also, Russell with Little and Jones *Life of Louise Norton Little*, 322. Russell presents the church register documents showing that the couple did indeed marry in Montreal, on May 10, 1919, with Uncle Edgerton present as well as a man named Johnathan Davis.

56 *Marcus Garvey: Look for Me.* A photo of an original UNIA application is shown in the documentary.

57 *Marcus Garvey: Look for Me*; also Grant's *Negro with a Hat*, 214.

58 For Eason's general information, see *New York Age*, December 28, 1918, 6. For Earl's search for "religious Garveyism," see Marable, *Malcolm X*, 20–22.

59 "President of Africa Will Be Elected by Negroes Here," *Brooklyn Daily Eagle*, August 18, 1920.

60 Carew, *Ghosts in Our Blood*, 118.

61 Tuttle, *Race Riot*, 244–45.

62 Menard, "Lest We Forget." For further understanding of the Omaha Race Riot from a national perspective, refer to McWhirter's *Red Summer*.

63 Menard, 162.

64 "Negro Assaults Young Girl while Male Escort Stands by Powerless to Aid Her," *Omaha Daily Bee*, September 26, 1919, 1.

65 Menard, "Lest We Forget," 154–57.

66 Tuttle, *Race Riot*, 245.

67 Quotes from the mob later to appear in the local newspaper: "String him up and let us fill his body with bullets." After a resident shot Brown seven times on the ground, the article states that "persons who were 'saner' shouted, 'Wait until we get him dangling into the air before you do any shooting.'" "Death by the Rope, Is Verdict of the Mob," *Omaha World-Herald*, September 29, 1919, 1–2.

68 Menard, "Lest We Forget," 161; Tuttle, *Race Riot*, 245.

69 The photo is on page 159 of the Menard article.

70 The historical marker is located at 3463 Evans Street.

71 Adam F. C. Fletcher, "A Biography of Rev. Dr. John Albert Williams," *North Omaha History*, May 8, 2019, https://northomahahistory.com/2019/05/08/a-biography-of-rev-john-albert-williams/.

72 Fletcher.

73 "In Memory of Hilda Florice Little (1921–2015)," *The Book of Memories*, April 6, 2015, https://gateway.frontrunnerpro.com/book-of-memories/2104633/little-hilda/view-condolences.php.

74 "Omaha Ban on Ku Klux," *Lincoln Journal Star*, September 23, 1921, 5; Schuyler, "Ku Klux Klan in Nebraska."

75 Schuyler, 235.

76 Schuyler, 246.

77 Grant, *Negro with a Hat*, 358–65.

78 Grant, 378.

79 Carew, *Ghosts in Our Blood*, 118.

80 Hill, *Marcus Garvey*, 10: 291.

81 In the most recent full Malcolm X biography, *Dead Are Arising*, 4. Les and Tamara Payne interviewed Wilfred Little in April 1991. During the interview, Wilfred not only told the Paynes that the Klan did indeed come but that it "helped greatly that his father was indeed not home."

82 Haley and X, *Autobiography*, 3.

83 Associated Press, "Dahlman Heads Fascisti of America," *Sacramento Bee*, May 3, 1923, 15. The short article goes on to report the comments made by a former member of the Klan, who says that the Fascisti's ideals are "similar to the ideals of the Ku Klux Klan but quite different from those which that organization practices."

84 One example of "rum runners" can be found in the "Rum Runners of Omaha Nabbed," *Fremont Tribune*, May 20, 1925. Two white Omaha men were caught by police and told the officers they were being paid $600 a trip to smuggle liquor between Chicago and Omaha.

CHAPTER 3

1 Perry, *Malcolm*, 2. Perry also interviewed Malcolm Orgias.

2 Carew, *Ghosts in Our Blood*, 151.

3 Carew, 151.

4 "Pres. Coolidge Given Deafening Welcome Today," *Falls City Journal*, October 8, 1925, 1.

5 "Largest Flag in World at Omaha," *Carroll Index*, October 8, 1925, 1.

6 Jesse J. Otto, "Dan Desdunes: New Orleans Civil Rights Activist and 'the Father of Negro Musicians of Omaha,'" *Nebraska History* 92 (2011): 106–17. Dempsey told *Ebony* magazine in February 1950 that the fight didn't happen because of financial reasons.

7 Vincent, "Garveyite Parents of Malcolm X."

8 Reginald Heber wrote "From Greenland's Icy Mountains," in 1819.

9   The format I chose was taken from this report filed by Louise Little and published in the *Negro World*, July 3, 1926: "The Omaha Division met on Sunday, June 13, in Liberty Hall, 2528 Lake St. The president, Mr. E. Little, presiding. Opening song from 'Greenland's Icy Mountains.' Prayer and preamble by the president. Musical selection. Prof. A. Vance was introduced and held his hearers' attention about matters of the organization. A membership drive was launched for the coming week, in which Mr. Vance will participate."

10   "The News and Views of U.N.I.A. Divisions," *Negro World*, May 22, 1926, 8.

11   See Gordon Lee, "The Ku Klux Klan in Wisconsin in the 1920's" (master of science thesis, University of Wisconsin-LaCrosse, August 1968). The Klan did not have a deeply significant presence, but Milwaukee was their initial target state headquarters. Also see Robert S. Smith, "African Americans," in *Encyclopedia of Milwaukee* (Milwaukee: University of Wisconsin-Milwaukee, 2016).

12   Carew, *Ghosts in Our Blood*, 115–19.

13   "The News and Views of U.N.I.A. Divisions," *Negro World*, January 29, 1927, 8. Louise Little was most likely the secretary reading from the *Negro World*.

14   "News and Views," January 29, 1927; "The News and Views of U.N.I.A. Divisions," *Negro World*, February 5, 1927, 8.

15   Hill, "June 1927," in *Marcus Garvey*, 6:561.

16   Hill, "Articles in the *Chicago Defender*," in *Marcus Garvey*, 7:3–5.

17   Also see Bill Miller, "Malcolm X: The Mystique," *Battle Creek Enquirer*, November 17, 1992, 1, 4, where area resident Hilda Miller recalls the Littles living for a brief time in Albion in 1927. A *Battle Creek Enquirer*, August 16, 1928, 15, newspaper clip shows the 717 address.

18   Haley and X, *Autobiography*, 5–6; "Special Report, Chas. B. Allen and G. W. Waterman, Michigan State Police, Case #2155, November 8, 1929," reprinted in Marable and Felber, *Portable Malcolm X Reader*, 9–14. Also "Interview of Earl Little, November 11, 1929," reprinted in Marable and Felber, *Portable Malcolm X Reader*, 5.

19   "Interview of Earl Little," 6. Philbert's words are from Strickland, *Malcolm X*, 21.

20   Strickland, 21.

21   Strickland, 21.

22   Haley and X, *Autobiography*, 6.

23   "Special Report," 11.

24   As quoted in DeCaro, *On the Side of My People*, 44.

25   Rory Brosnan, "Malcolm's First Lansing House," *Malcolm X in Lansing*, accessed June 19, 2021, Leadr.studio (page no longer extant). The article included the original documents of the court case.

26 If Earl set fire to his home, he would have been risking not only the lives of his family but also the reputation of the NAACP and the AME Church. See "Starting Evangelistic Drive at A.M.E. Church," *Lansing State Journal*, October 26, 1929, 3. The meeting was scheduled for 3:00 p.m. at the church on October 27.

27 Marable and Felber, *Portable Malcolm X Reader*, 13; Haley and X, *Autobiography*, 6.

28 Strickland, *Malcolm X*, 21.

29 Strickland, 22.

30 Sarata Seydi, "Charles St. 2nd house," Malcolm X in Lansing, accessed June 19, 2021, Leadr.studio (page no longer extant).

31 Little, "Our Family from the Inside."

32 Little; Haley and X, *Autobiography*, 9.

33 Strickland, *Malcolm X*, 23.

34 Strickland, 24.

35 Haley and X, *Autobiography*, 11–13. An early version of the *Autobiography* shows Malcolm handwriting this moment into Alex Haley's typed draft. Malcolm's words were, "We raised rabbits, but sold them to devils." Haley changed "devils" to "whites." A thank you to author Keith Miller for finding this detail.

36 Strickland, *Malcolm X*, 25.

37 Strickland, 25.

38 Haley and X, *Autobiography*, 12.

39 Haley and X, 12.

40 See "Man Run Over by Street Car," *Lansing State Journal*, September 29, 1931; "Street Car Death Was Purely Accidental," September 30, 1931; October 1, 1931, 1. Also, Earl's death certificate is reprinted in Strickland's *Malcolm X* on page 24.

41 "Man Run Over," 1.

42 "Ku Klux Klan Is Reorganized," *Lansing State Journal*, October 3, 1931, 1.

43 "No Foul Play: Malcolm X's Dad's Death Retold," *Lansing State Journal*, February 23, 1965, 18.

44 "No Foul Play"; Strickland, *Malcolm X*, 25. First fatality comes from Laurence's wife, Florentine, who said that Laurence told her about Earl's death.

45 Strickland, *Malcolm X*, 25. See also Russell with Little and Jones, *Life of Louise Norton Little*, 166. Russell reports that Earl's death certificate read 11:50 p.m. as the time of death; note that Hilda Little and Steve Jones Jr. collaborated with Russell on her important book.

46 Little, "Our Family from the Inside."

47 Letter from Malcolm X to Beatrice Clomax, June 11, 1952. This letter is a part of the collection at the New York Public Library's Schomburg Center for Research in Black Culture in Harlem (hereafter SCRBC).

48 For these debts, see Manning Marable and Garrett Felber's *Portable Malcolm X Reader*, 17–20. The amount was $1068.23, not including other potential expenses.

49 Marable and Felber, *Portable Malcolm X Reader*, 23. With inflation, $84 would be about $1,600 in 2024 dollars.

50 Strickland, *Malcolm X*, 26.

51 Strickland, 26.

52 Haley and X, *Autobiography*, 10–14.

53 Paul Lee was a close friend of the Littles. So little is on the public record regarding Hilda that Lee's comment in "Hilda Florice Little, Condolences," on April 8, 2015, means a lot for historical purposes. Also see Hilda's important contributions to Jessica Russell's 2020 biography, *Life of Louise Norton Little*.

54 Strickland, *Malcolm X*, 27.

55 Haley and X, *Autobiography*, 14.

56 Little, "Our Family from the Inside."

57 Letter from Malcolm Little to Beatrice Clomax, June 11, 1952, SCRBC. Malcolm was telling Beatrice that it was good that she was being strong-minded toward her children.

58 Little, "Our Family from the Inside."

59 Strickland, *Malcolm X*, 16.

60 Strickland, 15.

61 One of Louise's Sunday school students, Jenny Washington, remembered in a 1992 interview that Louise tried to make "the Bible and what we were studying come alive. We didn't just sit around and memorize Bible verses. We sorta felt like we were actually . . . in the situations that maybe some of the disciples were in." Jenny Washington, interview by Blackside, Inc., 1992, transcript and tape recordings archived at Washington University, St. Louis.

62 Letter from Malcolm Little to Mr. Philbert Norton Little, December 12, 1949, SCRBC; Jenny Washington, interview by Blackside, Inc.

63 Strickland, *Malcolm X*, 28.

64 Sonya Bernard, "Marshall Woman Tells of Her Brush with Fame," *Battle Creek Enquirer*, March 2, 1996, 3.

65 Malcolm Little Prison File, "Educational History."

66 Haley and X, *Autobiography*, 15.

67 Letter from Malcolm Little to Mrs. Henrietta Shah, March 25, 1951, SCRBC.

68 Strickland, *Malcolm X*, 33.

69 Strickland, 26.

70 Haley and X, *Autobiography*, 17. The Peter Pan Bakery and Plant opened in Lansing, Michigan around November 1937, per the article in an *Lansing State Journal*, "Good Bread Makes Good Friends," November 12, 1937, 37. It already had establishments in Kalamazoo and Battle Creek.

71 Haley and X, 16.

72 Haley and X, 16. A picture of the "relief food" can be found in Strickland's *Malcolm X*, 26.

73 Haley and X, 17. Proof of Philbert's Golden Gloves boxing success can be found in "Novice Class Finals Split," *Lansing State Journal*, January 26, 1941, 13.

74 Wilfred Little, interview by Malcolm X scholar Paul D. Lee, in *Detroit Black Journal*, a TV program that aired in May 1991 under the title "Tap Dance," https://abj.matrix.msu.edu/videofull.php/id=198-733-110/.

75 Haley and X, *Autobiography*, 18.

76 Perry, *Malcolm*, 22, 24. Perry states having interviewed Pleasant Grove principal Olive Roosenraad as well as the actual teacher, whose name was not given (394n).

77 Dick Lyon, a classmate of Malcolm's, quoted in Perry's *Malcolm*, 397n. The Lincoln Community Center was an extremely valuable asset located in an impoverished neighborhood. One of many examples showing the LCC's reach can be found in the *Lansing State Journal*, "Lincoln School Pupils Enjoy Handicraft Classes," April 14, 1939, 15.

78 Haley and X, *Autobiography*, 21; Strickland, *Malcolm X*, 32.

79 Strickland, 32.

80 See Erik McDuffie's article, "Louise Little" for her baptismal certificate.

81 Haley and X, *Autobiography*, 20.

82 Haley and X, *Autobiography*, 20. Doane family names found in Perry's *Malcolm*, 523n. Perry had interviewed the family. Doane is also mentioned in Malcolm's prison letters to Philbert at the SCRBC.

83 Letter from Malcolm Little to Philbert, December 12, 1949, SCRBC.

84 Letter from Malcolm to Beatrice Clomax, June 11, 1952, SCRBC.

85 Haley and X, *Autobiography*, 20–21.

86 Little, "Our Family from the Inside," 36.

87 Perry, *Malcolm*, 33; Strickland, *Malcolm X*, 32. A copy of the physician's certificate is included in Strickland's book.

88 Russell, with Little and Jones, *Life of Louise Norton Little*, 5.

89 See Haley and X, *Autobiography*, 27. Cyril McGuire's family took in Yvonne and Robert, according to Vickki Dozier, "Remembering When Malcolm X Was Assassinated," *Lansing State Journal*, February 22, 2015, A9.

90 Haley and X, 27. Bruce Perry deserves credit for finding and interviewing Dave "Ed" Roper. See Perry's *Malcolm*, 32–33.

91 Haley and X, 24. Thornton's revolver incident can be found in "Killed by a Companion," *Livingston County Daily Press and Argus*, September 27, 1899, 1.

92 Haley and X, 31. Mabel's Red Cross credential is in "Community Center Exercises Planned," *Lansing State Journal*, May 27, 1936, 33.

93 Haley and X, 24.

94 O'Sullivan is not mentioned in any of the prior Malcolm X biographies, yet Malcolm's prison file has her listed in "Employment History" as "Gertrude Sullivan" and provides a verified set of dates as to when he started and

finished (May 10, 1939–February 7, 1941) along with the two job titles. Information about Dr. O'Sullivan was found in "Dr. Gertrude O'Sullivan, Former Official Here, Dies," *Times Herald* (Port Huron), September 15, 1949, 1, 25. For her bouts with gender discrimination, see "Mason Poked Fun at Woman Doctor," *Lansing State Journal*, October 31, 1937, 6.

95 Perry, *Malcolm*, 35.

96 "Lansing Boy Leaves Detention Home Again," *Lansing State Journal*, April 3, 1941, 12. The boy's name was Kenneth O'Reilly, and this happened nearly two months after Malcolm had left Mason to live with Ella in Roxbury. Street address "E. South St." was on the 1940 Census record. On the ward, see Perry's *Malcolm*, 35.

97 Perry's *Malcolm*, 36, based on numerous interviews with Mason residents who knew Mrs. Swerlein (398–99nn); Haley and X, *Autobiography*, 31.

98 Haley and X, *Autobiography*, 32.

99 Information on Otto Grein, his name revealed by several local residents in interviews with biographer Bruce Perry, can be found in "WMU Hall of Fame to Induct Grein," *Lansing State Journal*, August 21, 1981, 22; "WMU to Induct Early Star Grein," *Lansing State Journal*, October 6, 1981, 23. Grein passed away in 1992. The lyrics for "The Cornfield Medley" were reproduced backward in the *Autobiography* (Haley and X, 35) and have been adjusted here.

100 "Harpy" was mentioned in Perry's *Malcolm*, 39.

101 Perry's *Malcolm* mentions "Harpy for President" signs (400n). "Pink poodle" is from Haley and X, *Autobiography*, 37.

102 Perry, *Malcolm*, 38.

103 Strickland, *Malcolm X*, 34.

104 Jazz musicians are mentioned in Haley and X, *Autobiography*, 33. Malcolm's work history, as listed in his prison file, doesn't list Matthew's Restaurant; however, Perry's *Malcolm* mentions a Matthew's Eatery, and a few of the Mason residents he interviewed mentioned that Malcolm sometimes danced for fun outside of the establishment (38).

CHAPTER 4

1 Collins with Bailey, *Seventh Child*, 50.

2 Marable, *Malcolm X*, 39.

3 Collins with Bailey, *Seventh Child*, 50, 53.

4 Collins with Bailey, 50–53.

5 Collins with Bailey, 50–53.

6 *The Malcolm X–Ella Little-Collins House: 72 Dale Street* (Roxbury: Boston Landmarks Commission Study Report, 1998), https://www.boston.gov/sites/default/files/embed/m/malcolm-x-report.pdf; Collins with Bailey, *Seventh*

Child, 54. In the commission report, the white family's head of household was Mary Linehan (*Malcolm X–Ella Little-Collins House*, 4n).

7   According to the *Malcolm X–Ella Little-Collins House* study report, Ella may have purchased the deed to the house, but she didn't buy the house back from the bank until August 12, 1941 (4). Ella paid the bank 4,100 dollars. By August 1941, Malcolm had been living in Boston for at least six months.

8   Strickland, *Malcolm X*, 34.

9   Cunningham and Golden, "Malcolm," 26. "Late November" comes from Jessica Russell's important biography *Life of Louise Norton Little*. Using primary hospital documents, Russell found that Malcolm and Ella visited Kalamazoo Mental Hospital to celebrate Louise's birthday on November 28, 1939. Malcolm and Wilfred also went back on June 24, 1940, just before Malcolm left for Boston.

10 Haley and X, *Autobiography*, 39.

11 Collins with Bailey, *Seventh Child*, 19.

12 Cunningham and Golden, "Malcolm," 26.

13 Haley and X, *Autobiography*, 39.

14 Collins with Bailey, *Seventh Child*, 20.

15 Russell with Little and Jones, *Life of Louise Norton Little*, 237. Russell's book contains vital contributions from Hilda Little, and Russell was also given access to Louise's Kalamazoo hospital files.

16 Haley and X, *Autobiography*, 43–45. For the description of Kaminska, see Perry, *Malcolm*, 43. Also see "Educator at Mason Takes Lansing Post," *Lansing State Journal*, March 2, 1941, 14. On the teachers, see "School at Mason Opening Wednesday," *Lansing State Journal*, August 31, 1939, 9; Brenda J. Gilchrist, "The Rebirth of Malcolm X," *Detroit Free Press*, November 8, 1992, 1G, 5G.

17 Location found on "Certificate of Death: Michigan Department of Health"; "Michigan Death Certificates, 1921–1952," entry for Earl Little and John Little, September 28, 1931, FamilySearch, https://www.familysearch.org/ark: /61903/1:1:KF39-SPM.

18 "Career Chart," assignment, n.d., Wright Museum. A different table also appears in the anthology *Malcolm X's Michigan Worldview* edited by Edozie and Stokes. Archivist Charles Ezra Ferrell's chapter, "Malcolm X's Pre-nation of Islam (NOI) Discourses," contains a chart of this assignment (127). While Malcolm was in Kaminska's eighth grade class, he still attended Mason High School's building. According to the 1939 Mason High School yearbook, they had students starting in the seventh grade. Technically, Malcolm was in junior high, but that terminology wasn't used at the time.

19 Placing "Orator" in two of the categories showed that Malcolm, even at this young of an age, had the idea that he already was a skilled speaker or knew he could be.

20 Haley and X, *Autobiography*, 40–42.

21 Brenda J. Gilchrist, "The Rebirth of Malcolm X," *Detroit Free Press*, November 8, 1992, 1G, 5G. Also in this article is a rare team photo of Malcolm on the high school football team. He is the tallest member on the team, and the only African American. Kaminska's daughter, Beth Waldvogel, confirmed to the *Detroit Free Press* that her father taught Malcolm X and said this: "I remember Dad saying that he was probably that teacher. But because the book used a different name [Ostrowski], he wasn't sure." For Beth, her father's place in Malcolm's timeline bothers her, saying Kaminska "was the least prejudiced person she knew." See also "Kaminska Joins Monroe Schools as Psychologist," *Times Herald*, June 30, 1957, 28.

22 Goldman, *Death and Life*, 29. Malcolm may have even alluded to this slight to his wife Betty and his daughters. Attallah Shabazz, Malcolm's oldest daughter, wrote the following about Kaminska in her foreword to a new edition of the *Autobiography*: "The teacher actually admired my father greatly and didn't want to encourage him to enter a field of study that he believed wouldn't allow my father to excel. Misguided, yet well intended. A teacher crippled by a country that offered little promise or future for its indigenous and colored inhabitants" (xiii).

23 Goldman, 45.

24 Letter from Ella Little to Malcolm Little, June 19, 1940, Wright Museum.

25 Letter from Ella Little to Malcolm Little, June 19, 1940. An old photo, possibly the one Ella included, is also at the Wright Museum.

26 Letter from Ella Little to Malcolm Little, April 4, 1940, Wright Museum.

27 Haley and X, *Autobiography*, 41; Carlton Jackson, *Hounds of the Road: History of the Greyhound Bus Company* (Bowling Green, OH: Popular, 1984), 65. Jackson's book states 1942 as the year Greyhound started conserving rubber (65), but other sources, including Greyhound, state that they'd been stockpiling supplies as early as 1939, believing war with Europe was imminent. "Greyhound Corporation," Encyclopedia.com, accessed April 29, 2024, https://www.encyclopedia.com/books/politics-and-business-magazines/greyhound-corporation.

28 Haley and X, *Autobiography*, 40.

29 Haley and X, *Autobiography*, 42.

30 Collins with Bailey, *Seventh Child*, 208–9. This important book quotes Ella, Collins's mother, extensively, and the August 17 letter is reprinted in full.

31 Haley and X, *Autobiography*, 44.

32 Sheila Schimpf, "Malcolm X: The Radical Leader's Life Is the Subject of Spike Lee's Provocative Movie and the Object of Fond Memories for Folks in Lansing, Where He Grew Up," *Lansing State Journal*, November 15, 1992, 1, 5. The article also quotes an eyewitness to the 1929 house fire, Betty Walker Steward. The family stayed with the Walkers after the fire.

33 Basketball information is based on four sources. The first is verification that "Malcolm Little" played center on the basketball team. "Basketball Practice

Speeded at Mason," *Lansing State Journal*, December 4, 1940, 19. The two games, Charlotte and Howell, were chosen because of their being mentioned in Haley and X, *Autobiography*, 35. The Charlotte game information was from "Charlotte Courtmen Edge Mason, 16–15," *Lansing State Journal*, January 11, 1941, 10. The Howell game was from "Early Lead Helps Mason Win, 43–35," *Lansing State Journal*, February 1, 1941, 10.

34 Joseph Wyman was the 1940–41 Mason High School orchestra director, confirmed through "More Than 250 Women Gather at Meet," *Lansing State Journal*, October 18, 1940, 19. The curtain story was remembered by two students and is in Perry's *Malcolm*, 43. Likewise, Malcolm's stopping of the music during a dance is in Perry's *Malcolm*, 43, and one of his sources was the Mason High School principal at the time, Clifford Walcott. *Lansing State Journal*, December 29, 1940, 4. My best guess is that this incident happened during homecoming. See also Haley and X, *Autobiography*, 36.

35 Malcolm Little Prison File. For Wilfred information, see Les and Tamara Payne's *Dead Are Arising*, 146. Les Payne interviewed Wilfred Little on April 26, 1991.

36 Haley and X, *Autobiography*, 43.

37 AfroMarxist Channel, "Ella Collins [Malcolm X's Sister] Interview Part 2," YouTube, accessed July 18, 2019, https://www.youtube.com/watch?v=uNVhf_sy_U8.

38 Collins with Bailey, *Seventh Child*, 22; Haley and X, *Autobiography*, 49.

39 Letter from Philbert Little to Malcolm Little, March 6, 1941; letter from Reginald Little to Malcolm Little, March 22, 1941, Wright Museum.

40 Letter from Christine Hoyt to Malcolm Little, February 7, 1941; letter from Peter Hawryliew to Malcolm Little, March 2, 1941, Wright Museum.

41 Haley and X, *Autobiography*, 51.

42 Collins with Bailey, *Seventh Child*, 23.

43 The April 1940 Census lists his age as "27," however. Earl's baritone voice is based off the fact that he was able to sing the low-note-loaded *Ol' Man River*.

44 The 1940 Census confirms that Earl Little was, as of April of that year, a "Prisoner" at the New Bedford House of Correction and County Jail.

45 Collins with Bailey, *Seventh Child*, 38. Several Boston newspapers list "Jimmy Carlton" as a singer on radio, such as the *Boston Globe*, October 4, 1935; November 15, 1935 (WEEI Boston radio); May 14, 1936; and April 23, 1936.

46 "Stars' Doubles Are at Irving," *Wilkes-Barre Record*, September 13, 1940, 21.

47 Malcolm Jarvis, as quoted in Strickland's *Malcolm X*, 51.

48 Strickland, 49; Collins with Bailey, *Seventh Child*, 61; Perry, *Malcolm*, 57, based off an interview with Malcolm's first cousin, J. C. Little.

49 Collins with Bailey, 39.

50 Perry's *Malcolm*, 407n, lists Earl Jr.'s death certificate date.

51 Perry, 58, based on Perry's interview with Ella Little.

52 Haley and X, *Autobiography*, 51.

53 "Car Hits, Kills Dr. Shag Taylor in South End," *Boston Globe*, November 6, 1958, 4. Taylor was 70 years old and just getting out of his car when another car hit him.

54 Cunningham and Golden, "Malcolm," 26.

55 Malcolm Little Prison File; Collins with Bailey, *Seventh Child*, 39.

56 Haley and X, *Autobiography*, 80. Beneficiary information can be found on the official document, published in Collins with Bailey, *Seventh Child*, in the second collection of photos, on the final page. Philbert's address can be confirmed from his letter to Malcolm in March 1941. Louise had been at Kalamazoo for nearly two years by this point.

57 "Interesting Panorama Unfolds along Route to New York City," *Boston Globe*, August 12, 1941, 9; Haley and X, *Autobiography*, 80.

58 Haley and X, *Autobiography*, 81–82.

59 "Interesting Panorama."

60 Haley and X, *Autobiography*, 82.

61 DeCaro, *On the Side of My People*, 62; Hans J. Massaquoi, "The Mystery of Malcolm X," *Ebony*, September 1964, 46.

62 Letter from Malcolm Little to Zelma Holman, November 18, 1941, Wright Museum. Zelma Holman became Zelma Davis later in life and passed away in December 2010. For the discussion of roller skating, see Carrie Ellett, "Keep On Rolling," *Lansing State Journal*, August 20, 1998, 36. On the kitchenette, see Les and Tamara Payne's *The Dead Are Arising*, 147.

63 Letter from Malcolm Little to Eloise Schack, ca. 1941, Wright Museum. The date on this letter, at first glance, reads January 17, 1941, but that is hard to believe. Ella did not secure the Dale Street house until November 1941, and Malcolm was in Michigan until February 1941. My best guess is that the date of the letter could either be November 17, 1941, or, less likely, January 17, 1942. The wording Malcolm uses in the letter to Zelma and to Eloise is very similar, especially his last line: "I do hope you will, for my sake, not take so long to answer as I did to write." Purple pen and blue stationery as well.

64 Letter from Malcolm Little to Mary Jane Smith, n.d. (but most likely November 1941, due to its similarity to the other two letters), Wright Museum. My guess is Malcolm was excited about his new bachelor pad at Dale Street and chose to write to all the girls he liked back in Michigan. Mary Jane Smith later became Mary Jane Huxtable-Koch and passed away in April 2020. Obituary, *Lincoln Journal Star*, April 22, 2020. See also *Lansing State Journal*, May 13, 1937, 6.

65 "Malcolm X: The Real Story," produced by Brett Alexander, aired December 3, 1992, CBS News. The date is from the Malcolm Little Prison File. Information on the Parker House is from Haley and X, *Autobiography*, and has been placed here because of Malcolm's description of hearing news

about Pearl Harbor, which would have been December 7, 1941, in between railroad jobs.

66 Lionel Hampton, quoted in "Malcolm X: The Real Story"; Haley and X, *Autobiography*, 66–67.

67 Letter from Gloria Strother to Malcolm Little, June 3, 1942, Wright Museum.

68 Strickland, *Malcolm X*, 55.

69 Beatrice Bazarian Prison File. The Tic Toc Night Club is mentioned in Malcolm's prison file and confirmed by a friend, Laurence Neblett, in Perry's *Malcolm*, 56. The year 1942 was decided because although Malcolm was reported in his prison file as saying he "approached and conversed" with Beatrice at the "Tic Toc Restaurant" in 1941, he also said that Beatrice's "husband was in the Army at the time," which, according to Mr. Bazarian's military records, wasn't until June 1942.

70 Beatrice Bazarian Prison File. On Joyce's cat, see "Dog, Lamb in Melee, Upset Pet Show . . ." *Boston Globe*, July 24, 1936, 7. Her cat's name was "Tiger."

71 Beatrice Bazarian Prison File.

72 Beatrice's prison file has her listed as living at 121 Dexter Avenue, her childhood home, until November 1945. This would mean on the surface that even after marrying Martin in February 1944, Beatrice lived with her parents.

73 Inscribed on Martin Bazarian's gravestone is "Pvt US Army," confirmed via his military archive records; Haley and X, *Autobiography*, 76.

74 Letter from Hilda Little to Malcolm Little, July 14, 1942; letter from Reginald Little to Malcolm Little, July 13, 1942 (12:31 a.m.), Wright Museum.

75 Letter from Hilda Little to Reginald Little, July 19, 1942, Wright Museum.

76 Letter from Hilda Little to Reginald Little, July 19, 1942, Wright Museum.

77 Yvonne Little, as quoted in Strickland's *Malcolm X*, 54.

78 The Malcolm Little Prison File lists Jimmy's Chicken Shack as a place of employment, although the 1942 to 1944 dates could be misleading, since the file shows that the listing was "unv."—unverified.

79 Wally Warner, "Tavern Topics," *New York Age*, March 7, 1942, 10; Doc Wheeler, *New York Age*, January 24 and 28, 1950. See also "Jimmy's Chicken Shack a Real Precedent-Maker," *New York Age*, August 6, 1949, 19, and an ad in the *Age* on January 28, 1950, 17. For Mr. Bacon's obituary, see *New York Daily News*, "Bacon," May 16, 1970, 115. Bacon was 64 when he died. For the picture of the chicken, see "Jimmy's Chicken Shack Harlem, NY 1930–1980's," *Harlem World Magazine*, March 24, 2018, https://www.harlemworldmagazine.com/jimmys-chicken-shack-harlem-ny-1930-1980s/. Malcolm's quote is from Haley and X, *Autobiography*, 129.

80 Giddins, *Celebrating Bird*, 54.

81 DeCaro, *On the Side of My People*, 67. DeCaro interviewed Atkins on July 17, 1992.

82 Atkins spoke with author Herb Boyd for Boyd's book *Baldwin's Harlem: A Biography of James Baldwin* (New York: Atria, 2008), 65. The biographer

was Louis DeCaro, from his Malcolm X biography, *On the Side of My People*, 64.

83 DeCaro, *On the Side of My People*, 64, from his interview with Atkins.

84 Capeci, *Harlem Riot of 1943*, 99–103.

85 Capeci, vi.

86 Haley and X, *Autobiography*, 125. Fletcher Henderson was scheduled to lead his orchestra at the State Armory Building in Wilmington, Delaware, two hours away, on July 31, 1943. "Fletcher Henderson to Play at Rally, Dance," *News Journal*, July 24, 1943, 10. Henderson was famous at the time for "Christopher Columbus," a "swing classic."

87 Ellison, who lived in an apartment a half mile south from Jimmy's Chicken Shack at 306 W. 141 Street, wrote to his close friend about the racial tension at the time, ignited in part by wartime conditions: "Negroes who once recognized some whites as friendly now arm themselves with knives when they go into white neighborhoods at night. They no longer trust white men." Ellison was 29 at the time of the riot. Letter from Ellison to Sanora Babb, July 4, 1943, in John F. Callahan and Marc C. Conner, ed., *The Selected Letters of Ralph Ellison* (New York: Random House, 2024), 162.

88 As quoted in Arnold Rampersad's *Ralph Ellison* (New York: Knopf, 2007), 166, from an op-ed Ellison wrote for the *New York Post* on August 3, 1943, titled "Harlem 24 Hours After—Peace and Quiet Reign."

89 Wilfred Little Shabazz, interview with Louis A. DeCaro, August 14, 1992, from DeCaro, *On the Side of My People*, 68. The Jarvis quote is from Strickland, *Malcolm X*, 54. Malcolm's quote is from Massaquoi, "Mystery of Malcolm X," 46. Malcolm mentioned in his *Autobiography* that security in Harlem tightened after the riot (125).

90 Cobey Black, "Black and Blue and Redd All Over," *Honolulu Advertiser*, June 9, 1976, 69; Robert Kerwin, "Seeing Redd," *Chicago Tribune*, December 9, 1973, 58.

91 Louie Robinson, "Redd Foxx—Prince of Clowns," *Ebony*, April 1967, 91; Foxx is quoted in Michael Seth Starr, *Black and Blue: The Redd Foxx Story* (Milwaukee, WI: Applause, 2011), 22–23, originally from a March 1971 *Penthouse* article. According to an article by Erik McDuffie and Komozi Woodard, Foxx and Malcolm did attend more serious events, such as Communist Party meetings. Malcolm was invited to the meetings by Vicki Garvin, but when the Communist Party speaker spoke poorly, Malcolm "put on his hat and coat" and left, telling Garvin that due to the speaker's speaking style, he wasn't interested in joining. McDuffie and Woodard, "'If You're in a Country,'" 507.

92 Robinson; Starr.

93 "Eighteen Years Old," *Brooklyn Citizen*, June 27, 1942, 7; "red hot" found on the backside of a 1940 postcard, courtesy of the New York Public Library Digital Collection, "Interior View of Small's Paradise, with Inset Portrait of Owner Ed Smalls," https://digitalcollections.nypl.org/items/7a926510

-e836-0135-7130-0f9d8f417c5f#/?uuid=7a926510-e836-0135-7130-0f9d8f417c5f.
Charles was the manager, and "Ed" was the owner. Room information came
from a series of advertisements in the *New York Age* archives; most helpful
was *New York Age*, July 22, 1944. See also Haley and X, *Autobiography*, 104.
Note that Malcolm gave Small's a strong spotlight in his autobiography,
even though his prison file does not mention him ever working there. It's
possible that Malcolm decided to spotlight Small's simply because in 1963,
when Malcolm started working on his book with Alex Haley, Small's was one
of the only places left. In fact, during the years Malcolm collaborated with
Haley on the autobiography (1963–64), Small's was co-owned by basketball
star Wilt Chamberlain and was rebranded "Big Wilt's Small's Paradise." Wilt
brought in Ray Charles for a three-night stay in 1961 and in March 1963 had
the sax legend King Curtis filling rooms on a nightly basis. Bottom line: If
you lived in Harlem and picked up the *Autobiography* when it was released
in 1965, you could clearly visualize the space Malcolm was describing.

94 Malcolm had been given a 4F rejection notice on October 25, 1943. Malcolm
served up a cocktail of behaviors to prove he wasn't fit for combat. Malcolm "was
found mentally disqualified for military service by the reasons of psychopathic
personality . . . sexual perversion and psychiatric rejection." In short, Malcolm
convinced them he was crazy. Les and Tamara Payne, *Dead Are Arising*, 187.

95 Beatrice Bazarian Prison File.

96 Haley and X, *Autobiography*, 106.

97 Haley and X, *Autobiography*, 106.

98 National Archives and Records Administration, *Hospital Admission Card
Files*, ca. 1970, NAI 570973, Record Group Number: *Records of the Office
of the Surgeon General (Army), 1775–1994*, Record Group Title: 112. Also
see Bazarian, Mehran Martin, US Veterans' Gravesites, ca. 1775–2019. All
information provided by NARA via ancestry.com.

99 Malcolm Little Prison File. "Dealing pot" is mentioned often in Malcolm's
Autobiography.

100 Malcolm Little Prison File; Beatrice Bazarian Prison File.

101 Letter from Malcolm X to Rev. Samuel Laviscount, November 14, 1950.
Words have been transcribed by Malcolm X biographer Louis DeCaro,
who documented the letter after Marla Blakey, Laviscount's granddaughter,
uploaded excerpts of the letter to a website back in the late 1990s. Only
Blakey would have the original letter in full.

102 Beatrice Bazarian Prison File.

103 Malcolm Little Prison File, "Calvin Peterson." According to the report,
Malcolm "never reported once" to the probation office, and thanks to an
apparently neglectful probation supervisor, his absence was never reported.

104 Malcolm Little Prison File. The police would have contacted Lennon for
confirmation in early 1946.

105 "Parisian Couple Are Married Here," *Palm Beach Post*, March 26, 1937, 8; "4 Gunmen Rob Sandwich Farm," *Boston Globe*, August 10, 1955, 24; "Palm Beach Notes," *Palm Beach Post*, April 11, 1937, 10; "Red Cross Call Reaches $12,838," *Palm Beach Post*, January 26, 1941, 11. See also Phelps, "Sexuality of Malcolm X," where Phelps included Lennon's passport photo.

106 In Haley and X, *Autobiography*, 152, Brown is called "Rudy," and Malcolm explains to Haley that "Rudy's mother was Italian." This can be proven by looking at Brown's prison file, which shows that Brown's mother's maiden name was Catalano. Also in the *Autobiography*, Malcolm believes Rudy "caught the first thing smoking," just after Malcolm had been arrested for burglary. In the prison file, Francis Brown was the only other listed defendant, and he was never found or charged. Also of note in Brown's prison file is that prison officials at the time vaguely noted that Brown's youthful effeminate nature meant he might need to be "segregated" from other men.

107 This debate—if Malcolm ever played for the other team—started with Bruce Perry's 1991 biography, *Malcolm*. In it, Perry quotes in his endnotes a letter he received from Jarvis stating that Malcolm had helped Brown with Lennon's talcum powder rubdowns (414). However, Jarvis, after being criticized for helping to create what many deemed a false narrative, told biographer Les Payne (working with his daughter Tamara on what would become his award-winning book, *The Dead Are Arising: The Life of Malcolm X*) plainly in a 1992 interview that Malcolm "hated the homosexuals." Another Malcolm X biographer, Manning Marable, not having heard Payne's interview with Jarvis, extended Perry's findings in his 2011 biography, *Malcolm: A Life of Reinvention*, and suggested that Lennon and Malcolm may have connected in such a way that impelled Lennon to reach out to Malcolm when he was in prison. Phelps's "Sexuality of Malcolm X" provides an all-encompassing and absorbing look into this debate. To better understand Paul Lennon's "double-life," *Gay New York* by George Chauncey is a great place to start.

108 Beatrice Bazarian Prison File.

109 The address in Miami was 1435 Collins Ave. Beatrice Bazarian Prison File, "Employment History." Also in the prison file are interviews with Beatrice's mother, Alice, and her husband, conducted by Framingham women's prison officials.

110 "Dice Game Raided; Seven Are Arrested," *Lansing State Journal*, October 19, 1942, 14; "44 Colored Boys at Y.M.C.A. Camp," *Lansing State Journal*, August 14, 1939, 12; "Pipe Stuns Negro during Fight Here," *Lansing State Journal*, September 29, 1942, 1; Perry, *Malcolm*, 84.

111 Malcolm Little Prison File; Marable, *Malcolm*, 80.

112 Little, "Our Family from the Inside," 16.

113 "Marriage Licenses," *Michigan Chronicle*, June 16, 1945, 7. Bertha and Wilfred had two children before Bertha passed away suddenly at the age of 26, on

August 29, 1949 (born June 18, 1923), while Malcolm was in prison. Wilfred later married Ruth Harriet Gray on April 3, 1951. On Jimmy Williams, see "Henderson Band Paradise Feature," *Detroit Free Press*, January 8, 1945, 12; Perry, *Malcolm*, 85.

114   Little, "Our Family from the Inside"

115   Ads for Caribbean Club begins running in the *Age* with Wally Warner, "Harlem Night Life," *New York Age*, July 28, 1945, 11. There was another man named Rhythm Red, a tap dancer who performed in revues and even sidewalks near Lenox Avenue but not as an emcee. See "Rhythm Red Revives the Art of Tap Dancing," *Herald Statesmen*, February 8, 1974, 10.

116   "The Caribbean Club," *New York Age*, July 28, 1945. See also "Lots of Girls and Comedy in Capitol Show," *Atlanta Journal-Constitution*, January 14, 1941, 8. As of 2023, this Harlem address would be between a McDonald's and a Harlem's Discount on what is now Adam Clayton Powell Boulevard.

117   Stuart Hall, "Calypso Kings," *Guardian*, June 28, 2002, 48.

118   Ulysses Boykin, "Jumpin' Jive," *Detroit Tribune*, December 20, 1941, 6; "Casino Presents 'Black-White' Revue," *Pittsburgh Press*, April 10, 1945, 8.

119   "Snookum Russell Closes Fine Tour with Roadshow," *Pittsburgh Courier*, August 3, 1940, 20; Sylvester's photo is included.

120   Haley and X, *Autobiography*, 137.

121   Fabre and Skinner, *Conversations with Chester Himes*, 14. Himes mentions Malcolm in a November 1964 interview with Francois Bott for the French magazine *Adam*: "I meant for [*Hollers*] to be a shock treatment, the same kind of treatment that Malcolm X wanted to inflict on the American public."

122   Himes, *If He Hollers*, 4. Himes, like Malcolm, served about seven years in prison for armed robbery (1929–36). While in an Ohio penitentiary, Himes developed his writing style and published several stories. See Lawrence P. Jackson, *Chester B. Himes: A Biography*, to learn more about Himes. In his excellent biography, Jackson states that Malcolm read *Hollers* in prison, but after reviewing primary source material related to the Charlestown State Prison library, it's doubtful they carried the book, and it would not have been able to get past censors. It's more likely that Malcolm read the novel *just before prison*, and its themes remained deeply on his mind during his first year behind bars.

123   Himes, 121.

124   Haley and X, *Autobiography*, 145–53. As Malcolm X scholar Keith Miller argues quite convincingly in his as-yet-unpublished manuscript, there is plagiaristic evidence showing that Alex Haley most likely lifted ideas, story lines, phrases, and names (like West Indian Archie) from Himes's Harlem detective novels. As Miller describes, Malcolm was killed before seeing past chapter 5 of the *Autobiography*. As for *If He Hollers*, Himes mentions in *Conversations* that he met Malcolm at least twice; once in Harlem in 1962 (60) and again in Paris in November 1964 (see Jackson, *Chester B. Himes*, 449). It would not be a surprise if Malcolm had told Haley how much he'd admired Himes's fiction.

If West Indian Archie was real, I'd suspect Egbert Moore as being him, due to Malcolm's time at the Caribbean Club just before leaving Harlem.

125 Strickland, *Malcolm X*, 57.

CHAPTER 5

1 Malcolm Little Prison File, "Commitment and Booking Data."

2 Malcolm Little Prison File.

3 Annette Gordon-Reed, *The Hemingses of Monticello*, 554. Reed shows that it was an article written by James Callender in the *Richmond Recorder* on September 1, 1802, that brought the relationship of Jefferson and Sally Hemmings into the public eye. Also see Gideon Haynes, *Pictures from Prison Life*, published in 1871. Conditions were also described as horrid in both Malcolm's *Autobiography* and Malcolm Jarvis's memoir.

4 *The Autobiography of Malcolm X*, 176.

5 Strickland, *Malcolm X*, 59.

6 "They Dug Out," *Boston Globe*, July 9, 1892, 1, 4.

7 "Prisoner Escapes at Charlestown," *Boston Globe*, February 25, 1946, 1, 3. Also see *Boston Globe*, February 27, 1946.

8 On page 60 of Strickland's *Malcolm X*, Malcolm's brother Philbert mentioned that he learned later that when Malcolm first entered Charlestown, he "was kind of a hell-raiser in prison, because he was trying to organize the people as though he was gon' break out and all this kind of stuff."

9 "Ex-Warden Lawes Called in Probe," *Boston Globe*, March 1, 1946, 1. In the same newspaper, Howard Belding Gill, Norfolk Prison Colony mastermind, also denounced Charlestown's prison conditions.

10 "Ex-Warden Lawes," 16.

11 "Ex-Warden Lawes." Also see *Boston Globe*, March 21, 1946, 8, which describes the requests of the newly established "State Prison Welfare Committee"—12 Charlestown prisoners who hoped to be given a bit of lee-way with the strict rules, such as writing two letters a week, instead of one. It was unclear which of the 16 requests the prison officials granted.

12 *Boston Globe*, March 21, 1946, 1, 16. Also, Haley and X, *Autobiography*, 166.

13 Haley and X, *Autobiography*, 167.

14 "Ex-Warden Lawes," *Boston Globe*, March 1, 1946, 1, 16.

15 Malcolm Jarvis Prison File, interview, "General Remarks and Personality Impressions," March 6, 1946.

16 Malcolm Jarvis Prison File.

17 The date comes from "Woman Drowned in Lake Tragedy: Three Lose Lives—Boy Saved at Hampton," *Boston Globe*, July 5, 1935, 21. The "whirlpool" quote is from Jarvis with Nichols, *The Other Malcolm*, 24. The book, which is a refreshing read and contains many helpful photos, has numerous timeline mistakes, however, since, to take one example, it states that Clifford drowned "around 1937."

18 Jarvis with Nichols, 23–25. Jarvis's Prison File mentions his 1936 bicycle theft and probation.

19 Jarvis's prison file mentions that the grocer job was 45 cents an hour.

20 Saturday movie dates are mentioned in his prison file. Jarvis's actual wedding date is hard to pin down, since in his memoir, *The Other Malcolm*, he lists February 16, 1940, on page 22, then gives 1941 on page 40 as the year they married. Jarvis's prison file says April 28, 1941, but on the same page, he's recorded as saying it was April 26, 1940.

21 Malcolm Jarvis Prison File, "Preliminary Record."

22 Malcolm Little Prison File, "Remarks."

23 Malcolm Little Prison File.

24 "Well Fed Prisoners at Charlestown Give Billfold to New Chef," *Berkshire Eagle*, March 16, 1946, 7; "State Prison Break Foiled," *Boston Globe*, March 19, 1946, 1, 9. Lewis Lawes was the former Sing Sing warden, and he'd been hired in March by Massachusetts Governor Tobin to complete a report of Charlestown and other prisons. The Lawes quote is in the *Boston Globe*, March 25, 1946, 1, 8.

25 Collins with Bailey, *Seventh Child*, 70; Haley and X, *Autobiography*, 167. Malcolm remembered it differently than Ella, saying they didn't have much to say to each other.

26 "Appellate Cuts Sisters' Terms; One, 18, Freed," *Boston Globe*, April 11, 1946, 12. The "historic" wording is a bit unclear: "Two young Watertown sisters, the first of their sex to make application for reduction of their Women's Reformatory sentences to the Appellate Division of the Superior Court."

27 "Girl, 18, Convicted of Burglary, Makes Appeal for Mercy," *Boston Globe*, April 2, 1946, 13; "'Tearful Bobby Soxer,' Facing 5-Year Term, Appeals for 'Justice,'" *Boston Globe*, April 3, 1946. Also, Beatrice Bazarian Prison File, "Outside Investigation Sheet: Interview with Captain Mahoney, Brookline Police Department at the Norfolk Court at Dedham," April 10, 1946.

28 Joyce Caragulian Prison File; Beatrice Bazarian Prison File, "Present Offense."

29 "Judge Walter Collins, 97, Dean of State's Judiciary," *Boston Globe*, February 11, 1975, 22.

30 Beatrice Bazarian Prison File, "Outside Investigation Sheet."

31 Perry, *Malcolm*, 107–8. Perry's source was his interview with J. C. Little. This can be more accurately verified once Perry's archives are made available to the public at Harvard's Houghton Library in 2041. Let's hope floppy disks can still be accessed . . .

32 Joyce Caragulian Prison File.

33 See the *Boston Globe*, January 10, 1946, 20, for "lewdness"; May 6, 1946, 7, for "assault" (stabbing Navy cook); and June 28, 1946, 10, for "larceny." "Two weeks apart" was in Beatrice Bazarian's prison file, in a letter written by Superintendent Miriam Van Waters to Beatrice's mother. For more about Van Waters and Framingham women's prison, see Estelle Freedman's *Maternal Justice: Miriam Van Waters and the Female Reform Tradition* (Chicago: University of Chicago Press, 1996).

34 Beatrice Bazarian Prison File, "Statistical Findings"; "Mrs. Wixon Starts Sentence at State Reformatory," *Boston Globe*, June 28, 1946, 10.

35 Beatrice Bazarian Prison File, "Chronological Sheet: April 31, 1946, 'Letter to Subject from Her Husband.'"

36 Beatrice Bazarian Prison File, "Notice of Home and Work." Bruce Perry, in *Malcolm*, noted that when he contacted Bea by phone, her response was "hostile" (xii).

37 Collins with Bailey, *Seventh Child*, 72.

38 Malcolm Little Prison File, "Massachusetts State Prison Psychometric Report." In 1946, this particular test, the Wechsler–Bellevue Test, was created by David Wechsler, a psychologist, but it wasn't until 1955 that he created a new version of the test that factored in a "non-white population."

39 Malcolm Little Prison File, "Family's Personal History," May 17, 1946.

40 Perry, *Malcolm*, 108. Perry had interviewed Jarvis for the book.

41 Malcolm Jarvis Prison File shows his June 6 transfer. He'd spend almost four years at Norfolk.

42 The John Elton Bembry Prison File shows his transfer date to Charlestown. Malcolm's words are from the *Autobiography*, 178.

43 The photo on the left is when he first entered Charlestown State Prison in 1943. The photo on the right is when he was released in 1948. As was the custom in Massachusetts at the time, prisoners were given a tailored suit and $10 before leaving prison.

44 John Elton Bembry Prison File.

45 John Elton Bembry Prison File states on multiple occasions that August 2, 1912, is his birthdate, including one verified instance. But in an interview with a prison official, Bembry gave the date July 25, 1912. This date is also repeated in the prison file.

46 John Elton Bembry Prison File.

47 John Elton Bembry Prison File. In his "initial interview," Bembry said that he liked school and didn't skip any grades. Another document states that he "probably" graduated high school.

48 Throughout his time at Norfolk, Bembry was considered highly skilled at dominoes and also played right field for the baseball team. See "Sports Comment," *Colony*, May 15, 1946, 14; "What Goes On Here . . ." February 15, 1946, 10.

49 John Elton Bembry Prison File.

50 John Elton Bembry Prison File. See also Associated Press, "15 Prisoners Are Punished," *North Adams Transcript*, April 30, 1946, 1.

51 John Elton Bembry Prison File.

52 John Elton Bembry Prison File.

53 John Elton Bembry Prison File. See also Jerry Bembry, "The Untold Story of the Inmate Who Helped Shape Malcolm X's Future," *The Undefeated*, February 2, 2020. Jerry Bembry was "Bimbi's" nephew, and this excellent

article, using a mix of prison file data and personal memories, humanizes Bimbi: "Uncle Elton would often express to his family his fondness for the man who Malcolm X became, but rarely spoke of the time they served together aside from a letter to my cousin, Clinton, in which he said he introduced the future Muslim leader to the work of Henry David Thoreau."

54 Haley and X, *Autobiography*, 167.

55 Haley and X, 168.

56 Henry David Thoreau, *Civil Disobedience* (New York: Penguin, 1995), 5, 10, 27, respectively. Thoreau's essay was originally published in 1849.

57 Haley and X, *Autobiography*, 168.

58 Malcolm Little Prison File, "Transfer Summary: From State Prison to Massachusetts Reformatory"; "Personal."

59 Perry, *Malcolm*, 108. Perry based his information on an interview with Bembry.

60 Hans J. Massaquoi, "Mystery of Malcolm X," *Ebony*, September 1964, 46.

61 Perry, *Malcolm*, 108–9.

62 Malcolm Little Prison File, "Transfer Summary."

63 Perry, *Malcolm*, 109.

64 Self-destructive comes from Perry, 109. For *Richard III*, see Reynolds, *Middle Man*, 199–200. Reynolds, Malcolm and Alex Haley's literary agent, recalls meeting Malcolm for the first time, writing that he and Malcolm riffed about Shakespeare, Malcolm recalling by heart the opening two lines of *Richard III*: "Now is the winter of our discontent / Made glorious summer by this sun of York." While it's not explicitly stated when exactly Malcolm read *Richard III*, I placed it here so it could live within his 1946 summer of Shakespeare.

65 Perry, *Malcolm*, 110.

66 Perry, 109, 401n. Perry interviewed Philbert Little.

67 This was from an episode of *Charlestown Live*, hosted by Tom Coots, his guest David Hennessy, vice president of the Charlestown Historical Society. Hennessy conveyed the information on the program, which aired in 2014 and can be found on their YouTube channel, CharlestownLiveTV.

68 "Skopp Executed after Praying Twenty Minutes," *Boston Globe*, August 18, 1945, 2.

69 "Skopp Executed after Praying," 1, 2.

70 John Noxon Prison File. The term *Down syndrome* was not around in 1943. Instead, words such as "mongoloidism" were used in the press in the 1940s.

71 Dorothy Wayman, "Ask Pardon for Noxon," *Boston Globe*, July 22, 1947, 1, 9.

72 "Wife Pleads for Noxon," *Boston Globe*, July 24, 1946, 1, 11.

73 Manning Marable believes the 14-million-dollar man was William Paul Lennon; however Rodnell Collins, author of *Seventh Child*, said that his mother, Ella, never heard from him. The quote is from Collins with Bailey,

Seventh Child, 71. One other possibility could be Abe Goldstein, who owned several clubs, worked with Malcolm for a longer period of time than Lennon and at least on the official record paid him the most on average out of any of the jobs listed in his prison file ($60). He was most likely "Hymie" in the *Autobiography*, and Malcolm had heard from someone that Hymie/Goldstein had been murdered, but he was at least alive long enough to provide a reply when contacted by prison officials to vouch for Malcolm's employment record, stating that Malcolm was "a bit unstable and neurotic but under proper guidance a good boy." Further support for the Hymie/Goldstein connection is that Goldstein owned a gasoline station on Long Island, where Malcolm went to bootleg. "Three Thugs Rob Gas Station Man," *Daily News*, June 18, 1935. Malcolm, while in prison, also told Alex Haley that when Reginald came to see him, they had a long conversation about how all white people were evil: "What about Hymie?" he asked Reginald, "who had been so good to me" (Haley and X, *Autobiography*, 174). These bits to me are more plausible than the Lennon angle.

74 Malcolm Little Prison File. Quotes are Malcolm's words from a letter he wrote to a Mr. Dwyer on July 28, 1947.

75 Malcolm Little Prison File, "Transfer Summary." The file redacts the names and leaves out how often they visited. Still, it's safe to say that Malcolm had a visitor at least ten times during his first stint in Charlestown.

76 "Reading in Prisons Will Be Studied," *Boston Globe*, May 21, 1929, 16. The Department of Education official was Kathleen Jones. The prisoner's name is J. R. M. "Books of Far West Most in Demand at State Prison," *Boston Globe*, August 6, 1924, 15; the article was reprinted from Charlestown State Prison's newspaper, *The Mentor*.

77 "Books of Far West." For court case, see "Inmate Argues His Case after Law Study in Prison," *Boston Globe*, March 25, 1940, 5. The prisoner's name was John T. Comerford. On magazine subscriptions, see "Asks Funds to Aid Freed Prisoners," *Boston Globe*, October 23, 1931, 31.

78 Malcolm Jarvis Prison File. Due to it being far less redacted, Jarvis's prison file clearly lists his November 12, 1946, court date information.

79 "Rites Saturday for Judge Good in Cambridge," *Boston Globe*, November 26, 1958, 22. A picture of him can be found in the *Boston Globe* on May 29, 1935, 9.

80 Malcolm Jarvis Prison File, "Spare Time Activities," August 17, 1946: "Subject plays in the 1st orchestra, spends his time in the company of other colored youths walking about, visiting or engaged in a musical jam session."

81 See Malcolm Jarvis, "An Evening Well Spent," *Colony*, November 1, 1946, 9. Jarvis and hundreds others listened to a program given by two "distinguished members of the Society of Jesus."

82 Malcolm Jarvis Prison File, "Transfer Summary."

83 Malcolm's handwritten letter to Ella was placed as an image in Jed B. Tucker's groundbreaking article, "Malcolm X, the Prison Years," *Journal of African*

American History, Spring 2017, 187. The original letter can be found at the Wright Museum.

84 Tucker, 187.

85 See Malcolm Little Prison File for date of transfer to Concord. Ella was in prison from January 7, 1947, to February 5, 1947, according to Perry's *Malcolm* (407n). Perry analyzed the criminal dockets available at the time from the Suffolk County Superior Court. The jail Ella was kept in is now the luxurious Liberty Hotel.

CHAPTER 6

1 "To Reform Reformatories," *Boston Globe*, March 10, 1884, 2.

2 For these stories, see the *Boston Globe*, April 30, 1947 (Walls); January 12, 1948 (Goode Jr.); January 21, 1947 (two fresh hoodlums). For the number 734 and average age, see Department of Correction, *Massachusetts Department of Correction: Annual Report of the Commissioners of Correction*, State Library of Massachusetts Digital Collections, 1947.

3 Haley and X, *Autobiography*, 166.

4 Perry, *Malcolm*, 112, based off Perry's interview with Arthur Roach.

5 *Boston Globe*, January 1, 1947; January 7, 1947; January 8, 1947. For a photo of Dolan, see "Harassed Boss of Reformatory Eats First Full Meal in 5 Days," *Boston Globe*, July 6, 1952, 48; "Maj. Dolan Given Dinner; Retiring from M.N.G.," *Boston Globe*, May 2, 1934, 8.

6 Department of Correction, *Annual Report of the Commissioners*, 1947, 39. For supplementary details on the farm, see the 1946 and 1948 reports.

7 Department of Correction, 39. Dining hall location verified via 1959 Associated Press photo of MR-Concord. In 1964, the institution started a total rebuilding process.

8 Department of Correction, 37.

9 According to Nash's prison file, he was a "Negro" and lived in the "poor and colored" sections in and around Lynn, Massachusetts, the second-oldest of ten siblings. His mother gave birth to him at 16, and his parents separated when he was 17. Robert had dropped out of school midway through the seventh grade but continued taking classes in "the art department" of "public schools," because his teachers believed he had a talent for "sketching." Robert most likely worked with Malcolm for a few months in MR-Concord's furniture department. He was given a five-year sentence for operating a motor vehicle without authority, after his "right to" operate had been "suspended." For his "leisure" in prison, Nash read "current magazines," such as *Life*, *Reader's Digest*, and *Collier's*; dabbled in wood carving; and attended "Catholic services regularly." In an interview with his mother, she

explained to the prison official that "Robert enjoyed dancing and singing. He was very proficient in both. It is his custom to become acquainted with all the latest songs."

10 William Paul Williams, "Monday Night Club Boxing," *Our Paper*, February 8, 1947, 46. Copies of *Our Paper* can be found in the Massachusetts Archives on the UMass Boston campus. Many of the articles deal with special sporting events, film summaries, poems, parole information, and holiday commemorations.

11 Willis's lengthy prison file starts with him getting two years for "using a car without authority." Nineteen at the time, Willis served some of his time on Deer Island, where he and two other young men tried to escape by heading into the water and hiding under a log. They kept their heads under water as long as they could, but a guard, scanning "between the island and Winthrop shore," eventually "saw one head appear; then two more heads." His sentence was changed to five years, indeterminate. Willis was transferred to MR-Concord and later that year, 1944, was given an infraction for having "home made playing cards." Willis's father died when he was two, and he dropped out of the seventh grade to help his mother but soon ran into a "gangster" named Ranahan, known for being an intimidating "prize fighter." His mother felt jail was a good way to escape the influence of gangsters, and Willis had hoped to join the Marines to support his mother and escape Ranahan's influence. Willis's weight fluctuated wildly while in prison, from 137 to 172 pounds.

12 William Paul Williams, "Monday Night Club Boxing," *Our Paper*, February 15, 1947, 53.

13 Johnston's prison file states that he was Black and worked as a dishwasher and farmhand before prison. He'd been charged with five counts of robbery and stealing money from five different individuals, and he was sentenced to five years. For Johnston's leisure, he read "sports and adventure stories," played football and baseball while attending Concord's school program "four nights a week" (he'd finished the eighth grade), and sometimes attended Protestant services. Johnston also worked in the furniture shop for three months, which meant he would have at some point been working near Malcolm.

14 William Paul Williams, "Monday Night Club Boxing," *Our Paper*, May 3, 1947, 142.

15 By the end of the year in December 1947, there were 517 men enrolled in school, out of 893. This means almost 58 percent of the prison body participated in the educational program. Department of Correction, *Annual Report of the Commissioners*, 1947.

16 Malcolm's prison file shows that he dropped out of Mason High School midway through the ninth grade.

17 Albert Lerer, "Study of the Education Program at the Massachusetts Reformatory" (master's in education thesis, Boston University, 1939), 55–60; Haley and X, *Autobiography*, 169.

322   Notes to Pages 151–158

18 The *Michigan Chronicle* is mentioned by Malcolm in an undated (possibly May 1948) letter to Philbert (SCRBC).

19 Lerer, "Study of the Education Program," 55–60.

20 Malcolm Little Prison File, "Conduct." The other two instances happened on September 4, 1947 (disturbance in shop), and December 18, 1947 (shirking, poor work). It was a tough year. Also see Perry, *Malcolm*, 112. Perry reported the chin "laceration" after reviewing MR-Concord medical records.

21 Godfrey Joiner Prison File, "Subject's Version of Present Offense."

22 Pritchett was sentenced to Charlestown on October 24, 1946, serving a three- to five-year sentence as an accessory for Joiner. He's on record as having known Malcolm at state prison and briefly at Norfolk, telling a biographer that he didn't think Malcolm was much of a troublemaker in prison. Charles Pritchett Prison File; Perry's *Malcolm*, 423.

23 Godfrey Joiner Prison File, "Transfer Summary." Pritchett ended up at Norfolk during Malcolm's first year there.

24 Perry, *Malcolm*, 424n. Perry interviewed Joiner for his book.

25 Little, "Our Family from the Inside," 30.

26 Little, 31.

27 Little, 31.

28 Little, 31–32.

29 Strickland, *Malcolm X*, 60.

30 It wouldn't surprise me if Malcolm, who didn't misspell these basic words in his letters to Ella and Philbert, purposely made misspellings as an attempt to pull on the educational heartstrings of Mr. Dwyer: *Can't you see how badly I need a strong educational facility?*

31 Malcolm Little Prison File, July 28, 1947, stamped by the MA-DOC on August 4, 1947.

32 Perry, *Malcolm*, 111; Heywood Hampton Prison File.

33 Hampton Prison File. Hampton was temporarily sent to MR-Concord for several weeks in May 1947, when he would have first met Malcolm, and then was sent to Charlestown for five months. He came back to MR-Concord in October 1947.

34 Perry, *Malcolm*, 111. Perry interviewed Hampton for his book. Also, Hampton's prison file confirms that he was at MR-Concord at the same time as Malcolm.

35 Perry, 106, based on Joiner's memory.

36 Collins with Bailey, *Seventh Child*, 71. Since Malcolm didn't work in the furniture shop at either Norfolk or Charlestown, this puts Collins's memory at Concord. "Poor and uncooperative" is in the Malcolm Little Prison File, "Mass. Reformatory Work."

37 Malcolm Little Prison File.

38 Haley and X, *Autobiography*, 169.

39 Haley and X, 170.

40 Haley and X, 170. Doane's two pigs come from a letter he wrote to Philbert, dated December 12, 1949 (SCRBC).

41 Bruce Perry's *Malcolm* put Joiner and Hampton on the record as saying that Malcolm's religious conversion happened at Norfolk (407n). Malcolm's autobiography does too. Also, Malcolm's first known letter to Philbert when he was in Norfolk does not have any kind of religious sentiment connected to Islam. Most likely, Malcolm's religious conversion occurred in early to late fall of 1948, at Norfolk.

42 "Car Hits, Kills Dr. Shag Taylor in South End," *Boston Globe*, November 6, 1958, 4; Charles Kenney, "The Politics of Turmoil," *Boston Globe*, April 19, 1987, 36. The quoted individual was politician Thomas I. Atkins, once a mayoral candidate and a member of the Boston City Council.

43 "Car Hits," 4.

44 Collins with Bailey, *Seventh Child*, 79–80.

45 This number also included Heywood Hampton, who was transferred to Norfolk in the fall of 1948. Godfrey Joiner also was transferred to Norfolk in mid-1949. Charles Pritchett, meanwhile, was transferred to Norfolk in 1947. All three men would end up seeing Malcolm pre- and post–Islam conversion.

46 Department of Correction, *Annual Report of the Commissioners*, 1948, 67.

47 Letter from Malcolm Little to Ella Little-Collins, March 28, 1948, Wright Museum.

48 Haley and X, *Autobiography*, 171.

CHAPTER 7

1 Map has been adapted and clarified with the help of Jessica McDonald; original is from Charles V. Jenkinson, *The Structures and Equipment of the State Prison Colony at Norfolk, Massachusetts*, unpublished, 1933, located in the Howard Belding Gill papers at Boston College. Jenkinson was a research engineer for the Bureau of Social Hygiene.

2 This was deduced from "Escape Timetable," *Boston Globe*, August 13, 1954, 3. Unit 2–2, connected to 2–3, is "behind Receiving Building."

3 Wooldredge, "Inside the Wall," 10–11. See also "New Prison at Norfolk, Massachusetts," pamphlet, 1930/1932, Howard Belding Gill Papers, John J. Burns Library, Boston College.

4 Wooldredge, 11; United States Bureau of Prisons, *Handbook of Correctional Institution Design and Construction*, 1949, 99–103.

5 "New Prison at Norfolk, Massachusetts."

6 "New Prison at Norfolk, Massachusetts," 14.

7 Malcolm Little Prison File. Norfolk clothes are mentioned in several issues of the *Colony* prison newspaper.

8   "New Prison at Norfolk, Massachusetts," 19. For more information on escapes, see M. N. Winslow, "Supt. Winslow Looks at the Record," *Colony*, March 1, 1946, 3. According to Maurice N. Winslow, between 1934 and 1946, "Twenty men . . . escaped . . . and all have been apprehended and returned." Since its start in 1927, a total of 60 men tried to escape, and only one managed to not be "apprehended."

9   See "Goldenberg Pleads Guilty to Murder," *Boston Globe*, January 22, 1931, 1 (photo included); "Master Mind in Plot for Escape at Norfolk to Go to State Prison," *Boston Globe*, July 15, 1947, 17; Wooldredge, "Inside the Wall," 15.

10 See map, adapted from Jenkinson source, for directional purposes.

11 "Orientation of New Men," *Colony*, January 1, 1949, 10.

12 "Orientation of New Men"; Haley and X, *Autobiography*, 171.

13 "New Prison at Norfolk, Massachusetts," pamphlet, 1930/1932, Howard Belding Gill Papers, John J. Burns Library, Boston College.

14 One could argue that Gill's vision was a forerunner to one of Norway's current correctional philosophies, called "the Normality Principle," implemented most famously by Halden Prison. Starting around 1998, the Norwegian government pivoted toward changing its prison system, emphasizing rehabilitation through job training, therapeutic counseling, and educational development. See Are Høidal, "Normality behind the Walls: Examples from Halden Prison," *Federal Sentencing Reporter* 31, no. 1 (2018): 58–66.

15 "New Prison at Norfolk, Massachusetts." See also Ashley T. Rubin, *The Deviant Prison* (Cambridge: Cambridge University Press, 2021).

16 Haley and X, *Autobiography*, 171. United States Bureau of Prisons, *Handbook*, 99–103; Lewis Parkhurst, foreword to "New Prison at Norfolk, Massachusetts."

17 Parkhurst, 7–8.

18 *Boston Globe*, March 16, 1922, 1.

19 "New Prison at Norfolk, Massachusetts."

20 "New Prison at Norfolk, Massachusetts."

21 Prout and Ross, *Care and Punishment*, 27. Gill was in his 90s when interviewed.

22 Prout and Ross, 27. See also "New Prison at Norfolk, Massachusetts."

23 "Orientation of New Men," *Colony*, January 1, 1949, 10.

24 Robert Loeb Cooper, "Forty Negro Prisoners: A Treatment Study of a Group of Inmates at the State Prison Colony at Norfolk, Massachusetts" (thesis, Boston University, 1933), 21–23.

25 "The Perfect Security State," *Colony*, June 15, 1950, 3.

26 "1946—Fourth Anniversary—1950," *Colony*, September 1, 1950, 8.

27 "New Prison at Norfolk, Massachusetts," 24–25.

28 Lester Wilkins, "Laundry," *Colony*, February 15, 1949.

29 Wilkins.

30 Wilkins. Also of note, and partly why I assume that Malcolm helped with sorting, was another familiar nickname drop earlier in the article. "[Clothing] is sorted and placed in the boxes by La Fontaine, Drake, Lewis" (Parker T., that is) and "Lindy." Without question "Red" Little is Malcolm, but "Lindy" could be another man fond of that dancing style. Or it could have been Malcolm's acerbic wit on display, surrounded by men who'd enjoyed a few of his Harlem or Roxbury tales as they waited for the washers and dryers to finish.

31 Jarvis with Nichols, *The Other Malcolm*, 8; Malcolm Jarvis Prison File.

32 Malcolm Jarvis Prison File.

33 Jarvis with Nichols, *The Other Malcolm*, 84. McHarg's name is found in *Colony* articles.

34 Haley and X, *Autobiography*, 171.

35 "New Prison at Norfolk, Massachusetts," 7; Perry, *Malcolm*, 425n. George Power remembers seeing Malcolm convert to Islam while at Norfolk. Perry also mentions Horace Dow as a house officer.

36 "New Prison at Norfolk, Massachusetts," 23; dining room picture, 27; Wooldredge, "Inside the Wall," 18–19.

37 Letter from Malcolm Little to Bazely Perry, July 25, 1949, as quoted in Perry *Malcolm*, 120.

38 Haley and X, *Autobiography*, 172.

39 Haley and X, *Autobiography*, 172.

40 "New Prison at Norfolk, Massachusetts," 5.

41 "Library Column," *Colony*, June 15, 1948, 13.

42 "In Memoriam," Colony, April 1, 1949, 8; Haley and X, *Autobiography*, 172. Also see letter from James Kerrigan to Sen. Lewis Parkhurst, September 9, 1938, Rauner Special Collections Library, Dartmouth College.

43 "Library Topics," *Colony*, April 1, 1949, 10. The United States Bureau of Prisons, *Handbook* cited 15,000 (99–103).

44 "Lewis Parkhurst, 93, Ex-Senator, Educator, Dies in Winchester," *Boston Globe*, March 28, 1949, 1, 21. Also see "Hanover News and Personals," *Landmark*, March 31, 1949.

45 "Wilder Parkhurst Dead," *Boston Globe*, September 26, 1904, 8.

46 Parkhurst, *Vacation on the Nile*, ix.

47 Parkhurst, 83.

48 Parkhurst, 83, 100.

49 Parkhurst, 96.

50 Haley and X, *Autobiography*, 172; "Lewis Parkhurst, 93, Ex-Senator, Educator, Dies in Winchester," *Boston Globe*, March 28, 1949, 1.

51 "Library Topics," *Colony*, April 1, 1949, 10.

52 "Rebuilds Lives of Convicts," *Boston Globe*, June 3, 1956, A-31. Magraw was Norfolk Prison Colony's educational director, and he would have seen and talked with Malcolm on a daily basis in Norfolk's school building. Magraw was also a Universalist minister.

53   Malcolm Little Prison File; Haley and X, *Autobiography*, 186–87.

54   Cunningham and Golden, "Malcolm," 24.

55   Malcolm Jarvis Prison File.

56   Malcolm Jarvis Prison File, letter from Malcolm Jarvis to his mother, January 30, 1949. The letter also reveals that Jarvis felt suicidal.

57   Jarvis with Nichols, *The Other Malcolm*, 39.

58   Boise Phillips Prison File. Phillips (1925–67) grew up in Youngstown, Ohio. After prison, Boise indeed boxed professionally from 1950 to 1955; his record was 7–33, with five of his wins knockouts.

59   Boise Phillips Prison File.

60   "An Evening at the Gym," *Colony*, May 1, 1949, 8; Perry, *Malcolm*, 114 (Perry interviewed Jarvis); Clif Keane, "Champion Bombards Challenger at Finish," *Boston Globe*, June 26, 1948, 1, 8.

61   The hospital remark was from Rafael Monserrate's interview with David Winslow, audio accessed in August 2020.

62   "Seize 2d Holdup Suspect with Girl Singer in Texas," *Boston Globe*, February 11, 1947, 1, 40; "Boxing News," *Colony*, July 1, 1948, 6.

63   Malcolm Little Prison File; Willie Roach, "Gym Notes," *Colony*, April 1, 1948, 10; Perry, *Malcolm*, 115.

64   Chester Hoynoski Prison File; "Boxing News," 7. Chester is listed at 181 in his prison file, but in the September 15, 1949, *Colony* (9), a C. Hoynoski is listed at 196. It's worth noting that Hoynoski's brother, Louis, 29, may have been Malcolm's opponent as well, since the *Colony* doesn't provide the first name, and an L. Hoynoski was listed as possible for a Labor Day boxing event two months later. I chose Chester because he was the only brother recorded as having fought an actual bout at Norfolk, losing by technical knockout to Al Lewis, a 32-year-old Black man from Tennessee. Louis's weight was much closer to Malcolm's, however, at 175, but he was significantly shorter (5'7" and three-fourths) and in his prison file listed as "feeble-minded" in a psychometric report from 1936, as well as "mentally retarded."

65   "Boxing News," 7.

66   Emily Sweeney, "Warden's Son Recalls Life at State Prison," *Boston Globe*, January 13, 2013.

67   "Phillips in KO over Dewan," *Colony*, July 15, 1948, 11.

68   "Field Events," *Colony*, July 15, 1948, 3; Malcolm Little Prison File.

69   Malcolm Little Prison File; Haley and X, *Autobiography*; various issues of the *Colony* newspaper, in particular, see "The Kitchen Situation," *Colony*, October 1, 1948, 13.

70   Letter from Malcolm Little to Philbert Little, n.d., SCRBC, box 3, folder 1. Malcolm flipped the words "divine" and "human" from Pope's original line in his 1711 poem, "An Essay on Criticism, Part I": "To err is human; to forgive, divine." Interestingly, Pope wrote this poem when he was 23, the same age that Malcolm used it in prison.

71 Letter from Malcolm Little to Philbert, n.d., SCRBC, box 3, folder 1.

72 Letter from Malcolm Little to Philbert, November 28, 1948, SCRBC.

73 "The Educational Program," *Colony*, October 15, 1948, 15.

74 "An Admirable Project," *Colony*, May 15, 1948, 6.

75 "The Lighter Side," *Colony*, November 1, 1948, 8.

76 Department of Correction, *Massachusetts Department of Correction: Annual Report of the Commissioners of Correction*, State Library of Massachusetts Digital Collections, 1948, 42. See also "Educational Program," 15.

77 "Rebuilds Lives of Convicts," *Boston Globe*, June 3, 1956, A-31.

78 Wooldredge, "Inside the Wall," 16; a slip of orange transaction paper is taped to the page. "New Quarters for Educational Division," *Colony*, March 1, 1936, 5; not sure if the blackboards had been redone before Malcolm arrived 12 years after they were first installed.

79 Author correspondence with Rick Nash, September 21, 2022.

80 "Lighter Side."

81 Author correspondence with Rick Nash, September 29, 2022.

82 John O'Connell Jr. and Greg O'Connell, interview by author, September 9, 2022. According to the sons, their father, who passed away in 1982, was also involved with the prison's boxing and basketball programs, before leaving Norfolk in the summer of 1950. O'Connell went on to become the superintendent of schools in Canton, Massachusetts, though in their early years they struggled. During O'Connell's prison teaching years, the growing family lived in the Mission Hills Housing Project, a low-income area at the time. The children always knew when payday was, because that was when they'd "eat like kings," only to then struggle for the rest of the month.

83 "Boston Slayer Suspect Back after 17 Yrs.," *Boston Globe*, August 19, 1941, 12; "The Educational Program," *Colony*, December 15, 1948, 14.

84 "Two Plead Guilty to Taxi Holdup," *Boston Globe*, June 10, 1946, 5. A *Boston Globe* article ("East Boston Men Get 4 to 6 Years for Series of Breaks," September 20, 1946, 12) gives more information and shows that Cavagnaro's sentence was extended by Judge John P. Higgins.

85 "Pair Who Assaulted Smith Art Graduate Get 7 to 10 Years," *Boston Globe*, February 24, 1947, 10; "Two Married Men Held in Attack on Smith Grad," *Boston Globe*, December 11, 1946, 1.

86 John Elton Bembry Prison File; Debate Fan, "A Protest," *Colony*, April 1, 1948, 1. The March 8, 1948, *Time Magazine* mention consisted of the following two lines: "Unbeaten in two years of competition with such universities as Princeton, Harvard and Boston, the Norfolk, Mass. Prison Colony debating team lost an argument to Brown. Subject: universal military training" (25).

87 Susan Tejada, *In Search of Sacco and Vanzetti* (Boston: Northeastern University Press, 2012), 279, 309. Cerise's full name appears in Karl Sax, "John George Jack. 1861–1949," *Journal of the Arnold Arboretum* 30, no. 4 (1949): 345–47.

88 Vigrolio, "Prison Debaters Will Challenge Anyone!" See also "Inmates Lose Valued Friend," *Colony*, September 15, 1935, 1, 8.

89 "Ace Prison Debater Loses Own Battle," *Boston Globe*, February 7, 1936, 17.

90 As far as local newspaper coverage is concerned, Norfolk's 1936 debate with the YMHA was the first to be covered. Norfolk defeated MIT in May 1937. Norfolk lost their first debate against Harvard in December 1937 but won the year after. "Harvard Defeats Prison Debaters," *Boston Globe*, December 13, 1937, 12; "Farnsworth Heads Crime Cure Group," *Boston Globe*, January 10, 1938, 2.

91 "Norfolk Debaters Win over B.U.," *Colony*, April 1, 1948, 7.

92 Haley and X, *Autobiography*, 189.

93 Murdo Margeson Prison File.

94 Murdo Margeson Prison File.

95 Murdo's mug shot in 1938 (left) and in 1961. Murdo Margeson Prison File.

96 Murdo Margeson Prison File, "Work Report."

97 Murdo Margeson Prison File. Murdo ended up a lifelong criminal, robbing banks long after mastering the art of debate. See Donald Goddard, *The Insider: The FBI's Undercover "Wiseguy"* [Billy Breen] *Goes Public* (New York: Simon and Schuster, 1992), for a depiction of Murdo as the "old man" who seems to know everyone and everything about life on the inside.

98 John J. Donovan, "Boy Attacked Widow to Raise Needed $10," *Boston Globe*, March 2, 1931, 1, 3.

99 Russell Noble Prison File; Donovan, "Boy Attacked." Also see Arthur Veasey III, "The Socialite and the Boy with the Rudy Vallee Hair," *Merrimack Valley Magazine*, April 9, 2020.

100 Donovan, "Boy Attacked." Also see "Noble, Young Lifer, to Write in Prison," *Boston Globe*, July 3, 1933, 2; "State Prison Inmates Show Esteem for Retiring Pastor," *Boston Globe*, August 28, 1939, 5.

101 "The Debate Season Opens," *Colony*, October 1, 1948, 11. John Elton Bembry, or "Bimbi," was released from prison on October 6, 1948, one day before Malcolm's first debate meeting.

102 "Debate Season."

103 "Debate Season"; debate club member, "Norfolk Debating Society," *Colony*, October 15, 1948, 13.

104 "Debate Season"; Roland Bradbury Prison File.

105 Haley and X, *Autobiography*, 185, 200.

106 See both of the previously cited debate summaries in the October 1 and 15 *Colony* issues. The *Autobiography* describes how Malcolm was "gone on debating," and this was his first experience seeing it (200). His debate assignment is mentioned on page 16 of the *Colony*, October 15, 1948.

107 John Noxon Prison File. Noxon is misspelled in the October 15, 1948, edition of the *Colony* (Noxin) but the spelling is restored in a future recap.

108 Haley and X, *Autobiography*, 175.

109 Haley and X, 172–73.

110 Haley and X, 172–74.

111 Haley and X.

112 Goldman, *Death and Life*, 33.

113 Haley and X, *Autobiography*, 174–75. Noxon's last name is not given in the *Autobiography*. Also see "Schoolboys Try Debating," *Colony*, November 1, 1948, 6.

114 "Ramblings," *Colony*, November 1, 1948, 5.

115 Haley and X, *Autobiography*, 189. In a letter to the Massachusetts commissioner of correction, Malcolm criticizes Charlestown Prison (where he was then, ca. 1950) for not carrying the work of Black authors, such as J. A. Rogers.

116 Various sources, including but not limited to *Colony* newspapers between 1948 and 1950, Malcolm L. Jarvis's memoir, and Wooldredge, "Inside the Wall," 23.

117 Haley and X, *Autobiography*, 189. Years after his release, Malcolm conveyed to his wife Betty Shabazz just how much time he had in prison: "And he says, 'Girl, when I was in prison, there was so much time that if a fly flew through a window, you would not say, "the fly flew through the window," you would say, "the fly flew through the lower right-hand quadrant and landed on its front legs."'" See Strickland, *Malcolm X*, 126.

118 Haley and X, 189. Window confirmed through various *Colony* articles, site visit.

119 "Library Topics," *Colony*, October 15, 1948, 13. Of *Days of Our Years*, the *Colony* writer wrote, "A great, warm human heart writes of his country and of himself and it will warm your heart also." In Malcolm's *Autobiography*, he tells Reginald that he's found new information in Milton's *Paradise Lost* to help support "Muslim teachings." As for Shakespeare, Malcolm was always reading Shakespeare, thanks in part to Bimbi's introduction and future debate topics.

120 Letter from Malcolm Little to Philbert, November 28, 1948, SCRBC.

121 Murdo [Margeson], "Schoolboys Try Debating," *Colony*, November 1, 1948, 6.

122 Murdo. The other two members on Kearney's team were "Rothwell" and "Nunnally."

123 Murdo. Murdo did not have anything complementary to say of Antosz except that he made a "fine first appearance." Cavagnaro wasn't even mentioned.

124 Rogers, *Sex and Race*, 1:29. Von Luchan was the name of the Berlin professor. A possible counter to this made-up argument could have been that, yes, physically we are products of environment, but the circumstances we are born into (a royal family, for example) would prove a far more effective influence toward success.

125 Haley and X, *Autobiography*, 200.

126 Amasa Howe, "Dewey Here," *Boston Globe*, October 28, 1948, 1.

127 "Debating Society," *Colony*, November 15, 1948, 7.

128 John Noxon Prison File; "Gov. Bradford Undecided on Noxon Petition," *Boston Globe*, September 8, 1948, 20. It's worth noting that Noxon's release didn't just bother Malcolm, but the entire Norfolk prison population, whose "morale dropped greatly," according to one researcher. "The men felt it was not right that a person found guilty of murder should be pardoned, while some of them served ten to fifteen years for armed robbery, in which no one was hurt." Wooldredge, "Inside the Wall," 48.

129 "Debating Society," 7. This was also the famous election where Truman, after winning, held up the *Chicago Tribune*'s erroneously printed headline *Dewey Defeats Truman*, thus symbolizing how Truman had been able to defy what the polls had been predicting.

130 "Norfolk Debaters Win over B.U." The two debaters were "Mo" Mahoney, a popular kitchen manager whose crime has been difficult to find because of his common last name and use of several first names. The other debater was Rupert S. Newhall, a "newcomer" and 32-year-old medical technician convicted of performing an illegal abortion, which resulted in the death of a 19-year-old woman. "Former Basketball Star Held in Death of Girl," *White River Valley Herald*, July 10, 1947, 1.

131 Debate club member, "Norfolk Debating Society," *Colony*, December 1, 1948, 7.

132 Debate club member. The Clark University debate result is on the same page.

133 Debate club member; "Pleads Not Guilty to 16-Year-Old Murder Indictment," *Boston Globe*, September 2, 1941, 18.

134 Debate club member. The reporter is most likely Murdo, but it could also be Russell Noble.

135 Debate club member. In short, Murdo went with the more conservative team to protect what they'd built.

136 "Clark University Defeats Norfolk Debaters," *Colony*, December 1, 1948, 7. Wendell Colson was the father of Charles Colson, a key member of Nixon's inner circle during his 1972 reelection bid. For this debate, Russell Noble was listed as the timekeeper and Murdo as the chairman. Bartlett may have been Black based on the fact that he told a *Colony* reporter that his favorite singer was Al Hibbler, and his favorite band was the Miles Davis Quintet.

137 Haley and X, *Autobiography*, 200. Also see "Educational Program" (December).

138 See "Marine Corps Filled: 18-Year-Olds Jam Recruiting Offices," *Boston Globe*, July 23, 1948, 2. After the "Elston Act" had been passed in June, 18-year-olds discovered that if they signed up now, they'd only serve for one year. But if they waited until 19, they'd need to serve for 21 months. As for Truman's executive order, signed on July 26, 1948, it states that "it is essential that there be maintained in the armed services of the United

States the highest standards of democracy, with equality of treatment and opportunity for all those who serve in our country's defense." A great book describing Woodard's case is *Unexampled Courage: The Blinding of Sgt. Isaac Woodard and the Awakening of President Harry S. Truman and Judge J. Waties Waringe* by Richard Gergel.

139 Haley and X, *Autobiography*, 200–201.

140 Pierre Van Paassen, *Days of Our Years* (Dial Press: New York, 1940), 307–9. Paassen's book was first printed in January 1939.

141 "Educational Program" (December), 14; Haley and X, *Autobiography*, 201.

142 Strickland, *Malcolm X*, 64.

143 Letter from Malcolm Little to Philbert, November 28, 1948, SCRBC. The letter is also the first time he mentions Elijah Muhammad, although he may have already started corresponding with Muhammad before this letter.

144 "Christmas Parties," *Colony*, January 1, 1949, 12.

145 Haley and X, *Autobiography*, 185.

146 Haley and X, 185.

147 Several sources were consulted for this section, but Raleigh, North Carolina, imam Mohamed Baianonie's webpage, "How Do I Pray" (Islamic Association of Raleigh, December 10, 2005, https://raleighmasjid.org/what-is-islam/how-do-i-pray/) was extremely helpful in understanding the step-by-step process of *Salah*. Also, Imam Mus'ab Abdalla helped me understand "mind over heart" and "heart over mind."

CHAPTER 8

1 Prisons that emphasize reform and rehabilitation used the title "superintendent," but "warden" could also be used. On his resume, Winslow made sure to state this, typing, "Same as warden." "Maurice N. Winslow: Resume," circa 1956. Special thanks to Rafael Monserrate for providing these and other Winslow documents. As for the epigraph, Malcolm wrote that passage on a Tuesday night. The original letter can be read in full at the SCRBC.

2 "Maurice N. Winslow: Resume," 2.

3 David K. Winslow, "Prison Reformer Winslow," letter, *Harvard Magazine*, November–December (year unknown), 115.

4 "Maurice N. Winslow: Resume"; Winslow, "Prison."

5 "Maurice N. Winslow: Resume"; Winslow, "Prison."

6 Emily Sweeney, "Warden's Son Recalls Life at State Prison," *Boston Globe*, January 13, 2013.

7 Department of Correction, *Massachusetts Department of Correction: Annual Report of the Commissioners of Correction*, State Library of Massachusetts

Digital Collections, 1948, 40. Winslow reported that the prison delivered nearly three million gallons of water to Norfolk during 1948.

8 "If I Were a Prisoner," *Colony*, August 15, 1949, 14.

9 "Both Sides of the Fence," *Colony*, April 15, 1948, 7.

10 Department of Correction, *Annual Report of the Commissioners*, 1949, 19–20. For times and locations, see many issues of the *Colony*. For this, I referred to "Religious Services," on page 15 of the September 1, 1949, issue.

11 "Religious Services." *Russian Orthodox* is only listed in the Department of Correction, *Annual Report of the Commissioners*, 1948, 10.

12 Malcolm Little Prison File.

13 Cunningham and Golden, "Malcolm," 35.

14 To learn more about Robeson, see the biography by Lindsey R. Swindall: *Paul Robeson: A Life of Activism and Art*.

15 See L. Cranmer-Byng and S. A. Kapadia, *The Rose Garden of Sa'di* (London: John Murray, 1919), 25. Note that *The Rose Garden* is another name for *Gulistan*.

16 See L. Cranmer-Byng and Syed Abdul Majid, *The Rubá'iyát of Hafiz* (London: John Murray, 1919), 46.

17 Letter from Malcolm Little to Philbert Little, February 4, 1949, SCRBC.

18 Letter from Malcolm Little to Philbert Little, February 4, 1949, SCRBC. It's possible that Malcolm found all these quotes in the same book: Charles H. Sylvester, *The Writings of Mankind*, vol. 2 (Epsilon Sigma Alpha Sorority, 1924). See "The Black Stone of Mecca: Malcolm X, Prison Letters, Tasawwuf Poetry, and Ethical Texts," published in *Khayál: A Multimedia Collection by Muslim Creatives*, 2023, found in Maytha Alhassan, "The Black Stone of Mecca | Audio Transcripts," Pillars Fund, June 27, 2023, https://www .pillarsfund.org/2023/06/27/the-black-stone-of-mecca-audio-transcripts/. In this excellent chapter, Maytha Alhassan, while going into detail about Malcolm's prison letters, mentions the book. In addition to Alhassan, Zaheer Ali leads the discussion, along with Omid Safi and Hussein Rashid.

19 Malcolm Jarvis Prison File, "Education" and "Administrative Chronology"; *Colony*, "Inmates Variety Show," December 1, 1948, 9. Two debaters, "Mo" Mahoney and Roland Bradbury, acted as emcees.

20 Malcolm Jarvis Prison File, letter from Jarvis to his mother, January 30, 1949.

21 Malcolm Jarvis Prison File, letter from Jarvis to his mother, January 30, 1949.

22 Malcolm Jarvis Prison File. See "Gunman Shoots Sergeant, Self," *Boston Globe*, January 25, 1949, 1 and 6. The picture of Robert Faulk tied to the bed is in this newspaper, as well as a description of him as a "dope-demented gunman," back when marijuana was believed to be incredibly dangerous.

23 Malcolm may have also crossed paths with Faulk, since both were incarcerated in 1947 at MR-Concord.

24 Malcolm Jarvis Prison File; "Two Arrested Here in Drug Raid May Be Links to Mexico," *Boston Globe*, February 4, 1949, 4.

25 Letter from Malcolm Little to Philbert, February 1949 (Tuesday night), SCRBC. Jarvis's prison file lists his psychiatrist visits on February 4 and March 4.

26 "Sgt. Cullinan Assailant Gets 25–30 Years," *Boston Globe*, February 20, 1950, 14. Buttrick again showed his propensity to charge Black men the maximum for associating in any way with white women. For nearly murdering a police officer, Faulk was given an 18-to-20-year sentence. For assault and battery with a dangerous weapon, he was given 8 to 10 years, but for three armed robbery charges and an assault "with intent to rape" a white woman, he was given 25 to 30 years.

27 Malcolm Jarvis Prison File, letter from Jarvis to his mother, January 30, 1949.

28 Malcolm L. Jarvis Jr., "How Malcolm X Influenced a Young Man's Life," *Hartford Courant*, March 7, 1993, 33. The description of Jarvis's prison attire might have been a mash-up of clothes from Norfolk and Charlestown prisons.

29 "The Prisoner's Cross," *Colony*, December 1, 1948, 11.

30 "Norfolk Debaters on Air Again," *Colony*, March 15, 1949, 13. The Haverhill matchups were broadcast over the radio. This helped to set up Malcolm's upcoming death penalty address.

31 "Gleanings," *Colony*, February 15, 1949, 11.

32 "Council Meeting," *Colony*, February 1, 1949, 15, and "Self-Sacrificing Benevolence," same issue, 9.

33 "Gleanings."

34 Letter from Malcolm to Philbert (but written for "all" his siblings to read), June 29, 1949, SCRBC. The passage in the epigraph also comes from the SCRBC.

35 Letter from Malcolm to Philbert (but written for "all" his siblings to read), June 29, 1949, SCRBC. Malcolm's conclusions here may have been supported by visits from Jarvis's friend, Abdul Hameed, who was a follower of the Ahmadiyya movement, a sect of Islam.

36 See William A. Maesen, "Watchtower Influences on Black Muslim Eschatology: An Exploratory Story," *Journal for the Scientific Study of Religion* 9, no. 4 (1970): 321–25.

37 Author correspondence with Rev. Michael Frank, formerly of Broadway Christian Church near Cleveland, Ohio, May 30, 2020. Rev. Frank was Broadway's minister for 41 years. He is also, full disclosure, my uncle.

38 Perry, *Malcolm*, 114. Perry was the biographer, and the "ego" line comes from an April 18, 1977, letter written by Adams to Perry. Unfortunately, Perry locked up his archives until 2041, so the entirety of that letter cannot be seen until then. J. Prescott Adams's obituary (*Boston Globe*, "Deaths," July 25, 1991, 50) does confirm he was a Jehovah's Witness.

39 Richard B. Turner, "The Ahmadiyya Movement in Islam in America," *Religion Today* 5, no. 3 (1988): 9–10.

40 Jarvis with Nichols, *The Other Malcolm*, 55. An alternate spelling of Hameed may have been Hamid.

41 Malcolm Jarvis Prison File. Malcolm also wrote this poem in a letter to "Brother Raymond" on March 9, 1950, adding a few lines at the end, after "Allah": ". . . both being in need of the house . . . a home . . . the Temple . . . the Complete Song and its Creator." See also "Malcolm X: Letter from Prison in 1950," *The Root*, February 19, 2015. The bracketed misspellings come from the typed letter, most likely completed by a prison guard. Malcolm's original handwritten poem from 1949 has not been found.

42 Letter from Malcolm Jarvis to Abdul Hameed, July 31, 1949. This letter was not found with the Jarvis Prison File sent by the MA-DOC; Jarvis's correspondence is located at the Massachusetts Archive, on the campus of UMass Boston.

43 Letter from Malcolm X to Philbert X, January 29, 1950. This is the first letter in the SCRBC collection in which Malcolm uses *X* at the end.

44 Letter from Malcolm Little to Philbert Little, August 9, 1949, SCRBC. Philbert lived in Detroit at the time.

45 Joiner, quoted in Perry, *Malcolm*, 437–38n.

46 Cunningham and Golden, "Malcolm."

47 Osborne Thaxton Prison File.

48 Osborne Thaxton Prison File, "Criminal Record."

49 Osborne Thaxton Prison File. Also, see "Two Jehovah's Witnesses Freed in Disturbance Case," *Boston Globe*, June 14, 1948, 1.

50 Betty Shabazz, "The Legacy of My Husband, Malcolm X," *Ebony*, June 1969, 176.

51 Strickland, *Malcolm X*, 63.

52 John A. O'Connell, "School News," *Colony*, August 15, 1949, 9.

53 Haley and X, *Autobiography*, 201–2.

54 Malcolm Jarvis Prison File, Osborne Thaxton Prison File, Russell Noble Prison File, Murdo Margeson Prison File, and Malcolm Little Prison File.

55 Roger D. Shepherd, "The Great Books," *Colony*, February 1, 1950, 7.

56 Works on the Great Books list included, among others, Darwin's *The Origin of Species*, Dante's *Divine Comedy*, the works of Homer, the *Confessions* of Saint Augustine, Geoffrey Chaucer's *Canterbury Tales*, R. H. Tawney's *Religion and the Rise of Capitalism*, and Marx and Engel's *The Communist Manifesto*.

57 "Lawyer-Educator Speaks at Institute Tomorrow," *News and Observer*, February 22, 1948, 16. Also see "Great Books Extend an Invitation to Learning," *Courier-Journal*, June 14, 1947, 6.

58 Shepherd, "Great Books," 7, 12.

59 Shepherd, "Great Books,"; Nell Battle Lewis, "Incidentally," *News and Observer*, March 7, 1948, 44. The *Encyclopedia Britannica* also helped finance the foundation.

60 Shepherd, "Great Books," 12.

61 Malcolm Little Prison File, "Education."

62 "Norfolk Debaters and Glee Club Take to Air Lanes . . . ," *Colony*, November 1, 1949, 4.

63 "Norfolk Debaters"

64 "Norfolk Debaters"; "The Prisoner Speaks," *Colony*, December 15, 1949, 13; "Tufts Defeats Norfolk Debaters," *Colony*, January 1, 1950, 5; "Radio Program," *Colony*, January 15, 1950, 12.

65 Murdo Margeson, "Argument for the Abolishment of the Death Penalty," *Colony*, December 15, 1949, 6. Murdo didn't qualify that some public lynchings in the South still occurred past 1900.

66 Margeson, "Argument for Abolishment."

67 "Radio Program," *Colony*, January 15, 1950, 12.

68 It's interesting that Malcolm uses the example of Lewis E. Lawes for ethos in his argument, the same warden who visited Charlestown Prison during Malcolm's first two weeks there. Lawes was indeed against the idea of capital punishment, at times citing the fact that, at least from 1919 to 1928, the homicide rate in states that had capital punishment was at least twice as high (8.3 per 100,000) as in states that had abolished the death penalty (3.6 per 100,000). E. J. Paxton Jr., "Capital Punishment: Older Than Civilization; Kentucky May Substitute Gas for Electric Chair," *Paducah Sun-Democrat*, March 17, 1946, 4.

69 This "167" fact appears to have come from an old essay written by the Reverend James Peggs, who did indeed query 167 capital offenders . . . but actually, according to Peggs, 164 had seen an execution. Malcolm was selling his research short, for once.

70 I can't help but feel this is Malcolm's most personal paragraph here, especially the "unreasoning fury" sentence. I imagine when he was writing this that he considered his own acts of crime in the past, since the level of emotional specificity is quite high. No source here . . . just Malcolm.

71 Malcolm Little, "Abolishment of Capital Punishment," in *The Prisoner Speaks*, WMEX 1510, January 15, 1950, 9. Malcolm X scholar Garrett Felber deserves credit for first bringing this document to light. See Garrett Felber, "Justice Breyer and Malcolm X," The Marshall Project, July 2, 2015, https://www.themarshallproject.org/2015/07/02/justice-breyer-and-malcolm-x.

72 "Rundown of the Orchestra," *Colony*, November 1, 1949, 10, 15; "Orchestra Notes," *Colony*, November 15, 1949, 7. Also "Past Movies," *Colony*, December 15, 1949, 5.

73 "Rundown."

74 Godfrey Joiner Prison File, correspondence, Mass. Archives.

75 Joiner Prison File, letter from Deputy Superintendent Edward Grennan to Herbert Tucker, December 15, 1949.

76 David Westerfield, "Paving the Way for Interstate 49," *Times (Shreveport)*, March 8, 1987, 1E, 2E. Verified through prison file.

77 Students dropping out midway through the school year was somewhat common. According to Winslow in the Department of Correction, *Annual Report of the Commissioners*, 1948, "There was, as before, a considerable turn-over of students due mainly to the fact that inmates were interested only in completing special projects of their own" (42). The Magraw quote is in Perry's *Malcolm*, 425n. For the epigraph quotation, the original letter can be found in the SCRBC.

78 Letter from Malcolm X to Philbert X (Little), January 29, 1950, SCRBC.

79 "H-Bomb," *Boston Globe*, January 29, 1950, 34. The US senator was Thomas Connally, a Democrat from Texas.

80 Gordon Englehart, "At Least Two Names, No Age Has He Who Scorns the Mark of Slavery," *Dayton Daily News*, April 22, 1948, 25.

81 Englehart, "At Least Two Names"; *Dayton Daily News*, June 3, 1948, and June 11, 1948.

82 Letter from Malcolm X to Philbert X (Little), January 29, 1950, SCRBC.

83 Haley and X, *Autobiography*, 216.

84 The original letter, dated March 12, 1950, sold for $12,500 at an auction in March 2018.

85 Letter from Malcolm X to Philbert X Little, March 26, 1950, SCRBC. By this time, Malcolm had been back at Charlestown for three days.

86 "Television? Earphones?," *Colony*, March 15, 1950, 5 and 12.

87 "Gleanings," *Colony*, March 15, 1950, 13.

88 Letter from Malcolm X to Philbert X Little, March 26, 1950, SCRBC.

89 United States Federal Census Records, 1950. MR-Concord's prison population was 835. The total number of incarcerated men at all three institutions was 2,416. Only 233 were Black. The only other individualized races listed were Native American and Chinese. This tabulation was done manually, over several days, and the handwriting was very difficult to read at times, so please leave a ½ percent +/– wiggle room.

90 Malcolm Little Prison File.

91 Malcolm Jarvis Prison File.

92 Malcolm Jarvis Prison File.

93 Osborne Thaxton Prison File.

94 Osborne Thaxton Prison File.

95 Margaret Rhodes, "Typhoid Is a Warm Weather Disease," *Douglas County Herald*, March 9, 1950, 2. Rhodes was a "County Health Nurse."

96 For more information on the Tuskegee Syphilis Study, see Stephen B. Thomas and Sandra Crouse Quinn, "The Tuskegee Syphilis Study, 1932 to 1972: Implications for HIV Education and AIDS Risk Education Programs in the Black Community," *American Journal of Public Health* 81, no. 11 (November 1991): 1498–505.

97 Letter from Malcolm X to Brother Raymond, March 18, 1950, Charles H. Wright Museum of African American History, Detroit.

98 Malcolm Little Prison File, "The Commonwealth of Massachusetts: March 20, 1950." The Boston University debate is mentioned in the Department of Correction, *Annual Report of the Commissioners*, 1950, 31, but it's unknown if Malcolm participated.

99 Osborne Thaxton Prison File, "March 21, 1950."

100 "35,000,000 Building Urged in Bay State," *New York Times*, August 16, 1949, 24.

101 Malcolm Jarvis Prison File, "March 22, 1950."

CHAPTER 9

1 "Ground to Be Broken Monday Morning for New State Prison," *Boston Globe*, October 11, 1950, 17. And also "Ground Broken for $3,425,000 State Prison," *Boston Globe*, October 16, 1950, 11. The epigraph passage was near the end of a letter to Brother Raymond. See The Root staff, "Malcolm X: Letter from Prison in 1950," *The Root*, February 19, 2015.

2 "Ground to Be Broken." The 590 number comes from the Department of Correction, *Massachusetts Department of Correction: Annual Report of the Commissioners of Correction*, State Library of Massachusetts Digital Collections, 1950, 15. The exact daily average was 594.

3 "Are You Wasting Time?," *Mentor*, 1950. The *Mentor* was Charlestown's prison newspaper.

4 Letter from Malcolm X to Philbert X Little, March 26, 1950, SCRBC. This letter also mentions how Malcolm was keeping up with the "Black Weeklys," or the *Michigan Chronicle* weekly newspaper, as one example: "In the Black weeklys I have read of racial tension in that city [Detroit]. What is really going on? Please keep me informed. I remember still when [my younger brother] Wesley was beaten up by that gang shortly after I came in here. It is just as well (as I said then) that I was in here. Allah must have known that even then. I am happy that Wesley has now grown up. May the incident never reoccur."

5 Leroy Thaxton Prison File.

6 Leroy Thaxton Prison File, "Psychiatrist's Report" and "Disciplinary Report." The incident happened on December 7, 1950, after 9:00 p.m., when Leroy was supposed to have been in his cell.

7 O'Brien was around 6'0", married, and had three grown daughters by this time. He'd been working in prisons, primarily Charlestown and Norfolk, since 1929. He and Winslow were close friends, and it was O'Brien who filled in for Winslow during World War II, when Winslow went overseas to help out with prison reform in Europe. See K. S. Bartlett, "State Prison's New Warden Can Face Crisis with No Sign of Nervousness," *Boston Globe*, March 20, 1949, 117. A picture of O'Brien with his family is included.

8 "Moslem Converts Get Concessions," *Dunkirk Evening Observer*, April 20, 1950, 2.

9 "Converts Expect to Pray from Their Jail Cells," *Paducah Sun-Democrat*, April 21, 1950, 12. Similar reports were reheadlined and paraphrased in the *Dunkirk Evening Observer* (NY), the *Burlington Daily News* (VT), and also two Boston newspapers. See Felber and Marable, *Portable Malcolm X Reader*, 59–61. I can't help but wonder if Malcolm was bluffing about the Egyptian consulate and, if necessary, would have simply called up religious friend Abdul Hameed.

10 Back at Norfolk, Malcolm's public efforts to express his "freedom to worship" at Charlestown were met with support. See "The Perfect Security State," *Colony*, June 15, 1950, 3.

11 Table 9.1 was made using prison files provided by the Massachusetts Department of Correction. For the two Massachusetts publications, see Felber and Marable, *Portable Malcolm X Reader*, 59–61.

12 "Lee," *Boston Globe*, March 23, 1950, 2. Elliott McDowell was also in favor of changing Lee's death sentence, but without Kellett putting his reputation on the line, the discussion of commutation would have never started. Also see "Death Sentence Commutation for Lee Asked," *Boston Globe*, April 13, 1950, 7.

13 This April 18, 1950, letter can be found in the Malcolm Little Prison File.

14 Malcolm Little Prison File, June 6, 1950, letter. If you are startled by Malcolm's use of "homosexual pervert," remember that this was 1950, and even superintendent Maurice Winslow used the same style of language in the Norfolk Prison Colony newspaper. Here's Winslow defending why Norfolk had a policy of not employing formerly incarcerated men: "But this institution does NOT BELIEVE: that a confirmed alcoholic should be given employment as a bar tender; that a known homosexual should be given custody of his own sex or otherwise placed in a position propitious to furtherance of his perversion." Winslow, "Comments," *Colony*, February 1, 1949, 12.

15 "Ousted Woman Penal Head Granted Hearing," *Berkshire Eagle*, January 10, 1949, 1. Van Waters survived McDowell's attempts to fire her, but her reputation was damaged.

16 Catch the pun/sarcasm?

17 Malcolm Little Prison File, letter from Malcolm X Little to Elliott E. McDowell, June 6, 1950.

18 Malcolm Little Prison File, letter from Malcolm X Little to Warden O'Brien, June 26, 1950.

19 Perry, *Malcolm*, 138.

20 Malcolm Little Prison File, letter from Warden John J. O'Brien to Elliott McDowell, June 29 [28?], 1950.

21 Paul W. Foster, "Commissioner Callahan May Be Seeking More Millions for Highways in State's Supplementary Budget," *Berkshire Eagle*, August 5, 1950, 10.

22 Foster, "Commissioner"; "Boston Firm Submits Lowest Bid for Wall at New State Prison," *Boston Globe*, September 14, 1950, 32. *The Bastille Concerto* was mentioned in Haley and X, *Autobiography*, 208. Jarvis's work was arranged into a 20-minute concerto by trumpeter Loz Speyer, a friend of Jarvis's son, professional drummer Clifford Jarvis. According to documentarian Anthony Collins, via our Dec. 2023 correspondence, a rendition of the concerto was played at Clifford Jarvis's memorial in 1999. A close listen hints at influences such as George Gershwin and Duke Ellington. To learn more about the Bastille Concerto, see the Facebook page "Clifford Jarvis Film."

23 Malcolm Little Prison File, John J. O'Brien, "October 3, 1950."

24 "2 Convicts Fail in Bid to Escape From Charlestown," *Boston Globe*, October 17, 1950, 14.

25 "Convict's Suicide Attempt Foiled by Prison Guard," *Boston Globe*, October 20, 1950, 17. Feeney would spend the next decade attempting to escape again from Charlestown in September 1951, at Norfolk in 1954, and at the new Walpole prison in 1959. By the end of the decade, he'd tripled the length of his original sentence.

26 Letter from Malcolm X Little to Henrietta Shah, October 16, 1950, SCRBC.

27 Jarvis with Nichols, *The Other Malcolm*, 97. Jarvis mistakenly puts this moment at the beginning of his Charlestown sentence. The Thaxton brothers were not at Charlestown when Jarvis was there in 1946. This moment would have happened between 1950 and 1951. I have been unable to find any additional material related to Leroy Ferguson and Charles O'Neil, who are also mentioned by Jarvis in the memoir. There was in 1949 a Rev. Leroy Ferguson, of St. Cyprian's Episcopal Church in Roxbury, seen in a March 6, 1949 *Boston Globe* photo.

28 Letter from Malcolm X to Philbert Shah, December 11, 1950, SCRBC.

29 Haley and X, *Autobiography*, 206.

30 Letter from Malcolm X to Philbert Shaw, December 11, 1950, SCRBC; "4 Cultists Go on Trial in Shooting," *Detroit Free Press*, December 21, 1950.

31 Wilfred Little, "Our Family from the Inside: Growing Up with Malcolm X," *Contributions in Black Studies* 13 (1995), article 2.

32 Letter from Malcolm X to Philbert Shah, December 11, 1950, SCRBC.

33 Little, "Our Family from the Inside."

34 Little, "Our Family from the Inside"; letter from Malcolm X Little to Henrietta Shah, March 25, 1951, SCRBC.

35 Redacted letter in FBI file, "Malcolm Little (Malcolm X)," FBI Records: The Vault, January 9, 1951, https://vault.fbi.gov/malcolm-little-malcolm-x. Also see Ferruccio Gambino, "The Transgression of a Laborer: Malcolm X in the Wilderness of America," *Radical History Review* 55 (1993): 7–31. Malcolm X

scholar Karl Evanzz believes Malcolm was writing to Elijah Muhammad, as do other scholars. Malcolm's official FBI file did not start until around May–June 1953, right around the time he was released on parole and formally made an NOI minister by Elijah Muhammad.

36 Redacted letter in FBI file, January 9, 1951.

37 Haley and X, *Autobiography*, 202.

38 Letter from Malcolm X to Philbert Shah, December 11, 1950, SCRBC; Payne and Payne, *The Dead Are Arising*, 274. The Paynes had interviewed Philbert in 1990.

39 Haley and X, *Autobiography*, 204.

40 Haley and X, 203.

41 Letter from Brother Malcolm X Little to Sister Beatrice, June 11, 1952, SCRBC, box 3, folder 3.

42 Haley and X, *Autobiography*, 203.

43 Haley and X, 203.

44 "Man Held in $1000 Here for Removal to N.Y. on Draft Charge," *Boston Globe*, October 22, 1951, 7; Haley and X, *Autobiography*, 204.

45 Haley and X, *Autobiography*, 205.

46 Jarvis with Nichols, *The Other Malcolm*, 70.

47 Malcolm Jarvis Prison File; Perry, *Malcolm*, 129, based on an interview with Jarvis.

48 Dale Carnegie, *How to Win Friends and Influence People* (New York: Simon and Schuster, 1936), 27. This is from a scanned copy of a 1943 edition, most likely the wording Jarvis read while in prison.

49 Malcolm Jarvis Prison File.

50 Malcolm Jarvis Prison File.

51 Malcolm Jarvis Prison File, "An Institutional History," compiled by E. Foley in May 1951.

52 Jarvis with Nichols, *The Other Malcolm*, 55.

53 The parole date comes from Jarvis's prison file, but it should be noted that it is the "Eligible for Parole" date, so there might be a more precise document out there showing the exact date Jarvis was released.

54 Cunningham and Golden, "Malcolm," 28–29. A photo of the ring was taken and shown on page 29. It is most likely Mrs. Estabrook's ring.

55 Malcolm Little Prison File. For Ella's offenses, Bruce Perry lists the court docket numbers in his biography, *Malcolm*, 406–7n.

56 Malcolm Little Prison File; Perry, *Malcolm*, 139.

57 Malcolm Little Prison File, "Parole Board." This note also shows the most likely date Malcolm was officially rejected by the parole board, May 29, 1951.

58 Malcolm Little Prison File, "Psychiatrist's Report."

59 Malcolm Little Prison File, report filed in May 1951.

60   Walter D. O'Leary, "Grossman to Give Prisoners a Chance," *Boston Globe*, January 25, 1951, 3.

61   O'Leary, "Grossman"; "Obituaries: Civic Figure, Philanthropist Col. Maxwell Grossman, Business Leader, at 66," *Boston Globe*, June 14, 1963, 32.

62   Malcolm Little Prison File. Letter typed from the handwritten scan sent by the Massachusetts Department of Correction.

63   Malcolm Little Prison File, note from Grossman acknowledging receipt, June 21, 1951. Grossman informed Warden O'Brien that the transfer board would decide on Malcolm's request "in the very near future."

64   "Cultists Beat Policemen; Two Shot," *Detroit Free Press*, June 17, 1950; "4 Cultists Sentenced for Assault," *Detroit Free Press*, January 26, 1951.

65   "4 Cultists Convicted in Shooting," *Detroit Free Press*, January 13, 1951, 13; letter from Malcolm Little to Philbert Shah, December 19, 1951, SCRBC. See also "4 Cultists Go on Trial in Shooting," *Detroit Free Press*, December 21, 1950.

66   For those interested in investigating the Paul Lennon angle, one article, published in the "Nab 3 Ex-Convict Suspects in Cape, Saugus Robberies," *Boston Globe*, August 13, 1955, 3, contains a picture of Paul Lennon and a young Black chauffeur named John I. Grant, who the *Boston Globe* reports as being 25 in one article and 38 in another. The article describes how Lennon's house was robbed by several white men, who "bound and gagged" Lennon, Grant, and Lennon's gardener. In an earlier report, they were also "stripped of their clothing." One of the robbers, according to Lennon, who at 63 "suffer[ed] from a heart condition," gave Lennon "one of his heart pills during the Cape holdup, when [Lennon] feared that the excitement would bring on an attack." If it wasn't Lennon who reached out, it could have been Abe Goldstein, Malcolm's former employer at the Lobster Pond.

67   Letter from Malcolm X Little to Philbert Shah, January 15, 1952, SCRBC.

68   Little, "Our Family from the Inside."

69   Letter from Malcolm X Little to Philbert Shah, January 15, 1952, SCRBC.

70   Letter from Malcolm X Little to Philbert Shah, January 15, 1952, SCRBC.

71   Inkster address confirmed in Malcolm Little Prison File. The 4336 Williams Street home had been restored by a team led in part by Dawon Lynn, Chaka Wilson, and Dr. Tareq A. Ramadan as of late 2020. In February 2022, it was added to the National Register of Historic Places. See Oralandar Brand-Williams, "Inkster Home of Malcolm X," *Detroit News*, February 2, 2022.

72   Frances Burns, "Care of Criminals Needs Overhaul," *Boston Globe*, November 30, 1952, 22-A.

73   "Proposed Bill H-1461," *Colony*, February 1, 1949, 4.

74   Little, "Our Family from the Inside."

75   Letter from Malcolm X Little to Beatrice Clovis, June 11, 1952, SCRBC.

76   Letter from Malcolm X Little to Beatrice Clovis, June 11, 1952, SCRBC. In case this line made you wonder what Dr. King was doing during this

time, here is a passage from a July 18, 1952, letter King wrote to his then-girlfriend Coretta Scott. In it, the 23-year-old King, then a PhD student at Boston University, shows his frustration with capitalism, albeit in poetic fashion: "I imagine you already know that I am much more socialistic in my economic theory than capitalistic," King wrote to Coretta. "And yet I am not so opposed to capitalism that I have failed to see its relative merits. It started out with a noble and high motive, to block the trade monopolies of nobles, but like most human systems it falls victim to the very thing it was revolting against. So today capitalism has outlived its usefulness. It has brought about a system that takes necessities from the masses to give luxuries to the classes." Read in full at Martin Luther King Jr., "To Coretta Scott," Stanford Martin Luther King, Jr. Research and Education Institute, July 18, 1952, https://kinginstitute.stanford.edu/king-papers/documents/coretta-scott.

77 Carnegie, *How to Win Friends*, chaps. 1, 8.
78 Letter from Malcolm X Little to Beatrice Clovis, June 11, 1952, SCRBC.
79 SCRBC.
80 Malcolm Little Prison File, letter from Philip J. Flynn, supervisor of Massachusetts paroles, to Gus Harrison, state supervisor of paroles, June 27, 1952.
81 Letter from Malcolm X Little to Beatrice Clovis, June 29, 1952, SCRBC. This letter is the last prison letter available. As far as what has been reported, there are no prison letters between June 30 and August 7, the date of Malcolm's release.
82 Malcolm Little Prison File.
83 "Dozen Riots in 3 Months," *Boston Globe*, July 23, 1952, 7.
84 "Heat to Continue Here, Weather Bureau Says," *Boston Globe*, July 23, 1952, 1.
85 Paul V. Craigue, "Convicts Hold Guards," *Boston Globe*, July 23, 1952. This edition of the *Boston Globe* has riot-related articles on six other pages, but Craigue was an eyewitness to this event, since he was the "Globe Man" the men reported to during negotiations in the auto plate shop.
86 Craigue, "Riot," timetable of prison riot, 8.
87 Craigue, "Riot," timetable of prison riot, 8.
88 Edgar J. Driscoll Jr., "Crowds Jam Prison Gate Area, Worry about Hostages Inside," *Boston Globe*, July 23, 1952, 21.
89 "Rioters 'Let Off' with 10 Days Solitary," *Boston Globe*, July 24, 1952. At first the damage was estimated at over $70,000, but a week later, it more accurately totaled $17,469.21. See "Prison," *Boston Globe*, July 30, 1952, 4.
90 Malcolm Little Prison File, "Parole Board Memorandum"; letter from Philip J. Flynn to Mr. Gus Harrison, August 6, 1952; Haley and X, *Autobiography*, 208. Strangely, Malcolm either misremembered or falsified (or Alex Haley misremembered) Shorty's parole in the *Autobiography*, which states that Shorty

was "up for parole" but not able to get someone to sign for him. It's possible that Haley, when crafting the narrative, accidentally took threads of Malcolm's own first parole denial retelling and put them into Shorty's storyline.

91 Haley and X, *Autobiography*, 209.

92 Weather is from the *Boston Globe*, August 7, 1952, and Malcolm's words from the Haley and X, *Autobiography*, 209.

93 Haley and X, *Autobiography*, 209.

94 Haley and X, 209.

95 United States Bureau of Public Roads, and American Association of State Highway Officials, *United States System of Highways, Adopted for Uniform Marking by the American Association of State Highway Officials, with Additions and Amendments Subsequently Approved 1950*, map (Washington, DC: Library of Congress, 1950), https://www.loc.gov/item/00562124/. The Interstate Highway System was not established until Eisenhower pushed forward the Federal Aid Highway Act of 1956. Malcolm's journey to Detroit was country-road slow.

96 Vicki Garvin, "Malcolm as I Knew Him," *Arm the Masses*, February 1993, 18. Copy found in the Vicki Garvin papers at the SCRBC.

97 The letters are dated January 29, 1950 (Norfolk), June 29, 1950 (Charlestown), and January 9, 1951 (Charlestown).

98 Pulled from a combination of three sources: "Malcolm Little (Malcolm X)," FBI Records: The Vault, file 1, pp 4–10, https://vault.fbi.gov/malcolm-little -malcolm-x; Malcolm Little Prison File (for parole); Carson, *Malcolm X*, part 3.

EPILOGUE

1 "Prison Population," *Colony*, March 15, 1949, 3; Wendy Sawyer and Peter Wagner, "Mass Incarceration: The Whole Pie 2022," *Prison Policy Initiative*, March 14, 2022. The Mandela quote is from the excellent UNESCO report compiled in Krolak, *Books beyond Bars*. See also E. Ann Carson, "Prisoners in 2020—Statistical Tables," Bureau of Justice Statistics, December 2021, https://bjs.ojp.gov/content/pub/pdf/p20st.pdf.

2 Sawyer and Wagner, "Mass Incarceration."

3 According to Laura M. Maruschak and Emily D. Buehler, Black prisoners account for 39.1 percent of 2019's prison population, whereas white prisoners total 38.9 percent. The percentage of Hispanic prisoners was reported at 18.6 percent. Of all the prisoners, 88.4 percent are US citizens. Maruschak and Buehler, "Census of State and Federal Adult Correctional Facilities, 2019—Statistical Tables," Bureau of Justice Statistics, November 2021,

https://bjs.ojp.gov/library/publications/census-state-and-federal-adult
-correctional-facilities-2019-statistical-tables.

4 See Michelle Alexander, *The New Jim Crow: Mass Incarceration in the Age of Colorblindness* (New York: New Press, 2010); Shane Bauer, *American Prison: A Reporter's Undercover Journey into the Business of Punishment* (New York: Penguin, 2018); John Pfaff, *Locked In: The True Causes of Mass Incarceration—and How to Achieve Real Reform* (New York: Basic, 2017); James Forman Jr., *Locking Up Our Own: Crime and Punishment in Black America* (New York: Farrar, Straus and Giroux, 2017); Danielle Sered, *Until We Reckon: Violence, Mass Incarceration, and a Road to Repair* (New York: New Press, 2019).

5 Howard Manly, "Malcolm Blazed Path for Others at Norfolk," *Boston Globe*, November 19, 1992, 31, 36. Manly also asked if men kept "separate" the views of Dr. Martin Luther King Jr. and Malcolm X. Shabazz said no, for the most part: "[Malcolm X and Martin Luther King Jr. are] two spirits emanating from the same African-American soul. . . . One side wants to compromise and appeal to the good graces and mercy of the oppressive system. On the other side was Malcolm, who said things that a lot of blacks didn't have the courage to say" (36).

6 Author correspondence with William Mongelli, September 2021.

7 The following is a list of seven criteria MCI-Norfolk staff must follow when "excluding" certain books from their collection. This is from the "MCI-Norfolk Inmate Orientation Guide," a Norfolk procedural document based on the 103 CMR 478 "Library Services" regulation, via William Mongelli correspondence. A book is forbidden if it

a) Depicts or describes procedures for the construction or use of weapons, ammunition, bombs or incendiary devices. b) Depicts, describes, or encourages methods of escape from correctional facilities, or contains blueprints, drawings or similar descriptions of any correctional institution within the Commonwealth. c) Depicts or describes procedures for the brewing of alcoholic beverages, or the manufacture of drugs. d) Is written in code. e) Depicts, describes or encourages activities that may lead to the use of physical violence or group disruption. f) Encourages or instructs in the commission of criminal activity. g) Sexually explicit material of a graphic, violent, or disturbing nature or material which features nudity.

8 Nelson Alves (superintendent), "MCI-Norfolk Inmate Orientation Guide," November 17, 2020, 42. In 2021, Alves, via Reginald Dwayne Betts's Freedom Reads initiative aimed at developing prison libraries, turned Malcolm's cell into a microlibrary where men can gain access to a variety of books, curated by Betts, within the dormitory unit. See Adrian Walker, "Prison Advocate and Macarthur 'Genius' Turns What May Be Malcolm X's Former Cell into a Library and Place for Hope," *Boston Globe*, November 25, 2021.

9 So, too, has Jed Tucker, as a part of the vital Bard Prison Initiative (BPI), serving mainly New York state prisons.

10 Correspondence with Mongelli, September 2021.

11 Correspondence with Mongelli, September 2021; Williams, *Blue Rage, Black Redemption*, 295.

12 Williams, *Blue Rage, Black Redemption*, 249.

13 Williams.

14 Woodfox, *Solitary*, 199.

15 Woodfox, 251, 297–98.

16 Special thanks to MCI-Norfolk superintendent Nelson Alves for allowing me access to the grounds and librarian Nancy Hughes for helping with library content.

17 For more information about the Harriet Tubman project, please contact Jacqueline Fonseca, the coexecutive director as of May 2024. The quote is from the website *Free Fuquan*, which has been taken down as of May 2024.

18 As of August 2023, according to one prison official, at least 60 men at Norfolk asked for meals that adhere to a "Muslim diet."

19 The number of jails is from Wendy Sawyer and Peter Wagner, "Mass Incarceration: The Whole Pie 2020," *Prison Policy Initiative*, March 24, 2020. The number of prison libraries is from Vibeke Lehmann, "Challenges and Accomplishments in U.S. Prison Libraries," *Library Trends* 59, no. 3 (2011): 490–508.

20 It's worth a shot, though. Go ahead . . . Give this to your local prison and see what happens, and let me know.

21 As cited in James Tager and Ariel Fishman, "Literature Locked Up: How Prison Book Restriction Policies Constitute the Nation's Largest Book Ban," *Pen America*, September 2019, 12–13. Another stunner from Pen's issue briefer was that Pennsylvania's DOC had ordered a switch to e-books in September 2018. Incarcerated individuals could no longer receive physical books as a gift. Now, their only choice is to buy a $149 tablet with 8,500 preselected titles. For those lucky enough to afford such a device, they will not find *The Autobiography of Malcolm X* as one of the choices, nor even Anne Frank's *Diary of a Young Girl*. But those in love with Tony Bennett's music can rejoice . . . his autobiography passed censors.

22 Haley and X, *Autobiography*, 195. Krolak, *Books beyond Bars*, 9, 11. It's been estimated that one-in-seven Americans (not incarcerated individuals, but free citizens) are functionally illiterate, or lack the basic reading skills to complete a job.

SELECTED BIBLIOGRAPHY

The following sources were either cited or
consulted during the creation of this book.

PRINTED WORKS

Abdat, Fathie Bin Ali. *Malcolm X and Christianity*. Master's thesis, National
University of Singapore, 2008. CORE. https://core.ac.uk/download/pdf/
48631743.pdf.

Ambar, Saladin. *Malcolm X at Oxford Union*. Oxford: Oxford University Press, 2014.

Baldwin, Lewis V., and Amiri Yasan Al-Hadid. *The Cross and the Crescent: Christian
and Muslim Perspectives on Malcolm and Martin*. Gainesville: University of
Florida Press, 2002.

Bodmer, Frederik. *The Loom of Language: An Approach to the Mastery of Many
Languages*. New York: Norton, 1944.

Boyd, Herb, and Ilyasah Al-Shabazz, eds. *The Diary of Malcolm X (El Hajj Malik
El-Shabazz), 1964*. Chicago: Third World, 2013.

Breitman, George, ed. *By Any Means Necessary: Speeches, Interviews, and a Letter
by Malcolm X*. New York: Pathfinder, 1970.

———. *The Last Year of Malcolm X: The Evolution of a Revolutionary*. New York,
Merit, 1967.

Capeci, Dominic J., Jr. *The Harlem Riot of 1943*. Philadelphia: Temple University
Press, 1977.

Carew, Jan. *Ghosts in Our Blood: With Malcolm X in Africa, England, and the
Caribbean*. Chicago: Lawrence Hill, 1994.

Carson, Clayborne. *Malcolm X: The FBI File*. New York: Carroll and Graf, 1991.

Catalogue of Books in the Library of the Massachusetts Reformatory at Concord, Mass.
Concord: Massachusetts Reformatory, 1885.

Clarke, John Henrik. *Malcolm X: The Man and His Times*. New York: Macmillan,
1969.

Collins, Rodnell P., with Peter A. Bailey. *Seventh Child: A Family Memoir of Malcolm X*. New York: Kensington, 1998.

Cone, James H. *Martin and Malcolm and America: A Dream or a Nightmare*. Maryknoll, NY: Oris, 1992.

DeCaro, Louis. *On the Side of My People: A Religious Life of Malcolm X*. New York: New York University Press, 1996.

Dyson, Michael Eric. *Making Malcolm: The Myth and Meaning of Malcolm X*. Oxford: Oxford University Press, 1995.

Edozie, Rita Kiki, and Curtis Stokes, eds. *Malcolm X's Michigan Worldview: An Exemplar for Contemporary Black Studies*. Lansing: Michigan State University Press, 2015.

Epps, Archie, ed. *Malcolm X: Speeches at Harvard*. New York: Paragon House, 1991.

Evanzz, Karl. *The Messenger: The Rise and Fall of Elijah Muhammad*. New York: Vintage, 1999.

Fabre, Michel, and Robert E. Skinner, eds. *Conversations with Chester Himes*. Jackson: University Press of Mississippi, 1995.

Fanon, Frantz. *Black Skin, White Masks*. New York: Grove, 1967.

Frazier, E. Franklin. *The Negro in the United States*. New York: Macmillan, 1949.

Gallen, David, ed. *Malcolm X: As They Knew Him*. New York: Carroll and Graf, 1992.

Giddins, Gary. *Celebrating Bird: The Triumph of Charlie Parker*. New York: William Morrow, 1987.

Goldman, Peter L. *The Death and Life of Malcolm X*. Champaign: University of Illinois Press, 1973.

Grant, Colin. *Negro with a Hat: The Rise and Fall of Marcus Garvey*. Oxford: Oxford University Press, 2008.

Haley, Alex, and Malcolm X. *The Autobiography of Malcolm X: As Told to Alex Haley*. New York: Ballantine, 1965.

Hall, Rodney, ed. *Poems from Prison: Jack Murray, Max Williams, Eric Mackenzie, Robin Thurston*. Brisbane, Australia: University of Queensland Press, 1973.

Haynes, Gideon. *Pictures from Prison Life: An Historical Sketch of the Massachusetts State Prison*. Boston: Lee and Shepard, 1871.

Herskovits, Melville J. *The Myth of the Negro Past*. New York: Harper and Brothers, 1941.

Hill, Robert A., ed. *The Marcus Garvey and Universal Negro Improvement Association Papers*. 10 vols. Berkeley: University of California Press, 1983–89.

Himes, Chester. *If He Hollers Let Him Go*. New York: Doubleday, 1945.

Jamal, Hakim. *From the Dead Level: Malcolm X and Me*. London: Andre Deutsch, 1971.

Jarvis, Malcolm, with Paul D. Nichols. *The Other Malcolm: "Shorty" Jarvis*. Edited by Cornel West. Jefferson, NC: McFarland, 2001.

Joseph, Peniel. *The Sword and the Shield: The Revolutionary Lives of Malcolm X and Martin Luther King Jr.* New York: Hachette, 2020.

Junker, Buford Helmholz. *The State Prison Colony at Norfolk and the Norfolk Plan for Treatment.* Unpublished bachelor's thesis, Harvard University, 1933. Harvard Law School Library.

Karim, Benjamin. *Remembering Malcolm.* New York: Carroll and Graf, 1992.

Kelley, Robin D. G. *Race Rebels: Culture, Politics, and the Black Working Class.* New York: Free Press, 1994.

Khayyam, Omar. *The Rubaiyat of Omar Khayyam.* New York: Collier, 1972. First written in the late eleventh or early twelfth century.

Kondo, Baba Zak A. *Conspiracys: Unravelling the Assassination of Malcolm X.* Washington, DC: Nubia, 1993.

Krolak, Lisa. *Books beyond Bars: The Transformative Potential of Prison Libraries.* Hamburg, Germany: UNESCO Institute for Lifelong Learning, 2019.

Lewis, Elma, and the Norfolk Prison Brothers. *Who Took the Weight: Black Voices from Norfolk Prison.* Boston: Little, Brown, 1972.

Lincoln, C. Eric. *The Black Muslims in America.* Boston: Beacon, 1961.

Lomax, Louis E. *When the Word Is Given: A Report on Elijah Muhammad, Malcolm X, and the Black Muslim World.* Westport, CT: Greenwood, 1963.

Marable, Manning. *Living Black History.* New York: Basic, 2006.

———. *Malcolm X: A Life of Reinvention.* New York: Penguin, 2011.

Marable, Manning, and Garrett Felber. *The Portable Malcolm X Reader.* New York: Penguin, 2013.

McWhirter, Cameron. *Red Summer: The Summer of 1919 and the Awakening of Black America.* New York: Henry Holt, 2011.

Melville, Herman. *Moby-Dick.* New York: Macmillan, 2016. First published in 1851.

Merz, Leon, Jr. *Norfolk Prison Colony: Ideal and Actuality.* Unpublished bachelor's thesis, Harvard University, 1934. Harvard Law School Library.

Milton, John. *Paradise Lost.* New York: Penguin, 2000. First published in 1656.

Morris, James McGrath. *Jailhouse Journalism: The Fourth Estate behind Bars.* Jefferson, NC: McFarland, 1998. Updated edition by Routledge in 2002.

Myrdal, Gunnar. *An American Dilemma.* New York: Harper and Brothers, 1944.

Natambu, Kofi. *Malcolm X: Critical Lives.* Indianapolis, IN: Alpha, 2001.

Norrell, Robert J. *Alex Haley: And the Books That Changed a Nation.* New York: St. Martin's, 2015.

Parkhurst, Lewis. *Education in the State Prison at Norfolk, Massachusetts.* Boston: Thomas Todd, 1938.

———. *A Vacation on the Nile: A Collection of Letters Written to Friends at Home.* Ithaca, NY: Cornell University Library, 1913.

Payne, Les, and Tamara Payne. *The Dead Are Arising: The Life of Malcolm X*. New York: Norton 2020.

Perry, Bruce. *Malcolm: The Life of a Man Who Changed Black America*. Barrytown, NY: Station Hill, 1991.

Prout, Curtis, and Robert N. Ross. *Care and Punishment: The Dilemmas of Prison Medicine*. Pittsburgh, PA: University of Pittsburgh Press, 1988.

Reed, Annette Gordon. *The Hemingses of Monticello*. New York: Norton, 2008.

Reynolds, Paul R. *The Middle Man: The Adventures of a Literary Agent*. New York: William Morrow, 1972.

Rickford, Russell. *Betty Shabazz: A Remarkable Story of Survival and Faith before and after Malcolm X*. New York: Sourcebooks, 2003.

Robertson, David M. *Denmark Vesey: The Buried History of America's Largest Slave Rebellion and the Man Who Led It*. New York: Knopf, 1999.

Rogers, J. A. *One Hundred Amazing Facts about the Negro with Complete Proof: A Short Cut to the World History of the Negro*. Middletown, CT: Wesleyan University Press, 2014. First published in 1934.

———. *Sex and Race*. Vols. 1–3. Middletown, CT: Wesleyan University Press, 2014. First published in 1940.

Russell, Jessica, with Hilda Little and Steve Jones Sr. *The Life of Louise Norton Little: An Extraordinary Woman: Mother of Malcolm X and His 7 Siblings*. Independently published, 2020.

Sawyer, Michael E. *Black Minded: The Political Philosophy of Malcolm X*. London: Pluto, 2020.

Shabazz, Ilyasah. *Growing Up X*. New York: Random House, 2002.

Shabazz, Ilyasah, cowritten with Tiffany Jackson. *The Awakening of Malcolm X*. New York: Farrar, Straus and Giroux, 2021.

Shakespeare, William. *Macbeth*. Hollywood, FL: Simon and Brown, 2018. First published in 1606.

Strickland, William. *Malcolm X: Make It Plain*. New York: Viking, 1994.

Terrill, Robert E. *Malcolm X: Inventing Radical Judgment*. Lansing: Michigan State University Press, 2004.

Tuck, Stephen. *The Night Malcolm X Spoke at the Oxford Union: A Transatlantic Story of Antiracist Protest*. Oakland: University of California Press, 2014.

Turner, Richard Brent. *Soundtrack to a Movement: African American Islam, Jazz, and Black Internationalism*. New York: New York University Press, 2021.

Tuttle, William M., Jr. *Race Riot: Chicago in the Red Summer of 1919*. New York: Macmillan, 1970.

Williams, Stanley "Tookie." *Blue Rage, Black Redemption: A Memoir*. Pleasant Hill, CA: Damamli, 2004.

Wood, Joe, ed. *Malcolm X: In Our Own Image*. New York: St. Martin's, 1992.

Woodfox, Albert. *Solitary: Unbroken by Four Decades in Solitary Confinement. My Story of Transformation and Hope*. New York: Grove, 2019.

Wooldredge, Henry L. "Inside the Wall of the Norfolk Prison Colony at Norfolk, Massachusetts." Bachelor's thesis, Dartmouth College, 1952. Dartmouth College's Rauner Special Collections Library.

ARTICLES

Baldwin, Lewis V. "Malcolm X and Martin Luther King, Jr.: What They Thought about Each Other." *Islamic Studies* 25, no. 4 (1986): 395–416.

Bradley, David. "Malcolm's Mythmaking." *Transition* 2, no. 56 (1992): 20–46.

Branham, Robert James. "'I Was Gone on Debating': Malcolm's Prison Debates and Public Confrontations." *Argumentations and Advocacy* 31, no. 3 (Winter 1995): 117–37.

Cunningham, Bill, and Daniel Golden. "Malcolm: The Boston Years." *Boston Globe*, February 16, 1992, 18–42.

DelSesto, Matthew. "Norfolk's 'Model Prison Community': Howard Belding Gill and the Social Process of Prison Reform." *Prison Journal* 101, no. 2 (2021): 127–46.

Eakin, Paul John. "Malcolm X and the Limits of Autobiography." *Criticism* 18, no. 3 (1976): 230–42.

Franklin, H. Bruce. "The Literature of the American Prison." *Massachusetts Review* 18, no. 1 (1977): 51–78.

Gill, Howard. "The Norfolk State Prison Colony at Massachusetts." *Journal of Criminal Law and Criminology* 22, no. 1 (May 1931): 107–12.

Kelley, Robin D. G. "House Negroes on the Loose: Malcolm X and the Black Bourgeoisie." *Callaloo* 21, no. 2 (1998): 419–35.

Kempton, Daniel. "Writing the Dictionary: The Education of Malcolm X." *Centennial Review* 37, no. 2 (1993): 253–66.

Lehmann, Vibeke. "Challenges and Accomplishments in U.S. Prison Libraries." *Library Trends* 59, no. 3 (2011): 490–508.

Little, Wilfred. "Our Family from the Inside: Growing Up with Malcolm X." *Contributions in Black Studies* 13, article 2 (1995): 7–47.

Manly, Howard. "Malcolm Blazed Path for Others at Norfolk." *Boston Globe*, November 19, 1992, 31 and 36.

Marable, Manning. "Rediscovering Malcolm's Life: A Historian's Adventures in Living History." *Souls* 7, no. 1 (Winter 2005): 20–35.

McDuffie, Erik. "The Diasporic Journeys of Louise Little: Grassroots Garveyism, the Midwest, and Community Feminism." *Women, Gender, and Families of Color* 4, no. 2 (2016): 146–70.

McDuffie, Erik S., and Komozi Woodard. "'If You're in a Country That's Progressive, the Woman Is Progressive': Black Women Radicals and the Making of the Politics and Legacy of Malcolm X." *Biography* 36, no. 3 (2013): 507–39.

Menard, Orville D. "Lest We Forget: The Lynching of Will Brown, Omaha's 1919 Race Riot." *Nebraska History* 91, no. 1 (2010): 152–65.

Morris, Albert. "Massachusetts: The Aftermath of the Prison Riots of 1952." *Prison Journal* 34, no. 1 (April 1954): 35–37.

Muhammad, Najee E. "The Educational Development of Malcolm X." *Western Journal of Black Studies* 26, no. 4 (Winter 2002): 240–48.

O'Connor, Tom, and Jeff B. Duncan. "The Sociology of Humanist, Spiritual, and Religious Practice in Prison: Supporting Responsivity and Desistance from Crime." *Religions* 2, no. 4 (2011): 590–610.

Phelps, Christopher. "The Sexuality of Malcolm X." *Journal of American Studies* 51, no. 3 (August 2017): 659–90.

Sanford, R. N. "Psychological Work at the Massachusetts Prison Colony." *Psychological Exchange* 4 (1935): 59–61.

Schuyler, Michael W. "The Ku Klux Klan in Nebraska, 1920–1930." *Nebraska History* 66, no. 1 (1985): 234–56.

Smallwood, Andrew P. "The Intellectual Creativity and Public Discourse of Malcolm X: A Precursor to the Modern Black Studies Movement." *Journal of Black Studies* 36, no. 2 (November 2005): 248–63.

Tager, James, and Ariel Fishman. "Literature Locked Up: How Prison Book Restriction Policies Constitute the Nation's Largest Book Ban." *Pen America*, September 2019. https://pen.org/wp-content/uploads/2019/09/PEN-America-Literature-Locked-Up-Report-9.23.19.pdf.

Tucker, Jed. "Malcolm X, the Prison Years: The Relentless Pursuit of Formal Education." *Journal of African American History* 102, no. 2 (Spring 2017): 184–212.

Vigrolio, Thomas. "These Prison Debaters Will Challenge Anyone!" *Federal Probation Quarterly* 25, no. 1 (March 1961): 27–31. (*Vigrolio was serving life in prison at Norfolk at the time.)

Vincent, Ted. "The Garveyite Parents of Malcolm X," *Black Scholar* 20, no. 2 (March/April 1989): 10–13.

Waxler, Robert P. "Changing Lives through Literature." *PMLA* 123, no. 3 (2008): 678–83.

PRISON FILES (MASSACHUSETTS DEPARTMENT OF CORRECTION AND MASSACHUSETTS ARCHIVES)

Bazarian, Beatrice (Mass. Archives)

Bembry, John Elton (MA-DOC)

Bradbury, Roland (MA-DOC)

Brown, Francis E (Mass. Archives)

Cappucci, Chester (MA-DOC)

Caragulian, Joyce (Mass. Archives)

Hampton, Heywood (MA-DOC)

Hoynoski, Chester A. (MA-DOC)

Hoynoski, Louis E. (MA-DOC)
Jarvis, Malcolm (MA-DOC;
    correspondence at
    Mass. Archives)
Johnston, Floyd (Mass. Archives)
Joiner, Godfrey (MA-DOC;
    correspondence at
    Mass. Archives)
Little, Malcolm (MA-DOC)
Margeson, Murdo (MA-DOC)

Nash, Merlin (Mass. Archives)
Nash, Robert D. (Mass. Archives)
Noble, Russell (Mass. Archives)
Noxon, John, Jr. (MA-DOC)
Phillips, Boise (MA-DOC)
Pritchett, Charles (MA-DOC)
Thaxton, Leroy (MA-DOC)
Thaxton, Osborne (MA-DOC)
Willis, Frank R. (Mass. Archives)

ARCHIVES

Charles H. Wright Museum of African American History—Detroit, MI
Howard Belding Gill Papers—Boston College—Chestnut Hill, MA
Massachusetts Archives—Boston, MA
New York Public Library—Schomburg Center—Malcolm X Collection and
    Papers—New York, NY
University of Massachusetts—Amherst, MA

INTERVIEWS/CORRESPONDENCE

Alves, Nelson. August 2023. MCI-Norfolk superintendent.
Collins, Anthony. December 2023. Put together a performance of Malcolm
    Jarvis's Bastille Concerto.
Hughes, Nancy. August 2023. Current MCI-Norfolk librarian.
Mongelli, William. September 2021. Former MCI-Norfolk librarian.
    Correspondence.
Nash, Rick. September 2022. Son of Richard W. Nash.
O'Connell, Gregory M. August 2022. Son of John A. O'Connell.
O'Connell, John, Jr. August 2022. Son of John A. O'Connell.
Shabazz, Ilyasah. 2019 to 2024. Daughter of Malcolm X.
Winslow, Dan. August 2023. Grandson of former MCI-Norfolk
    superintendent Maurice Winslow.
Winslow, David. Accessed August 2020. Conducted by Rafael Monserrate.

INDEX

Page numbers followed by *f* and *t* refer to figures and tables, respectively.

PATRICK PARR was born in New York and raised in Cuyahoga Falls, Ohio. He graduated from Catawba College with a degree in Literature and Creative Writing, and earned a Master's in Writing from Seton Hill University. For over a decade, he taught English and Writing at various universities, such as the University of Washington and the University of Southern California. His previous books include *One Week in America: The 1968 Notre Dame Literary Festival and a Changing Nation*, and *The Seminarian: Martin Luther King Jr. Comes of Age*, which was a finalist for the Washington State Book Award. Shorter work has appeared in *The Atlantic*, *Politico*, *History Today*, and *The American Prospect*, among others. Parr lives with his wife near Tokyo, and is a writing professor at Lakeland University Japan.